Social Media Metrics
SECRETS

Social Media Metrics
SECRETS

DO WHAT YOU NEVER THOUGHT POSSIBLE WITH SOCIAL MEDIA METRICS

John Lovett

WILEY

Wiley Publishing, Inc.

EXECUTIVE EDITOR: Carol Long
SENIOR PROJECT EDITOR: Kevin Kent
TECHNICAL EDITOR: Steven Groves
PRODUCTION EDITOR: Kathleen Wisor
COPY EDITOR: Kezia Endsley
EDITORIAL MANAGER: Mary Beth Wakefield
FREELANCER EDITORIAL MANAGER: Rosemarie Graham
ASSOCIATE DIRECTOR OF MARKETING: David Mayhew
MARKETING MANAGER: Ashley Zurcher
BUSINESS MANAGER: Amy Knies
PRODUCTION MANAGER: Tim Tate
VICE PRESIDENT AND EXECUTIVE GROUP PUBLISHER: Richard Swadley
VICE PRESIDENT AND EXECUTIVE PUBLISHER: Neil Edde
ASSOCIATE PUBLISHER: Jim Minatel
PROJECT COORDINATOR, COVER: Katie Crocker
COMPOSITOR: Chris Gillespie, Happenstance Type-O-Rama
PROOFREADER: Louise Watson, Word One
INDEXER: Robert Swanson
COVER IMAGE: © Chad Baker / Lifesize / Getty Images
COVER DESIGNER: Ryan Sneed

Social Media Metrics Secrets

Published by
Wiley Publishing, Inc.
10475 Crosspoint Boulevard
Indianapolis, IN 46256
www.wiley.com

Copyright © 2011 by John Lovett

Published by Wiley Publishing, Inc., Indianapolis, Indiana

Published simultaneously in Canada

ISBN: 978-0-470-93627-6
ISBN: 978-1-118-14903-4 (ebk)
ISBN: 978-1-118-14902-7 (ebk)
ISBN: 978-1-118-14901-0 (ebk)

Manufactured in the United States of America

10 9 8 7 6 5 4 3 2 1

For my loving wife, Kara, and our three
wonderful boys, Jackson, Chase, and Brooks

About the Author

John Lovett is a veteran industry analyst and expert consultant who has spent the past decade helping organizations to understand and measure their digital marketing activities. As a Senior Partner at Web Analytics Demystified, Lovett regularly consults with leading enterprises to offer strategic guidance for building innovative digital measurement programs. These programs typically incorporate Web Analytics, CRM, marketing automation, multivariable testing, behavioral targeting, voice of customer, and social analytics technologies that assemble data at the point of the customer. In addition to working with enterprise organizations, Lovett is also a trusted advisor to vendors within the digital measurement community. His deep industry knowledge and forward thinking perspective help vendors and clients alike to transcend mediocrity by changing the shape of business using strategic measurement practices.

Prior to joining Web Analytics Demystified, Lovett was a Senior Analyst with Forrester Research, where he was responsible for analytics and optimization technologies. Currently, Lovett is the Vice President on the Board of Directors for the Web Analytics Association and has pioneered efforts like the Web Analyst's Code of Ethics with the WAA Standards Committee. He is co-founder of the Analysis Exchange program, which is introducing eager students to analytics by helping nonprofits with mentored analysis. This program has already helped hundreds of nonprofits to benefit from digital data and learn analytics. Lovett lives in New Hampshire with his yellow lab, wife, and three boys.

About the Technical Editor

Steven Groves is co-author of *ROI of Social Media: How to Improve the Return on Your Social Marketing Investment* and is the online and social media strategist for ProfitStreams, a closed-loop marketing platform developer in Denver, Colorado. He is an international speaker, educator, and blogger on social media in CPG/FMCG, retail, and technology companies and has worked with marketers around the world, driving home the message that marketers need to build ROI into their marketing, regardless of whether they are using social or traditional methods. Connect online at www.ROIofSocialMedia.com, Facebook, or LinkedIn.

Acknowledgments

This book couldn't have been possible without the help, guidance, and contributions from an ecosystem of generous contributors. First and foremost, I'd like to thank Jim Sterne, who graciously referred me to my publisher, John Wiley & Sons. Jim is both a friend and a mentor, and I'll be thanking him for his sage wisdom for many years to come. I am also grateful to my business partner, Eric T. Peterson, whose guidance over the years has shaped the way that I think about analytics. Additionally, my sincere thanks goes out to the following influencers, organizations, and individuals for sharing their ideas, thoughts, and shards of brilliance about social media: Simon Abramovitch, Eric Beane, Connie Benson, David Berkowitz, Christopher Berry, Rohit Bhargava, Constantin Basturea, Casey Carey, Jeff Clark, Mikey Cramer, Adam Greco, Steven Groves, Ericka Gutierrez, Chris Harrison, Cory Hartlen, Zach Hoffer-Shall, Jeff Jordan, Sheldon Levine, Alex Mann, John McKean, Alex Nagler, Kenny Norton, Jim Novo, Anna O'Brien, James O'Malley, Jeremiah Owyang, Katie Paine, Bob Page, Judah Phillips, Stefanie Posavec, Guy Powell, Lizzie Schreier, Brian Solis, Jason Thompson, and Robert Tuttle, and to all those who unknowingly influenced me with their thoughts and words about social media measurement.

Contents at a Glance

Contents

Foreword

Trying any new initiative, especially social media, should involve a measured approach. In fact, if you can't measure the impacts of your new investments, how can you hope to improve them? With that said, measurement is key in both established programs that you're seeking to optimize and new media investments. Yet measurement, which we've identified as a top priority inside of organizations, has been generally afflicted by ineffective efforts and flat out wrong tactics. Most organizations don't really know how to measure anything, including the new frontiers of social media, based on business objectives. In the specific case of social media, too many organizations are simply relying on the low-level metrics provided by social networks as a sole means of social media measurement. This book teaches you how to go beyond those counting metrics to arrive at truly valuable measures of success that you can use to manage your business.

John Lovett is a former colleague from Forrester Research and an outright thought leader in this space. I was pleased to engage on a research project with John, who brought his measurement expertise in analytics and coupled it with my focus on social media marketing to build the "Social Marketing Analytics Framework." Our initial framework identified how to measure based on business goals like dialogue, advocacy, support, and innovation, not on mere counting metrics like fans or retweets. John demonstrated a quick adaptation of the framework and built the detailed formulas that have now become a standard for many practitioners leading the social analytics charges at today's modern corporations. And his work in this book takes our framework, as well as new ideas and concepts for strategically measuring social media, to even greater heights.

More often than not, we find companies lack a measurement strategy, and they are unable to develop one because of the complexity of APIs and the noise of data exuding from the ever-changing social networks. These companies have difficulty creating their own formulas tied to their business objectives and thus fall short of effectively measuring their social media activity. Companies who succeed in developing a measurement strategy not only are better able to demonstrate ROI to their executives and glean more investments, they are also able to improve their programs to connect with customers. This book contains many of the secrets that can help you get there.

Don't aimlessly measure, instead develop a measurement strategy and put your social media metrics to work for you and your bottom line.

—Jeremiah Owyang
Partner, Altimeter Group

Read This First

Social media is all the rage these days. With over a half a billion people on Facebook alone, consumer participation in social media has become ubiquitous. Marketers and businesses are active participants, too, with 90 percent of CMOs reporting activity in at least three social media channels in 2010.[1] Your company is probably one of the many already involved with social media, or perhaps you're ready to begin, but there's one crucial question that most companies are working frantically to answer: *How do you know if social media is working for you?*

Responsible businesses cut straight through the hype of social media to answer this burning question by developing an understanding of social media effectiveness using measurement. Yet, this is also where most organizations falter. Understanding requires defining your social media metrics and analyzing data to make sense of your operations in a programmatic way. Building a program of social media measurement is a complex undertaking that requires knowledge, skill, and collaboration, but it will be one of the most important tasks that you'll take on this year and in the years to follow. It's imperative because there's a desperate need to understand the impact that social media has on your business. And I guarantee you that it will impact your business; it's just a matter of how much and how quickly. The tide is rising for social media, and those in the know will have measurement programs in place to map out their future adventures in social media and chart their successes against the past.

Who This Book Is For

If you're brand spanking new to social media, this book may be a daunting indoctrination to the challenges of measuring this medium. By design, I wrote this manuscript with the intention that it would pick up where other works on the topic of social media metrics left off. There are some fabulous works published on how to get started in measuring social media, including *Social Media Metrics* (Wiley, 2010), authored by Jim Sterne, that you should read first. His book and others like it set the context for thinking about social media measurement, and I attempted to take that one step further by working to define the metrics, categorize their uses, and build

[1] "CMOs on Social Marketing Plans for 2011." BazaarVoice and The CMO Club, 2011.

a framework for operational success. All this may be a bit unnerving for the casual reader, but don't despair, it's entirely comprehensible if you apply just a modicum of business acumen.

That said, *Social Media Metrics Secrets* is prescribed for everyone from the novice to the social analytics elite. This book is meant to be a hands-on guide to strategizing and measuring social media efforts with a business mentality. Yet, I took on a big challenge in writing this book because I wrote it for two very distinct audiences.

This book is for:

▶ **The everyday businessperson:** For those of you journeying into social media as executives, directors, managers, marketers, analysts, or all-around bricoleurs, this book will help you define your measures of success and effectively measure social media.

▶ **The seasoned professional:** For my peers and colleagues and the multitude of social savvy pros who are well versed in the ways of social media and digital analytics, I aim for this book to reveal a secret or two for your social media measurement coffers.

So, whether you're the stalwart champion for social media, a newly minted community manager, a solo practitioner, or even if you just inherited social media measurement, I welcome you into the pages of this book.

What This Book Covers

The core of this work is focused on social media metrics, but it covers a lot of ground outside of the measures and metrics you'll need to quantify your social media activities. For the most part, I aim to help you design and implement a sustainable program for social media measurement. Yet, my approach doesn't dwell too much on channels or even specific technologies because I believe that these elements are secondary to strategy. That said, I do spend a fair bit of time discussing vendors, including how to select them and what capabilities they offer. But overall, you'll find that the approach I take is pragmatic and timeless in the way that it doesn't place undue emphasis on channels, vendors, or trendy tactics that may not stand the test of time.

An early secret that I'll share is that this book turned out to be a massive research project. I embarked on this project of revealing the secrets of social media with a clear and elaborate plan of what I wanted to accomplish. After laying out the different types of metrics and my framework for putting metrics to use, I realized that this was just the beginning. Simply having metrics is potentially debilitating if you aren't equipped to use them and incorporate analysis into a business strategy. Thus, I had to go further to explain not only how social media metrics can fit into your enterprise applications, but also how it applies to the social media ecosystem at large. This is where I turned to research. There are so many bright and creative practitioners using social media today that new information, new ideas, and revolutionary practices are emerging every day. Rather than spout only what I know about social media and measuring its impact, I chose to tap into my social network of relationships that span social media consultants, practitioners, and peers to offer so much more than I could do alone. Thus, much of the information contained in this book includes lessons learned from my experiences, stories of others' successes, and ideas generated by some of the brightest minds working in social media today.

Readers should recognize that the data, statistics, examples, and case studies were all researched in 2010 and the first half of 2011. Although I worked to update all my figures and data points prior to publication, appreciate that this book represents a snapshot in time. I'm sure that many of these examples may look trite in years to follow. In fact, I took some sly pleasure in knowing that looking back on my statements about the unfathomable size of our data stores or the velocity at which a viral video accelerates today would pale in comparison to what will be possible with social media tomorrow.

Where Are the Secrets?

Social Media Metrics Secrets is organized into three sections that illuminate what it takes to successfully measure social media. However, as you're probably aware, this is no easy task, so there's a great deal of information about the current state of social media and how to convince your company that this channel is right for your organization that fills in the background of how to make this happen. Each of the three parts in this book contains some key pieces to assembling the big picture of social media measurement. Yet, I realize that some of you might want to jump straight to the metrics, so here's the secret to finding the goods.

The actual metrics of social media in this book are organized in four key sections. It's likely that these sections will be the pages that become dog-eared and coffee-stained as you reference them often to validate and confirm your efforts when building social media metrics. These key sections are as follows:

- **Counting metrics (Chapter 1):** These are the most basic and readily available metrics in social media. They're likely the ones that you are already collecting today because they are typically offered by social networks, platforms, and applications to shed light on tactical performance. Counting metrics include fans, followers, users, viewers, visitors, subscribers, and so on.

- **Business value metrics (Chapter 3):** These metrics will be the basis for communicating the successes and failures of social media to stakeholders across your organization. Business value metrics are designed to strike executives and managers at the very core of their corporate mandates. These metrics are specific to roles within the executive suite, legal department, human resources, sales staff, service teams, and marketing functions. Business value metrics include revenue, market share, customer satisfaction, and so on.

- **Outcome metrics (Chapter 4):** These metrics help measurers of social media align their operational programs with their corporate goals. These metrics are crucial in quantifying the effectiveness of social media and for making course corrections while efforts are underway. These are the Key Performance Indicators (KPIs) of social media. Outcome metrics include reach, velocity, interaction rate, conversion rate, sentiment ratio, and so on.

- **Foundational measures (Chapter 5):** These foundational measures will be the underlying formulas used to calculate your own customized outcome metrics and business value metrics. They are somewhat complex, so I saved them for later in the book, but these measures will enable an exponential leap in the value and insights you gain from social media metrics because they are specific to your unique business. After you establish a familiarity with basic metrics and social KPIs, foundational measures will launch your measurement program into overdrive. Foundational measures include interaction, engagement, influence, advocates, and impact.

For those of you who want the full immersive experience, the following sections outline what you can expect to find in each of the three parts of *Social Media Metrics Secrets*.

PART I: ADDRESSING THE SOCIAL DATA DILEMMA

In Part I, I dive right into the metrics, skipping over the social media 101 platitudes that you've likely heard a dozen times or more. But there are some meaty points about social network growth, Big Data, and data visualizations that I felt compelled to write about. These topics set the stage for the metrics you'll eventually use and, therefore, are important to understanding what you're getting into. Further, I also spend a good deal of time talking about preparing your business to accept social media. So many things about this medium are new that change management tactics are required for any business to assimilate to social media. I've included a number of mini case studies, anecdotes, and examples of what to do and what not to do with social media data. There's much to be learned from ancient history, and measurers of social media are advised to learn from the mistakes of the early pioneers in social media exploration.

PART II: MANAGING SOCIAL MEDIA WITH ANALYTICS

Part II gets into the crux of social analytics by defining the essential elements of collecting and analyzing social media data. I lay out the fundamentals of aligning your measures of success with business goals and objectives that should set the stage for developing your social media measurement programs. More importantly, I offer the mathematical calculations that you can apply immediately to begin quantifying your social media KPIs. These foundational elements are the building blocks of the Social Analytics Framework that I describe in great detail. This framework is based on a tested methodology that both large and small businesses have applied to evaluate, assess, and explain their social media activities. Of course, I wouldn't want to leave you without a long-term plan for success, so this section closes out with a solid chapter delineating continuous optimization. There, I describe what it takes to track elusive social metrics like reach, engagement, and virality.

PART III: FINDING THE BIG SOCIAL MEDIA PAYOFF

Part III of *Social Media Metrics Secrets* explores what it takes to correlate social media initiatives with your business success. Since there are entire books written on the subject of social media return on investment, I intentionally contain my coverage to measurement and mapping returns back to the desired outcomes of your social media efforts. Here I relied on research to reveal some of the secret costs behind managing a social media operation and how you can build a business case for social media. And I describe specific methods to help quantify both "hard" and "soft" metrics of social media. From there, I take a deep dive into the current technologies available across the social technology spectrum today. This section details the different types of social media technologies, such as social search, social analytics, social engagement, social platforms, and social management software, and when your organization might need each one. To do this, I create a blueprint for defining your business requirements and also evaluate a series of leading social analytics vendors against an assessment matrix of 75 criteria. All of this culminates into a glimpse at what's possible in the future. I touch upon the burgeoning trends in mashing data and location-based services as well as what it takes to execute and manage an ethical social measurement program.

What You Need to Use This Book

To use this book, all you really need is a desire to participate in social media. For some this will be a curiosity and for others a passion, but either way, this book is about helping you to quantify your goals in social media and recognize when you achieve them. Some consumers may find value in the metrics contained within these pages, but this book is really designed for businesses to learn how to measure their forays into social media.

Additionally, you don't need any specific tools or social media platforms to utilize the lessons contained within this book. In fact, many of the secrets I share don't cost a thing, as free tools and open resources are plentiful in social media. But be advised that there is no quick fix or silver bullet contained within this book. Most of the secrets I share will require you to make them your own by applying your insights and recommendations. Thus, the most important thing you need to effectively use this book is your open mind.

On a recent podcast featuring Jay Baer and Amber Naslund, authors of *The NOW Revolution* (Wiley, 2011), the discussion turned to tools required for measuring social media. I listened intently to see if their expert opinions aligned with my own. I was elated to hear Amber proclaim that tools don't make a good social media measurer. She declared that the human brain was the most important social media tool, and I agree wholeheartedly—so much so that her statement prompted my Tweet depicted in Figure I-1.

FIGURE I-1: A live Tweet captured during a social media measurement podcast.

Features and Icons Used in This Book

The following features and icons are used in this book to help draw your attention to some of the most important or useful information in the book, some of the most valuable tips, insights, and advice that can help you unlock the secrets of social media metrics.

Also keep an eye out for Quick Response (QR) codes in the margins like the one you see here. These codes hold data that will lead you to web sites and additional interactive resources. You'll need a smartphone or a tablet device to snap a picture of the codes using a QR code reader application. There are many free ones available and I'm using RedLaser at the moment. If your mobile device didn't ship with a built-in QR code reader, a brief search in any app store should reveal a whole slew of code-reading options. Give it a try by scanning the QR code in the margin to visit the socialmediametricssecrets.com web site that accompanies this book.

> ▶ Watch for margin notes like this one that highlight some key piece of information or a juicy link to some awesome resource.

bit.ly/my_book.qrcode

SIDEBARS

Sidebars like this one feature additional information about topics related to the nearby text.

TIP The Tip icon indicates a helpful trick or technique.

NOTE The Note icon points out or expands on items of importance or interest.

CROSSREF The Cross-Reference icon points to chapters where additional information can be found.

WARNING The Warning icon warns you about possible negative side effects or precautions you should take before making a change.

PART I

ADDRESSING THE SOCIAL DATA DILEMMA

Going Pro with Social Media

Welcome to the wonderful world of social media metrics!
Social media has unquestionably entered the mainstream as consumers flock to jump
on every social bandwagon, buggy, and freight train that drives past. This frenzied
enthusiasm has helped the largest social networks to amass hundreds of thousands of
users that rival the world's most populous countries, while new platforms and channels
emerge unabated. The early sparks of social media innovation have flourished into a
raging inferno of opportunity for consumers and businesses alike.

These businesses include everyone from the largest global fortune 100 to the
smallest mom-and-pop shop, who are winning and losing every day with social media.
The losers are detached from their customers because they are unable to hear the

outpouring of ideas and feedback over the drone of their antiquated toiling. Conversely, the winners are tapping into consumer needs and wants and using social media as a method to:

- ▶ Increase their brand exposure
- ▶ Initiate dialogue with customers
- ▶ Generate interactions with their owned media
- ▶ Facilitate customer support
- ▶ Assemble legions of loyal advocates
- ▶ Spur corporate innovation
- ▶ Do much, much more

As consumers race to nascent social media channels, businesses are impelled to embrace the medium or risk losing their competitive edge. And most are electing to comply with the masses.

Research from numerous sources indicates that nearly 80 percent of organizations doing business today are using at least one form of social media for their marketing efforts. However, usage does not always include measurement, which leaves companies who deploy social media without measures of success effectively running blind. According to data from the Web Analytics Association, 35 percent of survey respondents cited measuring social media as the biggest challenge they will face in 2011. Among organizations in this group, nearly 65 percent are *still* planning to establish and implement social media Key Performance Indicators (KPIs) in 2011—meaning that they haven't deployed these measures yet. Thus, while social media is rampant, many organizations are still working to get their measures and metrics in place to quantify this powerful new medium. And hopefully, that's why you're reading, too.

Throughout this book, I will detail what it takes to measure the many facets of social media. I'll introduce you to concepts that will allow you to construct a foundation for understanding the impact of your social media efforts. I'll reveal the details behind social media metrics that go beyond just counting fans and followers to identifying real business value. I'll offer methods to create a collaborative working environment whereby social media spans your entire organization. And I'll help you elevate your social media game plan to truly benefit your business.

The secrets of social media metrics that I share will save you countless hours of time and frustration by allowing you to employ metrics that help identify social media activities that are critical to your business. Although the pages of this book

▶ Going pro with social media requires a level of accountability that is only present with a program of measurement securely in place.

hold many secrets and strategies to get you started on your way to a professional career in social media measurement, *you* are the key ingredient. By understanding what it takes to apply a holistic program of social media measurement, you can use social media as an instrument for success. Yet, make no mistake, it's a big job, and there's no shortcut to going pro with social media. Making the jump from amateur to professional requires not only the skills to go pro, but also extensive planning and preparation. Entering the world of social media as a professional means having a plan for success and the metrics to quantify it. It's hard work, but the benefit of going pro is that you get paid. At the same time, social media is fun, exciting, and ever-changing. With the guidance and secrets offered in this book, you'll be equipped to execute your social media endeavors with well-defined metrics that can accelerate your brand awareness, increase your customer pipeline, and elevate your bottom-line sales. So, if you're ready and want to learn more, let's go.

DEMYSTIFYING SOCIAL MEDIA METRICS

Almost since its inception, the entire genre of social media has mystified businesses and individuals alike. To many, it's foreign, it's ambiguous, it's not exactly clear what social media is and what it isn't. Confusion and bewilderment are common emotions evoked in businesses working to understand and participate in social media. And this makes measurement all the more challenging. Yet, making sense of measurement is what I do. Although I do not claim to be a social media guru, a shaman, a ninja, or a virtuoso by any account, I have built my professional career on measuring online properties. In fact, my business partner Eric T. Peterson wrote the original book called *Web Analytics Demystified,* and that's the name of the consultancy that Eric founded where we both ply our trade today. Much of the knowledge that I have and the secrets that I share throughout this book emerged from my years as an industry analyst at the world's leading research organizations; from what I learned from Eric about KPIs, metrics, and measurement; and from experiences with clients in my years of consulting. Thus, the secrets of social media measurement don't come from guru-ism, but rather from diligence, experience, and hard work.

You'll quickly see that I take a pragmatic approach to social media metrics, which is steeped in the fundamentals of measurement. To attempt to measure social media in any other way is akin to chasing the newest shiny object. All too often in my consulting practice, I encounter organizations that do just that. They approach social media as if it's some kind of three-headed hydra that they've never encountered before. Although it may be true that they haven't seen the specifics of the platform or the behaviors of their customers, social media is just another channel for your business and it should be treated as such. To approach it any differently creates an unwarranted mystique that typically needs to be unraveled before starting on the real work of measurement. Yet, with all this said, the "newness" of social media creates opportunities for organizations to deliver metrics, insights, and simply beautiful information that often slip through the grasp of many traditional digital measurement technologies.

Starting from a Solid Measurement Foundation

I can tell you with complete confidence that measurement can be simplified, but it's not easy. It's challenging because to measure effectively, you must not only understand the mechanics of the digital properties and be able to evaluate data with statistical rigor, but you must also comprehend the desired outcomes of your efforts from a strategic business point of view. These diametrically opposed skills require a balance of art and science in measurement. Finding individuals who have the technical chops for measurement along with the business acumen is exceedingly rare. What's even more uncommon is finding an individual who has these qualities and the ability to effectively communicate results and findings to a wide range of stakeholders across an organization. These are rare skills indeed.

Thus, after spending the past decade focusing on online businesses and the art and science of measuring them, there's one construct that I've identified that really works. We use this construct as a foundational element in our consulting practices at Web Analytics Demystified, and it has helped countless organizations to approach and understand digital measurement. It's called the "Trilogy of Measurement," and it includes People, Process, and Technology. Each of these elements is critical to building a solid foundation for digital measurement, and the absence of any single one can be debilitating. We've applied this trilogy to our consulting practice with great success because it offers the basic building blocks for any measurement effort. This is true for social analytics as well. Let's take a look at each of the components within the "Trilogy of Measurement."

ALLOCATING PEOPLE

One of the most important secrets that I can share with you is that people are the most valuable asset in any measurement initiative. Although many businesses will look to technologies and tools as the panacea for their measurement woes, technology alone cannot deliver insights, nor can technology answer the tough questions about your social media programs. And it certainly cannot shape data into stories

▶ People are your most important asset in any measurement initiative. Everything else becomes secondary if you don't have people capable of creating measures of success, conducting analysis, and delivering insightful recommendations.

that resonate with the goals and aspirations of your business. These tasks require people. Metrics can help you to present the facts and communicate them in a way that transforms data from numbers on a page to meaningful recommendations for operating a successful business, yet metrics are not the endgame. The endgame is communicating across your organization about the successes (and failures) that you experience by participating in social media. The reality is that you will have failures, and the metrics you instill will help you to learn from them and to avoid them in future endeavors.

Additionally, the people responsible for measurement within your organization will hold the knowledge. Successful measurement programs have analysts who not only collect and analyze data, but also educate the business on the metrics that matter. People are the liaisons that translate business needs into meaningful metrics and key performance indicators (KPIs). They also transcribe raw data from low-level metrics to business value. Yet doing all of these things requires that organizations recognize the value in the data and the analysts who make sense of it. Historically, the role of data analyst has been a thankless task that conjured up visions of statisticians crunching numbers with slide rules and pocket protectors. Yet, as data proliferates and digital channels become a mainstay for conducting business, measurers of digital media are gaining their rightful recognition. Organizations that are on the bleeding edge of innovation have voracious appetites for data, and their consumption is making them healthy with knowledge. As social media increases in importance for everyday business operations, the data that emerges from it and the measurers that create, manage, and analyze the metrics that arise will be the rainmakers within their respective organizations. It's people who make this happen.

BUILDING PROCESS

Having the right people and adequate numbers of them is paramount to attaining success with your social media measurement endeavors. Yet, another critical secret that I'll share with you is that no one individual can build a successful program of measurement singlehandedly. Measurement requires a chain of individuals because effective measurement originates from strategy, and then flows through a management process to operations; from there measurement is embedded within execution and evaluated across all stages of an initiative. The loop is closed when measurement surfaces back up at the strategic level and is assessed in terms of performance. This cycle is a continuous exercise that is made possible through process. Process dictates how measures are created, how they are socialized and shared, and how they're implemented within an organization. Further, process ensures that all efforts are measured and that they support the strategic initiatives set forth by the organizations. Process makes measurement scalable and process brings together the appropriate stakeholders to ensure that programs can be evaluated in a business context.

The problem is that most businesses don't have processes in place for measurement. Nor do they take the time to ensure that measurement is consistently applied in a manner that is meaningful to the business. Companies that operate in this way tend to launch social programs, experiment with ideas, and deliver inconclusive results. This fails to benefit the organization and often results in program termination or constricted budgets. Operating in this manner is the quickest route to market and often the easiest for companies getting started with social media. However, this is shortsighted and flat out wrong. It will end up hurting individuals in the long run, as measurers will struggle to find value in trivial metrics and executives will fail to recognize the benefits that social media can deliver to their organizations. It doesn't have to be this way. You can circumvent the pitfalls of failed efforts that came before you by insisting upon a big-picture view of your social media activities and how they will ultimately fit into your business strategy. Although every detail and nuance doesn't need to be perfect at launch, by developing a process for measurement that utilizes a framework that is both scalable and repeatable, you will achieve greater gains. Using process is the best way to foster collaboration and facilitate an environment where knowledge is transferred across a diverse group of people.

UTILIZING TECHNOLOGY

▶ Social media measurement technologies change and evolve quickly. Be sure to develop key business requirements and take the time to find vendors that meet your needs, because switching vendors can be costly.

Technologies are perhaps that sexiest of the three parts of the trilogy. Who doesn't like a new technology solution? But as I stated earlier, technologies are typically not a one-stop solution for measurement problems. The technologies are only as capable as the operators who guide them and pull the levers and switches to calibrate them to your unique business. In social media measurement, so much can be accomplished using free tools and creative ingenuity that technologies can often hamper an organization's ability to build a solid platform for measurement. Don't misconstrue this; technologies are important and in many cases essential to effectively measuring the progress of social media. But often technologies can get in the way of seeing the realities of your social media progress. The advice that I offer to my clients and to the readers of this book is to select your technologies after you've secured adequate staff for conducting analysis and developed a strategic plan for measurement. I offer this guidance because any measurer of social media worth his or her salt will go to great lengths to identify business requirements for technologies that will serve their measurement needs. I go into much greater detail on this subject in Chapter 8, so feel free to skip ahead if you need to find a vendor ASAP. Just ensure that it's not the first thing that you do.

The reality is that to effectively measure social media, you will need a technology assist. There's simply too much information pouring in every minute to process everything using makeshift tools and Excel spreadsheets. You may find that basic technology resources are part of your social media measurement toolset, but in my experience, organizations (and especially large enterprises) typically require multiple tools to measure all the moving parts of their social media activities. This is true because so much of what we do in social media is stretched across platforms and channels. For example, you may initiate a social media campaign with a video, where data about the number of views and embeds may come from your video player of choice. From there, if the video is embedded within your Facebook page, you may use Facebook Insights to garner information about the demographics of your viewers—how many "liked" or commented on the video and who they interact with inside the Facebook platform. But, let's assume that you have a call to action within the video that leads viewers back to your primary web site. Here you may require Web Analytics tools to understand referral source, content viewed, and conversion events. Each of these steps in this hypothetical example requires you to measure your initiative with a different tool.

Using Metrics and Measures of Success

I want to make something crystal clear before diving any deeper into the world of social media metrics: metrics must have meaning. Without meaning, otherwise known as context, metrics are just numbers. For this reason, it's critical that measurers of social media know what they are working toward. It's also important to understand that any good program of measurement will have multiple layers of metrics used to assess, explain, and manage social media operations. I go into greater detail about how to do this throughout this book, but I think it's worthwhile to lay out the groundwork here.

> ▶ All your social media metrics must have meaning that's revealed by presenting metrics in the context of what they represent and what they mean to your organization.

UNDERSTANDING THE FOUR TYPES OF METRICS

Effective measurement programs almost always include metrics that work from the top of the organization on down. When I talk about working from the top down, I'm referring to the fact that everything you do from a measurement perspective should support the goals at the top of your organization. As such, it's often important to create metrics that are designed for communicating to the top of the corporate ladder and across senior executives that preside over each of your departmental areas.

Additionally, it's imperative that the metrics you use are consistent and repeatable because in many cases, advanced metrics will build upon the base metrics that you apply to measuring your social media programs. Following these high-level and foundational metrics, you need operational metrics that provide insights into the success of individual initiatives, which hopefully are designed to support your big-picture goals. These are the key performance indicators that should fire off bells and whistles when they deviate from predefined thresholds. From there, you should have tactical metrics as well. These are the granular details that shed light on the day-to-day execution of your social media efforts and allow you to measure progress in micro detail. These tactical metrics are important because some days the needle doesn't move too far and you'll need detailed measures that give you the boost you need to come into work the next day.

To help you wrap your head around these different types of metrics, allow me to elaborate on four types of metrics that I believe are key to the success of any measurement program:

▶ **Foundational measures:** Nearly all measurement programs will rely upon a handful of metrics that persist across channels and apply almost universally to measuring all sorts of social activities. I call these the foundational metrics because many of the business value and outcome-based metrics that follow are calculated based on the definitions created within your foundational metrics. While I go into much greater detail about the foundational metrics in Chapter 5, five key metrics that I've identified include interaction, engagement, influence, advocates, and impact. The nature of foundational metrics is such that you will need to use the calculations you build to define other measures of success, so in a way they are the building blocks of social analytics. As such, they must be defined in a way that applies to your business, and they must be calculated consistently each and every time.

▶ **Business value metrics:** Depending on your organization, your senior leaders may want the excruciating details of your social media activities (especially if they're investing in them), but in most cases, executives should only receive a handful of pertinent metrics that reflect how your social media efforts are contributing to overarching corporate goals such as revenue, market share, and customer satisfaction. I describe these as business value metrics because they hold significant meaning for key stakeholders across your organization. For example, metrics that matter to your chief officers will differ from those that are important to your legal team or to your human resources department. Further still, marketers will require different metrics than your salespeople.

As a measurer of social media, you will quickly realize that aspects of social interaction with consumers extend well beyond the confines of any single platform or channel and that social will pervade the recesses of your entire organization. As such, you need to develop business value metrics that hold meaning for different departments and managers within your company.

► **Outcome metrics (KPIs):** Following business value metrics, the next level of measurement detail that I typically advocate for is outcome metrics, also known as Key Performance Indicators or KPIs. These metrics take into consideration an objective that you are working toward such as generating awareness, creating a dialogue, encouraging interaction, facilitating support, promoting advocacy, or spurring innovation.

> **NOTE** I also refer to outcome metrics as Key Performance Indicators (KPIs), which is a commonly used term in traditional Web Analytics. I use the terms synonymously throughout this book.

Outcome metrics can vary according to your business needs and they will fluctuate depending on the type of social campaign that you're working on, yet the metrics contained within this category typically enable you to manage progress toward your desired outcomes. In most cases, outcome metrics enable you to evaluate social media activities from varied perspectives such as before, during, and after a campaign goes live in the field. Outcome metrics also require social media measurers to collaborate with stakeholders to determine success factors up front so that you know what you're measuring toward. This method of establishing and predetermining measures of success is key to aligning strategies with tactics and provides a means to track performance over time. When deployed correctly, outcome metrics (as well as business value metrics) can be tracked over time and used to create benchmarks. These benchmarks can be used to gauge the performance of one campaign against another or the effectiveness of one channel over another.

► **Counting metrics:** Finally, counting metrics are the lowest level of measurement and usually represent the minutia of social media metrics. Here, I'm referring to fans and followers, visits and views, and clicks and click-throughs. The list goes on and on, with rows of data that may or may not have an impact on your business. Although I do believe that counting metrics are critically important, I also know that far too many organizations use these low-level metrics as their primary source of information and they wonder why they cannot determine the value or success of their social media efforts. Counting metrics can answer questions such as how much, how many, how often, and how far, but they usually can't tell you how successful you are. The important thing to know about counting metrics is that they reveal the tactical details of your social media campaigns. But they must be trended over time and presented in context. Simply knowing how many is irrelevant if you don't have a basis for comparison, such as percent change or competitive share. This is why placing metrics in the context of your business is paramount for any organization.

Armed with these four types of metrics, you'll be ready to tackle the biggest challenges in social media measurement. And quite possibly you'll make the jump to a professional program of measurement.

GRADUATING BEYOND EXPERIMENTATION

To a great extent, businesses have been forced to view social media as experimental. You haven't had much choice. The intent, design, and execution of numerous social platforms were founded on creativity and inspiration rather than clear financial motivation. Take Facebook, for example; Mark Zuckerberg didn't create "The Facebook" with the intention of generating the largest advertising platform in the world. Instead, he developed a method to enable college students to find one another online. On Facebook, Zuckerberg was initially opposed to advertising and any forms of monetization in favor of growing the network of participants. This model didn't leave room for business participation. Or consider Twitter—the notion of broadcasting your thoughts to the masses in 140 characters or less is a foreign concept to many. Businesses are challenged to recognize the value in this new medium. I recently heard Guy Kawasaki speak at a measurement conference and he quipped: "If your first reaction to Twitter was, it's stupid, then you passed the IQ test." My point is that many social media platforms are experimental at first. Yet, the good ones build substantial user bases; they survive beyond their initial growing pains and often constitute the basis for thriving marketing opportunities. As part of an organization, or even as an individual building a personal brand, it's your responsibility to differentiate frivolous platforms from those that will serve your business aspirations.

▶ Many social media opportunities may appear shallow at first glance because it's often difficult to recognize business potential. But don't underestimate the power of social media when a platform attains critical mass.

Getting Serious about Social

Regardless of whether you recognize their potential at first glance, the reality is that many forms of social media are not frivolous at all; they're opportunities lying in wait. Although this certainly isn't true for every emergent social medium that hits the streets, there are channels that will become indispensible to businesses. Finding these solvent channels isn't a matter of identifying the most populated networks, but rather distinguishing online habitats that resonate with your unique audience. Fortunately for businesses, the need to be an early adopter of the latest social channel *du jour* isn't paramount. Yet, the need to do it right is imperative. For this reason, I recommend resisting the temptation to rush into participation in every new social media activity; instead take a considered and strategic approach that will pay long-term dividends.

▶ Don't assume that just because Facebook is the most popular social network, you need to focus on it. Your audience may not be there. Take the time to identify channels that work for you.

WITNESSING A DIGITAL TRANSFORMATION

One of the first steps to participating in and measuring social media must be taking the time to recognize what's occurring within your macro environment. This includes understanding your changing customer base and your evolving competitive set as both change with social media. Collectively, we're undergoing a tectonic shift in behavior because of social media, which is transforming the way that businesses operate. The way I see it, there are three distinct phases that lead to social media transformation. These include emerging platforms, participating consumers, and assimilating businesses. Let's take a look at how these phases emerge:

▶ **Platforms emerge:** Whether you take examples from Mark Zuckerberg (co-founder, Facebook), Biz Stone (co-founder, Twitter), or Dennis Crowley (co-founder, Foursquare), building a social media platform from concept to fruition requires not only genius, but also perseverance. Although many undoubtedly questioned the value of these solutions, others recognized the potential that each held for connecting people in new and meaningful ways. The platforms provided a catalyst for interaction among individuals and eventually for businesses to interact with their audiences in inventive ways. Much as the industrial revolution enabled machinery that produced an infrastructure to spur innovation, social media is giving rise to new methods of interconnectivity that will forever transform the way humans coexist.

▶ **Consumers participate:** For the most part, social networks thrive when the number of people participating reaches critical mass sufficient to sustain the population without significant outside intervention. This means that conversations and interactions are forthcoming from the user base and the creators can allow the community or network to evolve within the construct they set forth. That's not to say that you should allow your users to run amok without guidance or supervision—you shouldn't. But you must allow consumers the latitude to create, develop, and collaborate. The most successful social initiatives are ones where consumers champion the cause and become active participants. When this occurs, an effort is successful in moving from a unidirectional monologue to a bidirectional or multidirectional conversation.

> **NOTE** Much of social media is about facilitating a dialogue between brands, customers, and other consumers. Many of the metrics in this book identify ways to quantify these *interactions* between people and the distances their conversations travel.

▶ *The game has changed and it's time to interact with consumers in a more meaningful way.*

▶ **Businesses assimilate:** The final stage of transformation is when businesses participate (or are allowed to participate) in social networks via participation, advertising, content creation, or other means. As you'll learn later in this book, business participation is contingent upon transparency and genuine interactions. Used-car salesperson tactics won't work here, as consumers don't want to be sold to in every social interaction. Instead of putting on your sales hat, initiate a dialogue with customers and add value by offering information that comes with the authority of your brand. Too many failed attempts exemplify that businesses cannot treat social media as yet another broadcast medium.

ADAPTING TO SOCIAL SAVVY CUSTOMERS

The challenge that most businesses and the marketers that serve them face is keeping up with their ever-changing customers. Back in the day when customers had only three channels to choose from and audiences were captive, changes could be anticipated and, to some extent, influenced by marketers. Yet, today the bars of captivity are nonexistent and a proliferation of choice is the norm. Further, consumers have embraced social channels as a means to gain information about brands, products, and services without the bias of the marketers behind the message. Instead they turn to their friends, families, and social networks to gain information and awareness about products and services. The result is that businesses must work harder to satisfy their customers and to control the message they put forth from their respective organizations. However, this is much more easily said than done. Organizations are struggling to adapt to the new social customer.

According to a report produced by Forrester Research called "The CMO Mandate: Adapt or Perish" (http://www.forrester.com/rb/Research/cmo_mandate_adapt_or_perish/q/id/57245/t/2?action=5), marketers are struggling to keep up with the frenetic pace of consumer change. According to the research, the evolving ecosystem of media, technology, and devices is forcing change for marketers. In response, 75 percent of marketers surveyed are planning to reorganize their teams in 2011 in an attempt to better deal with consumer actions in a transformed digital environment. (See Chapter 3 for more on organizing your business for social media metrics measurement.) These reorganizational measures are a direct response to shifting digital and social marketing activities for 65 percent of organizations surveyed. Yet, Forrester points to another study by Accenture Interactive that calls out a "crisis of confidence" affecting two-thirds of organizations that faced problems when implementing digital marketing initiatives. The primary fear reiterated by Forrester is that only 4 percent of marketers claim that they are prepared to tackle the digital marketing opportunities before them. This is a direct reflection of the complexity of marketing across new and emerging social media channels.

Yet, despite the gloom and doom painted by research organizations, as a measurer of social media, I can assure you that you do have a fighting chance. Bear in mind that you will need to evangelize for social media within your organization and to indoctrinate the uneducated, but you can succeed if you approach social media as a business activity. Throughout several sections of this book, I will elaborate on what it takes to measure social media and expose your organization to the value of this important task. Yet, the primer is summed up with the following:

▶ **Embrace the digital transformation:** There's no question that the social media train is rolling fast. Your chances of chasing down your customers and asking them to revert to your antiquated ways is futile. Thus, you may as well embrace the social media craze and determine how you can effectively use social media to drive your business into this century. However, this is no easy task for many old-school organizations that still fail to recognize the consumer metamorphosis to digital. If you work at an organization that is impervious to change, you will undoubtedly meet with resistance and continually battle against a prove-it mentality. Throughout the chapters of this book, I offer secrets to initiate the skeptics. You'll learn to establish a bulletproof social media measurement plan that maintains the culture of your

▶ Consumers today not only hold a position of empowerment, but many also feel entitled to use (sometimes abuse) social media as a service channel for unwarranted gain. Don't pander to consumer bullying, but do recognize that the tables have turned.

organization and aligns with the goals of your senior leadership. Using the framework I offer, you can demonstrate the value of social media while minimizing exposure to the pitfalls and risks of social media. These are the secrets that will enable you to make the transformation and bridge the digital divide.

▶ **Use measurement to understand behavior:** As you work to keep pace with consumer activities across digital channels, you will quickly find that their digital footprints cover much ground. This means that you must understand customer and prospect behavior, not just on the digital properties that you own (such as your web sites and mobile properties), but also on proprietary social networks (such as Facebook) and distributed channels (such as Twitter and Yelp), which likely extend beyond your "controllable" comfort zone. Measuring these earned media outlets becomes increasingly more difficult because you often cannot simply place tracking codes on the page to watch as visitors come rolling into your digital stores. Instead, you need to listen and get creative about the ways in which you assemble digital data and measure the implicit and explicit preferences of consumers. Throughout this book, I expand upon the ways in which you can collect digital data and reveal secrets about the complexity of understanding behavior through measurement. Although these are not simple tasks, the importance of measuring behavior across social channels is critical. These acts of measurement not only reveal behavioral characteristics, but also inform you about what works with social media, which channels are most effective, and where revenue can be generated from social media activities.

▶ **Hold on by letting go:** Whether you've already gone pro with social media or are working toward that end, one of the key concepts to grasp is that consumers are empowered by the shift to social technologies. For businessperson or marketer who has spent the past decades reaching customers on their terms with controlled messages and carefully crafted campaigns, this is a foreign land. Yet, these newly minted consumers who emerged from digital liberation don't want to be boxed in with one-sided marketing messages and generic sales collateral. In fact, they're averse to these tactics. Instead, they're conditioned to ask their networks for guidance or to call out brands directly when they have a problem. These new digital consumers do not want to be shown the way; they want to lead. And for a brand working to retain any semblance of connection with customers, compliance is the only option. Thus, many organizations have opened their brands to consumer ideas and empowered them by sincerely valuing their opinions. These organizations are succeeding with social media not because they're clutching to consumers, but because they are letting them go. With the secrets and examples I share within this book, you too can strengthen ties with your customers by offering them more freedom and strengthening your relationship with social media.

INCORPORATING 10 SOCIAL MEDIA MUST-HAVES

If I haven't scared you off yet, allow me to share with you what I believe to be the 10 social media must-have secrets. These indispensible elements are so important to social media participation that your organization cannot be serious about social media until you adopt these 10 must-have items. Anything short of this list means that you're either struggling to prove to your company that social media is impor-tant (if so, keep reading) or still testing the waters with social media (if so, read on to change your outlook). In either case, take my word for it, social media will impact your organization, and adopting this list by assigning action items for your business will raise the stakes for any social media program.

1. **Strategy:** Venturing onto the social media playing field without a strategy will almost certainly result in failure. Social strategies can take myriad forms that need not be extraordinarily complex, but they do need to portray a clear plan for what you're doing and why. A sound social strategy will provide vali-dation for your social activities and a reference point to keep you on track.

2. **Audience:** Understand that social media is about connecting with people. If your business doesn't command an audience or if you don't have the need to interact with individuals, social media may not be for you. Alternatively, if you do have a need to connect with people, understanding your audience— whether niche or mainstream—and where they spend their time online is key to deploying any social initiative.

3. **Commitment:** Launching a social media program requires multiple levels of commitment. For starters, know that any social activity that you undertake will require commitment. A Facebook page needs content and curation; a Twitter account implies that you'll respond; and any other effort will man-date interaction. If you're present on social media, consumers will find you, and failure to respond is fatal. Further, commitment from your organization to support social media is a must-have. Organizations that engage in social media without backing from the business will continually struggle.

4. **Content:** A steady stream of content and creative ideas is critical for social media programs. Whether you sell blue jeans or big ideas, your participation in social media requires giving your audience something to talk about. The most successful social media campaigns start by seeding conversations and then stepping back to let their customers take their ideas and run. This typically leads to productive interaction, but be sure to keep the guardrails on your social activities so they don't go too far astray.

5. **Staff:** To effectively participate in social media requires people to deliver, manage, and interact with the outside world. Although small organizations may be able to get away with a limited staff dedicated to social media, don't expect that you can assign an intern to manage your social media programs. This is not only shortsighted, but also irresponsible. Social media is just as important to your business as customer service or product development. Even if this isn't the case for your company today, social media has the potential to eclipse other channels in terms of its criticality to your business.

6. **Identity:** Social media requires a genuine and authentic approach, which is often determined by the identity your organization portends. As you'll see within the pages of this book, consumers trust each other more than they trust your brand because of social media. Faking it, pretending to be something you're not, or even offering a callous face via your social media programs will often result in consumer outcry. When developing your social media programs, give careful consideration to the identity that you want to put forth.

▶ Measurement is a must-have of the highest priority.

7. **Metrics:** Of course, this is my personal favorite and the impetus for writing this book. If you're not measuring your social media efforts, you're wasting everyone's time. Measurement not only allows you to put a stake in the ground for what you're working toward but also creates milestones and checkpoints to determine how successful you are. Any social media initiative that launches without measurement is effectively a blind effort.

8. **Policy:** Social media will potentially span to the farthest reaches of your organization, meaning that it will become an indispensible tool for interacting with—and learning from—customers. Yet, as social media becomes accessible to many within your corporate environment, there must be a common understanding of what's acceptable and what is not. For these reasons, a corporate social media policy is a must-have for any organization. I go into greater

details about policy in Chapter 9, where you'll learn to build one that sets the standards for conduct and holds your peers accountable for their social media actions.

9. **Crisis management:** Despite best-laid plans, you will inevitably encounter a snafu or two along your social media journey. Have a crisis-management plan in mind that documents standard operating procedures and includes escalation steps up to DEFCON 1, which can get you through the worst of times. Action plans can be borrowed from other, pre-existing plans within your organization, and they will mitigate unexpected social surprises and give you a jump on any fire-fighting activities that come your way.

10. **Fortitude:** This social media must-have is important because social media practitioners will inevitably meet with skepticism, resistance, and failure. Fortitude is a must-have because you will fail. The vast majority of social efforts are built on the foundations of failed ideas. Though social media has moved beyond the experimentation phase, there is still a great deal to be learned from failure. And the best experts around will advise you to fail fast and fail often so that you can learn from the bad ideas and progress quickly to the good ones.

Once equipped with these 10 social media must-haves, you'll be ready to attack the plethora of social challenges that lie ahead. I do, however, want to call your attention to the fact that my list of social media must-haves doesn't include any channels or technologies.

I differ from many social measurers and strategists who will rattle off must-have channels for your social business. It's my strong belief that social media channels (that is, Facebook, Qzone, Bebo, Orkut, Twitter, and so on) are secondary to your strategy. I'm wary of anyone who recommends a channel before they understand your business. And clearly I don't understand your business yet. Channels are important and I will certainly address them throughout this book; however, no single social media channel is pervasive and they don't belong in a list of social media must-haves.

For me, technologies are similar to channels. All too often, I witness organizations that get wrapped up in technology decisions and place the importance of technology in front of other aspects of their social media programs. I am a proponent of using social technology for discovery, analysis, engagement, delivery, and

▶ Channels will come and go, but key social media program elements—including strategy, audience, commitment, content, staff, identity, metrics, policy, crisis management, and fortitude—are timeless.

management, which I discuss in detail in Chapter 8, yet placing your technology before your strategy is a mistake. Organizations are advised to develop their strategies to define clear and actionable goals for social media, as well as to identify the staff and support necessary to fortify a robust social media program before considering technologies. The technologies will help, but they are not a panacea for staff or planning.

Matriculating to the School of Social Media Measurement

Even before you embark on your social media journey by putting out social media campaigns and building social programs, it's relatively safe to assume that somebody out there is already talking about you in some social sphere. (Well, unless of course you're working for a stealth startup or an obscure off-the-map organization, in which case you'll have to attract your own attention with social media.) But most corporations—brands, products, and even individuals—have some notoriety online. However, to find this you need to start measuring. I call it "measuring" because that's the way that I think of capturing conversations about your company, products, and/or services. It's a way to quantify what is being said about you and your brand and who's doing the talking. If you already know that measurement is a hard sell within your organization, feel free to adopt your own vernacular to make it more familiar or appealing to your stakeholders. Call it listening, call it learning, call it research, call it what you will, but understand that what I'll be focusing on throughout this book is quantifying your social media escapades and the impact that they have on your organization.

Measurement starts with paying attention to the world around you and then, when you do get around to putting your own initiatives into the field, measuring their effectiveness with precision and purpose. Measurement offers a straight line to accountability. Regardless of what type of company you work for, this should resonate. If not, I suggest you start taking notes now to build a business case for social media and amass ammunition for your internal argument. For those of you who are already on board, let's take a look at the "curriculum" for the school of social media measurement.

ACCEPTING LEARNING AS A PRIMARY OBJECTIVE

As a brand, or even as an individual, the primary objective for social media should be to learn. Although some may argue that this isn't their primary objective ("I'm in this for the money!" or "I'm working to gain more customers!"), I maintain that

▶ Find ways to introduce social media measurement to your organization in familiar terms. This may mean calling it "listening" or "research," but be sure that your terminology resonates with key decision makers.

for every social media effort, the underlying goal should be to learn. Any effort designed to generate revenue will also bring lessons about what worked, what failed, who responded, and who didn't. Similarly, if you're working to build a bigger customer base, you'll want to note which tactics attracted new prospects, which new prospects proved to be qualified, which channel performed better than another, and so on. These informational tidbits provide knowledge about how to perform better on subsequent actions. Any social media effort that's worth putting forth is worth learning from—without question.

To accomplish this and actually benefit by learning from your social media efforts, you need to measure. Although this is basic measure 101 material, you'd be amazed at how many organizations forget that quantifying success is a critical component of evaluation. All too often, companies push initiatives or campaigns out the door without taking the time to identify success or to implement measures that will determine acquisition of their desired outcomes. This is a travesty of time and resources! Failure to measure your social media activities is the cardinal sin of contemporary marketing. Measure with the intent to learn and work toward delivering better products, services, and messages to consumers. Doing this will not only enable you to get smarter about your social media activities, but it will also allow you to prove what worked and to showcase your success in order to gain more resources or funding for ongoing opportunities.

> ▶ Every social media effort that leaves your organization is a learning opportunity. Measure to learn what works, how you can do better, and what not to do in future activities.

OPTIMIZING EFFORTS WHILE UNDERWAY

For many readers of this book, your social media efforts are already in flight, and you're looking to find ways to effectively measure your progress. That's great, but it's also hard to do. I tend to use the analogy that creating measures of success while a program or campaign is already in the field is similar to attempting to change the wing of an airplane while it's flying at 30,000 feet. Luckily for measurers of social media, you can often do this without resulting in a crash-and-burn scenario by learning how to implement a pre-flight plan for even the toughest measurement projects. This will force you to plan ahead and will ultimately make life easier on you and your business counterparts for future social media itineraries.

Think about social media measurement as a work in progress. The good news is that you can continually refine your practices and embellish upon specific tactics to incrementally improve your offerings. The bad news is that your work is literally never done. Once you think you've got something figured out, you can dig deeper into the data and find anomalies or trends that will require you to adjust your course and completely change direction. Yet, accepting learning as a primary objective and becoming a student of social media measurement takes the frustration out of these hurdles and hopefully makes them fun. Done right, measuring social media allows you to become a hero within your organization, because you'll be able to report when things are going well and you'll be able to predict when the train is about to run off the tracks. And if you're optimizing along the way and doing this effectively, you will be able to make a profound impact on many aspects of your business.

BECOMING A PERPETUAL STUDENT OF BEHAVIOR

▶ Social media in some respects is a giant focus group that allows you to hear and see what customers think about your company, your products, and your services. Don't miss out on an opportunity to understand what others think by failing to listen.

If there's one guaranteed constant in social media, it's change. I can assure you that no matter how well you think you've got things figured out, they are destined to change. Technologies are changing at an astounding rate. With emerging social media platforms and a proliferation of devices with which to connect to these new media, change is interminable. Consumers are fickle in this way, too. They'll change their devices, their minds, their attitudes, and their loyalties faster than you can say "Jack Robinson." What's worse is that in my experience consumers will tell you one thing and then act in a way that is entirely discordant with what they told you they'd do. Stopping short of plugging every customer into an fMRI (functional Magnetic Resonance Imaging) machine and reading their brainwaves with neuroscience, you're reduced to listening to what they say and watching what they do. Yet, these two methods of understanding customers can be incredibly powerful if applied correctly.

Successful measurement pros not only understand human behavior, but in many cases, they can also anticipate it. This has been going on in traditional analytics for years, with the ability to build predictive models and look at segments of individuals who behave in a certain way. By using this knowledge and learning from it, measurers of social media can identify cues that indicate a propensity for action. You would be amazed at how consumer behavior follows recognizable patterns when you start to look at the data. Yet, this is possible only if you are measuring your efforts and spending the time necessary to become a student of human behavior. I'll emphasize this throughout the pages of this book, but fundamentally, social media is about people and the way they interact with businesses and each other. By studying these traits and nuances of these behaviors, you can learn a lot about your social efforts and determine how to deliver and build the most efficient and effective social media campaigns. But first you need to recognize that behavior is an ever-changing thing and getting ahead requires planning and diligence.

MOVING BEYOND COUNTING METRICS

As you read earlier in this chapter, companies are becoming more aware of the need to measure their social media efforts, which is increasing competition and leading to better overall measurement awareness. Yet, many organizations erroneously take only the metrics they're offered and assume they're done. Out-of-the-box measures delivered by platform providers, social media channels, and even listening tools are just the foyer into the world of social media metrics. Organizations that take the time to develop outcome metrics and calculate business value metrics do more than just count the number of individuals that enter their social media properties. They begin to understand how their initiatives are working in the context of their unique business goals.

I'm already on record as saying that the vast majority of businesses today are using the wrong metrics for tracking social media. This statement was based on the fact that most companies look to fans, followers, visits, and views as the primary metrics by which they track social media. These metrics represent what I call the digital trivia of social media. Yes, they are important numbers, but by most accounts they are just numbers.

> Most measurers of social media begin and end their metrics by collecting digital trivia. If you want to deliver business value, you must go further.

Unfortunately, nearly a year after I first made this statement, things still haven't changed much. Organizations commonly fall victim to reporting counting metrics as the measures of success for their social media initiatives. Not only is this potentially misleading for your organization, but it could be placing your social media programs in jeopardy. As budgets shift toward social media activities, the priority should be on demonstrating accountability and producing results—not counting up fans and followers. No program of social media should exist without a means to quantify whether or not it's working. And by and large, organizations that rely solely on counting metrics are hard pressed to demonstrate value.

COUNTING METRICS BY CHANNEL

Despite the derogatory things I've already said about counting metrics, they are a necessary evil. Counting metrics will provide you with some value if you recognize them for what they're worth and ensure that you work to place them into context (as in percent change month over month), while also aspiring to develop outcome metrics and business value metrics as you get comfortable with measuring social media.

So, think of counting metrics as the freebies of social analytics. Most platforms make this data widely available and I, too, will give up a slew of counting metrics that will give you a reference point for what to expect. The following metrics are the basis for understanding the volume, activity, and demographics of users interacting with your social media endeavors.

SOCIAL NETWORKS	MICROMEDIA	BLOGS	MEDIA SHARING
Users	Followers	Posts	Visits
Active users	New followers	Comments	Views
Fans	Unfollows	Views	Followers
Page views	Updates	Time spent	Uploads
Tab views	Mentions	Bounce rate	Downloads
Updates	ReTweets	Engagement	Likes
Check-ins	Reach	Votes	Dislikes
Likes	Impressions	Shares	
Interactions	Amplification	Likes	
Comments	Velocity	Bookmarks	Comments
Discussions	Impact	Subscribers	Favorites
Reviews	Influence	Trackbacks	Trackbacks
Posts	Lists	Referrals	Shares
Referrals	Clout	Conversions	Embeds
Feedback	Generosity		
Impressions	Signal		
Video plays	Authority		
Audio plays	Engagement		
Photo views	Share of voice		
Video uploads	Topic trends		
Audio uploads	Sentiment		
Photo uploads	Keywords		
Age	Themes		
Gender	Relevance		
Location	Resonance		

Keep in mind that this list is just getting started. There are many more counting metrics available for different social channels, platforms, and technologies. This list is not meant to be comprehensive, and don't you dare stop reading here and assume you're done. Now that we've identified the low-hanging metrics, it's your job to shuffle, categorize, and apply these in ways that make sense to your business. Better yet, start combining metrics to create your own calculated metrics that can become the outcome metrics for your business.

WORKING TOWARD PROFESSIONAL METRICS

Although measurers of social media certainly work at various levels of sophistication, I've found that most talk about counting metrics when they refer to measuring their efforts. You often hear about celebrities and the number of followers they have on Twitter, or when companies tout their Facebook presence, the number of fans is usually the reference point they offer for demonstrating success. Those that are slightly more conscious about driving value for their organizations may cite content metrics like page views, posts, or mentions. Yet, all of these are the granular details that represent program performance and not business performance.

Fortunately, this is changing for some chief marketers as they begin to align their social media efforts with bottom-line results. A recent study from Bazaarvoice and the CMO club found that marketing leaders were shifting their social media measurement focus from counting metrics to business value metrics. Table 1-1 reveals findings from studies conducted in 2010 and 2011, whereby executives were asked to report on how they plan to measure the effectiveness of their social media marketing activities. Although site traffic remains the top metric of choice, it shows promise that marketers are thinking about social media as a method to drive consumers back to their owned web properties. This jibes with the second most popular metric for 2011, which is conversion. Most often, conversions take place not on social networks but on a brand's owned web properties. Although this isn't always the case, the shift to directing traffic back to primary online destinations shows that marketers are working toward desired business outcomes. Further evidence of a shift toward value-based metrics is revealed in this data, with revenue and increased channel sales as the two metrics with the greatest levels of increased importance. Counting metrics such as fans, mentions, and contributors still rank highly in terms of importance, but it's reassuring to see that more organizations are thinking about the impact that social media can have on their overall businesses.

TABLE 1-1: The CMO's Social Media Marketing Value Metrics

	2010	2011	PERCENT CHANGE
Increased channel sales	4.0%	14.9%	272.5%
Other	2.9%	6.9%	137.9%
Conversion	32.6%	65.7%	101.5%
Revenue	29.1%	49.7%	70.8%
Reduced returns	12.0%	16.0%	33.3%
Number of positive customer mentions	52.6%	62.9%	19.6%
Number of contributors	42.9%	50.3%	17.2%
Number of fans/members	59.4%	62.9%	5.9%
Number of posts	40.0%	42.3%	5.7%
Average order value	22.3%	23.4%	4.9%
Site traffic	68%	68.0%	0.0%
Number of mentions	41.1%	41.1%	0.0%
Reduced call volume	11.4%	11.4%	0.0%
Number of page views	50.9%	43.4%	-14.7%
Do not track metrics	18.3%	6.9%	-62.3%

Source: Bazaarvoice and the CMO Club, "CMOs on Social Marketing Plans for 2011,"
January 27, 2011.

▶ Businesses are beginning to see the value in measuring beyond counting metrics.

Another positive sign is that the number of marketers not tracking social media metrics has dropped by 62 percent. This bodes well for measurers of social media, as a full 93 percent of organizations (at least those surveyed in this sample) are working to measure their social media efforts.

BECOMING A CURATOR OF METRICS

As a measurer of social media, it is your responsibility to discern numbers from metrics and to ensure that everyone within your organization recognizes the difference. Metrics must always be presented within the context of your business, even at the lowest level. Better yet, develop and communicate metrics across the three levels I've laid out here to effectively manage social media and communicate your successes throughout your organization. If you're successful, your colleagues will begin to ask better questions, and they won't tolerate hearing about fans and followers. Instead they'll be asking for percentage growth and impact on sales and delving deeper into the relevance of the metrics to their specific business needs. This allows you to elevate the conversations you have with peers and colleagues across your company and to demonstrate that measurement is a critical component in the strategic success of your social media activities.

It's important to understand that as a measurer of social media, you will need to collect metrics from all activities, including the trivial data that by itself doesn't offer much insight. Do this because the combination of metrics will often reveal important information about your organization and the ways in which you're interacting with consumers using social media. As a measurer of social media, you must become the curator of metrics to ensure that data is presented within the proper context and that your organization is using data in a meaningful and responsible way. By taking on the role of metrics curator, you assume the responsibility for defining, managing, organizing, explaining, and sharing metrics across your company. This is certainly no small task. With this responsibility comes the task of determining which metrics are comprehensible to various individuals across your organization and which are too confusing to share outside a small circle of data analysts. The role of metrics curator carries great responsibility in that the numbers you keep will eventually lead to the stories of social media success or failure. These stories will ultimately determine the longevity of many social media pursuits.

SUMMARY

In this chapter I described the underpinnings of a pragmatic approach to measuring digital media that works for traditional channels, established social media and even tenuous social platforms that are still in their early days. The details of this methodology will unfold throughout the pages of this book. Yet, as a curator of metrics, you must discriminate to determine which social channels and platforms are the right ones for your professional pursuits and which need time to mature before you consider investments. Putting metrics and foundational measures in place is the smartest way to determine if any given social media opportunity is right for you. You should start this effort by making learning your primary objective and then escalating this mentality to include greater levels of participation when you identify the right opportunities for your business.

Also recognize that there are different levels of metrics that you will use throughout your career as a measurer of social media. Identify and establish your foundational metrics and use these as a basis for establishing a common vernacular for analytics. From there, tactical metrics will provide a wealth of details about the health, performance, and growth of your social media programs. Yet, these metrics often don't mean much to the managers, directors, and executives within your business. Instead of fighting to force them to understand your way of measuring social media, adapt to their way of thinking by developing and reporting on outcome metrics and ultimately develop a set of business value metrics that resonate with your unique organization. It will take time to calculate these measures of success, but you will be infinitely rewarded as the work you do will be widely understood and appreciated throughout your company. I encourage you to read on to learn the secrets of how to develop social media metrics and how to effectively utilize them to find success in your social media endeavors.

CHAPTER 2

Riding the Social Data Wave: Churning Data into Information

IN THIS CHAPTER

- ▶ Deciding what data matter
- ▶ Applying your perspective to social media data
- ▶ Understanding the art and science of data analysis
- ▶ Establishing your virtual Network Operations Center

Collectively we've produced about 800,000 petabytes of digital data here on earth thus far. To put that into perspective, in a single petabyte you could fill 20 million four-drawer filing cabinets, or watch 13.3 years' worth of HD TV, or if you're hungry, one petabyte equates to roughly 52 tons of pepperoni pizza. So, 800,000 petabytes constitutes a staggering volume of data and represents a 62 percent growth of digital data creation in a single year. Findings from IDC's global digital output survey projected that we would grow data stores nearly as fast in 2010, and they're still counting to find out if they were correct. They also estimated that we'd surpass 1.2 zettabytes of digital data collected and stored. That's 1,200,000,000,000,000,000,000 bytes of data. According to Andreas Weigend, the former Chief Scientist at Amazon.com, the numbers would be even larger. He projected that in the single year 2009, individuals would generate more data than previously existed in the entire history of mankind, and give or take a few petabytes, his projection was correct. Now, I argue that we've been producing data all along; it's just that now we're attempting to collect it all. But that's just semantics because by anyone's count, we are amassing a ridiculous pile of data.

Regardless of how you do the math, our digital data stores are growing by at least five orders of magnitude each year. To put data creation into context, in the 60 seconds it's taken you to read the opening of this chapter, it's likely that 72,000,000 images were served up on Facebook; 2,900,000 Internet searches took place; 100,000 product searches were conducted on Amazon.com; 45,000 Tweets entered cyberspace; 24 hours' worth of video were uploaded to YouTube; and your heart probably beat somewhere between 60 to 80 times. And, if you're wearing your monitor, all of this data was recorded and stored for future reference.

Social media is a massive contributor to these increasing volumes of data and it's both a blessing and a curse. In this chapter, you'll explore how you can harness the deluge of data that's inevitably headed your way, assemble a vantage point for the influx of information, transform your data from measures and metrics into usable information, and establish an operational command center to keep tabs on your petabyte of knowledge.

> **NOTE** The size of a petabyte is 1,000 terabytes or 10^{15} bytes. The largest unit of measure is the yottabyte (10^{24}), which according to *The Economist* in 2010 is "currently too big to imagine."

HARNESSING THE DATA DELUGE

We live in a Big Data world, and there's no question that the data deluge is just beginning. I maintain that the origin of many modern data sources isn't necessarily new, but because of the digital medium in which we operate the realization of data becomes more apparent. What I mean is anything that can be captured and stored constitutes data. Cataloging the constellations or simple acts of communication that have been taking place since the Paleolithic era can now be construed as data. Humans by nature are social creatures, and we have evolved in part by communicating our needs, wants, and desires to one another. By simply sharing a gesture, stealing a glance, or uttering a sound, we've been communicating. Yet today, because so many of the ways in which we communicate take place using digital media, the multitude of our interactions are recordable and capable of translation to data.

Contemporary data fonts arise from our most basic Neanderthal instincts of finding food, seeking shelter, and procreating. Today, we can shake an iPhone app such as Urbanspoon to locate a restaurant serving a specific type of cuisine within 100 meters of our current location that has been reviewed and recommended by a critical mass of individuals within our extended network who all rated the experience an average of four out of five stars. Or we can surf to an online realty web site like Trulia .com to browse through home listings with sortable details that reveal square footage, number of bathrooms, days on the market, and how many other viewers looked at the property. We can do all this while also soliciting expert advice from realtors and residents about where to buy, what to expect, and when to lock in a low mortgage interest rate. Or what about clicking through the pages of a popular dating network such as JDate.com to find a soul mate with the perfect combination of a post-secondary pedigree education, compatible religious beliefs, and a desire to take long walks on the beach? These details are the data.

All of these facets of our daily digital interactions with others are capable of being sorted into rows and columns, tagged with metadata, and made searchable across social media platforms. These vast quantities of digital data will continue to proliferate along with so many other sources of data that it's simply mind boggling. So, the critical questions are these: Which data points matter to your social media endeavors and how do you unlock the power of data by translating data into metrics and metrics to knowledge?

▶ Almost every action we perform on social media sites (that is, clicking, reviewing, reading a blog, and so on) can be recorded as data. The challenge for measuring all this becomes determining why it matters.

Data Is Everywhere

Before unlocking the secrets of data, you need first to gain an understanding of what you're dealing with here. When it comes to your social media programs, the data you're amassing will ultimately come from a multitude of sources. You can decide if you want to manage a small trickle of information that is very specific to your company's brand or choose to drink from the Big Data fire hose and take in as much as possible. If you choose the latter, I caution you to beware of "noisy" data. Much of the data produced in social media activities is noise rather than signal.

- ▶ **Noise**, with regards to data, is the stuff that consumes your time and energy without offering much payout.

- ▶ **Signal**, on the other hand, is what you're looking for because it offers streamlined information that's relevant to your cause.

> **NOTE** Signal, or "signal to noise ratio," indicates that there is value in the message. This excludes someone Tweeting what they had for lunch, which is definitely noise. Typically, signal can be viewed as sharing information, tagging with a hashtag, making a reference via a hyperlink, or generally contributing to the conversation.

Data collection, and more so data analysis, requires effort. Whether it's chock full of signal or obfuscated by noise, you have to work at gaining data to make decisions about managing your social media activities. Finding the signal requires significantly more work, but it will inherently benefit you tenfold if you spend the time to strategize around your social media metrics. Expect to fine-tune your data collection tools using filters and Boolean logic to find an appropriate balance between signal and noise. Data is truly everywhere, but identifying data that's relevant to your cause is the challenge.

ACKNOWLEDGING BIG DATA

Big Data is a term that's entering the mainstream lexicon these days to describe the torrent of digital data that so many measurers are struggling to understand. Big Data is a moniker for data stores that grow from terabytes to petabyte, exabyte, or zettabyte proportions. These massive data sets present challenges not only of storage, but also of the scale required to process and analyze unprecedented volumes of data. To me, Big Data presents a need for analytical tools and processes for interpreting information and making sense of it all in an *analytical instant*, which I discuss later in this chapter. It's not so much about the volume of data that's stored, but rather the ability to use stored data in a meaningful way.

Yet, Big Data is the future. It's everyone's future because we live in the information age, and information is founded in data. The floodgates have opened, and data is permeating from every recess of our digital existence. You can choose to step aside and let the data rush past or jump into the data stream to find trends, patterns, and meaning that resonate with your business. Most organizations are leveraging a trickle of data today by placing tags on web pages, tracking applications, and listening to social conversations. Yet too few capitalize on the value of the information because they lack a strategy for putting data to work. Unfortunately, the scale at which data will grow when injected with social media sources increases exponentially, which intensifies the challenges for organizations working to use digital data to drive their businesses in meaningful ways. Consequently the vast majority of companies end up merely paying lip service to their data-driven mantras.

> **NOTE** According to Sir Tim Berners-Lee, the future lies in analyzing data—lots of data. Berners-Lee, founder of the Internet, talked about our future of data analysis as one that is dependent on journalists. He thinks they'll become a new breed of storyteller, empowered and authorized by data. Their interpretation of data would guide the awareness of the masses.
>
> According to the Guardian.co.uk's bloggers over at the OrganGrinder blog, Berners-Lee was asked who would analyze such data: Allegedly, Berners-Lee responded that "the responsibility needs to be with the press. Journalists need to be data-savvy. These are the people whose jobs are to interpret what government is doing to the people. So it used to be that you would get stories by chatting to people in bars, and it still might be that you'll do it that way some times. But now it's also going to be about poring over data and equipping yourself with the tools to analyse it and picking out what's interesting. And keeping it in perspective, helping people out by really seeing where it all fits together, and what's going on in the country."
>
> "Data-driven journalism is the future," he concluded.
>
> (See `bit.ly/bernerslee_data-driven_journalism` for more information.)

▶ More on data-driven journalism:

http://bit.ly/bernerslee_data-driven_journalism.qrcode

However, analysts taming the Big Data beast are doing so with the help of advanced technologies. Enterprise database vendors such as Oracle, Microsoft, IBM, and Teradata are delivering methods to process and store Big Data. Yet, many acknowledge Hadoop as the go-to system for handling Big Data. It's an open source project offered by the Apache Software Foundation that was initiated and led by Yahoo and leverages Google's MapReduce technique for high performance parallel processing. Yahoo was an early adopter of Hadoop and also a major benefactor whose initial investments helped the system to become commercially viable. But as an open source framework, Hadoop relies on an active community of developers globally for its success. As illustrated in Figure 2-1, Hadoop handles high volume data flows and uses a MapReduce process to enable utilization of data in distributed computing format. Companies like eBay and Disney are using Hadoop to store, parse, and process data in real time. Social media platforms like Facebook, Ning, and Twitter also use Hadoop to store weblog files and dimensional data, and as a source for analytical exploration and machine-based learning.

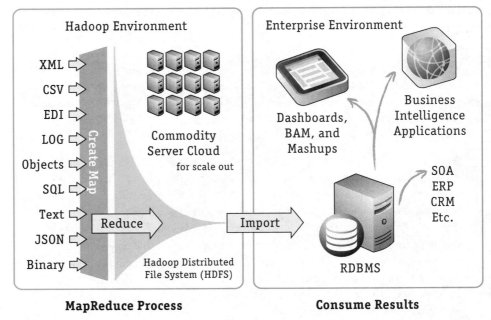

MapReduce Process   **Consume Results**

FIGURE 2-1: Using Hadoop to MapReduce Big Data.

WITH BIG DATA IT'S NOT ONLY SQL

Hadoop is a NoSQL ("Not Only SQL") database system. NoSQL is a relatively new datastore construct that emerged in 2009 as a method to handle increasingly larger data sets. It leverages distributed computing rather than a relational database management system (RDBMS). Numerous other NoSQL databases such as Cassandra, Cloudera, and Amazon SimpleDB have evolved to handle Big Data in a parallel processing environment that enables a hybrid handoff to a RDBMS.

Organizations that make data exploration a priority are most likely to attain leadership positions within their competitive environments. Yet, this capability to explore data, test hypotheses, and model scenarios manifests only after an organization has resolved its primary data needs. These primary needs include:

▶ The ability to effectively *capture the right sources of data* necessary to educate the business

► The efficient *translation of data to information* so that it can be understood by the masses

► The *automated reporting* required for key stakeholders to receive the data they need to conduct their jobs

All of this takes a significant effort, which is the prerequisite to having the freedom to explore data.

The 2010 Technology Forecast conducted by PriceWaterhouseCoopers entitled *Making Sense of Big Data* highlights that Big Data is meant for exploration because it can offer indications for what's to come. It's marked as exploratory because Big Data sets often require time, diligence, and creativity to reveal trends or insights. They don't necessarily afford empirical evidence at a glance. But investigative forays into data streams often deliver a competitive advantage for companies looking to get ahead in today's environment. Granted, not every organization is equipped to explore Big Data, but for those who are, insights await.

By analyzing Big Data flows, organizations can dramatically improve the following:

► **Customer retention:** By examining data generated from call center activity, help desk queries, web traffic patterns, and, of course, social media, organizations can anticipate customer problems before they arise. Technologies can be used to detect patterns that signify a propensity for churn and alert service agents into action.

► **Corporate awareness:** The act of fine-tuning listening tools to pick up on social conversations within Big Data sets allows you to protect your company brand or safeguard intellectual property. Big Data can easily be mined for competitive intelligence to cue organizations into potential market threats or greenfield opportunities.

► **Real-time operations:** Operating at the speed of the Internet requires that businesses make decisions and tailor offerings in real time. In some cases this requires navigating extensive data stores to determine product availability, offer eligibility, and customer prioritization in fractions of a second.

► **Ongoing optimization:** The ability to optimize business operations based on events such as weather, politics, social trends, or consumer uprising is increased with Big Data. As companies begin to amass larger sets of information, data can be mined for patterns that reveal behavioral psychology or even neuromarketing. These heightened levels of customer intelligence provide previously unavailable insights into human behaviors.

Despite the big social media platforms and enterprise vendors playing in the Big Data sandbox, it isn't just for big companies. With web log file data and social media data, it's actually quite possible to begin amassing your own Big Data set in relatively short order. Most Big Data sets consist of unstructured information typically found in web site log file analysis or social media data logs. Although you may not have a petabyte of information nor an immediate need for Hadoop in your organization, a nod of respect is due to Big Data because we'll all be working in the Big Data paradigm in the not-too-distant future.

THE SOCIAL MEDIA FIRE HOSE

One company that's betting big on the proliferation of social data is Gnip. This Boulder, Colorado–based company is feeding many of the biggest consumers of social media data today. And, I'm not talking spoon-feeding here either. Gnip has preconfigured APIs to extract data from the world's largest social media sources, including Digg, Facebook, Flickr, Google, Newsgator, SlideShare, Twitter, WordPress, and YouTube.

As of November 2010, Gnip had an exclusive partnership with Twitter, allowing them to sell up to half of Twitter's data at a pricey mark. The "halfhose," which refers to a randomized 50 percent stream of all Twitter messages, is available for just $360,000 U.S. annually. If your pockets aren't so deep, you can elect for the "decahose," which offers a randomized 5 percent Twitter blast for just $60,000 per year.

In reality, brands aren't likely to buy directly from Gnip to fill their datastores, but social monitoring vendors and developers looking to test their social media mettle probably will.

Most users of Big Data will be looking to the clouds for their data storage options. The sheer quantities of information being collected and the relative low cost of cloud-based storage space make a compelling combination. Many of today's analytical tools can also operate atop cloud-based data sets. Web analytics vendors have been doing this for quite some time, whereas other data analytics companies such as Quantivo and Aster Data are working to capitalize on the Big Data proliferation by enabling anywhere analysis capabilities.

AVERTING DATA OVERLOAD

Whether you're working with Big Data or not, it's pretty easy to get overloaded with data. Simply pointing a data collection tool at an opportunity can result in massive amounts of data. So you have to be careful. According to an article that appeared in *The Economist* on February 25th, 2010, in just the first few weeks of operation the data collected by the Sloan Digital Sky Survey's high-powered telescope surpassed the entire historic record of astrological data previously collected. Since launching in 2000, the survey has amassed over 140 terabytes of data contained within its archives. Yet a newer telescope expected to begin collecting astrological data in 2016 will exceed the past decade's 140 terabytes of data collection every 5 days. The proportions of these data are staggering. However, keep in mind that data collected by these telescopes and other machines are effectively sensor data. Sensor data is generated and collected by machines typically to serve performance, diagnostic, and research functions.

Consider the following example offered in the *GigaOM* article "Sensor Networks Top Social Networks for Big Data" by Stacey Higginbotham (http://gigaom.com/cloud/sensor-networks-top-social-networks-for-big-data-2/):

> For example, a Boeing jet generates 10 terabytes of information per engine every 30 minutes of flight, according to Stephen Brobst, the CTO of Teradata. So for a single 6-hour, cross-country flight from New York to Los Angeles on a twin-engine Boeing 737—the plane used by many carriers on this route—the total amount of data generated would be a massive 240 terabytes of data. There are about 28,537 commercial flights in the sky in the United States on any given day. Using only commercial flights, a day's worth of sensor data quickly climbs into the petabyte scale—for a single day. Multiply that by weeks, months, and years, and the scale of sensor data gets massive.

This type of sensor data will eventually outpace data generated from social media activity. Higginbotham estimates that in the next 5 years, the volume of sensor data will eclipse social media data by 10 to 20 times. Although not surprising, this shines a ray of hope on social media measurers for at least two reasons.

- ► First, the volume of data you'll need to monitor across social media initiatives is manageable in the grand scheme of things if you can work to focus your data collection priorities.

- ► Second, sensor-based data sets will likely offer opportunities for data exploration and mashups to add depth and knowledge to your social media data stores.

So, whether you have a Big Data set or a more reasonable quantity of information, the question becomes how to avoid data overload. The key is to know what you're looking for within your data sets. This is the part where you have to work to identify data that's relevant to your business and community using metrics. Although categorizing the heavens with a super-powered telescope is wicked cool, can you bring it around to benefiting your social media efforts? Unless you work for NASA, chances are probably slim. However, you might be able to get your community involved if you're both smart and creative.

As we all know, astronomers are a smart bunch. As data collected by the Sloan Digital Sky Survey began piling up, they knew they needed help to make sense of their data in a way that the machines weren't very good at. They were looking for visual patterns within their data that, among other things, would prove a theory that spiral galaxies have a tendency to rotate clockwise. They called on the world-wide community of amateur astronomers to help classify images using a clever online application they built called the Galaxy Zoo. The web site, pictured in Figure 2-2, shows the application used to classify the unearthly quantity of data collected by the telescope. The community sprang into action, and within the first 24 hours of launch the site was processing more than 70,000 classifications an hour. During the first year of the project, nearly 150,000 people participated, and they refuted the hypothesis that most galaxies rotate in a clockwise direction. As it turns out, about half of them do. But because they knew what they were looking for, the astronomers were able to analyze their data set and get the community involved.

Focusing your data collection efforts requires knowing what to look for and exploring data sets that are available to you. Whether the data sets are Twitter archives, galaxies in the universe, or the entire Internet as indexed by Google, you need to take a methodical approach to avoid data overload. I recommend the following steps for averting data overload:

1. **Set expectations for what you expect to learn from data.** Step 1 is the planning stage of any social media initiative and requires sitting down and thinking through what you're working to measure. You should have a clear idea of where you intend to point your measurement tools and what you hope to learn from the effort. More importantly, you must be able to articulate your rationale and set appropriate expectations for your measurement efforts. If your social campaign is about generating awareness, ensure that everyone from the executive team on down recognizes that your metrics for this campaign will be focused on media mentions and market share—not on contributing directly to the bottom line.

FIGURE 2-2: The Galaxy Zoo web site enlists help from the community of amateur astronomers to classify data.

2. **Categorize your specific social media measurement initiatives.** Step 2 requires you to examine your social media programs to determine which measures of success will reveal effectiveness. This will likely require you to create categories of data based on desired outcomes such as increasing exposure, creating dialogue, or facilitating interactions to narrow the scope of your measurement efforts. Maintain a tight focus on social initiatives by category, campaign, and/or channel to enable comparative data sources. This will position you to understand the value of specific data efforts and to avoid collecting and analyzing every data point under the sun.

   ▶ Step 2 must not be left off the to-do list or you'll end up with campaigns in the field that have no means of being tracked. That's the inverse of data overload.

3. **Implement tracking code wisely.** Test, QA, and validate data collection. Step 3 (in most companies) requires collaboration between the campaign designers and the technical resources that will actually implement tracking. This

involves knowing where to point your social media monitoring tools, where to place tracking tags for network initiatives, or how to deploy tracking across applications. It's a critical step to ensuring the data you're collecting is what you anticipate and what you can use.

4. **Activate your data collection in bite-sized chunks.** Step 4 allows you to get out from under the weight of an oppressive social media measurement strategy by treating distinct data collection efforts as individual projects. Although you should have an overarching strategy that ties together your measurement game plan, each campaign can be measured as an individual project and evaluated on its own performance over time or against comparative campaigns. This allows you to have a definitive time period for data analysis and enables you to learn from and improve on each measurement campaign.

5. **Analyze your data to separate the signal from the noise.** Step 5 is where you begin digging into the data specific to your social campaign and determining what's valuable and what's junk. It's an opportunity to parse out noisy data from your collection efforts or to omit channels that aren't adding value to your analysis. There's opportunity to get creative here by enlisting community members to perform analysis, as demonstrated by the Galaxy Zoo project mentioned earlier in the chapter. However, it's important to ensure clean, accurate, and usable data. Any data analysis effort will be exponentially more efficient if your data is clean and accurate. Take the time to fine-tune your data collection efforts.

6. **Refine your expectations, collection methods, and analysis.** Step 6 should serve as your third-down reality check. By this point, your campaign will be out in the wild and hopefully attracting the attention of your desired audience. You must revisit your expectations, your data collection efforts, and your analysis methods to ensure that the program is working according to design. If it's not, you must use this step to enact course corrections to get things in line. Much like a coach or a quarterback makes adjustments according to the defense, you need to refine data intake methods while the campaign is underway to ensure that you have the data necessary to evaluate success.

7. **Report your findings to key stakeholders within your organization.** Step 7 is the point where the rubber meets the road and you "officially" report metrics to your organization. I say officially because it's a good idea to offer preliminary metrics as indicators of social media program performance along

the way. This is especially true when multiple stakeholders are involved and you're working to build momentum for your initiatives. Additionally, it's a good idea to validate that the data you're collecting meets stakeholder needs.

In addition to these seven steps for averting data overload, an important eighth step to consider is constant evaluation. Even the best-laid social media plans can slip off track if no one is watching them. Accordingly, you should maintain ongoing measurement and analysis audits of campaigns in the field to ensure that your data collection efforts are still firing in their intended way.

▶ I recommend reserving your official blast of success metrics until the numbers stabilize, you gain confidence in your metrics, and no major changes are anticipated.

TRANSFORMING DATA INTO INFORMATION

In my experience the most egregious mistakes that companies make regarding their ability to process data originate from their expectations of the output they'll be able to generate with off-the-shelf technologies. Analytics solutions and social media monitoring tools are often sold with the promise that "actionable information is just a click away," a promise that an increasing number of companies have now realized is not usually the case. It turns out that these applications are best at parsing data and crunching numbers, and the act of translating the data and numbers into valuable business insights actually requires a lot of additional work.

To best explain this, at Web Analytics Demystified, where I'm a Senior Partner and Strategic Consultant, we use something we call "The Hierarchy of Analytical Needs." Based loosely on Maslow's Hierarchy of Needs, the hierarchy describes the amount of effort required to generate successively more valuable business outputs. Figure 2-3 shows data at the base of our hierarchy, which gives way to information, then insights, and then finally recommendations.

▶ More information on Web Analytics Demystified:

http://bit.ly/WebAnalyticsDemystified

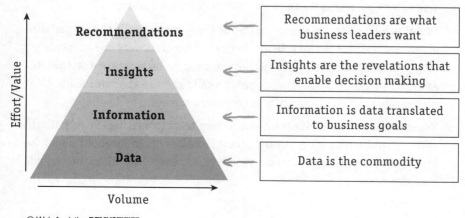

© Web Analytics **DEMYSTIFIED**

FIGURE 2-3: Web Analytics Demystified's Hierarchy of Analytical Needs.

The horizontal axis of our pyramid describes Volume and the vertical axis describes both Effort Required and the Resulting Business Value. The base of the pyramid contains Data—a high-volume, low-value, relatively low-effort output. As the organization is willing to invest effort, the data can be translated into information, insights, and ultimately actionable recommendations back to the business.

The differences in these outputs are subtle on paper but dramatic when manifest in the business context. Here's an example:

- **Data** is represented by the reports that most organizations have today, which are typically abundant, yet often of low value unless people know what they're looking for in the data.

- **Information** manifests when the data is put into context, usually via key performance indicators and dashboard reports examining data as it changes over time.

- **Insights** are the information coupled with analysis whereby individuals are illuminating observations with explanations and hypotheses.

- **Recommendations** are the insights presented with prescriptive actions the business can take to correct or capitalize on the data.

Consider this hypothetical example:

- **Data** tells an organization that its social media campaign sparked 1,375 mentions on non-owned web sites in the initial week after launch.

- **Information** tells the organization that these 1,375 mentions generated a firestorm of new visitor activity to the primary web site, as well as additional placements of the campaign content across social networks, which represented a 75 percent spike in new visitor acquisition traffic.

- **Insights** tell the organization that while Google is typically the biggest driver of referral traffic, the two primary sources of referrals were one advocate's blog and Facebook. Visitors from these sources spend more time on the site and click on the social media campaign's call to action at a significantly higher rate than visitors from other referral sources.

- **Recommendations** advise the management team to nurture the relationship with the influential advocate and invest more heavily in Facebook advertising, while presenting a clear plan to measure the results of these increased investments.

I present this hypothetical example to illustrate that organizations can generate substantially higher value output by using measurement and analysis practices. The Web Analytics Demystified Hierarchy of Analytical Needs is designed to propel organizations away from a profound dependence on data and toward a quest for information, insights, and ultimately recommendations.

The Proliferation of Social Data

As you ponder the enormity of Big Data and start to think about winnowing down your slice of the big social data pie, it's important to grasp the origins of social media data. For the most part, it's coming from people: people talking to one another, people posting images, people posting video, people creating content. As a brand, you must work to spark the conversation and to take part in the chatter, but most data out there shows that consumers trust each other more than they trust you. As such, your contributions to the proliferation of social data can be most effective if you build the platform and empower consumers with a soapbox to stand on or simply entertain them enough that they want to tell all their friends and return again and again. Don't get me wrong; there is plenty of opportunity to generate content and to give your social audience something to talk about. In fact, you pretty much have to do this or suffer brand anonymity. However, you need to acknowledge that consumers are predominately running the show when it comes to social media. That said, the next sections of this chapter explore some of the data components, creators, and participators of social media.

SPOTTING THE SOCIALLY CONNECTED

Social media isn't just for kids these days. In fact, according to a study conducted by Pingdom, the average age of a social network user is 37 years old. While the oldest user demographic exists on Classmates.com, LinkedIn is showing its gray hairs with a mean user age of 44 years old. Facebook users on average are seven years older than MySpace users; these groups have celebrated 38th and 31st birthdays, respectively. And Bebo clocks in with the youngest average user of all sites monitored in the study, with an average age of 28 years old. Figure 2-4 illustrates findings from the study that analyzed age statistics from 19 social networks.

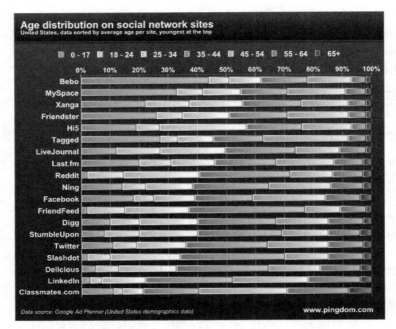

FIGURE 2-4: Age distribution of users across social networks.

According to data collected in 2010, a staggering 75 percent of online global consumers visit social network sites. The populations of these social networks is growing faster than the largest cities on earth as consumers find more and more ways to connect, share, and interact with each other online. By early 2011, Facebook was far and away the dominant social network destination, with a user population that surpassed the combined populations of the next top three networks (Qzone, Twitter, and Habbo). However, an important consideration is not just the size of the social network, but the audience that it attracts.

As the largest, Facebook has an eclectic user population that comprises 70 percent non-U.S. users. The site is available in more than 70 translations and over 300,000 people contributed to the multilingual versions by using Facebook's translation application. Similarly, Twitter's user population includes approximately 60 percent from outside the United States, and LinkedIn boasts members in over 200 countries. And these examples are just from the United States-based social networks. By evaluating where your audience exists, you can understand a great deal about where you should focus your social marketing efforts and where you can be assured to find your target audience. So, Facebook isn't the only game in town. As you're contemplating the geographic locale of your social audience, consider the following:

- ▶ Facebook had approximately 564 million users worldwide at the close of 2010, with at least half of these users logging in every day.

- ▶ The Facebook user population is almost 45 percent larger than the United States population.

- ▶ If Facebook were a country, its population would be the third largest in the world, after China and India.

- ▶ Orkut, the popular social networking site in India and Brazil, boasts over 100 million worldwide users and claims 80 percent market share in Brazil.

- ▶ Twitter CEO Evan Williams reported in the fall of 2010 that the company had 145 million registered users, and 60 percent of them were from outside the United States.

- ▶ LinkedIn has over 80 million members in over 200 countries and added a new professional at a rate of one every second in 2010.

- ▶ Vkontakte.ru ranked as the top social networking site in Russia with 111 million registered users, in a country where the average user spends 9.8 hours per month on social networks.

▶ Tune in to Erik Qualman's (@equalman) Social Media Revolution video for more social stats and prepare to be blown away (http://bit .ly/9NZuOh).

http://bit.ly/gqoLk8.qrcode

What's interesting is that many of the world's largest social networks as quantified by registered user populations are not very well known outside their geographic focus areas. Take, for example, Qzone, China's largest social network. The site experienced dramatic growth in part with teens and rural users because of its association with the wildly popular QQ messenger service. Yet, rival social networks in China, including RenRen, 51.com, and Kaixin001, are vying for the top network spot. Data about these organizations is not widely available, but sources like BloggerInsight (bloggerinsight.com) are digging into Asian markets and predicting a shakeup in Chinese social networks, with RenRen as a favorite.

> **NOTE** Qzone's billionaire owner, Pony Ma Huateng, is also the creator of QQ, a text messaging service that currently has 600 million active users in mainland China.

Similarly, social networks aimed at teens, such as Habbo, hi5, and Tagged, are relatively lesser known to general populations. Although these sites may fly under the radar for some, they've managed to amass a critical base of users to rank atop the most populated online social destinations. Table 2-1 is a list of the world's largest social networks (excluding dating sites).

TABLE 2-1: The World's Largest Social Networks

NETWORK	DESCRIPTION	GEOGRAPHIC FOCUS	REGISTERED USERS (MM)	YEAR FOUNDED
Facebook www.facebook.com/	The world's largest social network	Global	564	2004
Qzone http://qzone.qq.com/	A virtual world and social network	China	200	2005
Twitter http://twitter.com/	A microblogging network (140 characters or less)	Global	175	2006
Habbo www.habbo.com/	A social networking site aimed at teenagers	Global	185	2000
MySpace www.myspace.com/	A social entertainment destination	Global	130	2003
Windows Live Spaces http://spaces.live.com/	Microsoft's blogging and social platform	Global	120	2004 (MSN Spaces)

NETWORK	DESCRIPTION	GEOGRAPHIC FOCUS	REGISTERED USERS (MM)	YEAR FOUNDED
Bebo www.bebo.com/	A social experience to connect and share	Global	117	2005
Vkontakte http://vk.com/index.php	A social network for music, video, and entertainment	Russia	111	2006
Orkut http://orkut.com/	A network for meeting new people and building relationships	Brazil	100	2004
Friendster www.friendster.com/	An early social network focused on friendship	Asia	90	2002
LinkedIn www.linkedin.com/	A business-oriented site for professional networking	Global	80	2003
hi5 http://hi5.com	Social entertainment for the youth market	Latin America	80	2003
Tagged www.tagged.com/	A social discovery network for teens	United States	70	2004
Netlog www.netlog.com	A social network for European youth	Belgium	70	2003
Badoo www.badoo.com	A multilingual social network	Europe	69	2006

This information came from Wikipedia and CrunchBase.com.

In addition to being a global phenomenon, social media data is being produced at an astounding rate. Consider that 25 percent of search results for the world's top 20 largest brands link to user-generated content. There are over 900 million objects that people interact with on Facebook (for example, pages, groups, events, and community pages) and the average user creates 90 pieces of new content each month. And these users like to share. In fact, an estimated 30 billion pieces of content (links, news stories, blog posts, photos, and so on) are shared on Facebook each month.

When you factor in other social networks—like YouTube, which contains more than 100 billion videos, and Wikipedia, with over 15 million articles—that sheer volume of data becomes massive. It's been said that social media today generates more activity online than porn. That's probably a good thing.

ASSEMBLING A PANORAMIC PERSPECTIVE

Before you start to panic and try to determine how you'll ever keep up with all this social media data and the plethora of social networks, you need to put things into perspective. I can assure you that you do not need to drink from the social media fire hose upon taking your first sip. In fact, you'd be crazy to even try. There's simply too much data out there, too many opportunities, and too many wild geese to chase. Instead, to measure and manage your social media efforts effectively, you need a strategic vantage point and a foundation born of sensible metrics. This allows you to create a perspective on your social media campaigns and programs as they relate to your entire business—not all businesses, just your business.

Thus, your first order of social media measurement business is focusing your efforts on your target audience and categorizing your data into metrics that matter for your organization. Well, technically this isn't your very first step, since you will need a firm grasp on your corporate goals and business objectives before getting here, but these are initial steps for getting into the heart of your data. To do this, you need access points to perform social data analysis, to gain insights, and to generally explore information about your customers and your brand. I call these "data windows" and will discuss how you can create customized vistas to ensure the greatest opportunities for analysis. Of course, all this needs to happen instantaneously, so gaining that real-time jump on your data is critical as well.

Categorizing Your Data with Social Metrics

It's probably the analyst in me, or perhaps my forced left brain proclivity, which I'll cover shortly, but I have an insatiable desire to categorize things. For me it makes things more comprehensible, I can keep them straight, and it offers me the ability to explain what I'm doing to others in a meaningful way. I teach this approach when it comes to evaluating social data and social media opportunities. For example, if clients inform me that they want to measure fans on their Facebook pages, my first question is typically "why?" After the uncomfortable looks of shock and awe have passed, I start to dig in with questions that force clients to articulate how a greater understanding of the number of fans will relate to the client's business goals.

This usually takes a bit of education, patience, and more education to get there because most businesses simply believe that more fans equal more success. Well, sometimes more is better, but oftentimes, that's not the case. I'd argue for fewer fans who are highly engaged and regularly visit over a slew of apathetic fans who never come calling. But understanding motivating factors, like the fact that the company's Facebook page was initially created to build awareness for the brand and to offer a platform for conversation, tells me that acquiring more fans is a branding exercise. Thus, more fans equates to more exposure and more exposure can lead to increased interactions and perhaps, some day, more customers. This branding exercise might not result in a warm lead, but if all goes right in the process, that lead turns into a sale. At this point we're way downstream of the Facebook page, which is great, but I advise you to reel it back in to quantify the original intent. If building brand awareness is what you're after, you need to evaluate fans in that context.

> ▶ Always ask "why?" Don't develop metrics just to measure stuff. Ensure that you develop social media measures within the business context.

This approach can also help when you're determining which channels are appropriate for your specific social media initiatives. An extremely common question for companies starting out with social media is "How do I develop a Facebook/Twitter/Bebo/etc. strategy?" Aaaaarrrrgggghhhh! Strategies don't evolve at the channel level; they must start with your business. Be wary of anyone who jumps right in and starts rattling off best practices without first taking the time to understand your business. I never advocate starting with a channel strategy and will argue till I'm blue in the face that the channel cannot supersede your business rationale. Just because Facebook has half a billion users doesn't mean that you'll be able to sell widgets to them all if you create a fan page. The most critical first step is developing a perspective for why you're there in the first place. After that, you can begin to explore your channels, categories, and metrics.

▶ Categories also help to immediately frame the conversation with your colleagues or stakeholders.

When attempting to sort through data to arrive at your social media metrics, consider a data categorization approach. Categories can help to remind you why you're engaged in social media activities in the first place.

Recognize that metrics won't necessarily fit nicely into one single category and there will likely be crossover for any given metric. But you can use this to your advantage when presenting data within the context of your bigger social objectives. Although Table 2-2 is not a comprehensive nor exhaustive list of potential social media data categories and their corresponding metrics, it should serve to jump-start your thinking and get you going in the right direction.

TABLE 2-2: Social Data Categories and Corresponding Metrics

CATEGORY	SAMPLE METRICS
Branding	Impressions, Unique Visitors, Cost per Acquisition
Public Relations	Media Mentions, RTs, Referrals
Entertainment	Page Views, Time Spent, Engagement
Content Production	Posts, Comments, Trackbacks
Lead Generation	Downloads, Cost per Lead, Lead Conversion Rate
Direct Sales	Sales Conversions, Sales Lead Time, Avg Order Value
Customer Service and Support	Resolution Rate, Resolution Time, Cust. Lifetime Value
Customer Satisfaction	% Satisfied (+/-), Likelihood to Recommend, Affinity
Market Research	Trending Topics, Topics by Geography, Idea Impact
Competitive Intelligence	Share of Voice, Reach, Virality

WARNING Use metrics with calculated caution. All of the metrics offered in Table 2-2 and throughout this book must be considered in the context of your business. Not all categories nor all metrics will be applicable to every business. It's your responsibility to select metrics that matter to your business. Use the measures and metrics I offer in this book as a guide to build your own set of metrics that will become indispensable to your social measurement activities.

Creating Virtual Data Windows

I am going to come right out and tell you that I am not a database expert. In my business, I deal with databases because they hold the information I need to assess the performance of marketing and social media initiatives. But many of the technical aspects of databases are foreign to me. That said, I do understand that social media measurers need a perspective on data that will expedite their analysis, interpretation, and evaluation of any social effort. As such, "data windows" can offer a perspective into these technical aspects of measurement. A data window, by my definition, is *your* view into a table that contains information that *you* specify as important to *your* social media initiative. This can be totally transparent if you are a data geek or made simpler with a user interface such as those common to most social analytics tools. But, think about arranging your data windows in strategic locations so that you gain the best view of your brand, your customers, and your competition. Just like you might plan the placement of windows on your house to get the best views or the most sunshine, your data windows should be pointed at noteworthy customer vistas and business categories.

Now, as I said, I am not a database guru so I asked someone who is. Rob Tuttle is the Director of Solutions Marketing at Teradata and was kind enough to weigh in on my questions about data windows. In 1997, Rob led the development at NCR/Teradata of a product called "Behavior Explorer," which was described as a "window," specifically for marketing, into the customer data stored in the Teradata Warehouse at major financial institutions around the world.

Rob describes a data window as a view of the available, pertinent data that is customized for users or roles. According to Rob, "In database land, we call them views." From a user perspective, a view into the data can be developed for different users or user groups, based on their needs. They can see certain data elements and selected attributes, and tables have been pre-joined to allow easy retrieval of data from within the view. Views are especially valuable when you have lots of data, which is typical for social media, but much of it is not needed by a particular user or group. Thus, it helps to get the right perspective on your favorite slice of data.

Data views can serve many valuable purposes, which also apply to social media data.

▸ **Consistency:** A view can be constructed to provide consistency when underlying data structures change. The IT folks may need to change the underlying data model at some point, but the view can remain the same, so all of the reports and queries and analytics that have been built to use the "view" will continue to work unchanged. This protects the users and accessing applications from changes in the data structures.

▶ **Usability:** Views can be constructed for different users or roles using terminology that is more familiar to them. Data elements and attributes can be renamed with descriptions that make sense to the user in common English, rather than raw table names. With Behavior Explorer, Rob's team actually conducted focus groups to develop the names and relationships of different data elements that were used in their view for the marketing organization.

▶ **Security:** Views can be developed that limit the amount and type of data accessible (providing security) to a particular group or user. Marketing users might not be able to see certain fields that identify individuals by name when they do certain analysis, due to privacy rules. They might not be able to access credit card numbers themselves, but only a unique identifier for each credit card. And they might not need to see corporate financials or supplier information in their job roles, so that information is not accessible through their view. Limits could also be applied to the amount of history available to view (maybe only the last 25 months), or data could be retrieved from certain sources, but not others.

In a social media context, a "window" can help you focus on the signal within unstructured data. The greatest volume concern about social media is the raw text of a blog, a random post, or all the unstructured chatter. Normally, this data would be parsed and algorithms would determine the context of various words and strings, which would then be stored in a database. There may be hundreds or thousands of "key words" or terms (products, brand messages, people, and so on) that are identified and stored from these sources. Yet, business users may be interested only in some of the words, based on their organization or role. A "data window" could be constructed to provide them with a view into the use of only the terms or contexts that are pertinent to them. They may be limited to data sourced only from certain sources, blogs, Twitter IDs, wikis, and so on. This would be extremely useful if a group were tasked with monitoring certain blogs or sources.

Obviously, these are just a few of the ways that data windows can be used. Depending on your business situation, there are many other ways that you might want to "limit" or customize the view of the data available from social media sites. The point is to use data windows creatively to help you manage the data so you can start turning it into information you can use.

Acting in Real Time

As a stalwart Web Analytics guy, I always had a hard time with companies and clients who absolutely insisted on real-time analytics without good reason. So much so, that I even ranted about it on my blog way back in 2008 in a blog entry entitled "How 'Real' Is Real-Time Web Analytics?" I would typically ask why someone needed real-time data and what decisions were being made in real time. I did this because in the mid-2000s, there wasn't a whole lot that companies were doing with their data in real time. Web Analytics was largely a retrospective exercise that allowed analysts to look backward and determine how well their efforts on any given campaign, promotion, or web property performed. Web Analytics data usage was—and unfortunately largely still is—a reactive exercise that occurred postmortem. It was like looking in the rear view mirror, which is where this practice needs to stay. Needless to say, my views on real-time data have changed dramatically.

Real-time data is a prerequisite in social media. It's imperative. It is not an elective. It's become this way because consumers demand instantaneous response. Where it used to be okay to wait 24 hours for an e-mail response or perhaps even longer for an answer to a challenging query, it's decidedly insufficient today. Nowadays consumers hold a sense of entitlement and demand instantaneous results on everything from the smallest issue to the most egregious infraction. Their satisfaction, or lack thereof, can be broadcast to their following and amplified by empathetic listeners in a matter of seconds. Whether it's reporting breaking news in war-trodden streets, requesting support for a business solution, or relating the atrocities of an airline service worker, people now operate in the moment. Brands must be aware of this when considering the social measurement strategies and game plans.

These thoughts about real-time data are not exclusive to an organization's ability to intake data in real time but also relate to its ability to analyze and respond in short order. I call this the *analytical instant.* It's the ability to generate authentic, accurate, and informative social media output in an instant. In some cases, this can be accomplished with machines and technologies. These cases are most prevalent in marketing automation triggers based on implicit actions like clicking through a web site with a focus on specific content or demonstrating a propensity for action. However, automated triggers and computer-generated responses tend to fail almost completely in social media. Consumers expect humans to respond to their questions and inquiries and will quickly lose trust in an organization that doesn't respond in this way. This requires that organizations listen to their customers in the first place to even hear their cries. Then the secondary consideration is having the bandwidth

▶ My rant on real-time Web Analytics:

http://bit.ly/howrealisrealtimedata.qr

▶ Businesses must operate in an analytical instant. For data intake, decision processing, and expediting responses, businesses must react in microseconds, not hours or minutes.

to respond. This isn't always so easy either. In many cases, social media curators are empowered by their organizations to speak on behalf of the brand, but in other cases issues should be escalated to higher powers.

VISUALIZING INFORMATION AS KNOWLEDGE

We all learn differently. Those of you inclined toward the left side of your brain may be comfortable peering at rows upon rows of endless data complete with enough ones and zeros to fill a bathtub. Left-brainers are logical and thrive on structure and sequence to organize information. These are killer instincts for aspiring social analytics gurus because much of the data we analyze is organized in this way. Others—and I place myself in this camp—are right-brained and are more comfortable ingesting visual data cues. Sure, I still like to categorize things, but right-brainers look for patterns and configurations within data to find insights. This exploration of data through visualization is a right-brained exercise. I've been able to train myself to understand the numbers and the statistics behind analytics, yet my inclination is to gravitate toward the art of data interpretation rather than the science.

Appreciating Both Art and Science

When it comes to metrics that comprise digital measurement tactics, it's important to approach the topic with a mix of art and science. Although the cold calculations of science can add rigor and process to your social media measurement program, the interpretive side of analysis is often revealed through artistry, which warms the senses. In my experience, both are absolutely necessary, yet individuals often are just wired one way or another. Consequently, social analytics programs can take on a cold clinical feel or a more organic approach, depending upon who's orchestrating the effort. Finding the balance usually means building a team with characteristics indicative of both art and science. This section examines the art and science of analytics.

> ▶ Although staffing may prove to be a significant challenge, organizations that develop social media measurement programs using a balanced approach between art and science are much more likely to succeed as champions within the business.

BLIND ME WITH SCIENCE

The science of social analytics involves technology, mathematical calculations, and extensive domain knowledge to ensure accurate data capture of social media efforts. This translates to knowing how social networks, web sites, and applications function and what data is available from each in order to assemble the right measurement tools. In most cases, the scientific approach attempts to distill complex business functions into easily quantifiable units suitable for analysis. So, going back to the discussion from earlier in the chapter, using categories for classification and then segmenting data from these categories for analysis is a typical scientific approach. The output from this science-oriented method of analysis is commonly spreadsheets of data or dashboards that express important social metrics.

The challenge with the scientific approach to social analytics is that these data collection techniques are relatively new and certainly still evolving. Just keeping up with the ever-changing data collection rules on Facebook is enough to make your head spin, let alone tracking all the other networks and corners of the Internet where data may be lurking. Most of this data is unstructured and poorly understood. Even the best social analytics tools require analysts to interpret data and supplement additional insights to gain a solid perspective on data. However, if data scientists are too far removed from the business, interpretation of social data can easily miss the mark.

▶ Social media scientists dig into data to identify trends and insights about activities that can be explained and validated using data-driven facts.

ENLIGHTEN ME WITH ART

The art of social analytics explores people and their relationships by looking at experiences and attitudes, while requiring a deep understanding of the business to align social media efforts with corporate goals. This translates to knowing what you seek to accomplish with your social media initiatives and rooting out the people, platforms, and ideas that will help you get there. The artist's approach works to gain a big picture perspective on the social environment and determine which factors fit into the grand scheme of the organization. The acts of reaching out to communities, nurturing advocates, and fostering a dialogue are largely designed by social media artists who know the business goals they're working to impact and know how to motivate a community to do so. For artists, the message is equally as important as the medium, and they take care to craft a resounding message. Artists share this information with the business by shaping measures and metrics into stories or data visualizations that present data in the context of the business.

The challenge of the artistic approach is that it's dependent upon the business being engaged with social media efforts so that there is an understanding of what's being accomplished. This requires substantial educational efforts and ongoing training to ensure that stakeholders from around the organization know why efforts are being conducted and ultimately how these efforts will impact the business. Additionally, the art of social analytics requires time and resources to break free from automated reporting to deliver insightful analysis. It takes critical thinking and a trained eye to be able to craft a story from data; artists typically work toward this

▶ Social media artists have a big picture perspective of their social activities and ensure that efforts can be easily communicated and mapped back to business objectives.

end. Rather than presenting information as numbers on the page, artists attempt to bring data to life by relating information to stakeholders in a manner that enables information to jump off the page.

Table 2-3 highlights some of the characteristics of data scientists versus data artists. This table also alludes to the fact that both art and science are critical components of any social measurement program. In total isolation either discipline inevitably fails. Balance is therefore mandatory. As you contemplate your social media measurement efforts, take the time to determine whether you're inclined to lean one way or the other and work toward a more balanced solution.

TABLE 2-3: Balancing Measurement Art and Science

SOCIAL MEDIA GOAL	SCIENCE	ART
Architecting your social measurement environment	Cataloging data sources	Setting expectations
	Developing process	Educating stakeholders
	Enabling self-service	Ongoing training
Assembling your social measurement technologies	Powerful tools	Intuitive applications
	Flexible databases	Vendor relationships
	Rich statistical functions	Familiar business tools
Conducting your social media analysis	Structured analysis	Exploratory investigation
	Data mining	Hypothesis testing
	Empirical evidence	Logical explanations
Communicating your social media results	Spreadsheets	Visualizations
	Automated reports	Insightful interpretations
	Proof points	Storytelling
Underlying motivation	Accurate information	Business context

ART AND SCIENCE JUXTAPOSED

Word clouds are relatively common within social media monitoring applications because they can offer a quick glimpse of data that reveal trends and potentially interesting relationships. Word clouds function by making the size of each word relative to the number of times it appears in the text. Thus big words are more prevalent than small words. These are not the richest data visualizations, but they do offer insights about text that are easily digestible and geared for action. Wordle.net is a popular site for generating word clouds because it allows you to paste text, RSS feeds, or any URL into the tool to create a plethora of visual creations from text. This form of data visualization can be used in myriad ways, such as determining sentiment by visualizing comments spawned by a political debate or identifying trending topics across mainstream news sources.

The power of visualizing data using word clouds makes it more palatable for the right-brained. Take, for example, Figure 2-5, which captures a scientist's perspective of all of the words within this chapter, complete with frequency of use, in just two columns of a spreadsheet. I omitted common words such as "and," "the," and "a" to reveal the primary topics in this chapter. So, even a quick glance tells you that the chapter is about data. However, Figure 2-6 is a word cloud of the same data set that an artist might use to reveal so much more about the context and content contained within this chapter. Both are valuable, but which one is more compelling to you?

▶ Create your own word clouds using Wordle.net.

http://bit.ly/etoGQe.qrcode

Unique: 2992	Total: 15224	
393	DATA	
226	SOCIAL	
133	MEDIA	
72	TIME	
56	INFORMATION	
54	BUSINESS	
51	MORE	
51	REAL	
49	WILL	
45	NOT	
44	ALL	
43	BIG	
38	WE	
36	METRICS	
36	FIGURE	
35	ANALYTICS	
34	NETWORK	
34	WHICH	
34	ANALYSIS	
30	FACEBOOK	
30	USING	
30	VISUALIZATION	
28	MOST	
28	OTHER	
28	NEED	
28	ORGANIZATION	
28	EFFORTS	
27	WHILE	.
27	USE	
26	BECAUSE	
26	MANY	
26	OUT	
26	LIKE	
25	THAN	
25	TYPE	
25	WEB	
23	HOW	
23	USERS	
23	NETWORKS	
23	MEASUREMENT	
22	JUST	
22	TWITTER	
22	MAY	
22	SITE	
21	DIGITAL	

FIGURE 2-5: A data set showing all the words in this chapter in a spreadsheet.

FIGURE 2-6: The same data set containing all the words in this chapter, visualized as a word cloud.

Recognizing Beautiful Data

Whether viewed by a scientist or an artist, data can be incredibly beautiful. The incomprehensible waves of data headed our way hide mysteries, nuances, and remarkable beauty. Numbers can shift to colors, which morph into segments and then into patterns. Whether expressed in cylindrical rings, vibrant colors, or splintering paths, data patterns can emerge to stimulate the imagination and explain complexity with visual simplicity. The art of data visualization is a method for translating the scientific reality of numbers into a more accessible format that can be processed and understood by people in nanoseconds. Visualizations can expose relationships between numbers and offer context for information.

You've probably seen data visualizations before in the form of infographics. These data-rich methods of revealing information are becoming increasingly popular in mainstream media. Infographics are popping up in publications like *The New York Times*, *The Economist*, and *Harvard Business Review* with regularity. A practical data visualization shown in Figure 2-7 reveals how likely you are to get frisked by the police in New York City. *The New York Times*'s article "Stop, Question and Frisk in New York Neighborhoods," published on July 11, 2010, offers some shockingly stunning data expressions, including a practical data visualization that reveals how likely you are to get frisked by the police in New York City.

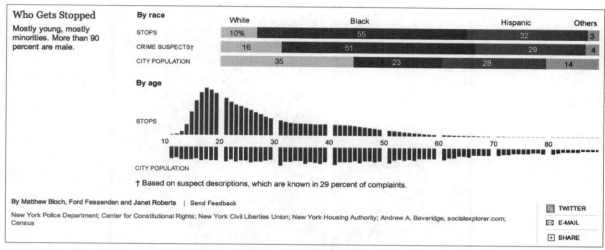

FIGURE 2-7: Who gets stopped in NYC.

Online sites like NYtimes.com are also providing engaging interactive infographics to allow users to relate with their content. Think you can balance the U.S. National budget more effectively than the current legislature? Well, the NYtimes.com's interactive Budget Puzzle offers you the chance to do better. The online data set allows you to sift through the national budget on a line-by-line basis to decide how you'll cut the projected 2015 and 2030 shortfalls of $418 billion and $1,345 billion dollars, respectively. These are tough decisions that certainly require introspection on your beliefs to make the tough decisions for the nation. The site is founded on data with calls to action for contributing to the conversation.

These infographics by *The New York Times* were generated by collecting data from publicly available sources and using it to inform, educate, and sometimes galvanize citizens. I expect that as we collectively amass more and more data, infographics will continue to gain popularity. While researching infographics, I found the image depicted in Figure 2-8 that shows an infographic describing infographics—a pretty clever idea put out by the folks at Darning Pixels, Inc.

As you've seen already in this chapter, there is a lot of data out there about social media itself—so much so that wrapping your arms around all this data is a challenging task. But creative companies like iStrategy are working with data to make it more comprehensible.

▶ Big data can often be effectively summarized using infographics that offer a familiar jumping-off point for learning about many different aspects of utilization and growth.

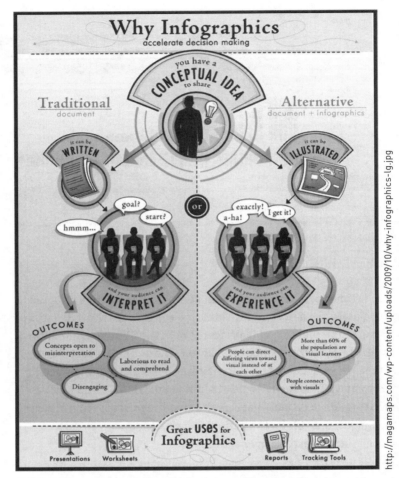

http://magamaps.com/wp-content/uploads/2009/10/why-infographics-lg.jpg

FIGURE 2-8: An infographic explaining infographics, from the Infographics Showcase.

For example, Figure 2-9 used data from the Burson-Marsteller Global Social Media Check-Up 2010 study to create an infographic that reveals compelling facts about social media use within big businesses. At a glance it shows you that 33 percent of the Fortune 100 have a corporate blog and that half of them have their own YouTube channels. What's even more impressive is that over half have dedicated Facebook fan pages and 65 percent are blasting messages via Twitter. This offers instant competitive intelligence to a large enterprise. Not that you should jump off every social media bridge, but if you need to understand where you are in relation to the competition, this type of infographic can tell you at a glance.

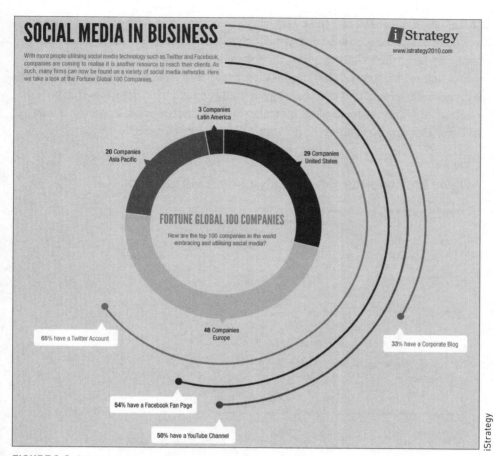

FIGURE 2-9: Social media adoption by the global Fortune 100.

Other informative and downright cool infographics come from David McCandless, who is a self-proclaimed data journalist with a passion for visualizing information. He's responsible for the Information is Beautiful blog and does miracles with data visualizations. David has generated numerous stunning data visualizations such as the Billion Dollar-o-Gram, Wikipedia's Lamest Edit Wars, Left vs. Right (political), and many more. Data visualizations that I find compelling include David's Hierarchy of Digital Distractions, which reveals the vast array of activities that keep humans from actually doing work, and "the Facebook breakup chart."

When looking at Facebook data, David and his team evaluated 10,000 Facebook status updates searching for key terms, indicating changes in relationship status. The output was the Facebook breakup chart that David described in his TedTalk shown in the YouTube snapshot in Figure 2-10. Their charted metrics included "breakup" and "broken up" and by searching publicly available profiles, they found a pattern in the data. Spikes indicating high frequency occurrences of these terms appeared just prior to Spring Break, on Mondays, before summer vacation, and two weeks before Christmas. Thus, the data for this analysis was trended and augmented with calendar events to reveal some key insights about dating. Be warned; if your relationship is on the rocks, data indicates that your not-so-significant other may be likely to abandon you before the holiday gift exchange comes due.

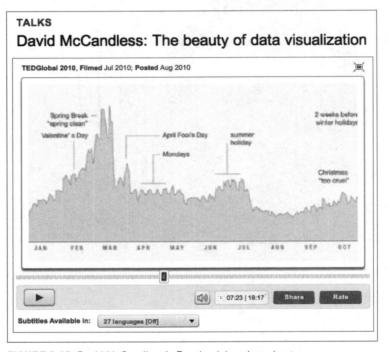

FIGURE 2-10: David McCandless's Facebook breakup chart.

NOTE   Check out a compelling video of David McCandless in his TED talk at `http://www.ted.com/talks/view/id/937`.

Beyond infographics, other data artists are doing remarkable work with stunning data visualizations as well. Some, like Stefanie Posavec, are translating text from literary works such as Jack Kerouac's *On the Road* into imagery. Figure 2-11 is a partial view of a visualization depicting the basic sentence structure within Part I of *On the Road*. Colors represent a character or theme in the novel (such as the protagonist, Dean Moriarty, represented in blue and work and survival in yellow). At a glance you can identify trends and relationships among characters, themes, and issues. These are the metrics on which the visualization is founded. The measures exist on each branch in the visualization, which starts with a chapter, then stems to paragraphs, then to sentences and words. The result produces a delicate flower-like image. While visually brilliant, this visualization is also highly informative. Other visualizations of this same work reveal rhythm structures within the novel.

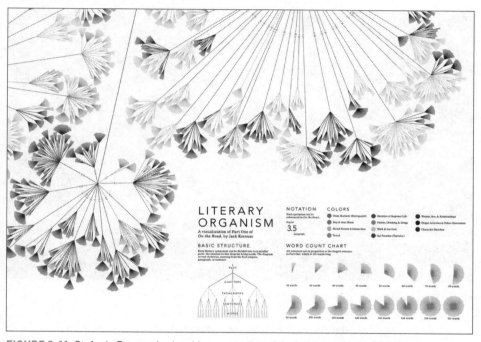

FIGURE 2-11: Stefanie Posavec's visual interpretation of Jack Kerouac's *On The Road*.

NOTE Edward Tufte is one of the pioneers of data visualization. Check out his work at www.edwardtufte.com/.

Chris Harrison, a Ph.D. student in the Human-Computer Interaction Institute at Carnegie Mellon University, also visualizes data. In one of his data visualizations, he took on the task of analyzing data from the Bible. He and Lutheran pastor Christoph Romhild set out to render more than 63,000 cross references within the text. These data artists admit that their visualization is "something more beautiful than functional," yet it reveals information about the Bible that isn't readily apparent in other interpretations of the work. Figure 2-12 is a visual depiction of the cross references contained within the Bible. According to a description extracted from Chris

Harrison's web site, "The bar graph that runs along the bottom represents all of the chapters in the Bible. Books alternate in color between white and light gray. The length of each bar denotes the number of verses in the chapter. Each of the 63,779 cross references found in the Bible is depicted by a single arc. The color corresponds to the distance between the two chapters, creating a rainbow-like effect." You can check out more of Chris Harrison's data visualizations at Chrisharrison.net.

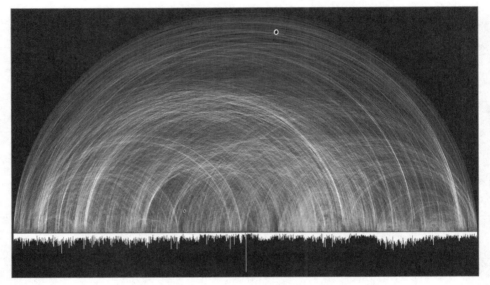

FIGURE 2-12: Chris Harrison's visualization of cross references within the Bible.

While I have strayed into some flat-out cool data visualizations here to illustrate my point, hopefully you can see that visualizing data can be highly informative. Whether you're using data to explain the progress of a social media program or trying to show your Chief Executive Officer that he is an outlier because he doesn't Tweet, you can make a solid case using data imagery. Personally, I am a huge fan of data visualization and expect to see a great deal more information visualized so that it's understandable by the masses.

Creating Your Own Data Visualizations

So it's all well and good to create stunning data visualizations about the Bible or *On the Road*, but you should be asking yourself how you can apply data visualization to your social media measurement efforts. Well, for starters, many social monitoring tools come standard with tag clouds that show keywords you're tracking and topics relevant to your brand. Additionally, analytics tools usually offer some visualization capabilities that allow you to add a visual dimension to your data. You can use these solutions to dive into specific topics and begin mining your data for deeper insights. Alternatively, you can start annotating graphs in PowerPoint to explain spikes in data with reference to causality. By laying information atop data sources, you can begin to add depth and understanding to the numbers. Oftentimes this is what it takes to convince a stubborn colleague or to finally secure buy-in for your social media efforts. In all cases, visualization requires that you think through the data and generate findings that are more than just numbers. You need to express data in interpreted form with insights and even recommendations to extract value from your data.

One of the more amazing discoveries I made while researching this book was IBM's Many Eyes data visualization platform. The site was created in 2007 and is dubbed an "experiment" by IBM Research and the IBM Cognos software group. In addition to being very powerful, the site is highly functional. The design of the site is pleasantly sparse, with tantalizing "Explore," "Participate," and "Learn More" navigational cues. But you will quickly get lost in the data visualizations. According to IBM, "Many Eyes is a bet on the power of human visual intelligence to find patterns. Our goal is still to 'democratize' visualization and to enable a new social kind of data analysis." The site is free to use and anyone can upload a data set and begin creating visualizations. Visualization types include the ability to

▶ Experiment with your own data visualizations on the Many Eyes data visualization platform at bit.ly/IBM_manyeyes.

- ▶ **Analyze text** in visual format using phrase nets, word trees, tag clouds, and word clouds.

- ▶ **Compare values** within data using bar charts, histograms, and bubble charts.

- ▶ **Visualize relationships** among data with network diagrams, scatterplots, and matrix charts.

- ▶ **See parts** of the whole with pie charts and tree maps.

- ▶ **Perform geographic analysis** using country and world maps.

- ▶ **Track changes over time** using line graphs, stack graphs, and categorized stack graphs.

Users can explore existing visualizations and add to or modify data sets. Information on this site ranges from data on the top 100 most popular web sites, as shown in Figure 2-13, to a histogram of the number of calories in fish, to favorite John Lennon songs as voted on by visitors to the Liverpool Echo web site. Using this site, you can extract data sets from your social media initiatives and create compelling visuals to regale your colleagues with stories of success.

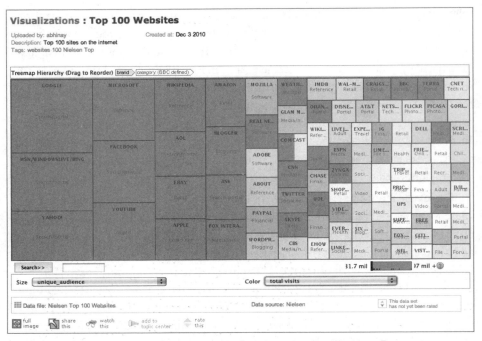

FIGURE 2-13: A data visualization of the top 100 websites, visualized on Many Eyes.

Another data visualization tool that you can use to identify trends on Twitter is called Twitter StreamGraphs, created by Jeff Clark of Neoformix. This nifty tool will chart the past 1,000 Tweets on any given topic and illustrate them in visual format. In Figure 2-14, I took the popular #measure hashtag (#measure is commonly used within Twitter to indicate Tweets that relate to analytics) and dropped it into the StreamGraphs tool to see what would show up. Right away I could see the popular topics and the tools allowed me to click on them to drill down to specific Tweets.

By simply exploring StreamGraphs and Many Eyes, as well as others like Fuselabs Social Gadgets (http://designer.socialgadgets.fuselabs.com/) and other free applications that are available for visualizing data, you can create your own meaningful interpretations of social media information. I actually created a list of Wicked Cool Data Visualization Tools to showcase some of the great things that people are making freely available out there (http://list.ly/list/As-wicked-cool-data-visualization-tools). I encourage clients to use these to break through to individuals in their organizations who cannot grasp the meaning of data in the form of columns and rows.

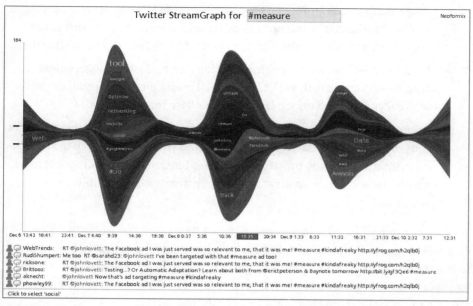

FIGURE 2-14: StreamGraphs visualization of 1,000 Tweets using the #measure hashtag.

> StreamGraphs is a fun visualization tool that you can use to track your brand keywords or trend topics that are meaningful to your brand.

WARNING Beware how and to whom you distribute these data visualizations. Callous managers may just tell you to quit messing around and get back to work. Admittedly, these data visualization tools won't work for everyone, but in my experience nothing works for everyone. Keeping some visualization tactics in your back pocket as a means to communicate information to others within your company could turn out to be the difference between communicating success and having another program go unnoticed.

ESTABLISHING A VIRTUAL NETWORK OPERATIONS CENTER

This chapter has covered a lot of ground already, but the biggest idea is yet to come. As you venture to the fringes of the Big Data abyss there is an ultimate window into the complexity of your social media beast. This window

- ► Affords an organization a unified perspective on its business operations as well as a process for managing the workflow of both inbound and outbound social media communications.

- ▶ Keeps your business informed by reporting on the key metrics that reveal the health of social media programs as delivered on your corporate web pages, your blogs, social networks, and communication outlets across the Internet.

- ▶ Triggers real-time alerts containing action items for myriad assignments to specific employees such as tweaking social media programs, communicating with consumers, and responding to competitive threats.

- ▶ Informs the marketing organization of the intimate campaign level details of your social media initiatives, but also informs the business about macroenvironmental concerns by functioning as an extension of the traditional teams within the enterprise—market research, customer service, public relations, and so on.

I'm describing a social media virtual Network Operations Center (vNOC). I envision this system as the organizational construct that facilitates multiple processes in the realm of social media data collection, analysis, triage, and response. It is an amalgamation of process and technology necessary to collect, analyze, plan for, and respond to a socially connected world in an analytical instant.

Clearly, a little bit of my background as a former analyst and consultant for Gomez (the performance management company now owned by Compuware) is showing through in my concept of a virtual NOC. Yet, the Network Operations Center (NOC) in any organization is the heartbeat of the network. If anything blips offline, online, or anywhere in between, bells and whistles start firing and people come running. The typical NOC possesses the ability to manage complex architecture spanning hardware, installed software, software-as-a-service, distributed applications, and much, much more.

According to Wikipedia,

NOCs analyze problems, perform troubleshooting, communicate with site technicians and other NOCs, and track problems through resolution. If necessary, NOCs escalate problems to the appropriate personnel. For severe conditions that are impossible to anticipate–such as a power failure or optical fiber cable cut–NOCs have procedures in place to immediately contact technicians to remedy the problem.

This description of a Network Operations Center that enables analysis, troubleshooting, communication, tracking, escalation, and emergency contingencies is ideal for a social media environment. The only difference is that a social media NOC is focused on people and their social networks, not on servers and systems. A social media NOC is the conduit for communication and, most important, for staying in touch with your customers.

Social media managers and measurers need a NOC! Each of the functions of a traditional network operations center translates fluidly to social media applications. Beyond a focus on people, my only modification to a traditional NOC is that the social media NOC is virtual—or at a minimum, part of it is. Although building out a facility with digital data eye candy is nice, it's probably not entirely necessary in most cases. However, if you're managing a social media presence that is the lifeblood of your brand, by all means build away. To help you conceptualize a vision of a social media vNOC, consider the following questions:

- ▶ Why do you need a social media vNOC?
- ▶ How do you assemble your own command central?
- ▶ Who is using something similar to a vNOC today?

Needing Your Virtual NOC

These command centers will serve enterprises that manage volumes of data and have a real business need to interact on an immediate basis. If you have a Facebook page as your social media beachhead, a vNOC is probably overkill. However, if you're working with Big Data, monitoring concurrent campaigns, interacting across multiple channels, and managing social platforms, a vNOC becomes pertinent.

Here are a few indications that your organization is ripe for a social media vNOC:

- ▶ **You're committed.** If you've generated a social media idea and released it to the world, it's your responsibility to keep up the effort. All too many social media ghost towns exist because social efforts went unchecked. If you are serious about social media, build a vNOC to manage it.

- ▶ **Data is critical to your operations.** If you've realized that making decisions based solely on intuition or gut feel is ludicrous, you may be ready. With the abundance of data coming your way, the choice to use it for gleaning insights and guiding the business is the only sensible thing to do. Use a vNOC to feed your business operations.

- ▶ **Consumers are your inspiration.** If you've entered the social arena to create a dialogue with your customers or to learn from them, you sure better be there when they want to talk. Whether it's a consumer on a rant or an advocate with a brilliant idea, you can tap into consumer intelligence using a vNOC.

▶ Further, if you rely on social media as a primary channel for any category (such as support, human resources, competitive intelligence, and so on), a vNOC is mission-critical.

> **Real-time interactions are vital.** If you've created a business that thrives on immediate response and five-nines availability, you need a vNOC. This is especially true if your social media campaign efforts span multiple channels and platforms where immediate response could be life-or-death.

> **Social media delivers competitive advantage.** If you're digging into social media because you recognize that innovation and competitive advantage awaits, you are definitely ready. Organizations on the forefront of change that are using social media to understand their audiences will be monitoring and managing their critical efforts using a vNOC.

Creating Command Central

Creating your version of the social media command control can be elaborate or elegantly simple. The concept is of a system that monitors your social activity and feeds stakeholders across your organization with information necessary to perform their job functions.

Virtualizing your social NOC happens in two ways:

> The most traditional form of NOC: the room full of computers, monitors, and so on. While these can be quite basic, you can also trick out your NOC by setting up a physical epicenter for your social operations, equipped with a bank of a dozen 42-inch HD monitors, flanked by half a dozen 24-inch screens and a 4 x 80-inch rear fired LCD/DLP projector.

> Alternatively, you could run this concept from a MacBook Air in a cubicle or from any location around the globe. The NOC can actually exist on transient machines within your organization. This setup would definitely require some heavy-duty support from the cloud, but it's doable and it's the future.

> Tomorrow's community managers and curators of social media will ultimately be plugged into their social activity via laptops and mobile devices 24/7/365, so you might as well plan now to take it with you.

Some traditional network operations centers are built for show by organizations that can afford to throw cash at that problem. So despite the fact that sitting in a dimly lit room with Oz-like controls surrounding him is any data geek's dream, this gig can really be run off a laptop. Sorry, folks, but remember, you are supposed to be social anyway, so you need to be talking to people. The virtual environment means that the vNOC can be monitored from an iPhone.

The vNOC that I envision can consist of a network of distributed computers with a central portal for access. This works because the data is pulled from a common record so that everyone has access to the same data, using the same data dictionaries and access protocols. The system should also include a workflow process to delegate actions to individual team members. These assignments can be specific to social media campaigns or issues for other departments in the enterprise such as product innovation, legal, or support. The vNOC acts like a ticketing system to assign accountability and track progress.

Actualizing Mission Control

Gatorade took the concept of a vNOC and made it a stark reality. Its social media "Mission Control" is the epicenter of the marketing function at Gatorade. The PepsiCo brand was working to reinvigorate its dwindling sports drink business and decided to use social media to fan the flames. The transparent walls of Gatorade's Mission Control exude the pulse of the brand as conversations are buzzing around at lightning speed. It's built with IBM hardware running Radian6 listening technology. And in true Gatorade style, it created a compelling YouTube video to showcase its Chicago-based digital HQ.

> NOTE Check out http://bit.ly/gatorade_MissionControl for more about the Gatorade Virtual Network Operations Center project.

What's interesting is that the video revealed the impetus behind Mission Control in captivating social media splendor, which is to engage with "millions of athletes and influencers," while monitoring "the pulse of the Gatorade brand." The mandate for the four full-time staffers within Mission Control is to listen, to create dialogue, and to track all things social. Early results indicate that more than 2,000 individual conversations with consumers have occurred; there has been a 9 percent increase in mentions of its G Series product, and a 60 percent jump in discussions about sports performance. (See http://adage.com/article/news/video-inside-gatorade-s-social-media-mission-control/146149/ for more information.)

Other brands are following the lead taken by Gatorade and erecting their own social media control centers. Dell, for example, is fully invested in social media and emphasizing the point with a "Ground Control" vNOC of its own. Dell's motivation is tracking conversations across all social media and using that information to improve its brand. Dell uses its new listening headquarters not only to listen and interact with consumers across social channels, but also to inform other parts of the business about actions that they need to take. In this way, Dell is executing on my vision of using the vNOC as a triage center to process requests and delegate tasks across the organization.

When I visited Dell's Ground Control at their headquarters in Austin, Texas, it was an impressive site indeed. The social media area was buzzing with activity both inside and outside the Ground Control vNOC. Dell uses social media in a way that impacts their entire business, and the physical location in Austin was more like a clearinghouse that executes on planning, training, and delegating actions to Dell employees across the globe. They've made a conscientious effort to empower their internal employees to use social media for interacting with customers. The map of the world on display in the social media floor at Dell revealed the 5,000+ employees that have already been trained to use social media as part of their jobs, and they have big plans for expanding this number throughout 2011.

Like Gatorade's Mission Control, the listening post is powered by a combination of technologies with Radian6 sitting at the center. It's expected that over 22,000 posts about Dell will be monitored on a daily basis. Some analysts, like my friend Jeremiah Owyang, are describing these types of social media command centers as the future of contact center operations. In a blog post, Jeremiah writes: "This isn't a revolution but instead evolution; in fact both types of centers will focus on issue resolution and customer satisfaction rates." He's right in that building a facility to handle customer requests via social channels isn't new; it's simply a new mode of response using Twitter and Facebook and other digital networks instead of telephones.

> **NOTE** Dell operates a Mission Control for social media too; see
> `http://bit.ly/Dell_MissionControl`.

If all this information about vNOCs and mission controls is making you scratch your head thinking that it's all just too much for your organization, don't despair. As I mentioned, these command centers don't need to be constructed with millions of dollars and plasma displays. You can shoestring a vNOC by simply organizing your company around a strategic concept of interacting with customers across social channels and informing your organization in real time. Whether this happens from a glass-encased mission control center at the heart of your marketing department or from distributed laptops around the world, it's more mentality than anything else.

> **NOTE** I encourage you to get started with a conceptual vNOC and prove that
> by listening you can move the needle on metrics that are important to your or-
> ganization. In doing this, you will quickly build a case for why social media is a
> critical component of your ability to connect with customers and perhaps even
> be able to justify a luxury vNOC of your own.

SUMMARY

Your key takeaways from this chapter should start with the realization that you're living in a Big Data world. The information that's available to a brand or an organization is monumental in both volume and possibilities. Although the rapid growth of social media data can be downright daunting, there are ways to manage it. Set yourself up for success by focusing on data that's most important to your business and setting expectations for your desired outcomes. I recommend breaking data collection and analysis into categories that allow you to consume data in bite-sized chunks. This task of categorization can also help to feed pertinent data to the right parts of your organization.

And speaking of data dissemination, the art of visualizing data is a powerful tool in your arsenal. Consider using infographics and data visualization techniques to offer information to business users throughout your company. While social media may still be foreign to many, the interpretation and business impact of your efforts doesn't need to be.

Finally, consider creating a virtual Network Operations Center to measure and manage your social initiatives. It will offer you a perspective on your social operations that facilitates rapid response, close customer ties, and enterprise collaboration.

CHAPTER 3

Activating Your Socially Connected Business

IN THIS CHAPTER

► Focusing on a people-centric approach
► Organizing your business for social media
► Gaining and sustaining social media buy-in
► Deciding where to start with social media metrics

The point at which you fully activate your socially connected business will determine if you hold any semblance of competitive sustainability or if you're destined to be a laggard within your industry. Although many, many organizations are already knee deep in social media, I honestly believe that it's not too late for new entrants. In fact, at this stage in the game, launching into social media with a well-defined strategy that includes the metrics necessary to quantify your desired outcomes is exponentially better than jumping in with a half-baked effort. Organizations that do the latter will inevitably end up losing more ground than they gain, or worse yet, they'll get brand-jacked by social savvy consumers. The imperative for activating your social organization will strike consumer-facing businesses first, but it will indeed filter through to business-to-business environments, non-profits, NGOs, and our global political and socioeconomic systems as well. Organizations that falter with social media will do so because they fail to recognize the power that social media bestows upon consumers.

▶ News flash: Your brand is already activated in social media because customers have done it for you. Catch up quick by listening first.

For these reasons, it's critical that you approach social media with a people-centric mentality. Remember that you're here in the first place because this is the new mode of communication between people. As individuals are figuring this stuff out, you need to be there to ensure that you have a voice in the conversation. That's a genuine, authentic voice, *not* the traditional interrupt method of marketing to customers. You may as well retire that tactic because shouting at customers ain't gonna work. Additionally, as a socially connected business you need to have your resources, technologies, and metrics tuned into your entire business. This chapter explores how to create a people-first perspective, how to organize for analytics, and how to demonstrate the value of social media across your entire organization using metrics. Once you achieve all this, your business will be primed for social media.

PARTICIPATING WITH A PEOPLE-CENTRIC APPROACH

This book is all about the metrics of social media and how to measure digital activity by understanding what it means to your unique business. However, I would be remiss if I didn't mention that metrics can sometimes interfere with your ability to connect with the real issues of importance. And in the case of social media, the real issues are people. The metrics are analogous to the gauges and dials you use to ensure that you're going in the right direction, but it's the interactions with people that constitute the essence of social media. Connecting with people requires getting out from behind the numbers and talking to them in a real and meaningful way.

Humanizing Your Approach

I've been a long time proponent of humanizing social media efforts by engaging in authentic and genuine actions. Regardless of the size of your brand, consumers will ignore you with vehement objection if you attempt to condescend to them from up on social media high. Further, if you try to dupe consumers with dubious tactics, they will inevitably find out and you'll be left looking foolish. Instead, you must relate to people across social media channels in a humanistic way. That's not to say that exuding professionalism and authority isn't required, because it is, but simply treating people with dignity and respect trumps all other cards in the social media deck.

When I started digging into humanizing the social media experience I called on Katie Paine of KD Paine & Partners to ask her to enlighten me with some of her knowledge on the topic. For those of you who aren't familiar with Katie's work, she's regaled as the Queen of Measurement and is definitely one of the sharpest social media measurers that I know. And she lives just up the road from me in New Hampshire. When we talked on a chilly winter day, Katie shared with me some fresh insights from a recent client interaction. Her client was just beginning to actively read Tweets and respond as part of their social listening strategy. For budgeting reasons her client wanted to do it themselves, which Katie was thrilled about because in her opinion, all organizations need to understand first hand what's being said about them and who is saying it.

We bantered a bit about the fact that today's social media tools are great for listening, but with commercial solutions it's too easy to watch the high-level trends and lose sight of who is really talking about you. In Katie's words, "These tools hide the people." They aggregate data and streamline consumption of information into pretty charts and graphs, but often the individual voices are muted. Katie went on to say that the way to remind social media measurers is to go in and look at people's Tweets or individual Facebook comments to see what people are saying about you. This is the social media equivalent of taking time to read open-ended customer survey responses.

> **NOTE** Katie Paine is the CEO and founder of KD Paine & Partners LLC and author of *Measure What Matters* and *Measuring Public Relationships: The Data-Driven Communicator's Guide to Success*. Check out her awesome blog at `http://kdpaine.blogs.com/`.

During our conversation, Katie shared a dirty little secret of her own with me that was pretty sobering. She believes that the vast majority of companies out there don't need a commercial social media monitoring tool for listening to their top 100 influencers (as ranked by high authority or high influence). Katie offered that the top 5 percent of brands get mentioned enough to warrant a tool, but with a little effort even big brands can track and monitor their social activity manually. She explained, "Mentions of all these brands and their competitors can be read without a tool. Once you actually read these things you can code them." When I pressed for more information, Katie revealed, "What's really important in social media is to understand not whether consumers like us, but do they trust us? Well, you can define the taxonomy for trust and actually start looking for that stuff."

What Katie was explaining gets to the heart of what you should be trying to accomplish from social media. If you're out there squawking on Twitter or putting up fancy Facebook pages, fine, but what's your objective? Aside from ultimately driving more sales, for most it's getting consumers to develop an affinity for the brand. Social media is a conduit for establishing that affinity and doing so in a very human way—by establishing trust.

When we eventually brought our conversation back around to metrics, Katie and I agreed that the tools are great, but in some cases, we (as social media measurers) do stuff that the tools cannot do. We look at sentiment for trustworthiness, we evaluate issues like green responsiveness or social good, and we look for key marketing messages that are subtly inserted between the lines. Ultimately, what we do is communicate with each other and the metrics must help us understand whether that communication leads back to our stated goals and objectives.

> The tools are a good way for a brand or company to get started and they're fun, but on the people side of social media, you need humility.

OFFERING GENUINE AUTHENTICITY

Companies that don't take the time to understand social media and attempt to treat social interactions only as sales opportunities are at serious risk of alienating their customers. Further, those that offer disingenuous social media efforts will ultimately draw scrutiny and lose credibility. Because of these reasons, embarking on a corporate social media journey is hard work. You can't simply set up a blog, campaign, or web page and then walk away and wait for individuals to flock together and sing your praises and offer you money. Instead, social media requires the tenacity of building and maintaining a presence and tending to individuals whenever and wherever they come, even when it won't result in a sale.

Yet, in numerous cases, brands are outsourcing their social response efforts to someone far removed from the brand who doesn't have a clue. These companies and their hired guns do nothing but surf around and deliver marketing messaging across social channels. It's a travesty, really, and you should avoid these tactics. Yet, there are ways to leverage offshore resources to delegate tasks to actually solve customer issues using social media without attempting to sell anything in the process. Positive examples stem from companies like Home Depot that respond to customer inquiries over social media channels with rapid response and relevant answers. Service issues are bound to happen, but the ability to address them in whichever channel a customer chooses is the new reality. Consumer Tweets directed at @Homedepot are met with near immediate response. Companies like Home Depot and many others both large and small are investing in service agents who are well versed in social media. These frontline agents who are tuned to the brand and the channels they support will have a resounding impact on the overall perception of their brand in the eyes of social consumers. Most importantly, they'll be satisfying customer needs and elevating the customer experience.

Ignoring customers is disingenuous and likely to dissuade customers from work-ing with you. There are many opportunities to sell, but when it comes to social media, take the time to listen and learn enough about every social media inquiry to deter-mine an appropriate response. This extends to working with agencies or external partners to educate them on how to do this also. It's worth pointing out the ramifica-tions of #FAIL actions to your partners and coworkers as examples of what not to do. These issues will continue to become more apparent as brands toe-dip their way into social media. But unless they do so with a genuinely human approach, they run the risk of tarnishing their reputations.

The consequence is that it's very easy for a consumer to turn off social media today by blocking out disrespectful or non-empathetic brands. This is a real threat because it's a shift in behavior. Before, when consumers received junk mail, they could simply toss it, and marketers would continue to blast them with offers until eternity, or the timing was right, whichever came first. But with digital media, tossing it means blocking you from contact, placing you on a do-not-call list, or relegating your e-mails to the spam filter forever.

> If you make an enemy of a digital native, you've probably got no chance of getting him or her back. The dialogue is killed. That's a new paradigm that social media marketers must contend with.

ADMITTING YOUR MISTAKES

There are a lot of wrong ways to do social media. Sites that are attempting social media forays often neglect the offerings they create, or worse yet, make serious blunders when it comes to interacting with people. Take Nestlé, for example, which was under fire in 2010 for using palm oil harvested by suppliers who were purport-edly destroying orangutan populations in Indonesia. Although this may sound like the start of a bad joke, the activists at Greenpeace took it very seriously and started a social media fiasco of epic proportion.

The issue came to a crescendo on Nestlé's Facebook page, which up until that point didn't receive much traffic and boasted only a modest following. As illustrated in Nestlé's public Facebook page in Figure 3-1, the Nestlé moderators threatened to censor any comments from people using altered versions of the Nestlé logo as their avatars. When individuals began criticizing the questionable tactic, they were met with hostile comments and downright rude behavior from Nestlé. Of course this cre-ated a social media firestorm that forced Nestlé back on its heels. As the company retreated to formulate a social strategy to deal with the current crisis on their hands, their Facebook page was effectively brand-jacked by consumers, who had a field day. Since then, Nestlé has cleaned up its act, but perhaps more importantly, with the help of social media Greenpeace was able to expose a problem to an audience that actually created change. This is just one example of how social media is impacting our world.

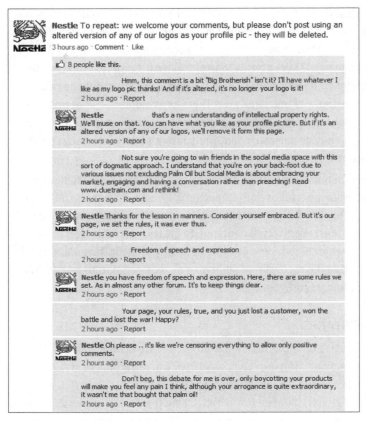

FIGURE 3-1: Nestlé's Facebook comments just hours after posting a censorship threat.

NOTE Greenpeace has fully embraced social media tactics within its arsenal of attention-grabbing tricks. In many cases, they're succeeding. Read more at `http://bit.ly/Greenpeace_SocialSuccess`.

Other examples of social media blunders are readily available. But, it's important to note that while some mistakes are social media *faux pas* that take place on social networks, other social disasters are simply exacerbated—or made public—by social media. For example, United Airlines committed a serious breach of trust by throwing and subsequently breaking a passenger's guitar. This now infamous event didn't originate online, but after hours of talking to United employees to gain some restitution, the victim was unsuccessful in resolving his rightful dispute. So, the musician/victim, Dave Carroll, took it upon himself to write a song about the incident and post it on YouTube. The "United Breaks Guitars" video was an instant viral hit and is now perhaps the most famous social media video exemplifying bad customer service (see the video at http://bit.ly/Unitedbreaksguitars). This cautionary tale shows how consumers are now empowered to tell their stories using social media channels.

The folks over at NVI, a Canadian web design and interactive agency, developed an interesting construct of the potential ways that companies can screw up social media. The idea was spawned in a blog post by Simon Abramovitch, who categorized actual events as captured by Michael Yeomans of *Advertising Age* in his SlideShare presentation called "Social Media Screw Ups" (http://www.slideshare.net/social mediainfluence/social-media-screw-ups). Yeomans calls out significant events that opened companys' eyes to the power of social media. Examples in the presentation include:

▶ Dell's awakening that resulted from one consumer's rant on "My Dell Hell," which educated Dell on the pains of customer service in a socially equipped world. (2005)

▶ Chevy's learning experience, during its "Design Your Own Tahoe" experiment, that consumers are fully in control and will often take your well-intentioned social media ideas to far off (and sometimes detrimental) places. (2006)

▶ Coca-Cola's explosive discovery that Mentos plus Diet Coke would equal the 12-million-view viral video phenomenon depicted in Figure 3-2, which was enough to teach them that social media places consumers in control. (2006)

▶ The unfortunate Comcast tech who was photographed sleeping on the job (on someone else's couch), which was broadcast across the Internet, forcing the telecom giant to focus efforts on customer service. (2006)

▶ Walmart's bust called "Walmarting Across America," where travelers Jim (a professional photographer) and Laura (a freelance writer) were in fact sponsored by Walmart to embark on their travels and report on the rosiest side of Walmart's effort. (2006)

▶ Sony's ousting for their fake blog and accompanying YouTube video called "All I Want for Xmas Is a PSP," causing them to retract the blog (now defunct) and issue apologies. (2006)

▶ Target's early attempts at ignoring social media, which prompted a written response to a blogger's concern that read, "Unfortunately we are unable to respond to your inquiry because Target does not participate with nontraditional media outlets." (2009)

The list of social media infractions goes on and on. But, the good news is that most of these misadventures forced the marketers—and their senior executives— to become more responsible about social media and to sit up and take notice. These events, whether triggered by social media or exposed as a result of it, sparked a realization that social media would profoundly affect their business. As a result, most of these brands have developed strong, if not leading, social media efforts subsequent to their early failures.

FIGURE 3-2: Diet Coke + Mentos YouTube video that racked up 12M views.

Simon Abramovitch of NVI spent some time thinking through each of the documented social media screw-ups and created a visualization, depicted in Figure 3-3, that classifies and organizes them. He identifies company behavior leading to the screw-up as Unprepared, Incompetent, Evil, or downright Foolish. In his blog post, "Social Media Debacles: 8 Ways to Screw Up Socially" (http://www.nvisolutions.com/ blog/social-media-optimization/social-media-debacles-8-ways-to-screw-up-socially/), Simon does a good job of describing three pairs of variables that he observed and how they relate to each of the events. In essence, by classifying screw-ups as either proactive or reactive, whether the screw-ups began online or offline, and whether the underlying intention was good or bad, a framework for describing social media screw-ups is developed. With this framework, people can analyze their current social media situations and learn from past mistakes stemming from the same combination of variables which they now face.

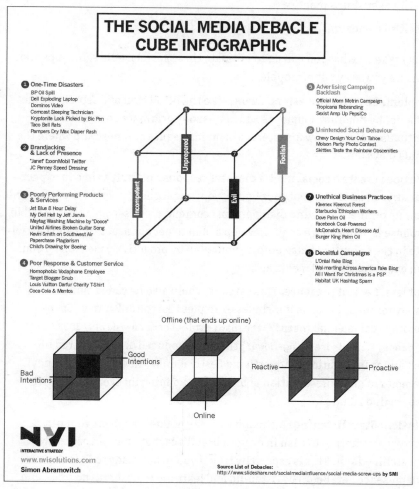

FIGURE 3-3: The Social Media Debacle Cube Infographic.

What I found particularly interesting in Simon's analysis was the determination that there are eight potential ways to blunder and get caught with social media. His screw-up synopsis includes:

▶ One-time disasters

▶ Lack of presence

▶ Poor performance

▶ Poor response

▶ Advertising backlash

▶ Unintended social behavior

▶ Unethical business practices

▶ Deceitful campaigns

Here's my take on what you can do to mitigate these social media screw-ups and how to measure your way out of trouble.

▶ **Problem: One-time disasters**: Events like the BP oil spill and reprehensible behavior by Domino's employees do not usually originate on social media, but that's typically how disasters gain mainstream awareness and where the drama plays out.

Solution: Create a social media disaster response plan. It's time to expect that any misadventures of your brand, your employees, or your executives will show up online. Following disingenuous contempt, the second worst possible response is no response at all. Develop a plan to get out a message and participate in the fallout, but also enforce your plan by proactively measuring your own employees' social media activity.

▶ **Problem: Lack of presence:** This category could also be called slander or parody response because it includes examples like the JCPenney "Speed Dressing" commercial (http://theinspirationroom.com/daily/2008/jc-penney-speed-dressing-down/) that was produced and submitted to the Cannes International Advertising Festival unbeknownst to JCPenney! Examples of misrepresentation of brands are popping up everywhere with disparaging results.

Solution: Start listening. Although you may not be able to prevent others from attempting to cash in on your brand's cachet, you can certainly be watching for it. This is especially true if you're not ready to launch your own presence yet. Begin by listening and learning to observe the tenor and cadence of your brand's social presence. Do this with proactive alerts triggered from your social listening technologies that will prompt your legal department to break out the cease-and-desist letters.

▶ **Problem: Poor performance:** Shoddy workmanship, sub-par customer service, and non-performing products have no place to hide in today's socially exposed world. Citizens like Heather Armstrong, author of a popular mommy blog called Dooce, aired Maytag's dirty laundry when she expressed her dissatisfaction

with a dysfunctional new machine to her Twitter following (http://www
.forbes.com/2009/09/02/twitter-dooce-maytag-markets-equities-
whirlpool.html). Next thing they knew, Maytag had a boycott on its hands.

Solution: Set expectations and make it right. This example was a tough one
because Maytag was there to respond with a new machine within a day, but
the stains had already set with Armstrong's following and the press. To add
insult to injury, Bosch, the rival manufacturer, swooped in and delivered a
new machine. Take back the reins by creating internal service level agreements (SLAs) for social media response times. Rapid replies will demonstrate
to consumers that you are not only listening, but also sympathetic and
responsive to their social cries for help. This includes welcoming the opportunity to make something right before consumers revert to social slander.

▶ **Problem: Poor response:** Official corporate communications like Target's
blogger response or individual employee messages like the unfortunate Twitter missive sent by one oblivious Vodafone UK employee reflect on an entire
organization.

Solution: Institute enterprise-wide social media training. Organizations
are past due to realize that any individual using a corporate account—from
intern to general counsel—speaks in the company's voice across social media.
Develop a social media policy similar to the ones referenced in Chapter 9. Yet,
having a policy alone is not enough: ensure proper training and compliance
with social protocol to mitigate embarrassment.

▶ **Problem: Advertising backlash:** Motrin admitted that they blew it with the
Motrin Moms ad that showcased Moms wearing youngsters as "accessories"
and suffering pain as a result. But only after the Twittersphere, blogosphere,
and YouTube simultaneously erupted.

Solution: Test market to your core audience. Social media is the new focus
group, so before putting something out there to face scrutiny from the masses,
test it. Develop satisfaction metrics and ask your influential fans and brand
advocates before launching mass social media to gauge invaluable opinions.
A *New York Times* article effectively re-Tweeted some good advice: "note to
self ... never piss off moms ... especially Twitter moms... they can be a nasty
bunch ;)" (http://parenting.blogs.nytimes.com/2008/11/17/moms-and-
motrin/).

▶ **Problem: Unintended social behavior:** With the best of intentions you hand-
craft a marketing campaign, only to have callous deviants stamp obscenities

▶ Jeremiah
Owyang created
a revealing Brand
Backlash category
structure to rank
just how poorly
some efforts fare
(http://www.web-
strategist.com/
blog/2008/11/17/
categorization-of-
brand-backlash-
storms/).

all over it. That's what happened to Skittles when they allowed Tweets to post uncensored on the homepage of their web site. After a sweet initial launch (couldn't resist the pun), the site was littered with negativity and off-color remarks, causing the company to recoil (http://econsultancy.com/us/blog/3374-skittles-launches-an-amazing-social-media-campaign).

Solution: Never relinquish total control. It's one thing to accept that consumers dominate the conversation, but another thing entirely to let them rule your owned media. It's your site: own it. That doesn't mean that you shouldn't listen and take part in the conversation or allow consumers to voice their thoughts and opinions in other places. Kudos to Skittles for rebounding from this episode and continuing to boldly venture into new media.

▶ **Problem: Unethical business practices:** While buying palm oil from an unethical supplier is certainly unjust, businesses today need to be extra diligent when it comes to not only their own practices, but those of their partners as well. There are just too many ways to go wrong today, and it's not worth taking the risk.

Solution: Become accountable to your customers. Shaking out the skeletons from every organization's closet won't be something that happens anytime soon. What can happen, however, is a new level of awareness when choosing business partners and engaging in business practices about the consequential effects a broadcast society has upon exposure. Use your social measurement tools to do your homework.

▶ **Problem: Deceitful campaigns:** The cosmetics brand L'Oreal learned a quick lesson from consumers after an agency launched a contrived blog on their behalf. The blog featured a supermodel-esque character that complained to be in need of anti-aging cream. Consumers realized it was fake within hours after the blog launched and the company scampered quickly to the powder room to try again.

Solution: Just don't do it. Consumers can increasingly spot fake social media in a New York minute. Transparency is the name of the game here. And if you've learned anything so far from this chapter, let it be that you don't want to get burned by consumers across social media. The backlash is detrimental. Measure this by keeping tabs on your agencies, partners, and internal colleagues with a system of checks and balances to not only figure out how they're tracking, but also what they're up to.

▶ *Social media is most certainly about connecting with people, but with the media properties you own, you control the conversation.*

Social media participants are human beings and when they engage in social media, they expect humans to respond. Every marketer I know is also a consumer, so take the time to think like a consumer before launching your next campaign. Ask yourself, "Is it genuine?" Then put yourself in their shoes. When you ask a question, do you want a response in the form of a press release? Or do you want a human to respond? Of course you don't want a PR person—or worse, a salesperson—selling you something that doesn't solve your immediate problem. You really just want someone who can answer the question. As social media managers, you need to make your colleagues live in your customers' shoes to make them understand this stuff.

TRAINING YOUR BUSINESS

One of the better stories I've heard about training your business was from Anna O'Brien, former VP Social Media at a major U.S. financial institution. Anna was the community manager who was responsible for social media communications at the Fortune 50 company. As all good community managers are apt to do, Anna was creating a plan for addressing comments aimed at the bank via Twitter. Her plan included detailed metrics such as quantifying incoming inquiries, calculating response times, establishing conversation volumes based on product line, and generally tracking social media interactions in a meaningful way to the business. Upon developing the plan, this community manager approached her legal department for clearance to proceed, which was a required step in developing communication plans with the bank's customers.

The legal department took a very literal approach in their line of questioning about Anna's plan for interactive communication. Their first response was "What will you Tweet back to these individuals when they write questions via Twitter?" Of course Anna answered that it would depend on what they asked. But legal insisted, "What exactly will you respond to these inquiries?" Uncomfortable with the newness of the channel, they forced the issue by insisting that Anna create a list of responses that she might offer to Twitter queries. As crazy as this sounds, Anna complied with the request and hatched a clever plan to prove a point about the error in their ways. Upon presenting a list of approximately 100 or so possible answers to customer questions and comments, the legal team got out their pens and began redlining. The result was a short list of about 24 corporate-approved answers that were permissible to send to customers via Twitter. Feeling frustrated but not surprised by the legal team's lack of understanding of the social universe, Anna left to begin amassing evidence of why this type of engagement would not work. You see where this is going, don't you?

As Tweets began rolling in, the "approved" messages didn't come close to answering customer questions. For example, when a customer asked, "I am a college student with limited credit history. I don't know which credit cards to apply to," Anna's best response option was "We're sorry for the inconvenience; I will share that information with our internal team." When she gathered enough evidence for her compelling case, Anna brought some poignant examples to the team of legal eagles and very politely asked which of the inadequate approved responses she should use? Anna's example made an impact, and with time she was granted approval to answer Tweets with appropriate responses using a real human voice. Although not every organization will require this degree of hoop-jumping, it's a pretty good example of a business being disconnected from the potential of social media. Yet, it's also an example of an organization that's protecting itself with a calculated approach. Luckily the legal team was able to learn about social media and has since become one of the organization's greatest internal proponents. This was all thanks to the help of one savvy community manager. Nice work, Anna.

Growing Social Relationships

So, hopefully you are beginning to see that social media requires a people-centric approach for both delivering and managing it within your business. Once you master this mindset, it's imperative to find ways to judge the value of your social relationships to determine which people can help you and which are better at helping each other. That's where the metrics come in. Metrics can help you to discern relationships that work and those that don't. They can also give you a sense of where you need to focus and how to accomplish your social objectives. Yet, it's also about the strength of your relationships and how far and wide they go. It's my belief that the social graph will play a profound role in identifying individuals and how important they are to any given initiative. If you think about social media across your owned digital properties as a web of interconnected relationships, that's just the beginning. The social graph extends well beyond your control to the farthest reaches of the Internet. The attitudes, affinities, and ties between individual relationships will provide immense insights into how consumers relate to one another and how their behaviors can be influenced by their social graph.

HARNESSING THE SOCIAL GRAPH

Mark Zuckerberg, founder of Facebook and *Time* magazine's 2010 Person of the Year, is credited with coining the term "social graph." He used the phrase to describe relationships between people and ultimately his vision for the Facebook platform, of connecting people across the globe. Yet, Brad Fitzpatrick originally defined the social graph as "the global mapping of everybody and how they're related" in his 2007 blog post called "Thoughts on the Social Graph" (http://bradfitz.com/social-graph-problem/). With the explosive growth of Facebook, over half a billion users, and a rapidly burgeoning Facebook Connect, it's quite possible that Facebook could own the social graph. But this manifestation of the social graph and others, such as Google's social circle, means that connectivity will affect your brand because it's ubiquitous.

Yet, the social graph isn't about Facebook or Google or Orkut or any single social network. These are enabling technologies that allow consumers to connect with one another using social media. The challenge today is that there are too many choices for how to interpret social graphs and where to apply them to business. Jeremiah Owyang summarized the issue way back in 2007 in a blog post he called "Explaining what the 'Social Graph' is to your Executives" (http://www.web-strategist.com/blog/2007/11/10/what-is-social-graph-executives/) as follows:

> The Social Graph is the representation of our relationships. Today, these graphs define our personal, family, or business communities on social websites. Unfortunately, we're duplicating our same Social Graph on multiple websites, resulting in inaccurate data and time spent managing it. Despite many challenges, our Social Graphs should be self-managed from a single trusted source, replicated to websites of our choosing, thus resulting in accurate, efficient, relationship management.

Social graphs have the ability to relay information about individual users and the networks of people that they associate with. As Jeremiah points out, one challenge is that social graphs are often replicated across multiple networks, creating seemingly more information when in fact much of the data is duplicated elsewhere. Yet, despite the fact that multiple social graphs may exist, the value of the social graph for a business lies in the ability to recognize a connection between individuals and their social graph. For example, a group of people may be included in a common social graph simply because each individual "liked" a brand's new social media campaign. These individuals don't know each other, but they've explicitly (and publicly) indicated an interest that links them to each other. As a marketer or data scientist, you could begin to explore this information and look for other similarities within the data to identify segments of the social graph that are most likely to purchase, those that are affluent and likely to become valuable customers, or those that indicate behaviors that are indicative of less profitable customers. This information can empower you with knowledge about how to market to these different segments of individuals and which social networks they're most likely to spend time on.

▶ Think about social media across your digital properties as a web of interconnected relationships.

▶ Check out the social graph InMaps and other cool stuff at LinkedIn Labs:

bit.ly/LinkedIn_labs.qrcode

In other cases, you might have information about an individual's social graph like the one depicted in Figure 3-4. This is a visualization of my personal social graph from LinkedIn (visualize yours at http://inmaps.linkedinlabs.com/), and it makes sense to me because I know *how* I'm connected to each of the individuals on this visualization. The majority are connections I've made from my work in analytics and measurement, yet I've also got pockets of former colleagues that represent networks of individuals. Additionally, you can see that my social graph of actual friends and family as represented here on LinkedIn is quite small in comparison to the other groupings of individuals. While this all makes sense to me because I know these people represented on this visualization, as a marketer or measurer of social media, your job is to find the connections between different nodes and the strengths of those social connections on any individual's social graph. Once you hold that nugget of information, then you can start to leverage the power of the social graph to strengthen the connections between people and your brand by keying into their interests and behaviors.

> **NOTE** Recognize that bonds between individuals within any social graph carry varying degrees of strength that aren't always readily apparent in digital communications. My ties to friends and family are stronger than my ties to business acquaintances, yet a social graph visualization doesn't reveal this fact.

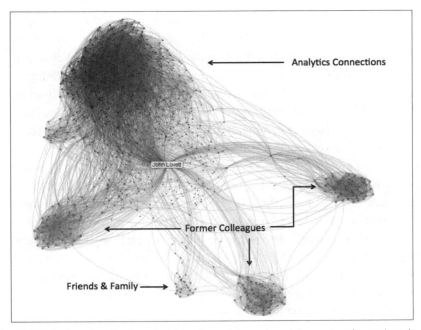

FIGURE 3-4: A visualization of a LinkedIn social graph and the context for each node.

The relevance of the social graph becomes immediately apparent when you identify the context of the graph and the information contained within it. Thus, by recognizing that each of the individuals connected in the top grouping in Figure 3-4 have analytics in common, you can begin to utilize that information for marketing purposes. Moving forward, this contextual relevance will have a profound impact on marketing and business as people inevitably become more interconnected through social media. Early signs are already appearing. If you've been paying attention to Facebook advertising lately, you may have noticed ads popping up with your friend's faces next to them. The savvy marketers at Facebook determined that seeing your friends' avatars next to advertisements that they "liked" significantly increases the chances that you'll click on the advertisement as well. That's using the social graph.

RECRUITING COMMUNITY MANAGERS

Here's an analogy. Imagine, if you will, a party planner. A good party planner starts with an idea and shapes it into an event. This requires understanding not only how to effectively plan a party, but also what topics, themes, elements, and people go together to ensure that guests enjoy themselves and all have a good time. Regardless of the occasion, party planners must think about many details that will ensure a successful event, from planning the timing of the event, the desired attendees, the entertainment, and numerous other details right down to the flavor of cake served at any good party. And planning the party is typically only where the work begins. During the event, the host or hostess is quickly consumed with greeting guests, making introductions, and sparking conversations by finding commonalities among attendees.

Community managers are much like party planners in that their jobs require diligent planning and tireless effort. But unlike party planners, who typically receive respite following a big event, social media community managers aren't so lucky. During my research on community managers I caught up with Connie Benson, Director of Community Strategy & Social Media for the vendor Alterian SM2. Connie was fresh back from a trip to India, where she had been doing some training, and she shared with me some secrets about the day-to-day responsibilities of a successful community manager.

Connie dove right in and began explaining that a key role for any community manager was to facilitate the cultural shift internally within an organization by training the staff and empowering employees to use the social web. Immediately I was puzzled because I thought that being a community manager is all about interacting with the outside community, but here Connie was explaining to me the

▶ Being a community manager isn't all about interacting with the outside world. The first task of a good community manager is often evangelizing for social media within the organization.

importance of circulating within an organization and floating between business units to evangelize for social media. As we talked it became apparent that this made complete sense. The business needs to understand social media and the ways in which it can be used to connect with consumers. And this works best if the internal communications occur before interacting with actual consumers.

The community manager is the liaison between the business and consumer and effectively knows both. They make the introductions. In a traditional lead-generation organization, a sales team may set up hundreds of meetings and convert only a small fraction of those meetings into business. When interacting across social channels, salespeople can tune in to the conversation and approach prospects at the right time during their buying cycle, which can be entirely more productive. Connie explained that community managers can help to identify these prospects and recognize when they're ripe for the picking. Once an organization begins to see the effectiveness of this type of sales approach, they begin to fully embrace social media as a feeder channel for their business.

Measuring these activities is largely dependent upon the team—for sales, it may be more qualified leads, or for product marketing, it might be new ideas. Yet, the role of the community manager is to determine how each internal team within the business might benefit from social media. In an ideal world, a community manager would know everything about every product to identify marketplace cues and conversational chatter that might be relevant to a specific part of the organization. But in the real world that's nearly impossible, so empowering the staff about the capabilities of social media and training them what to look for is a realistic and infinitely more scalable approach.

Most community managers and social strategists will find that they need to interface not only with consumers and their internal peers, but with their agencies as well. Depending on who your company works with on the agency side, you may find that they're either very innovative with regard to social media or decidedly traditional. Traditionalists may try to sell you ideas and even create blog posts for you and suggest that you submit them to your community as byline articles. Yet, according to Connie, this is a bad idea.

▶ First of all, it treads pretty close to deceit (see the previous information about deceiving your customers).

▶ Secondly, it's unlikely that their style will adhere to your own.

Other issues arise, such as who will respond to the comments. The agency? You? Rather than taking this approach, Connie suggests that a substantially more effective alternative is to connect the agency with a specific line of business to determine their needs and develop a social media story around the product. In fact, Connie's secret belief is that the future for public relations is that they create the story and use social media as the distribution channel. The role of the community manager is to ensure a genuine fit with the brand and to make the connection between internal teams and the agency. This method shifts the burden of work from the community manager and succeeds in getting the business directly involved with social marketing programs. If done correctly, this approach can produce very effective content that resonates across social media.

▶ Good things happen when content is genuine and not placed.

When it comes to metrics, community managers in many cases default to the lines of business that they support. In the role of liaison, the community manager simply looks to make the match and then gets out of the way to allow the newly introduced parties to do their thing. Yet, according to Connie, if there was one single underlying metric, it would be brand visibility. She stated, "Without brand visibility what are you? In my company our executives want more and more brand visibility...so that's my KPI. And I'm trying to empower my people to talk to me and to each other to help increase it."

Connie went on to talk about soft metrics (brand visibility) versus hard metrics (revenue) and described how she works to relate the two. By showing increases in conversations from last quarter to this quarter, Connie can demonstrate which of the company's social efforts are working. With data as evidence, no one argues that it's not. And by overlaying this data with sales revenue and making correlations where there are spikes, it becomes really compelling. Of course, in B2C organizations with short sales cycles, this is substantially easier, but it's still possible to do in a B2B sales environment with a sales cycle that extends 6 months or longer. Fundamentally, using social media facilitates a shift in strategy for many organizations. It's a shift from outbound cold calling to warming up leads and enabling them to easily find inbound avenues. With enough inbound volume that's tuned in to relevant and timely messaging, some companies may be able to discontinue their cold calling entirely. Yet, this will only happen in organizations that are connected to their prospects and customers across social channels in a very meaningful way. Community managers can play an integral role in seeking out these connections and hooking their audiences.

CELEBRATING BRAND ADVOCATES

A whole lot has been written about social media influencers and brand advocates, but when it comes to growing your social media relationships these two groups are likely to be critical to your success. The distinction I make is this:

- ▶ **Brand advocates** often have no official connection to the brand except that they are product users.

- ▶ **Social media influencers** are often individuals who have been sought out because of their ability to sway a specific audience toward a given predilection.

Although influencers may hold an audience, brand advocates typically hold passion. This passion is often very contagious as it spreads through the power of word of mouth. Advocates are the ones who will recommend your product to friends and relatives without provocation. They also tend to write reviews and offer support to their social networks without any thought of compensation or recognition. These characteristics can be an extremely powerful voice for your brand because they typically have no bias and almost always reflect the authentic and genuine attitudes of individuals.

▶ Building trust is a key social marketing function where Advocates and Influencers can help.

Companies engaging in social media are beginning to embrace their brand advocates because they are extremely powerful allies. At a time when consumers are bombarded by advertising from every channel, the last thing they need is more marketing speak directed at them. Research conducted by InSights Consulting found that among consumers surveyed, the most credible sources of social media information about a brand are fellow consumers. No surprise here. But after their peers, consumers look to the brands themselves. This actually represents a migration from previous thinking indicating that brands are gaining credibility within social channels. Next on the list of sources of credible information, the believability meter sinks dramatically to journalists and then marketers, finally sinking to competitors. Brian Solis writes about this in his blog post "In Social Media, Consumers Offer Rewards to Deserving Brands" (which you can find at http://www.briansolis.com/2010/05/in-social-media-consumers-offer-rewards-to-deserving-brands/). It shows the credibility slide of trust where consumers listen to each other first. Yet, if you're a brand manager, take this as a good sign, because you may have a fighting chance. Nonetheless, consumer advocates still dominate the credibility factor and as such, they're people you want on your side.

If you want an example of a brand that has enthusiastic brand advocates, check out LEGO. Figure 3-5 shows the LEGOFan homepage (http://shsl.org). It's a non-sponsored, non-authorized, non-endorsed, "official fan-created LEGO site." These fans have taken it upon themselves to build and maintain a site dedicated to their passion of stacking tiny blocks. Here, you can join a LEGO User Group (LUG), find out about the latest news on LEGO video games, or recover building instructions to your long lost LEGO set. Now that's dedication! But LEGO isn't sitting back and letting their brand advocates do all the work. The LEGO Group recently launched its own LEGO Click community that brings together inventors, explorers, tinkerers, artists, and idea people of all ages. They're embracing social media by linking out to both Twitter and Facebook, while also providing an iPhone app that will turn your photos into LEGO creations.

FIGURE 3-5: LEGOFan official fan homepage.

Bringing It Back to the Business

When it came time to connect all the dots and see how companies are actually executing within their respective businesses, I called on Eric Beane, who is the Director of Analytics & Optimization at the agency VML, to gain his perspective. Eric put me in touch with James O'Malley and Mikey Cramer on his Emerging Media Team in New

York. They work with brands like SAP, Hershey's, and Gatorade to help develop, execute, and measure social media campaigns. The team tackles a broad range of activities ranging from activating events across social media to guiding the overall social strategy for their clients. They work to quantify their efforts using metrics, which they monitor on behalf of their brand partners.

One of the key secrets that the Emerging Media Team shared with me was that despite meticulous planning and diligent efforts, the social media metrics they create tend to change over time. For them, it's an iterative learning process because the tools, metrics, and initiatives are changing constantly. They use metrics to drive content strategy and media buying, but as much as their efforts are working, they succeed because they look at data from many perspectives and can evolve to meet the flow of ideas and initiatives stemming from their clients. In some cases, this is challenging because many brands have multiple sub-brands, and the target market for each one is very different. What works for VML is identifying content that drives specific conversion events. Whether it's an actual online conversion that includes a transaction or simply a conversion like consuming content, registering for an event, or sharing with another individual, they focus on measuring these consumer activities.

One of the challenges that VML has with some clients is that they want to correlate social media numbers to their traditional measures of success, like television ratings. Although some brands are beginning to include calls to action in TV ads that include vanity URLs for Facebook Fan pages, measuring the direct impact of online social activity from television is still largely a harlequin's trick. Instead, teams can establish baseline measures for normal traffic and growth patterns and evaluate that against time periods when non-digital campaigns are active. Additionally, using advertising data, they can determine markets where ads play and map those against web traffic as identified by geography. Using these tactics, brands can begin to understand the impact that television and other media have on digital channels.

Although VML works with some of the largest and most sophisticated brands on the planet, sometimes there is a disconnect between the organization and the social media managers within it. The social managers are typically very engaged with the agency when it comes to planning the metrics for measuring the success of every initiative before things go out the door, but the rest of the organization isn't always as cooperative. At times, campaigns launch without tracking codes or campaign IDs in place, thereby making measurement extremely difficult. When situations like this occur, the VML team has to scramble to get the right metrics and tracking in place because ultimately measuring this stuff is their responsibility. Although these are worst-case

▶ Metrics change over time! Don't get stuck in your ways and be prepared to modify and optimize your measurement efforts.

scenarios overall, clients who work directly with the agency tend to get it, but in many cases at the company-wide level, their organizations are not there yet.

One of the tools that VML uses to help their clients activate their social organizations is communication of metrics through dashboards. They develop and use their own custom dashboards such as the one depicted in Figure 3-6. They develop these dashboards by talking to clients and determining the best ways to display information according to their key performance indicators. This typically involves several data views including an executive overview, a marketing channel view (which includes social media, e-mail, Facebook, searches, and so on), and then a performance view that demonstrates success. Dashboards are extremely useful and relevant for VML clients in supporting their strategies because they are developed using the same language that their clients use and include specific measures of success that apply across the business. Using these tools, marketing managers can evaluate the impact of social media activity resulting from a newsletter drop or isolate individual user segments to determine the success of Facebook ads by demographic characteristics.

> ▶ Organizations often launch campaigns and expect metrics to magically appear, when really analytics pros have to make metrics happen. Don't launch an effort without measures of success; plan ahead and collaborate on metrics and measurement tactics.

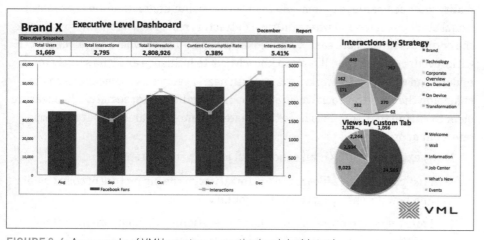

FIGURE 3-6: An example of VML's custom executive level dashboard.

When I asked the Emerging Media Team at VML to share some thoughts on what lies ahead for digital measurement across the spectrum of clients they work with, the immediate answer was "mobile." More and more mobile devices and social mobile applications like FourSquare are changing the game for social media measurers. Incorporating the logistics of mobile into their strategies in terms of how it's reported, and how these location-based services are overlaid onto other metrics, starts to show very interesting trends about customers and the networks that they're in. Yet, for most brands the lines are blurring between mobile, social, and fixed web properties.

Increasingly, it's about the ability to provide a brand health report that reveals metrics from multiple channels. Although clients may request a seemingly simple social media report, there is data hidden behind overlays that provide web analytics traffic information, sales data from another system, and customer profile information from yet a third solution. More and more, their job is about breaking down data silos and convincing organizations to look at data holistically, rather than isolating success in individual channels.

ORGANIZING FOR SOCIAL MEDIA

As you work to activate social media within your organization, it's a good idea to start with an honest assessment of the challenges that lie ahead. For some, instituting a social media program will be a joyous occasion that meets with widespread acceptance, whereas others will undoubtedly meet with resistance and criticism. In reality most companies fall somewhere in between, but understanding the organizational allies you have and where internal detractors reside will allow you to navigate the corporate ranks more easily. Additionally, depending on where social media fits within your company, you'll have to know whom to influence and who's likely to understand what you are working toward. In nearly every case, someone needs to champion the cause for social media and, more specifically, for social media measurement to ensure that programs have the greatest chance of making it out the corporate front doors.

In my experience, this is an educational journey at every step.

1. First you need to educate the organization on the big picture of social media and how it's changing the world around you.

2. From there, it requires a game plan to determine how your organization—whether large or small—will contend with these changes.

3. And then of course, once your plan is under way, you will continually need to reiterate the values and demonstrate the fruits of your efforts.

Using metrics allows you to do this more easily because metrics become the proof points that indicate where you were yesterday and where you are today. Further, they can also be used to indicate where you're headed. But many companies still need a wake-up call to jump start their thinking and to spur them into action. For the individuals who lead these organizations, I wrote the following letter to the C-Suite.

DO YOU EVEN KNOW YOUR CUSTOMERS?

This letter originally appeared in Exact Target's "10 Ideas to Turn Data Into Results" report. It's part of their "Letters to the C-Suite" series and this is my letter.

To The Executive Team:

Do you even know who your customers are anymore? Chances are you probably don't. You catch fleeting glimpses of them as they open your emails or pop onto your website for a quick visit. You might even momentarily engage with them when they drop into your store to browse around or see your products firsthand. Or maybe you meet them ever so briefly as they feign interest in your brand by "liking" something you posted on Facebook. If you're doing it right, your business is collecting feedback across many customer touch points.

But you only really hear them when they shout from the rooftops, irate and full of vim. That's probably where you begin to learn what's on their minds. But do you even know that it's the same person who was showing you all that love during your last promotion? Probably not.

In actuality, few companies really know their customers. Whether your customers are end users or other businesses, how they interact with your brand, where they discover new information, and how they communicate are changing at an astounding rate. Customers are increasingly unaffected by traditional marketing conventions, and their tolerance for redundant messaging, static content, and conflicting brand information is nonexistent. They don't see your organization like you do—in departmentalized silos of categories, products, business units, and operating divisions. To them, you're just that brand they either love, hate, or treat with ambivalence. That is, until you knock their socks off by impressing them with your service, support, and relevance. Yet, to really deliver value to your customers, you need to get to know them. This starts by remembering the interactions you have with them and building off of these activities.

Digital communication is the new reality, and treating customers through digital channels is synonymous with how you'd treat someone you meet in person. Listen to what they're saying and respond with appropriate dialogue. But most importantly, remember these things (because upon your next conversation, your customer might just remember you).

(continues)

DO YOU EVEN KNOW YOUR CUSTOMERS? *(continued)*

Your memory of customers exists at the database level. By maintaining customer profiles and appending them with attributes that contain history, activity, and propensity (among other things), you can truly begin to have meaningful interactions. To do this effectively, the database must contain information from all your touch points.

This includes transactional systems, web analytics, call centers, mobile devices, social media, ATMs, stores, email systems, and whatever else you're using to reach out. Bringing your data together through integrations enables you to achieve a holistic picture of your customers. A little scared by this? Well, you should be.

Customer behaviors are going to fundamentally change the way you engage with your audience. If you're not equipped, they're going to take their conversations (and their wallets) elsewhere. By integrating your data, you open opportunities for new customer dialogues.

Take my word for it—it's happening now.

Your Agent For Change,
John Lovett

Selling Social Media Internally

I had the good fortune of hearing Lizzie Schreier of Allstate Insurance speak on a number of occasions. Lizzie tells a fascinating and entirely entertaining account of activating social media in a highly regulated, risk adverse environment such as the one at Allstate Insurance. A few years back, the organization made a commitment to become more focused on its customers and to enable them to connect with one another using social media. At the time, Lizzie was part of the web team and became the internal champion for developing the organization's first social media experience.

Lizzie's undertaking meant that she had to find a way to institute social media that would adhere to the high standards of the Allstate brand and conform to the requirements of the insurance industry. As such, she determined that the best place to start was to get legal on board by getting them comfortable with the value that social media could bring to the organization. According to Lizzie, the legal team at Allstate is top-notch and their thorough understanding of the risks and rewards associated with social media was a prerequisite to getting any idea or initiative off the ground. When I talked about her process, she commented that the rigor of the Allstate legal team made her step up her game to develop a compelling case and to formulate a bulletproof social media strategy before any outbound communication ever occurred.

Lizzie informed me that she approached her task of seeking internal approval for social media by planning things in bite-sized pieces. Doing this made the moving parts of her social media strategy easier to control and easier for others to understand. While she had formulated a long-term vision of what the big picture looked like, she also knew that she was only capable of taking on so much at one time. Part of this strategy was introducing social media in business-friendly terms. Lizzie exemplified by telling a story about scheduling an initial meeting with the head attorney to discuss the concept of a new message board that she was thinking about. Going into the meeting, Lizzie wasn't sure what to expect so she hoped for the best and prepared for the worst. The topic was certainly of interest because the short meeting Lizzie intended drew significantly more attorneys than she expected. But instead of trying to bulldoze them into a social media plan complete with buzzwords, PowerPoint slides, pros and cons, and amazing benefits that the organization would realize, Lizzie did something revolutionary. She simply talked to them. She went in and started a conversation about social media to determine how much the legal team knew about it, what their fears were, and what she needed to do to assuage their concerns. She also knew that because Allstate hadn't participated in social media previously, there would be hesitation. Thus, she looked at it differently and instead of walking into the meeting with her social media guns blazing, she associated social media with "content syndication" and other terms that the legal team was already familiar with. When she was satisfied with her initial fact-finding mission, she adjourned the meeting and left to revise her strategy. But not before she fully understood what the lawyers viewed as red flags when heading into social media.

NOTE Visit http://bit.ly/Allstate_TwitterStream to see Twitter comments that posted during Lizzie Schreier's eMetrics presentation.

As it turns out, social media has some serious implications for industries like insurance because if individuals deliver and take advice from one another on a company-hosted web site and there is ever a tragedy that occurs, the company could be legally responsible in a court of law. Thus, this first meeting was very valuable in refining the social media strategy because Lizzie was able to see from the legal team's perspective, work within their guidelines, and get things approved more quickly. Armed with this information, Lizzie developed a plan and formulated an education strategy that would enable her to gain buy-in for the social program and indoctrinate the Allstate staff on what it means to participate and actually connect users to one another using social media.

The new program was dubbed "Syndicated Content for Organic Search," which was entirely brilliant, because a "social media" program didn't align with corporate culture and could have been denied before it ever got off the ground. In Lizzie's wisdom she realized that to get the program moving, she needed to not only exemplify the benefits that Allstate would receive, but also emphasize that it would flourish through organic growth. This was her method of communicating to her internal stakeholders in a language that they understood, a language that also indicated that customers would be involved in growing the social media program. Since the legal team was already familiar with SEO, an effective program that had shown great results for the organization in the past, she hitched the two together. While this may seem like a stretch, really the social aspects of creating the message board that was Lizzie's initial plan truly was syndicated content, and it would ultimately be searchable.

By collaborating with her legal team and other internal stakeholders, Lizzie discovered what the lawyers were concerned about and how they needed to manage social media in order to protect their assets and the Allstate brand. So she did her homework and uncovered nice examples that explained what she was talking about, using comparable industries. By selecting businesses that were similar to insurance in terms of the issues that they might have to deal with, she built a compelling case. And looking at those other industries and explaining with examples helped to elevate their comfort level. Her strategic plan included setting up guidelines, defining terms, and creating filters that legal was 100 percent comfortable with. She went on to identify things to look for and point out potential red flags. This strategy also included an escalation procedure borrowed from pre-existing e-business teams at Allstate. The legal team was instrumental in helping other areas of the organization to build processes for handling customer complaints, so Lizzie jumped on the chance to leverage their processes and guidelines—this was a comfort zone for legal because they helped create them. All this happened before anything went live.

Through diligent planning and by getting to know her own organization, Lizzie was granted approval to proceed with her plan to develop the site that appears in Figure 3-7. Syndicated Content for Organic Search was launched with the approval of leadership and legal. The kicker was that you couldn't talk about insurance on the insurance forum. For the first few weeks, people talked about vinyl siding, potty training, and all sorts of topics that had nothing to do with insurance. But after a month or so, there was talk about insurance. During this time the team began to grow comfortable with the concept, and Lizzie was diligent about feeding them information and reports on the progress of the effort. She realized that in order to continue with the program and keep it running, she had to establish a trust level. When there was a problem, legal needed to know that she was there and accountable with a plan, a goal, and a benefit. Once it was live, the proof of what was happening and constant communication made the program work.

So here's the recap:

1. Do your homework.

2. Educate your audience.

3. Tailor your language for internal stakeholders.

4. Walk before you run.

5. Prove, communicate, enhance, repeat.

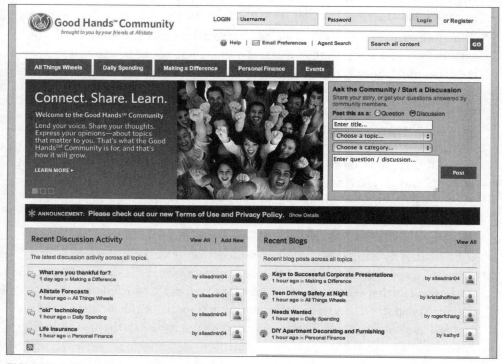

FIGURE 3-7: Allstate Insurance community site.

I offer this story about Lizzie and Allstate primarily because I found it entertaining and because it worked for her. Keep in mind that this may not work for you. There's lots of great advice in here, but Lizzie was successful because she took the time to understand her company and determine how social media would fit within their organizational guidelines. If your business has fewer limitations you may have an easier time, or perhaps there's more you have to contend with. In either case, this is an example of a well-planned approach.

Finding a Home for Your Social Programs

▶ Because social media encompasses all aspects of your business, no single department or team should own it. Instead, implement social media as a shared service.

A lot of people ask me where social media should live within the organization. I often get this question about more traditional digital measurement functions as well. And the short answer is that no single department or team can—or should—own social media. It's bigger than any individual group because social media will encompass all aspects of your business. Although marketing may be the first to grasp the flash of social media, it will pervade public relations, customer service, human resources, market research, IT, and the legal department of your organization. It's not a question of where it should live, but rather it becomes a question of how social media can become a shared service across your entire business.

Building this shared service requires that social media managers work closely with many groups across the organization. Although social media activities may be the outward-facing efforts that consumers see and interact with, they should be orchestrated internally to ensure that they reflect the goals of the organization and match the agendas of disparate groups across the company. Operating in this way mandates that programs launch with consistent frameworks and measures of success in place so that companies can quantify their efforts and track the results of social media. This is important because all too often, measurement is an afterthought and analytics pros are discriminated against as "those web guys," who operate at arm's length from the business. In these unfortunate cases, which I see a lot of, digital measurement is perceived as a skunkworks project that would be lucky to kick out a few innovative ideas. Yet, in reality, the success of many social media programs is determined by teams of centralized resources that understand how technologies work, and more importantly, how consumers interact with the outbound efforts. And most definitely that success is quantified by the metrics that are inherent in well-designed programs. The alternative is launching programs without indicators of success and questioning whether any given effort had an impact on the organization. Not a good way to operate.

Organizations that do leverage a centralized team of resources effectively manage social media efforts across the entire company. This team typically works with different lines of business to shape their ideas for reaching customers in new and innovative ways using social media. Oftentimes, ideas can work congruously with existing programs already in the field, thus creating efficiencies and leveraging existing networks. By managing social operations through a centralized resource, organizations have the ability to see the big picture of social efforts to ensure the most effective opportunities.

Jeremiah Owyang conducted some fascinating research on this topic by interviewing 140 corporate social strategists to ask where their social media programs reside within their respective organizations. Not surprisingly, marketing was the number one answer, followed by corporate communications. However, what was most interesting in his findings was the organizational structures applied at these companies. Figure 3-8 illustrates the five ways that companies organize for social media. The most popular and the one I suggest using is the hub and spoke model. This construct employs a centralized team of cross-functional social media resources that manages technologies and processes while supporting the lines of business as spokes. The hub effectively acts as a Center of Excellence and distributes knowledge, information, and best practices to the supported business units within the spokes. Following the hub and spoke model, companies use centralized (29 percent), multiple hub and spoke (18 percent), decentralized (11 percent), and holistic (1 percent) models to manage their social media efforts. Jeremiah does a marvelous job of explaining his findings in great detail in his research and on his blog (http://www.web-strategist .com/blog/2010/11/09/research-most-companies-organize-in-hub-and-spoke- formation/). I highly recommend that you take the time to read his work.

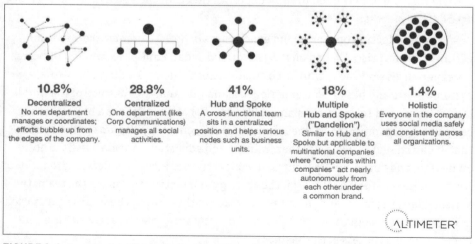

10.8%
Decentralized
No one department manages or coordinates; efforts bubble up from the edges of the company.

28.8%
Centralized
One department (like Corp Communications) manages all social activities.

41%
Hub and Spoke
A cross-functional team sits in a centralized position and helps various nodes such as business units.

18%
Multiple Hub and Spoke ("Dandelion")
Similar to Hub and Spoke but applicable to multinational companies where "companies within companies" act nearly autonomously from each other under a common brand.

1.4%
Holistic
Everyone in the company uses social media safely and consistently across all organizations.

ALTIMETER

FIGURE 3-8: A centralized/decentralized social media operations construct.

Ultimately, there's no single place that social media will fit within every organization. In some cases, marketing owns it because they're using social media in the most outward-facing ways. In other cases, public relations grabbed it because they were supposed to be good at interacting with the public. But for many companies, the answer to where social media should live within the organization can be answered by a cross-functional steering committee that governs the Social Center of Excellence. Organizations that use this construct for the measurement and management of their social media operations gain a global perspective on performance and impact across their companies. It's a system that enables continuous monitoring and response that places accountability on every part of the organization by having a designated representative that takes part in the planning and activation of social programs. This certifies that all parts of the business remain informed about social media initiatives and that each has a say in their execution. Granted, this situation won't work for all organizations, but for those that need to force collaboration and dictate participation across a diverse group of people, it is a viable answer. The challenge is ensuring that decisions get made at the governance level and that there is an execution function with adequate resources to actually do the work required.

Integrating Social Media within the Enterprise

> ▶ Social media is still new to nearly everyone. Prudent businesses will take the time to understand what they're getting into so that their practices don't wind up on a list of what not to do with social media.

There are a great many ways to integrate social media within your business, but success will largely depend on the corporate culture inside your company. Hopefully, the fact that you are reading this book means that you're ready to take the corporate plunge and are amassing a case to demonstrate how social media can impact your entire organization. But a critical step in the process, as demonstrated by the lessons learned from big brands cited in this chapter, is that training and education must be a part of the process.

As I was reflecting on stories and experiences of how to integrate social media within the enterprise, I called on my good friend Judah Phillips to gain insights on his experiences working within large organizations. Judah is a digital measurer extraordinaire and has unique experience managing analytics at some of the world's largest media and Internet companies. We agreed that education is a big part of successfully incorporating social media within an organization. Yet, one of the secrets that Judah shared with me was that training and education in social media is both an in-work and out-of-work activity. In-work activities include understanding why the business is using social media, the strategy and tactics, the goals, the team, the stakeholders, the tools, and the measures. Each of these things helps an organization assimilate social media and develop a level of assurance that the activities are contributing to the success of the business.

Yet, outside activities enable organizations to see how social media is transform-ing the ways consumers interact with businesses. This includes understanding how social media is playing a role in macro business strategies through experiential learn-ing. In contrast to the inside view, where the business develops assurance that social media is helping the cause using metrics and pragmatic means of validation, outside activities assuage fears about the uncertainties of social media by establishing a level of comfort through utilization. As social media in the form of networks, applications, and location-based services pervades our daily interactions, the importance of these solutions becomes more apparent. What this means is that the more exposure manag-ers, directors, and executives have to social media in their daily lives, the more com-fortable they will become with utilization of social media in business.

As I steered our conversation back to metrics, I asked Judah how social media measurers can communicate the value of social media within large enterprises. He began by offering that from a measurement perspective, you need to ensure that the social media metrics are defined, standardized, and agreed upon by consensus. This means working within a construct (similar to the hub and spoke model) where collab-oration between brand managers and social media measurers is not only possible, but paramount. Additionally, Judah went on to say that your metrics must be accurate and verifiable. If you are providing access to tools with data and reports, you need to ensure people are trained to use the tools and understand the data and how to inter-pret the reports, or at minimum have access to well-resourced analytical teams to do so. This alignment is key to ensuring consistent understanding of the data. Within any organization, as the social media measurement strategy evolves and new people participate, strategies and tools change, training activities and overall corporate resourcing for social media need to accommodate.

When I pressed Judah about communicating the value of metrics and data across the enterprise, he shared that value is communicated across two dimensions: brand and direct response. According to Judah, modern Internet companies have little choice but to participate at some level in social media. Thus, the impact on the brand is measurable at the simplest levels (followers, fans, percent of social media–exposed unique visitors), but is still hard to measure in the context of multiple channels. For example, social media "fans" may likely engage with your brand with or without social media, thus how do you understand the incremental impact of social media on an established brand—and how do other channels (such as paid search) impact and/ or complement it? Judah communicated that the contribution of social media needs to be understood "incrementally," because 80 percent or more of your customers in the social channel may likely buy from you regardless of social media, and the major-ity of them probably already know your brand.

Judah went on to say that direct response is easier to communicate because you can measure registration, membership, conversion, revenue, and profit contributed directly from social media—in the context of first or last click or other attribution models. Where direct response for social media gets trickier is trying to estimate the incremental impact across a multichannel marketing mix—in other words, attribution across multiple advertising exposed touches during a given time period.

Based on our conversation, we agreed that the way you communicate social media within a large enterprise is:

1. Carefully

2. Within context

3. Based on business need

4. Focused on incrementality

5. Dedicated to improving profit or brand equity

Typically a business needs to create internal alignment to agree on what constitutes critical information about social media. Do this first at the highest levels and then widen your focus accordingly to meet the needs of specific groups or teams at both the macro and micro levels. You then make the overall corporate social media data available in a common, easy-to-access location (such as on an intranet or standard report on a SharePoint or network share) and ensure that the group/team needs are delivered on an agreed-upon schedule and method (perhaps in sync with or separate from the overall corporate media reporting/analysis).

Soliciting Executive Buy-In

As with any program that spans the reaches of your corporate organization, social media efforts should gain support and endorsement from senior executives. In stalwart organizations this is more challenging than in innovative young ones, but each holds its own obstacles. But it's changing today as media consumption patterns morph and new modes of conversation become commonplace. Because social media is so pervasive, no one—not even executives—can gloss it over. Just like data, it's everywhere.

My belief is that universal change will occur when digital natives come of age within the workforce and social media becomes ingrained within everyday tasks. We are starting to see this now as internal corporate communication tactics are reliant upon social applications like Salesforce.com's Chatter. Yet, we're also seeing the digital elite begin to rise up the ranks at major corporations. Companies like Barnes

& Noble are shuffling their ranks by appointing e-commerce veterans like William Lynch to leadership positions. Lynch is the current CEO who is charged with leading Barnes & Noble (nyse: BKS) into the future. The 39-year-old executive joined B&N in early 2009 as president of BN.com, and in just over a year he was promoted to CEO. His pedigree is pure digital; he has held roles such as EVP Marketing & General Manager of HSN.com, and before that he co-founded Gifts.com in 2004. After Lynch's appointment to CEO in March 2010, one TechCrunch writer summed it up nicely in a March 18, 2010 article, "Barnes & Noble CEO Steps Down, BN.com President William Lynch Takes Over," by stating: "In short: he's all about digital, baby" (http://techcrunch .com/2010/03/18/barnes-nobles-ceo-steps-down-bn-com-president-william- lynch-takes-over/). This new breed of executive will be much more receptive to social media tactics and likely to support their use in overall corporate strategies.

Another digital native is Raul Vazquez, who works for Walmart. Some might say that the $204 billion enterprise is traditional in its ways, but now it's partially in the hands of Mr. Vazquez, who holds the title of EVP and President of Walmart West. His previous post was President and CEO of Walmart.com, where he received accolades from Bill Simon, EVP and COO, for effectively managing Walmart's fastest-growing marketplace segment. This 39-year-old was also featured as #4 on *Fortune Magazine*'s "40 under 40." It's young executives like Lynch and Vazquez who will become agents for change within their organizations. These tuned-in executives will not fear data and social activities, but instead they will embrace them and look to ways that new media can bring their organizations into the future.

However, many organizations that are still dominated by old-world mentalities have social initiatives sequestered within marketing teams that fail to effectively gain an audience with the C-Suite. Even worse, there's no connection to the business. Despite the growing recognition of the value of digital data and analytics, these diminished perspectives are still a reality today, and measurement and analysis professionals find themselves working to prove the value of their efforts. This is especially why analytics—social or business—need to inform your business and why the business needs to corroborate with digital measurement and analysis teams. This is the feedback loop that enables the business to become connected with social initiatives and priorities by giving them a chance to weigh in on what matters to their respective roles within the business. This is similar to the way that consumers offer feedback, direction, and new ideas for curators of social media. But to do this, you must present a panoramic view of what you're capable of delivering and how it will help your organization, as well as have a seat at the table and an opportunity to showcase the benefits of social media.

SOCIALIZING YOUR BUSINESS

The outlook for measuring social media within your business is promising. The good news is that marketers and social media planners are building on their efforts and driving forward in a progressive manner. Even if many companies are not measuring all that well today, they're finding value and reasons to keep building upon their successes. But it's a challenge to know what they want their metrics to tie back to. Although it's really easy to use metrics as a means to count things (such as people, posts, visits, and views), this fails to quantify business value. Yet, marketers can only get away with this fuzziness for so long without having something to show for it. Therefore, measurers of social media need to dig deeper to investigate what matters to the business and identify ways that social media efforts can contribute to those causes. Most measurers are sticking with it and surpassing the fad stage of social media to incorporate it into their overall businesses. And they're proving it, because 2009 investments in social media increased in 2010 and even greater increases are expected for 2011.

People managing social media need to proactively reach out and talk to HR departments and customer service teams to make connections happen. The fact is that working relationships with these teams are not well established.

Steps toward socializing your business:

1. Listen
2. Collaborate
3. Engage
4. Facilitate
5. Learn

While thinking about ways that organizations can socialize their businesses, I caught up with David Berkowitz, the Senior Director of Emerging Media & Innovation for agency 360i. David is a social media veteran and, among other things, he helps businesses to understand that social media is a measurable asset.

When I asked David how organizations are gaining executive buy-in for social media, he commented that oftentimes buy-in is gained from outside the organization. According to David, "The rock stars and social media foot soldiers who make organizations more social are typically resident within marketing departments. They have to work hard to plug in the rest of their organizations." He went on to comment that from the agency side it's rewarding when he can bring parties together to show them the value of social media. In his experience, when agencies can get the ear of senior management, it's an incredible opportunity, and you need to be selective about how you use it. But it's where a lot of nudging can come from. Agencies, consultants, and even new blood can bring credibility to social media ideas and concepts that insiders have been advocating for all along. Yet, sometimes higher-ups just need to hear it from someone on the outside. A lot of change can come from the outside and many organizations are in need of external expertise. Of course, companies can nurture buy-in from the inside as well, but inside it's murkier because it requires figuring out who is connected to whom.

At this point, social media isn't slipping under the radar of any executive's vantage point. As David Berkowitz said, "Social media itself needs no PR." Companies today are primarily struggling to determine how it fits within their organizations. Other organizations are still wondering how much they need to care about social media—but there is a growing consensus that it's a big deal. There isn't much concern that social channels like Facebook won't be around, but there's still the question of how much you have to deal with this stuff. For some marketers, social media is just a pain. They're not used to the conversation and don't have a tightly planned program to handle social media. And consumers don't do themselves any favors by engaging in mob behavior—or swarming over deals—or even engaging in bribery. Offering cheap deals is a great way to get people to like you, but it can devalue your brand. According to David, generally there's a learning curve for figuring what works, and most companies are still finding their way.

KICK-STARTING YOUR SOCIAL MEDIA METRICS

I would be doing you a disservice if I simply provided a big whopping list of metrics and sent you on your merry way. I very much want and encourage you to use metrics for every program down to the countless details, but setting you loose with a bag full of metrics would ultimately come back to haunt you. Instead, I urge you to consider your audience. Whether you work for a Fortune 50 brand, a mid-sized business, or own your own shop, some metrics will matter more for your company than others. You're exploring social media for business here and the impact that it can have on your organization. As such, you need to think about why your organization is involved with social media in the first place. It's not simply to say that you have a Facebook page or a Twitter presence. It's because somewhere along the way you recognized that social media can have a dramatic impact on what you do as an organization. Take this realization and transform it to metrics that showcase your success as a corporate entity.

Detailing Your Own Detriment

Many measurers of social media will gravitate to readily available counting metrics to showcase the progress they're making with social media. You can easily immerse yourself in the low-hanging fruit of counting metrics because they are there for the taking. But that's essentially what you're doing when using these data. You're counting. Although it's great to know that your Facebook page has 100 or 100,000 fans, it's just a number. Without context that number doesn't really add up to much.

The specific details that reveal nuances of your social media campaigns and programs are indeed very important. But mostly, they are important to you. You are there to determine what's working and what is not, and you can demonstrate this through metrics. But metrics at that most basic level are designed to help you understand your efforts and ultimately to take action. Hopefully those actions are designed to improve your business. But remember that you are the specialist here. While social media will undoubtedly impact your entire business, not everyone will know how to—or even care to—measure its effects. Thus, creating the measures of success, identifying metrics that will allow you to recognize issues, and establishing benchmarks to determine when an initiative is overperforming are all part of the behind-the-scenes work of a measurer of digital media.

Imagine, if you will, a mechanic who takes great pride in fixing your automobile. When you complain about sputtering or improper acceleration, he may describe for you in the greatest detail how the inner workings of your engine were not performing and how he recognized these issues and valiantly fixed them. If you're not a car person, somewhere during the part where your mechanic is describing the imbalanced ratio of air to fuel passing through your carburetor, your eyes glaze over. He'd still be talking about the fact that a ratio that should have been 14.7:1 was actually 13.5:1 and that was building carbon deposits on your spark plugs, causing them to turn black and, thus, the sputtering, which of course would be described in the most mechanically detailed iteration you've ever heard. Additional factoids regarding the negative effects that this scenario had on your automobile would be forthcoming and would likely result in a spontaneous combustion lecture. Yet, all the while, the only thoughts running through your mind are these: "Did you fix my car? How much will it cost? Is the problem resolved?" In many cases, this is how your managers and senior executives will feel if you attempt to drag them down into the minutia of every social media metric. Sure, some will be interested and you should be able to pull metrics to appease the most curious managers. But for the vast majority, simply telling them what you found and how you fixed it is the preferred method of communication.

▶ Resist the temptation to start your social media measurement efforts by counting. Trust me, you will rely on these granular metrics, but it's a poor way to showcase value across your organization.

Speaking Business Value

Communicating to your organization about the gritty details of social media without boring them to death is a skill indeed. In fact, it's one that you will utilize throughout your digital measurement career. Moreover, your ability to communicate this information in business terms will very likely be the difference between ascending the ranks to decision maker or hovering somewhere slightly above number crunching miscreant.

Social media metrics must deliver business value to the recipient. This means that you should stop in your tracks before skipping into your boss's office to report that your Twitter following increased by 13 percent this week. Ask yourself why that matters. It could be that increasing awareness in microblogging channels is a top priority, but what do those additional followers really get you in terms of business value? In Chapter 4, I detail ways to align your social media measures with business objectives, so feel free to skip ahead if you just cannot wait. But here, I offer metrics specific to different roles within your organization that should help to kick-start your thinking about what and how to report progress using social media metrics.

> **WARNING** The metrics that follow do not represent a comprehensive list of all things to measure. This is a starting point to get you thinking about metrics that apply to specific roles within your organization. Yet, organizations will differ dramatically in their analytical needs. Use the following metrics as a guide to help develop measures that matter to your business.

METRICS FOR EXECUTIVES

Business metrics must start at the top. The senior executives at your organization will no doubt be interested in social media, and they're going to want to know what you are up to. Business metrics are the language that you will use to communicate. While you're doing the busy work of detailing measurement plans for specific initiatives and educating the organization on how to think and use social media to their competitive advantage, formulate a plan for how to summarize for your most senior executives.

This plan should hit squarely upon the metrics that matter most to your top decision makers. Although this will vary across organizations and industries, there are a handful of issues that every executive that I've ever worked with really cares about. The following list discusses three social media metrics that are suitable for senior executives.

► **Revenue:** Determine whether the social media efforts that you put forth have an impact on the top or bottom line of your organization. Doing this requires analytics to identify activities that lead back to dollars. This absolutely dictates work on your part to plan, track, and reconcile social media activities. Although you may not be able to attribute sales directly back to every social move, it is entirely possible to make correlations for many activities. Your ability to quantify this impact will make an impression on your top executives.

► **Market Share:** Size up the opportunity in the market by knowing how much market share your organization owns and how much is owned by your competition. This is critical information for any executive. It reveals how well you are doing from a competitive perspective while exposing what's there for the taking. Competitive intelligence is key information for any senior executive, and social media measurement offers unique opportunities to quantify your advantage.

► **Satisfaction:** Remember where this chapter began: with a focus on people. Businesses function because of their ability to service people, and social media presents a means to do this in contemporary fashion. Keeping customers happy is a primary concern for most executives because it reflects upon their ability to earn revenue. Satisfaction is also a leading indicator for loyalty, long-term sales, and ultimately success. By rolling up social media metrics to formulate a satisfaction score, you can keep your executives informed.

METRICS FOR LAWYERS

As Lizzie Schreier from Allstate showed, lawyers are a nervous bunch. And social media can extend their fears by orders of magnitude simply because for most, it is the great unknown. Yet, corporate legal departments must have a vested interest in social media because serious fallout can occur for companies with inattentive practices. I strongly recommend taking the time to understand the fears of your legal department and working with them rather than against them.

Working with legal is also critically important because there are realities of liability, risk, and infringement that present genuine threats for organizations. One of my clients is a pharmaceutical company that must comply with "Adverse Events" laws as governed by the FDA. These laws state that if an identifiable patient reports an adverse event about a specific drug, such as nausea or bleeding, in any public or private communication, the organization is required to report these side effects to consumers in all of their warnings. Technically, this would include instances when an identifiable patient Tweets out side effects they're experiencing with any given drug.

While the criteria for this example are more detailed than I explained here, it represents a liability issue for organizations that decide to even listen to social media conversation. If you hear it, see it, or read it, you are responsible.

Given these considerations, social media managers should arm their legal teams with information. I suggest creating the following metrics for apprising lawyers of your corporate social activity:

- **Social Liability:** Understand the events that can be construed as liability concerns, such as customer confidentiality, competitive assaults, and defamation of character, and chart them over time. When liability situations arise across social media channels, keep your legal teams apprised of the situation using metrics that indicate frequency, origination, and resolution. This can be very helpful at mitigating issues before they become problems.

- **Social Risk Quotient:** Taking the liability metric one step further, chart your company's risk over time to illustrate your actual exposure to risk and where it surfaces.

- **Infringement Alerts:** Watching the marketplace for intellectual property infringement, copyright infringement, and other types of brand borrowing activities is the legal department's responsibility. Social media monitoring tools can make this infinitely more accessible by scouring the social web for brand infractions or other instances of infringement. Limit these activities by identifying them with alerts and then issuing cease and desist letters.

► Keep the Social Risk Quotient metric to yourself until you have stable metrics. It has the potential to educate your organization about the realities of operating in a socially connected world, but you don't want to get your programs shut down because of a high risk quotient.

METRICS FOR HR

Since I'm talking about managing risk and watching social channels for liability, I thought that I would introduce metrics for the biggest source of liability that you have, your coworkers. Human resource workers aren't new to social media. In fact, a little social research is a great way to determine whether your prospect is worthy of hiring in the first place. And prospects can be downright oblivious. Just ask one job prospect that Tweeted the following: "Cisco just offered me a job! Now I have to weigh the utility of a fatty paycheck against the daily commute to San José and hating the work." Cisco employees happened to be listening and responded with a Tweet of their own, "Who is the hiring manager? I'm sure they would love to know that you will hate the work. We here at Cisco are versed in the web."

Although this may be a cautionary tale, the fact is that employees—even after they're hired—will do foolish things. All organizations should create a social media policy and enforce compliance across their entire organizations. HR pros will be forever indebted to you as the measurer of social media if you create metrics that alert them to dubious behavior. This will allow your company to track policy compliance as well as keep tabs on how your brand is represented in public. The unfortunate reality today is that all employees, whether officially endorsed or not, represent your organization. There's too much transparency not to protect your brand, and using social media to do this can be entirely effective.

Table 3-1 showcases the metrics that come in handy for business leaders, legal departments, and human resources staff.

TABLE 3-1: Social Media Metrics for Business Leaders, Legal Departments, and Human Resources

Metrics for Executives	Revenue Impact Market Share Satisfaction
Metrics for Lawyers	Social Liability Social Risk Quotient Infringement Alerts
Metrics for HR Pros	Policy Infractions Conduct Alerts Social Recruitment

METRICS FOR SALES, SERVICE, AND CRM

When you begin to look at areas of your business that can be profoundly impacted by social media, sales and customer service should rise up pretty quickly. Although sales teams aren't likely to abandon their dialing tactics and in-person meetings altogether, social media is proving to be an effective feeder channel for leads and opportunities. Once you've hooked your sales team up to the power of social media, it's likely that there will be no turning back. Similarly, once you offer consumers a taste of social customer service, there's no turning back either. However, you may not have much choice in activating the latter because the competitive environment is dictating that social customer service is a must-have for any organization. For me the real beauty of interacting across these social channels is the opportunity to build closer and stronger ties with customers.

> Doing this allows you as a brand to build trust and advocates that will do your bidding for you. Sometimes all it takes is a single positive interaction to build a lasting relationship.

The list of business value metrics starts to expand for each of these roles within your organization. Although I recommend that senior executives receive only a handful of metrics on a recurring basis, directors and managers can do with a few more. These metrics should still be laser focused on the value that social media brings to their part of the business. And of course, at each level, additional metrics will be available to appease the curious.

Table 3-2 offers a sampling of metrics that are likely important to sales professionals. The ability to identify leads and referrals from social media will become increasingly important as more and more opportunities are sourced in this way. Metrics will enable sales pros and the social media measurers that support them to identify where the best leads come from and how to chase down the biggest-ticket, fastest-closing deals out there.

TABLE 3-2: Social Media Metrics for Sales, Service, and CRM

Metrics for Sales	Social Referrals
	Social Leads
	Cost per Social Lead
	Percent Qualified Leads
	Percent Closed Leads
	Lead to Close Duration
	Lead to Close Touches
	Average Social Transaction Value
	Social Customer Value
	Social Win Rate
Metrics for Customer Service	Social Inquiries
	Inquiries by Category
	Resolution Rate
	First Response Resolution Rate
	Resolution Time
	Inquiry to Resolution Touches
	Percent of Satisfied Customers
	Revenue per Service Inquiry
	Cost Savings per Inquiry
	Churn Rate for Social Customers
Metrics for CRM	Percent Social Customers
	Most Effective Channels
	CRM Campaign Response Rate
	CRM Campaign Conversion Rate
	Active Advocates
	Advocate Influence
	Advocate Impact
	Loyalty Strength
	Customer Value by Segment
	Social Customer Lifetime Value

Social media is firmly planted within customer service for many organizations at this point already. Although some consumers abuse the transparency of social media by simply griping about poor service and generally detracting from a brand, many are genuinely looking for issue resolution. The onus is on organizations to balance these two sides of the community and treat each with a dignified response.

I recommend keeping a log or tagging all customer service inquiries that originate via social channels to first get a sense of the volume that you're dealing with on a regular basis. This will give you a sense of the resources needed to manage this new stream of customer interactions. From there it's a good idea to categorize your service inquiries to recognize any patterns and trends that could alert you to bigger issues with your products and services. Following these metrics, traditional call center metrics apply to social media. Table 3-2 offers a list of metrics that can help you to understand the performance of service across social media channels and deliver a strong comparative for effectiveness and costs of taking care of customers using social media versus other channels.

The ability to build deeper and more meaningful relationships with customers using social media channels delivers an entirely new mode of interaction. Not only is it new, but it's also powerful. As quickly as customers can flame your brand, they can also spread goodwill. Managing the relationships you have with customers will impact the things that they say about you and ultimately determine if they recommend you to a friend, or throw you under the bus. Avoid this latter scenario by getting to know your customers, understanding their preferences, and reaching out with meaningful marketing messages.

Savvy social media measurers will track their ability to sidle up to customers with metrics that reveal the growth of social media channels that they operate in and campaigns that they respond to. Table 3-2 illustrates these metrics as well as advocacy metrics that can help quantify the results of your social relationships.

METRICS FOR MARKETERS

Data from the Altimeter Group's survey of Corporate Social Strategists (http://www
.altimetergroup.com/2010/11/altimeter-report-the-two-career-paths-of-the-
corporate-social-strategist-be-proactive-or-become-social-media-help-desk
.html) showed that social media resides with the marketing departments at 41 percent of organizations they surveyed. Following this group, 30 percent reported that corporate communications is responsible for social media, and 11 percent place it within the web or digital department. Yet, when you strip away the specificity from these departments, aren't they all really marketing functions? If you agree with me on that account, that's 82 percent of organizations that place social media in close proximity to their marketing teams. As such, it's no wonder that marketers will have the most metrics.

There's a ton of value in social media for brand marketers, PR pros, product teams, and all aspects of marketing. Yet, in many cases, public relations professionals grasp social media more quickly than others within an enterprise. This is because social media is really just an extension of what they already do. The only difference is that it's the newest channel and there are still kinks to be worked out. Yet, PR in general is about getting out the message and working to plant that message in all the right places. Of course, there's also damage control, so that comes with the territory as well.

Table 3-3 identifies a set of metrics for public relations professionals and marketers.

For public relations, understanding the volume of chatter is important to gauge just how much ground you'll need to cover when listening and responding to social media. From there, determining just how much of that conversation you own and how far it resounds is also important. And PR pros also hold responsibility for getting their company name in lights, so monitoring citations, both positive and negative, will be good metrics for them to watch.

▶ All the metrics presented in this chapter are merely primers to get you thinking in the context of business value metrics. There are certainly more, and there is definitely overlap among corporate functions for what's important to watch.

TABLE 3-3: Social Media Metrics for Marketers

Metrics for Public Relations	Social Mentions
	Share of Voice
	Conversation Reach
	Press Release RTs/Mentions
	Influential Press Citations
	Detrimental Press Citations
	PR Disaster Response Time
	Disaster Recovery Rate
	Influencer Mentions
	PR Referrals/Leads
Metrics for Marketing	Brand Awareness/Visibility
	Customer Acquisition Growth
	Campaign Effectiveness
	New vs. Returning Visitors
	Interaction Rate
	Engagement Rate
	Conversion Events
	Campaign Virality
	Brand Sentiment
	Community Growth

So remember that I am talking about business value metrics. When I created this short list of metrics for marketers in Table 3-3, as well as all the lists in this section, I was thinking about the most fundamental business functions and how social metrics would highlight their performance. I emphasize this because there are infinitely more metrics that will be of significant importance to marketing.

Yet, when you get right down to it, branding, acquisition, engagement, and growth are really the elemental functions of social media marketing. Now, don't make the mistake of thinking that there won't be other functions that are also important because it's likely that you will need additional measures of success. This is the list I arrived at when boiling it down to the most basic functions. Like all good calculated metrics, there are lots of individual measures of success that make up each of these metrics. Take engagement, for example. I go into great detail about the complexity of calculating engagement in Chapter 5. These kick-start metrics should put you into the right frame of mind to understand business value metrics. And these are just a few of them.

Connecting Metrics to Managers

Although the entire list of 59 business value metrics that I offer to kick-start your social measurement program is important, each metric is not imperative for every job function. For this reason it's critically important to align metrics with individuals who care about them. The challenging work is opening the conversation to understand what it is that each stakeholder cares about and translating these cares into actual measurable metrics. In most cases, it requires education, conversations, and collaboration to enable managers across your business to articulate their needs. To do this requires understanding what social media is capable of delivering and then having clear and articulate goals to work toward. In environments where this isn't present or where collaboration isn't forthcoming, it becomes very challenging to truly spread the power of social media.

The good news is that most companies are opening their eyes to the possibilities and embracing social media at all levels within their organizations. Managers are hungry for social media metrics, and offering them a short list of metrics that matter to their job function will be infinitely better received than telling them how many followers the company brand has on Twitter. You possess the capacity to dazzle your colleagues by first listening to their fears, needs, and opinions about social media and then shaping a program that fits those criteria. Marching into a manager's office and telling her that you've found the answer to her troubles is not a recommended starting point. Take the time to listen, explain what's possible, and then formulate a plan with the manager's participation. In my experience this is a solid way to gain acceptance, buy-in, and ultimately favor with your colleagues.

SUMMARY

I'm here to tell you that social media can impact multiple areas of your business, but you will have to sell it internally. From HR to finance to market research, social media metrics have that capability to offer insights and revelations to teams that aren't yet aware of the possibilities. However, it's exceptionally difficult to expose these potentialities by communicating in trivial metrics that don't matter to your organization. Although the most basic measures are undoubtedly important to you and to understanding tactical performance, you must communicate the value of social media efforts in business language. This requires translating your lowest level metrics into measures of success that matter to key stakeholders across your company.

Creating these business value metrics requires understanding the goals, fears, and aspirations across your company. Once you understand this, the secret is to translate internal objectives to consumer facing initiatives. Your success as a measurer of social media will ultimately be determined by how well you communicate these efforts in business terms. Organizations that do well with social media begin by taking a people-centric approach and working to develop a genuine and meaningful conversation with their customers. Additionally, by organizing for social media in a way that enables all aspects of the business to become involved and participate, companies are reaping rewards. Yet, most important is the ability to translate business objectives into measurable metrics. The lists that I've provided in this chapter are a starting point, but each list needs to be tailored to your organization and the individuals within it.

MANAGING SOCIAL MEDIA WITH ANALYTICS

Embracing Social Analytics

Social Analytics is a relatively new doctrine that was born of necessity. Consumers forced brands to expand their interactions from traditional channels such as web sites and call centers to new and emerging social media ones. Upon entering this new realm of correspondence, which empowered consumers with unbridled free speech to a vast audience of attentive listeners, organizations and their brand managers desperately needed a method to understand emerging customers' behaviors and a means to manage their interactions across these new channels. As such, Social Analytics was adapted from the established field of Web Analytics where web site owners quantified user behavior by monitoring their activity. This chapter defines Social Analytics and describes the components necessary to use this discipline as a definitive management tool.

DEFINING SOCIAL ANALYTICS

When working to define Social Analytics, I set out to leverage the collective intellect of my own social network of Web Analytics and social media connections to crowd-source a widely acceptable definition.

I began with a blog post that drew comments from influential vendors, consultants, and practitioners from across industries. Word got out through Twitter and spread to other channels spawning a Facebook discussion (see "How do we define Social Analytics?" as posted on Facebook: **www.facebook.com/topic .php?uid=300923039757&topic=14759**) and other ongoing dialogues about the meaning and purpose of Social Analytics. After numerous iterations and valuable feedback from the field, I arrived at the following definition:

Social Analytics is the discipline that helps companies measure, assess, and explain the performance of social media initiatives in the context of specific business objectives.

UNDERSTANDING THE DISCIPLINE OF SOCIAL ANALYTICS

▶ Check out these social media measurement frameworks from John Lovett and Jeremiah Owyang (http://bit.ly/SM_ framework_1), Peter Kim (http://bit. ly/SM_framework_2), and the UK IAB (http://bit.ly/ SM_framework_3).

So, now that you have a working definition of Social Analytics, what does it really mean? For starters, it's important to realize that Social Analytics, up until this point, is largely modern-day alchemy. Numerous vendors and consultants have developed independent methodologies for measuring social initiatives and spinning these activities into gold, yet there's certainly no consensus for a standardized process among the initiated. What most have agreed upon is the fact that it is possible to quantify social media behaviors, to understand social media's effectiveness, and to discern the impact that social media has on your business. Although the science of calculating and understanding these facets of social media is still emerging, the art of interpreting exactly what to do with Social Analytics information is entering a renaissance.

To help organizations and social media managers grasp the essence of Social Analytics, it may be helpful to expand upon what Social Analytics is all about. For starters, Social Analytics is a method for businesses to understand the effects of their social media efforts.

It is the construct that will contain all of your specific metrics necessary to analyze every minute detail of social media. This relies on mathematics and statistical analysis. If no one told you there'd be math involved, then unfortunately you were lead astray. Social Analytics is the solution by which you can systematically analyze quantitative metrics on a recurring basis to gauge successes, failures, and critical situations as they happen. It also allows you to look at the interactions you have with customers and prospects in a holistic manner to get the big picture. Social Analytics helps you to understand how people perceive your brand and how they respond to your corporate products, services, and marketing messages. It lets you dive into the numbers and quantify actions of multiple users to find out what's working for specific segments or geographic markets. Perhaps most importantly, Social Analytics empowers you with data necessary to make informed decisions. The real end game with Social Analytics is using the data to make recommendations to the organization about how things are working, or not, and how they can be improved. Social Analytics collects and organizes this information by making it available for use by you and your colleagues to make decisions. The technologies that collect data and enable analysis facilitate this process of Social Analytics, and you make it happen.

▶ Social Analytics is not meant for consumers. It's a business discipline that enables informed decisions.

Developing a Triple-A Mindset

I'm going to start by making this really simple before diving down into the complicated details. You can follow me as far as you choose to go, but if you only walk away with one thing about Social Analytics, let it be the Triple-A Mindset. The *Triple-A Mindset* is **A**udience, **A**ctivity, and **A**ctions. This is a concept that will help you put your social media initiatives into the right perspective and remind you why you're doing all this work in the first place.

▶ The Triple-A Mindset tells you the who, what, where, and why of social media.

You need to push and get creative on developing the how, but if you embark on social media by thinking of your Audience, their Activity, and your Actions, you will be starting from a good spot. Here's a breakdown of the three components that shape the Triple-A Mindset:

▶ **Audience:** Social Analytics helps organizations to understand people and determine where they congregate online. These people are your fans, followers, or friends and Social Analytics reveals the who, where, and how they change over time. Social Analytics captures where your audience spends time online, whether it's on blogs, forums, chat rooms, or social media platforms. Audience metrics can also include demographic or socialgraphic characteristics about your following. And further, audience metrics can help discern

different types of people to identify thought leaders from dabblers or celebrities. Audience metrics tell you who is out there and where you can find them.

▶ **Activity:** Social Analytics enables organizations to quantify activity created
by your brand, instigated by your audience, or initiated by your competitors.
Activity reveals how your audience reacts to campaigns or messages, how they
spread information across various social channels, and the level of attention
they give to you and your brand. There's nothing passive about activity; it's
the energy, buzz, and moxie that your social media programs exude. Social
Analytics can pick up on this activity within your specific initiatives or those
outside your circles of influence. It can also help to determine how to engage
new audiences or identify new hot topics or trends.

▶ **Actions:** Social Analytics guides organizations with data to illuminate which
actions you should take to achieve your business goals and objectives. Once
you recognize who your audience is and what activities they participate in,
this information should lead you to take actions that will contribute to your
desired outcomes. Here is where Social Analytics really has an opportunity
to leave its analytical predecessors in the stone ages by transcending mere
data collection and reporting to truly driving actions. Social media managers
who use Social Analytics in its intended form will create workflow processes
around social media that trigger actions and spark new programs as dictated
by your audience and activities.

Collecting Data

Despite the fact that there is no one-size-fits-all approach to measuring social media,
there are some common elements that are shared across Social Analytics. These
include collecting data, performing analysis, reporting results, and driving actions.
You can think about these elements in the context of Demystified's Hierarchy of
Analytical Needs (which I discuss in more detail in Chapter 2), because they build on
one another. You need data as a starting point to begin your analysis. From there you
draw insights and formulate hypotheses. And this leads to providing recommendations and taking actions that will ultimately benefit your business and your customers. Social Analytics requires people, processes, and technology to get the job done.
Assembling this analytical triumvirate begins by understanding the mechanics of
Social Analytics, which I describe within this chapter.

Data collection is the foundation of Social Analytics because it provides organizations and managers a set of information to work with for conducting analysis and

▶ There's
no magical
technological
solution that you
can throw at this
problem. Social
Analytics, like
social media itself,
requires people to
function.

driving actions. Numerous data-collection methods exist, yet many are dependent upon the information provided by each social media channel. These data sources are derived using a number of methods, but the primary ones are scraping, API extraction, and platform extractions. The following sections take a look at each one in more detail.

SCRAPING DATA

Data scraping is a data-collection tactic that works well for public social media channels like blogs, forums, or ratings and reviews. These sources can be scraped from the Internet using spidering tactics. Scraping requires technology to facilitate the data-collection process, which can be as simple as setting a Google Alert or as high tech as solutions delivered by a social media monitoring vendor. Monitoring technologies like those offered by Alterian's SM2, Radian6, or Social Radar offer the ability to initiate data collection based on keywords, which is effectively a scraping technique. Figure 4-1 shows the Alterian SM2 interface, which offers a Search Setup Wizard for entering keywords. Using tools like this, managers can track a list of branded keywords, competitive keywords, or topical issues to determine where conversations are taking place across the Web. Scraping works well for external web properties that are not owned by the business. This includes mainstream media, competitive sites, and social channels.

▶ By "spidering" the Internet, search engines systematically index the Web. With social media, these crawlers are typically focused on keywords, topics, or brand names.

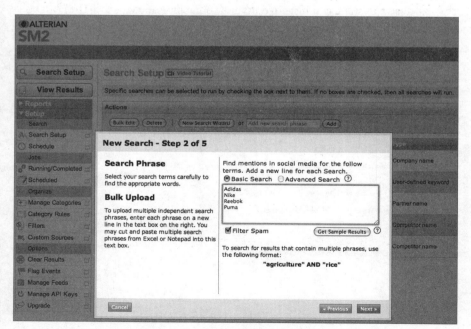

FIGURE 4-1: SM2 offers a keyword Search Setup Wizard that helps users track mentions across the Web.

Social media managers should be cognizant of the fact that scraping can effectively open up a fire hose of data if not properly managed. Thus, it's important to take a calculated and deliberate approach to data scraping so that information collected can be used effectively. I'll talk more about this effective use of data and a focused approach later in this chapter.

API DATA EXTRACTION

Another method of data collection is typically made available from social media channels when they open access to data through an Application Programming Interface (API). Nearly every online property, from Amazon to Zillow, offers an API these days. APIs are also abundant in social media channels, and Twitter is perhaps the best example. They've made all of the functionality present on Twitter, including data collection, available via API access methods. This is why an abundance of Twitter clients like TweetDeck, Seesmic, and others can essentially replicate Twitter content and make it accessible via any number of customized graphical user interfaces (GUIs). The Twitter API also enables data collection and analysis for tools like Twitalyzer or Klout to offer calculated scores for individuals based on data. For example, Twitalyzer calculates a metric they call Impact, which uses data points extracted from the Twitter API. When calculated within the Twitalyzer interface, as shown in Figure 4-2, these measures combine to deliver a composite Impact score that can be used to compare Twitter users.

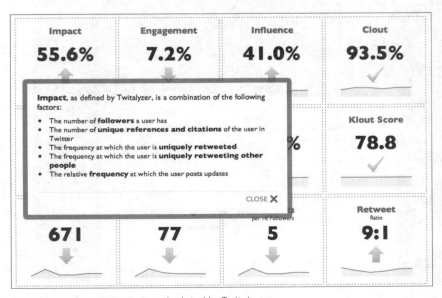

FIGURE 4-2: Impact score as calculated by Twitalyzer.

The Twitter API makes the underlying data available for presentation or analysis in any way a developer or analyst can imagine. Thus, it opens the flexibility of the medium to the masses and enables unlimited creativity. Yet, for your purposes, specific user's Tweets, Tweets that contain hashtags relevant to your organization, or Tweets that mention your brand can all be accessed and extracted using the Twitter API. These data sources can be aggregated within a social media monitoring tool, an Excel spreadsheet, or even a Google document for analysis, reporting, and management.

► Twitter provides a whole wiki full of useful information about extracting data from the platform using its APIs and for building applications using Twitter data on its web site at http://dev.twitter .com/.

PLATFORM EXTRACTIONS

Several social media platforms such as YouTube and Facebook also provide metrics within their solutions that illuminate trends, user growth, and other key metrics. Armed with administrative access to your company's accounts, you can break open the vault of data offered by these solutions. Although calling it a vault may be generous. In the case of Facebook, the analytics offered through Insights are somewhat lacking when compared to enterprise Web Analytics solutions. Currently metrics are offered on a daily basis 24 hours after the day has closed, so that's far from the real-time data you could expect from most Web Analytics vendors. But they do provide a bevy of useful info like referral traffic to apps from ads within Facebook, fan activity, and page interactions. Additionally, there's demographic data about fans that is depicted in a number of formats, one of which is displayed in Figure 4-3.

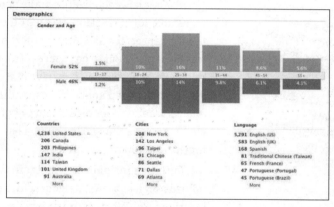

FIGURE 4-3: Gender, age, and geographic metrics are displayed in this Facebook Insights screenshot.

NOTE Eric Eldon did a great write up on the Facebook Insights features on the popular blog "Inside Facebook" back in April 2010, just before the features were released to the public in Summer 2010. Check it out here: http://bit.ly/ FB_Insights—although I expect that by the time this book is published there will be even more changes.

An example of fan interaction data from Facebook Insights can be seen in Figure 4-4, which reveals the total number of interactions, wall posts, comments, and likes as well as the demographic metrics for the UMASS Amherst page.

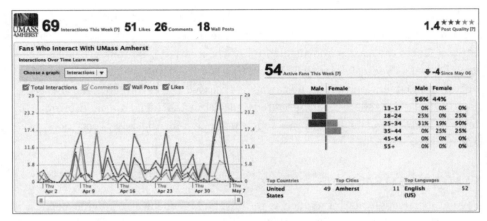

FIGURE 4-4: Facebook Insights offers interaction metrics for fan pages including comments, posts, likes, and demographics.

▶ Looking to go deeper with Facebook Analytics? Read my in-depth blog post on how to view Facebook data within most Web Analytics solutions at http://bit.ly/ FB_Analytics.

Although Facebook does make much of the juicy info included in Figure 4-4 accessible for extraction via an API, they also offer export functionality from the Insights interface as well. To export data, all you have to do is extend the permission for the application to gain access from your users through the innocuous notification alert and then you can have at it. At the time of this writing, Facebook Insights doesn't offer deep analytical capabilities like customized metrics or segmentation analysis. Yet, it does offer plenty of off-the-shelf data to keep the average social media manager busy. That's not a bad deal considering all this information is offered for the low, low price of free.

YouTube's insights are similar in that video owners can track information on their uploads such as views, demographics (gender and age), popularity, and geographic locations. YouTube administrative users get access to a metrics summary page shown in Figure 4-5, and there are also granular details provided for each section within the summary.

▶ Savvy social media curators could manually pull information about their competitors or watch for referral sources that spark strong viral activity to stay a step ahead of the competition.

Perhaps in a move to become more transparent, YouTube also makes data available to the general public that reveals total views, likes/dislikes, comments, and virality, among other attributes. These details are revealed in Figure 4-6, and are accessible to any interested YouTube viewer. Although it's not entirely clear how the average consumer would use this info, YouTube is helping to educate the masses by simply sharing the details specific to each video. On the other hand, social media managers can use this information to understand many things about not only their own videos, but also those of their competitors. Export functionality to get this data out of YouTube exists within the Insights interface only for video owners, which is available daily in 24-hour snapshots. This data can be downloaded in CSV format; however, data from other peoples' videos cannot be accessed directly from the YouTube platform.

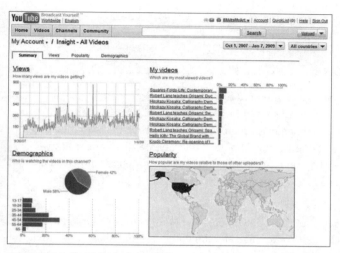

FIGURE 4-5: YouTube Insights delivers a summary page of views, popularity, and demographics.

► YouTube offers a plethora of counting metrics for brands and organizations that manage video channels.

► YouTube also makes data about video views, links, and audiences available for all to see.

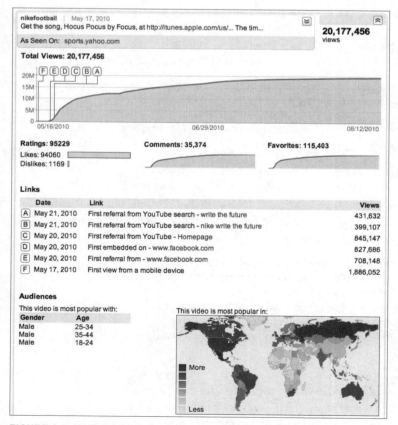

FIGURE 4-6: YouTube video metrics are revealed by clicking the drop-down menu on the Views tab.

GUERILLA MONITORING TACTICS FOR CASH-STRAPPED MANAGERS

I recognize that not every business can shell out big bucks for a commercial social media monitoring tool. Luckily, there are a number of free tools out there that can add pieces of Social Analytics data to your big picture. Some of these tools include Klout, SM2, and Twitalyzer (mentioned in this chapter), and Google Analytics is also a spectacular free tool. However, I do recommend pulling Social Analytics data sources together at some level to gain your strategic perspective, and this typically requires aggregation and technology.

For those of you who want this type of aggregated solution but don't have the budget, you can avoid tin-cupping it around the office to raise enough dough for that shiny new social media management tool. Instead, there are a number of creative ways that you can use to capture data with freely available solutions and some old-fashioned ingenuity.

Several social media smarties have developed ways to leverage data extraction using "push" methods instead of "pull" ones like the API takes advantage of in the previous example. You can essentially bootstrap a guerilla-monitoring dashboard using any combination of RSS feeds. Here are two methods that I found particularly useful:

▶ "Monitoring Social Media Metrics," by Rhea Drysdale. Originally published on the "Outspoken Media" blog on 6/26/09

▶ "How to Build a Reputation Monitoring Dashboard," by Marty Weintraub. Originally published on the "aimClear" blog on 3/16/09

In Rhea's blog post, she lays out a crafty way to create a Google Doc spreadsheet to track social media mentions across a number of different platforms. By using the Google Doc function `"=ImportFeed"` you can draw data from Twitter, Yelp, YouTube, or any other channel with an RSS feed using the syntax `ImportFeed(URL, query, headers, numItems)`. Rhea provides the following examples:

```
=ImportFeed ("http://www.yelp.com/syndicate/biz/
   6PdMtDkLAg_kDYCEi6VBwA/rss.xml", "items title", true, 15)
=ImportFeed ("http://search.twitter.com/
   search.atom?q=freshbooks+followfriday", "items title", true, 15)
=ImportFeed ("http://gdata.youtube.com/feeds/base/
   videos?q=palm%20pre&client=ytapi-youtube-search&alt=rss&v=2",
   "items title", true, 15)
```

By dropping these into your spreadsheet, you can start to play with the data and format it in a way that is most valuable to you or your organization. The beauty of this is that the data will update on the fly and you can segment and format to your heart's content. And—what a bonus—it didn't cost you any more than the time you put into it.

Performing Analysis

When it comes to Social Analytics, the act of performing analysis is critical. Analysis is the catalyst that propels social media managers from report jockeys to critical thinkers who can translate data into information and information to insights. This requires planning up front so that the measures and metrics you collect have a purpose. It also requires humans to do the work. (Sorry, folks, there's just no way around this one.) Whereas reporting can be automated to generate beautiful outputs of metrics and measures delivered swiftly to intranets and inboxes around your organization at precisely 7:47 a.m. on Monday morning, analysis just doesn't come easy.

THE ANALYSIS SKILLSET

Organizations that effectively deliver more than just reporting have dedicated resources for analyzing data and putting together the pieces of social media analysis. While true analytical talent is difficult to come by, the right person to perform analysis on social media understands the business first, the medium second, and finally the technology required to perform analysis. Thus, identifying individuals within your company who understand your business and the goals specific to your organization is the ideal starting point. If that's you, congrats. You can learn many of the analysis skills necessary for Social Analytics by jumping in and getting involved.

The following list covers a look at a few of the requirements for a successful Social Analytics rock star.

- ▶ **Must have:** A strong business acumen and understanding of the specific business of your company and your industry
- ▶ **Must have:** A willingness to learn about new communication channels and embrace change
- ▶ **Must have:** A strong technical understanding of digital technologies and social media platforms
- ▶ **Must have:** A high comfort level for working with disparate sources of data and ability to see the big picture in the details
- ▶ **Must have:** Impeccable communication skills and ability to articulate ideas and findings to senior management
- ▶ **Nice to have:** Some statistical training that will come in handy when drawing inferences or making recommendations from data
- ▶ **Nice to have:** A background in Web Analytics or data analysis

▶ **Nice to have:** Experience collaborating with agencies and other external parties to communicate data needs and provide direction

▶ **Nice to have:** 250 or more Twitter followers

▶ This was an actual "preferred qualification" for a job posting at Best Buy. See the sidebar "Creating the Killer Job Description" for more details.

CREATING THE KILLER JOB DESCRIPTION

Not sure how to draft the killer job description necessary to attract some stellar talent? Not to fear, you could always steal a page out of Best Buy's book and crowd-source the job description for your next social media hire. That's what Best Buy CMO Barry Judge did on his blog when seeking a Senior Manager for Emerging Media Marketing. After receiving a good deal of buzz for listing 250+ Twitter followers as a "preferred qualification" for their new hire, the company decided to allow the masses to weigh in with their ideas.

Mr. Judge asked the Best Buy community to contribute their ideas on the job responsibilities, basic qualifications, and preferred qualifications for the position. The request drew hundreds of comments and responses.

Reporting Results

Reporting is certainly a key function of the Social Analytics discipline. It's the information stream that keeps your colleagues alert; reporting highlights both successes and failures and gets people to take action. Yet so many organizations fail miserably at reporting by delivering streams of useless, unread, and unloved reports. In many cases, brightly colored reports of digital drivel do not contribute to a greater understanding across the organization, nor do they adequately showcase the impact of social media efforts on the business. As a social media manager, you need to take a stand against bad reporting and just say no!

Developing good reports requires several key components that I'll dive into here:

▶ **Make reports understandable:** All of the data and information contained within a Social Analytics report must be clear and understood by every recipient in your organization. You can jump-start the education process by enlightening users across your company with friendly training sessions. But also be sure to include definitions and cues for calculated metrics or complex terms within your reports. I can assure you that most of your colleagues won't remember until you drill it into them with repetition.

- **Keep reporting simple:** Again, most of your colleagues probably don't speak analytics. So rather than making it harder for them by sharing your new language of techno geek within your Social Analytics reporting, keep the jargon to a minimum and keep the reporting simple. Simplicity is often the best way to shed light on a complicated matter, and it also gives you the opportunity to showcase your brilliance when asked.

  ▶ That's a key component here; always have details behind your simple reports to drill down into the nitty-gritty upon request.

- **Deliver information on a need-to-know basis:** Be respectful of your colleagues' time by delivering only information that is critical to their jobs. Everyone is busy, including you, but it's your job (or your direct report's job) to disseminate information that will help the social media aspects of your business move forward. That typically means creating multiple versions of reports with details becoming more granular as you deliver them on down to the lower floors of your corporate headquarters.

- **Automate reporting for an easier life:** Reporting is one of the more tedious tasks in analytics, so be sure to leverage automated capabilities available from many commercial Social Analytics solutions. This will save you headaches and time in the long run as reporting can consume massive amounts of precious time if not conducted in an efficient way. It's important to also provide some analysis with your reporting to offer context for your recipients. Report automation frees you up to perform the more critical task of analysis, so it's important.

> **TIP** If you get asked to run a report by different colleagues more than three times, it's a good idea to save it and begin generating it as a regular report. Chances are that others can use it too and that the information is valuable. On the other hand, if the same colleague asks you to run the same report three times, teach him how to fetch it himself!

- **Revisit reports regularly and check in with recipients:** This is a best practice for ensuring that reports are actually used by recipients throughout your company. Some people with admittedly dysfunctional organizations advise shutting off automated reporting altogether to see how long it takes colleagues to notice. I can't in good faith offer this recommendation, but rather I suggest that you communicate with stakeholders who receive your reports to ensure that they're getting what they need from your reporting and that the reports meet their unique business requirements.

Driving Actions

The ability to drive actions from Social Analytics is perhaps the most difficult and equally the most important aspect that you as a social media manager can control. Social Analytics doesn't stop at data collection and analysis. It carries these capabilities through to create action items for individuals throughout your organization. Don't use Web Analytics as your template here because the entire field of Web Analytics has failed miserably at driving actions. But you have a chance to be different! In fact, it's time to use Social Analytics as a discipline to advance the entire field of data consumption, analysis, and action. You can help do this by changing the way in which beneficiaries of Social Analytics output mechanisms act and react to data.

Perhaps one of the best ways to drive actions with Social Analytics is to ensure that your metrics matter to the business. I'll talk more about this later in the section on developing your Key Performance Indicators (KPIs) later in the chapter. But just to get you started, keep these few secrets in mind as you think about your ability to drive actions using a Social Analytics data and reporting:

▶ **Create imperatives:** Managers who can demonstrate why specific actions are necessary will ultimately find more success with their programs. You can accomplish this by keying into goals and objectives that are mission-critical to your organization. For example, if competitive market share is a priority for your business, a key metric like Share of Voice can be highlighted to illustrate your competitive market share within specific channels or demographics. If Share of Voice is declining, everyone on your marketing team should know that something must be done to recover. This urgency can spark new campaign ideas, increase social media activity, or even empower you to reach out across new channels. But the point is to find a metric that matters and make it visible to people within your organization. Doing so will create an imperative for action.

▶ **Build a sense of urgency:** Somewhat similar to creating imperatives with your Social Analytics metrics, building a sense of urgency is essential in helping to drive actions. There are a number of ways that you can accomplish this, but one method is to establish benchmarks for key social media metrics and leverage alerting functionality to notify individuals when a metric falls below a designated threshold. An example of this is setting a threshold for response times on social media service inquiries. If you determine that customer questions that originate via social media channels should be answered within 2 hours, for example, any issue that doesn't receive a response within this time frame would violate the threshold. Alerts would go out via an automated social monitoring tool or other customer service technology solution and individuals would be compelled to respond. If these thresholds continually fall below the desired levels, it will also become clear that you need to change the way that your staff responds to service inquiries.

▶ **Delegate responsibilities:** Building off of the other tactics for driving actions with Social Analytics, delegating responsibilities to specific individuals is a best practice. Here, the trick is to hold specific individuals within your company accountable for taking action on key social media initiatives. This will likely span across your organization and not be limited to your marketing group, but be careful not to position your social programs in such a way that they create problems for stakeholders across your business. Rather, position your programs in such a way that each area of the business has the ability to positively impact customer experiences; this is one way of empowering your staff. More often than not, you need to leverage a social media tool or other technology to create workflow processes necessary to assign tasks to specific individuals. For example, you can delegate product-related service inquiries that arise through social media channels to agents who have in-depth knowledge about such products. Alternatively, brand managers may be notified when chatter specific to a certain campaign occurs so that they can be aware of the conversation and respond if appropriate.

> **TIP** Creating calls to action from your Social Analytics programs requires planning early on in the process. For each of the examples cited here, the need to plan your metrics strategically, to create thresholds of acceptable metrics, and to assign responsibilities to designated individuals requires that these issues be considered before social media programs launch.
>
> Yet, all too often in the rush to get a new idea out the door these premeditated steps are abandoned. Don't let this happen to you by insisting on measurement as an early stage requirement of any social media activity.

ALIGNING SOCIAL OBJECTIVES WITH CORPORATE GOALS

So hopefully, by now I've drilled into you the notion that Social Analytics requires planning and premeditated actions. These factors are absolutely necessary to ensure success with social media metrics. Yet, where do high-performance social media managers start? In nearly every business case I've seen, the starting point is at the top of the organization. In most cases, the CEO or sometimes an executive team establishes a vision for the company. From this vision, the leaders set corporate goals for the organization. Everything else rolls downhill from there.

Corporate goals should be well known throughout an organization and often times exist because of the ideals upon which your company was founded. Hopefully, you can rattle off the goals of your company because they are in the forefront of your mind. But if not, take the time to jot them down and go a step further by shopping them around to your colleagues to ensure that the corporate goals that you believe to be true are shared by the rest of your company. This is important for social media managers and analytics managers in general because corporate goals are the glue that bonds you together with your peers. These corporate goals apply to any group, department, team, or channel within your company and that solidarity gives you a starting point. Corporate goals can provide the common cause between you and your CFO. By aligning social media strategies with the corporate goals and the vision set forth by your organization, your metrics will matter. They'll matter because you'll be reporting on activities that are in pursuit of goals that everyone from the executive team on down cares about.

▶ *Do you know your company's corporate goals?*

Accepting Your Mission

Prior to formulating your social strategies and getting deep into the weeds of measures and metrics, it's a good idea to confirm what you're working towards. You can do this by talking to your colleagues or potentially by picking up the company handbook and ensuring that you understand the mission statement of your company. I know, this may sound corny, but trust me, if you can align your objectives, strategies, and tactics to illustrate that you're contributing to the corporate mission, you will have much greater success than being labeled as the social media maverick.

I discovered a lot about different types of organizations by simply evaluating their mission statements. Take a look at Table 4-1.

So whether these mission statements give you a warm and fuzzy feeling or not, they reflect what each of these brands is trying to achieve. The challenge becomes translating these lofty worded visions into measureable goals, objectives, strategies, and tactics. But that's where you come in.

TABLE 4-1: Mission Statements of the World's Most Socially Engaged Brands

BRAND	MISSION STATEMENT
Starbucks	To inspire and nurture the human spirit—one person, one cup, and one neighborhood at a time.
Dell	To be the most successful computer company in the world at delivering the best customer experience in markets we serve.
eBay	To provide a global trading platform where practically anyone can trade practically anything.
Google	To organize the world's information and make it universally accessible and useful.
Microsoft	To help people and businesses throughout the world realize their full potential.
Nike	To bring inspiration and innovation to every athlete* in the world. *"If you have a body, you are an athlete."
Amazon	To be earth's most customer-centric company; to build a place where people can come to find and discover anything they might want to buy online.
SAP	To make work become a more personally enjoyable and rewarding experience.
Intel	Delight our customers, employees, and shareholders by relentlessly delivering the platform and technology advancements that become essential to the way we work and live.
Yahoo!	To be the center of people's online lives by delivering personally relevant, meaningful Internet experiences.

Note: All mission statements were collected from each company's web site.

Despite that these mission statements were carefully crafted to convey goodwill and meet with shareholder approval, there are key ingredients in each one that social media managers can pick up on to build out measureable objectives. You should dissect your mission statement to extract its essence. You will have to work to identify possible objectives that could align with measurable objectives. Keep in mind here that this is merely an exercise to get you thinking about Social Analytics and how you can align your measurement tactics with overarching mission statements. There are numerous ways to do this and there will certainly be conflicting priorities and factors that dictate specific measures. That said, this exercise will hopefully get you in the right frame of mind to align the vision of your company with some specific business objectives.

▶ Share your social media objectives with colleagues and key stakeholders to solicit feedback prior to cementing them into your Social Analytics programs.

Simply collecting data without applying meaningful analysis or directing the data to validate working hypotheses is insufficient. Luckily, you have an opportunity to transcend antiquated thinking by using Social Analytics to start from a point of meaningful, actionable data. Data, and subsequently, metrics that contain the inherent ability to take action are ones that are developed with a specific business objective in mind. Organizations must take a methodical, pragmatic, and common sense approach to measuring social marketing initiatives using business objectives.

Developing a "Waterfall Strategy"

Organizations that do apply resources to Social Analytics and use data effectively almost without exception always have a plan for what they want to accomplish and how they will get there. Most often, this emerges from a discipline that I call the "Waterfall Strategy."[1] By starting at the top of an organization and identifying the corporate goals, the Waterfall Strategy provides a common direction for each member within the company to work toward. From there, the Waterfall Strategy cascades to include business objectives, which align the goals with management strategies necessary to monitor meaningful activity. Next, come the measures of success, which allow organizations to apply metrics against their strategies and quantify progress. Finally, as shown in Figure 4-7, the Waterfall Strategy includes operational tactics that dictate individual programs, campaigns, and channels.

FIGURE 4-7: The Waterfall Strategy aligns goals with objectives, metrics, and tactics.

Across each of these four tiers of the Waterfall Strategy, organizations can measure progress towards their desired outcomes. To do this, goals must be both specific and measurable. Keep in mind that the vision of your organization is typically not included in the Waterfall Strategy because it's highly unlikely that you as a manager of social media will be able to shape or change the vision laid out by your executive leadership. Even if you could, you wouldn't necessarily want to, as the corporate vision must consider all facets of your business. Social media is but one avenue that you will use to reach people and should be considered in that context. Therefore, the Waterfall Strategy begins with corporate goals and then cascades to specific social media business objectives, measures, and tactics.

[1] I originally developed the Waterfall Strategy in 2010 to guide my consulting clients at Web Analytics Demystified. This methodology has been expanded and adapted for use in Social Analytics and is used by numerous organizations across the globe.

Using a SMART(ER) Methodology

Another thing to keep in mind here is that the discipline of Social Analytics shouldn't always force you to re-create the wheel for every action or piece of analysis that you do. Remember that social media should extend across all aspects of your business and permeate the organization on multiple levels. As such, ingrained processes or existing methodologies can be applied to Social Analytics. This can help you as the manager of social media by giving you a jump start on establishing processes for managing social media and also by delivering familiar management tools to your colleagues.

Take a look at the SMART methodology as one example of a process that you as a social media manager might want to employ within your organization. SMART is a mnemonic created in the early 80s to help businesses create meaningful goals or objectives.[2] It stands for **S**pecific – **M**easurable – **A**ttainable – **R**elevant – **T**imed. Managers can use this methodology as a means to define goals that have all of these characteristics and therefore have more impact within the organization.

SMART helps managers to create goals within the context of information that will not only move the business forward, but also provide the insights necessary to make informed decisions. Table 4-2 illustrates the concepts behind the SMART methodology and includes an adaptation to make you even SMARTER than you already are. The E stands for *E*valuate and the R is for *R*eevaluate. Both are key activities to include when evaluating your Social Analytics goals because they enforce a method of verification and validation.

▶ Social media frameworks don't have to be prognostic concepts from the future. Social Analytics is about business, so by keeping it simple, understandable, and familiar, you'll win the allegiance of your colleagues.

TABLE 4-2: The SMART Methodology for Creating Goals

S	Specific	Targeted for a unique audience, outcome, or purpose
M	Measureable	Quantifiable as a single instance or benchmark over time
A	Attainable	Realistic in the ability to achieve and replicate
R	Relevant	Applicable to the intended medium, audience, or channel
T	Timed	Delivered within appropriate or necessary intervals
E	Evaluate	Verify that goals meet the requirements of the business
R	Reevaluate	Validate the sustainability and applicability of goals over time

[2] The original documentation of this concept is attributed to Doran, George T. "There's a S.M.A.R.T. way to write management's goals and objectives." *Management Review*, Nov 1981, Volume 70, Issue 11.

By using a plan that includes a strategy embedded with specific measurement tactics, organizations can systematically develop social media programs and campaigns that can directly impact progress towards corporate goals. It's important to note that while there may be only a handful of corporate goals, there can be many objectives, measures, and tactics that work towards advancing the company to achieve its targets. And not all of these goals will necessarily have a direct impact on the bottom line. However, each initiative requires planning and strategy as well as collaboration across the enterprise.

IDENTIFYING COMMON SOCIAL BUSINESS OBJECTIVES

Business objectives are the social media initiatives that you pursue to achieve your goals. Think of them as the path you're taking to accomplish a goal. Objectives are the designs you put in place to reach your aspirations in social media. It's probably worth reiterating here that a goal, in simple terms, is the end that your business seeks to attain. These goals should be specific, measurable, attainable, relevant, and timed. Yet, objectives can be somewhat softer, because they will ultimately point you in the direction that you need to go with measures of success and tactics.

Objectives should be uniquely configured to your specific company. Although I set out to identify a handful of common social business objectives in this chapter, not all of these will be relevant to every organization. In the same way, you may find that your company has a dozen other objectives necessary to meet your corporate goals. But bear in mind that the objectives will lead to measures of success and then to operational tactics so they should be carefully considered. Six common social media business objectives that can serve as jumping-off points for your Social Analytics program are as follows:

- ► Gaining exposure
- ► Fostering dialogue
- ► Generating interaction
- ► Facilitating support
- ► Promoting advocacy
- ► Spurring innovation

The following sections explore these objectives in more detail.

Gaining Exposure

Exposure is the brand marketer's gold. It's about putting an idea into the social media centrifuge and watching it go viral. When ideas are really good, the centrifugal force pushes them way out beyond your known audience to ones who've never heard of you. Exposure is a powerful aspect of social media and certainly an objective for you to measure.

> **NOTE** Social media exposure is the ability to make your brand, products or services known to the masses. This works through the power of the interconnected social networks. Exposure enables relatively obscure companies like Blendtec to introduce their products to millions of potential new customers by relying on the virality of social media to spread the message.

While exposure can be native to social channels, exposure is sometimes about presence in traditional media as well. In these cases exposure can be about simply recognizing a brand because of print, television, outdoor advertising, or any other means and how that spreads via word of mouth and social media. Organizations that include digital cues in traditional media such as listed URLs or the use of QR codes provide a means to track referrals from traditional media.

This translation from traditional to digital channels is where you can really highlight the benefits of social media. Do this by quantifying the amplification made possible from social media. Exposure requires:

- **Getting your big idea out there.** Whatever industry you're in or whatever it is that you do, social media can help spread the word. Find your audience and use the social media channels that they're tuned into to release your message. Keep in mind that every idea won't take, but make sure that you continue to make content available to maintain a presence for your brand.

- **Offering methods for sharing.** Exposure is about how ideas spread through social medium and that requires you to enable people to share. Of course, the message must be good, but you can also make it easy to share content by building share functions into your social media.

- **Controlling the message.** In social media you do not always have the luxury of controlling the message, but in the category of exposure you do. Think of exposure as the way that you want consumers to see you brand and what you want them to know about your products. When planning to use the business objective of exposure, ensure that you're building awareness for products and services in a strategic way.

SUPER BOWL AD FANS—START YOUR ENGINES

Super Bowl television advertising spots cost more per second than any other form of media buy today. In 2011, the going rate was $3 million USD for a 30-second spot. And for the many who were glued to their devices monitoring #Brandbowl (the Twitter hashtag for discussing the best commercials), the commercials and the social media frenzy that accompanied each one were more exciting than the game itself. Yet, Volkswagen preempted the game-time hype by leaking their commercial on YouTube on Friday, a full 3 days before the actual game. It immediately went viral. When I captured the screenshot in Figure 4-8, just 24 hours after the commercial's YouTube launch, over 10 million views already occurred. Currently, it has been exposed to 35.5 million viewers, just a few short months later. The ad was clever and entertaining and undoubtedly it hit home with many viewers with relevance. My favorite commentary of the ad comes from Penelope Trunk who wrote in her blog post, "Volkswagen Super Bowl Ad is an Anthem to Gen X" (`http://blog.penelopetrunk.com/2011/02/03/volkswagen-super-bowl-commercial-is-an-anthem-to-gen-x/`), that she loved the ad "because it captures the shared experience of Generation X." I think she's right.

FIGURE 4-8: Volkswagen's early release Super Bowl commercial on YouTube goes viral.

Fostering Dialogue

The business objective of creating a dialogue between an organization and its customers is grounded in the fundamental concept of using social technologies to facilitate a conversation between people.

Such dialogue requires that brand managers act in a genuine and real manner.

Dialogue involves starting a conversation and offering your audience something to talk about while allowing that conversation to take on a life of its own. Such conversations can ultimately traverse the Web through multiple networks and platforms, gaining momentum and building merit, thus providing knowledge back to the organization. Dialogue requires:

▶ **Building awareness by initiating the conversation.** Organizations do this by creating original content on blogs, communities, or any other social channel that offers information as a catalyst for discussion. This conversation can be addressed directly or socialized to extended networks via additional social channels like Twitter.

▶ **Engaging with individuals to determine their response to ideas, thoughts, products, and activities generated by your organization.** Here, the task is to elicit feedback through blog comments/microblog formats/community sites/and more, and to follow updates and new conversation streams as they develop on the source channel as well as on external channels.

▶ **Responding to individuals on behalf of your brand through genuine interactions.** This demonstrates a willingness to communicate with individuals in an environment that is familiar to them and often times one that is outside the control of your business. Sounds scary? Perhaps, but it validates that individuals can influence the products and services offered by your brand and instills trust among your followers.

> ▶ Always remember that social media is just another way for humans to interact with other humans. It's not about brands reaching customers or robots talking to numbers; these are real people operating in a new and evolving channel.

THE OLD SPICE MAN ON A HORSE

The marketers of Old Spice took the business objective of creating dialogue to new heights with their "Smell Like A Man, Man" campaign. Figure 4-9 shows the reputable Man on a Horse as seen on the Old Spice YouTube channel. What started out as a television commercial blossomed into a full-blown social media success because the brand was able to capitalize on the buzz and maintain

(continues)

THE OLD SPICE MAN ON A HORSE *(continued)*

a dialogue with their customers. In addition to the television spots, the company delivered YouTube videos featuring the relatively unknown man on a horse. These prompted such a heavy stream of dialogue that the geniuses behind this campaign began delivering personalized video responses to Twitter comments and other forms of outreach by consumers. The result was a highly entertaining, directly personal, and engaging dialogue that a men's body wash product (of all things) was able to generate.

FIGURE 4-9: The man that your man could smell like, as featured on YouTube.

Generating Interactions

The business objective of generating interactions is your organization's ability to persuade visitors, customers, or prospects into responding to your social media calls to action.

NOTE Interactions are social media conversion events. Whenever a person interacts with your social media initiative in the manner that you designed, it's an interaction. Whether it's visiting your website, downloading information, or transacting with you online, your ability to generate interaction is a critical business objective.

Think about interactions as the events that you want people to accomplish when they explore your social media initiatives.

Interactions can be directly tied to revenue, used as lead generation vehicles, or they can be purely for entertainment value. Yet, use your ability to move people from a passive state of social media consumption to an active state of decision by compelling them to interact. Interaction requires:

- **Compelling calls to action.** When developing your social media initiatives, you should be thinking about what it is that you're trying to get people to do. If you're thinking strategically about social media, these acts should align with your business goals, and therefore, you need a call to action. Give social media participants a strong message so you get their attention.

- **Offering a value exchange.** In addition to getting people's attention, you also need to persuade them to interact with you. Sweeten the deal by articulating what an individual gains from interacting with your brand. This isn't about giving away free goods, but simply about communicating the value offered through your activity.

- **Creating choice.** When it comes to interacting with your brand, consumers will oscillate in their desires to share information or commit to an interaction. Regardless of how trivial the interaction might be, you should offer choice to individuals by allowing them to interact directly from the social channel when possible or by offering up additional means of contact and communication.

> **NOTE** Hallmark is generating interactions using Facebook. They are one brand that is capitalizing on the sheer volume of active Facebook users by enabling those users to choose, customize, and send cards entirely within the Facebook platform. The greeting card company has taken some of the pain out of sorting through the card aisle in your local drugstore by bringing the process online. With just a few clicks of the mouse, you can have your card literally signed, sealed, and delivered.

Facilitating Support

The business objective of support is perhaps the most straightforward. It also represents the revolutionary shift in consumer empowerment enabled by social media. Individuals can now turn to social media channels to expose their service issues to the world. They can sing your praises for the world to hear, but just as easily throw you under the bus. Consumers are also beginning to expect near instantaneous responses to their social outcries, so it's likely worth your while to listen up.

Consumers who are listening will develop impressions of an organization or brand based on your ability to respond in a timely manner and upon the quality of your answers.

Regardless of whether it comes from you or your customers, the capability to provide support through social channels is imperative. Support requires:

▶ **Resolving service issues through social media channels** via direct company response and crowd-sourcing alternatives. Organizations that encourage support inquiries via social media channels can potentially decrease call center support costs and should track metrics such as number of issues resolved by company, number of issues resolved by customers, shift in volume of service issues online versus offline, and change in cost per service issues online versus offline.

▶ **Expediting issue resolution** with quality and integrity. Social media channels hold potential for speedy resolution of issues with less friction than traditional IVR solutions. Organizations should measure these efforts using comparable call center metrics such as issue resolution time, issues resolved without escalation, and quality of response. Quality can be measured using survey tools and ratings/ranking of resolution.

▶ **Satisfying customers** is the pinnacle of support and requires quality, integrity, and speed. Organizations can monitor satisfaction levels using traditional online survey tools to acquire feedback as well as by monitoring social channels for comments about service interactions. Companies should monitor the number of product or service use mentions as well as mine sentiment within product and service use mentions.

> ▶ Although support can come from consumers to consumers, you better listen in as well to correct any misinformation and to set the record straight if necessary.

COMCAST USES TWITTER AS A SERVICE CHANNEL FOR CUSTOMERS

Comcast is one organization that has grasped the social media revolution firmly with both hands. They've deployed a team of service agents to respond to inquiries ranging from heated to benign over Twitter. Figure 4-10 shows the actual Twitter account of "ComcastCares," which leverages real people like Bill to interact with customers about service issues. The company uses technology from Radian6 to monitor incoming Tweets and assign them to agents for prompt response. Much has been written about the ComcastCares method of servicing clients over new and emerging channels, and they are certainly on the forefront of this new communication imperative.

FIGURE 4-10: @ComcastBill is shown here on the ComcastCares Twitter page.

Promoting Advocacy

The business objective of consumer advocacy enlists the support and dedication of individuals who are ambassadors for certain products, brands, or organizations despite having no official connection.

You will likely need to offer some perks to your faithful, but these can be as simple as breaking early news or offering advanced opportunities.

Advocacy allows businesses to extend their reach beyond their immediate circles of influence by taking advantage of word of mouth and viral activity. Advocacy requires:

- **Encouraging word-of-mouth activity** by promoting and endorsing conversations shared by individuals through channels such as ShareThis, AddThis, Twitter RTs, tags, and more. This information can be tracked over time to determine velocity of word-of-mouth activity and recognizing contributions through acknowledgement.

- **Developing relationships with individuals who have an affinity towards the brand**—or those who can be won over—who also have clout or influence over others. Organizations can establish these relationships through brand advocacy programs or by less formal means, yet identifying and determining the influential individuals is achieved through learning and dialogue.

- **Nurturing existing relationships** with customers is a proven method of building advocacy within an easily identified segment; it's the low-hanging fruit of advocacy. However, organizations must rely on varied measurement methods of determining customer satisfaction, life-cycle cues, and indicators for action. These metrics are typically derived from a number of disparate applications.

▶ More often than not you don't need to compensate advocates financially. Most will act upon the sheer recognition from you or your brand, and you'll be amazed at the love they can show. That is, of course, assuming that you're doing things right.

BREAST CANCER ORGANIZATIONS USE GENUINE ADVOCATES

Social media advocates can originate from many places. Advocates are often celebrities or loyal extremists, but they can be regular people too, as seen in Figure 4-11. Susan G. Komen for the Cure is a movement for breast cancer awareness and treatment that uses everyday people and their compelling stories as advocates. Those affected by cancer can learn from others like them and learn about the services offered by organizations like Susan G. Komen for the Cure.

FIGURE 4-11: Susan G. Komen for the Cure wins survivors as loyal advocates.

Spurring Innovation

The business objective of innovation is an extraordinary byproduct of engaging in social marketing activity. Organizations that are truly listening to their customers take cues from social media comments, suggestions, and conversations to source and identify product needs, service requirements, and other innovative opportunities. Companies on the forefront of customer-centric innovation are tapping into their audiences for ideas, support, and promotion with great success.

Innovation can also stem from the collective knowledge base amassed by social information, which can be mined for insights and ideas. Innovation requires:

▶ **Gathering customer insights via social media channels with a clear mission of identifying market needs and service opportunities.** Organizations will benefit from mining product ideas offered by the community through platforms, ideation sites, Facebook, Twitter, or other channels. These ideas should be tracked by source, frequency, and channel to expose the most lucrative sources of innovation.

▶ **Processing ideas and community feedback as a means to drive products and services requires receptive product managers.** Organizations that source innovation from social media must set egos aside and acknowledge that the collective mass can be more innovative than the creative few. This can be measured by tracking product ideas and comparing innovations developed from traditional methods with those having social origins.

▶ **Delivering new products and services to the market with credit and acknowledgement to customers.** Microsoft is currently taking this approach with its Windows 7 commercials. While somewhat in jest, the campaign features individual consumers and the ideas and contributions they made for improving a mass-marketed product. Companies can bolster this awareness through advocacy programs and measure effectiveness by the number of ideas/posts/updates shared by customers, the velocity of product ideas, and the influencers identified from ideation.

STARBUCKS ENCOURAGES ITS CUSTOMERS TO DRIVE INNOVATION

Starbucks is one of the early pioneers using social media to spur innovation. Their MyStarbucksIdea web site, shown in Figure 4-12, is a fertile breeding ground for new ideas that leverages their loyal audience of caffeinated fans. The site not only allows individual customers to submit ideas that they believe will make the customer experience at Starbucks better, but they also allow customers to vote on ideas, thereby leveraging their audience to help prioritize development and innovation. If you said this to a company even just five years ago, they may have told you that you were nuts. Now Starbucks is succeeding in its mission to "inspire and nurture the human spirit" through this creative means of interacting with customers.

(continues)

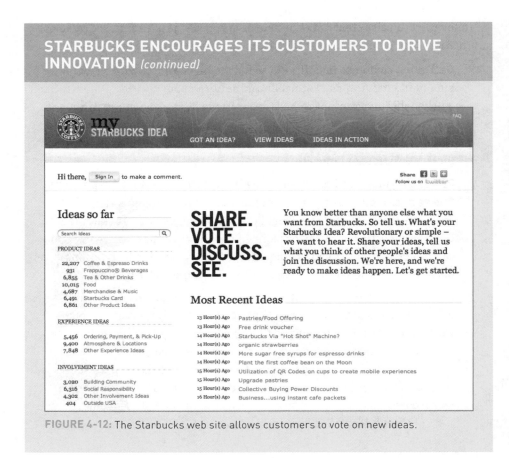

FIGURE 4-12: The Starbucks web site allows customers to vote on new ideas.

These six social media business objectives are by no means comprehensive. Nor are they appropriate for every business or manager looking to execute on a social media initiative. However, they are common objectives to many social media managers that are embarking on a quest to deliver services and maintain pace in this new communication arena.

In addition to these objectives, there is a seventh objective, one that should be obvious but that some companies will still fail to take advantage of: learning from the open conversation. Realize that every conversation with an advocate, every dialogue with a detractor, every support incident and insight gathered from the crowds, although potentially difficult to measure, are opportunities to learn. The best businesses will embrace these opportunities and formalize the learning process through social media, keeping track of each critical insight, dialogue, and complaint as part of their long-term organizational growth.

DEVELOPING KEY PERFORMANCE INDICATORS

Most organizations will use both metrics and Key Performance Indicators (KPIs) to quantify and report on social media activity. Yet, it's important to understand that not every piece of social media data that you collect should be reported to your entire organization. This is why it's so important to begin by understanding your corporate goals, objectives, and strategies. At the highest level, data you collect and the metrics you calculate should all point to programs that align with your corporate Waterfall Strategy goals. However, for the most part, your social media metrics will make up the granular details of your programs or social channel activities that help you to manage the day-to-day operations of social media. Your KPIs will be the benchmarks that report on the pulse of your activities and provide the best insights about success, failures, and progress. But, like it or not, most executives, directors, and even managers in your organization probably don't care about the details of your social media success. To them it's minutia. That's why I recommend sharing only a handful of your measures and metrics with your business colleagues so that you do not overwhelm them with data. It's your job to intake all the individual pieces of data and weave them into a comprehensible story that matters to the organization. KPIs can provide the "Ka-Pow" headlines to your stories.

But before I get into the specifics of developing KPIs to map to your specific business objectives, it's important to define what precisely a KPI is. All too frequently, I see the term bandied about and associated with measures that do not constitute true indicators of success. Not all metrics are KPIs, and not all KPIs are worth sharing. Organizations will likely have a plethora of metrics that offer information about social media activity, but KPIs are the measures that map back to specific objectives and define progress toward those objectives. Some of these should be the most visible data points in your organization regarding the health of your social media programs. Yet, others can be used to test hypotheses, validate assumptions, or collect interesting data to be used at a later date. For those of you reading between the lines, I'm applying some Web Analytics rigor to the nascent social measurement field. By reading this book, you are on the forefront of the Social Analytics movement, so pay attention.

DIFFERENTIATING BETWEEN METRICS AND KPIS

Metrics are:

▶ Numbers that are derived from analytics, social media monitoring, or social media platform solutions without any type of modification

▶ Presented in tabular format or visually in bar charts or graphs

▶ The data flow that acts as the lifeblood of your social media operations

Examples of Social Analytics metrics include:

▶ Fans, followers, visits, views, view-throughs, new visitors, returning visitors, active users, inactive users, likes, dislikes, ratings, reviews, downloads, uploads, embeds, shares, bookmarks, comments, sentiment, top keywords, referral sources, influencers, key influencers, and so on

Key Performance Indicators (KPIs) are:

▶ Presented as rates, ratios, and averages (typically not raw numbers)

▶ Presented visually as tachometers, thermometers, and stoplight-colored symbols indicating change

▶ Triggers that should cause you to jump into action when benchmarks deviate from the norm

Examples of Social Analytics metrics include:

▶ Share of Voice, Audience Engagement, Conversation Reach, Active Advocates, Advocate Influence, Advocacy Impact, Resolution Rate, Resolution Time, Satisfaction Score, Topic Trends, Sentiment Ratio, and Idea Impact

NOTE My business partner Eric T. Peterson wrote *The Big Book of Key Performance Indicators* in 2006, which was the groundbreaking work in defining Web Analytics KPIs. Much of it is still relevant today and Eric's giving it away for free (`http://bit.ly/demystified-books`).

If metrics are the data flow that acts as the lifeblood of your social media operations, KPIs are your vital signs. Think about KPIs as the temperature, pulse, respiration, and blood pressure of your social media activities. Without KPIs, it's difficult to tell if your programs are alive, let alone functioning properly. KPIs should be the first thing that you check when you log in each day, and they should be monitored constantly to determine the status of your programs. Green-light KPIs should give you a sense of assurance and allow you to get on with interesting analysis or new social media planning. Failing KPIs can be indications that something is awry with your social programs and you better make a diagnosis quickly to find out what's wrong before they flat line. With measures this important, you can begin to see why it's critical to get your KPIs right.

When established correctly, KPIs provide context for your social media progress, they set expectations for what to expect, and they mandate actions when things aren't looking so good. The next sections take a closer look at these three key ingredients of successful KPIs.

Providing Context

All KPIs must have context because without it, KPIs are just numbers that don't necessarily mean anything to the uninitiated. You and your data-loving chums may fully understand what your KPIs mean, but mere mortals typically need contextual clues. Context offers a basis for comparison for your KPIs and in turn provides a greater level of understanding for all who receive them. While some of your KPIs may be calculated metrics that result in integers, you can still provide context by offering them as percentages, ratios, or averages with month-over-month comparisons. This will provide the context needed for socializing the measures beyond your analytical network of peers.

Hopefully, the previous example reveals how important it is to offer KPIs in context. But it's also critically important to understand that this is true of all metrics, not just KPIs. So the next time you or one of your colleagues tells you that a fan page has 30,256 followers, ask the questions: So what? Is this trending upward? Has it been 30,256 for the past six months? Is 30,256 even good compared to our competition?

CONTEXT REVEALS HOW GOOD GOOD REALLY IS

I'll use an example to drive home the point about putting metrics into context. Say you launch a new social media initiative around an issue that is important to your business. You can tune the dials of your social media monitoring tools to scrape data from across the Web and identify all of the conversations taking place that contain keywords related to your specific issue.

The results of this tremendous effort may yield a list of sites where these conversations are taking place and also tell you that your company's brand name was mentioned 1,275 times over the first 30 days of the campaign. You quickly tally these data to come up with a "social media mentions" metric and get ready to show your boss how well you're doing.

But wait, before you start celebrating your social media success, how do you know that 1,275 mentions is good?

One thing to look for when you scrape all those sites for your key issues is mentions of your competitors as well as mentions of your own brand. In doing this, you can come up with a Key Performance Indicator called "Share of Voice" that not only reveals the number of times your brand was mentioned, but also the relative proportion of mentions you received when compared to the competition.

Thus, Share of Voice will reveal a percentage of mentions within the context of your competitive set and show you that 1,275 is actually 75 percent of all brand mentions of you and your competition. Now you have some information worth sharing.

Setting Expectations

The act of developing KPIs can be an important mechanism for you to teach your colleagues about the value of Social Analytics and to guide them on what to expect. Use it as a way to educate your peers about the capabilities within your social media measurement tools as well as to inform them of the data that they can get from you. By socializing your KPIs you can solicit feedback and attain buy-in from stakeholders across your business. They will have a much greater understanding of the business value you can deliver and will also know what the metrics are telling them.

In my consulting practice, I've found that individuals who have a vested interest in analytics take a much more dedicated approach to using data as a management device. Those who have metrics thrust upon them are more often than not intractable when it comes to trying to use unfamiliar data. With this in mind, take your KPI ideas, concepts, and early findings to individuals throughout your company to ask their opinions and ensure that you're on the right track. If this is done with the right approach, your colleagues will thank you for it and the metrics will have much greater significance for your peers.

When you properly set expectations for your KPIs, everyone on your team and everyone within your organization is capable of recognizing success. By clearly setting expectations, the definitions become solidified and the business of identifying success becomes much simpler. It's imperative to set these expectations up front and with stakeholder approval if possible.

Mandating Actions

Often times, companies with innovative social marketing campaigns and even bright individuals fail to grasp the concept of actionable metrics. In researching this book, I conducted dozens of interviews and scoured countless blogs written by very smart people, but the vast majority of them were misguided in their social measurement tactics. Many use counting metrics such as page views, number of posts, number of comments, time on site, trackbacks, and conversions as isolated metrics to evaluate the performance of their social marketing endeavors. These metrics are important in understanding the health of your audience, but they are not generally indicative of success.

Be sure to develop KPIs in such a way that when they fluctuate you have a clear idea of the actions required to remedy the situation. This can be accomplished by establishing thresholds for performance where deviance outside the threshold forces an action by you or a member of your team. Failure to take action from variances in any given KPI will lead to yet another worthless metric. Any KPI that changes dramatically should cause you to celebrate or go running for help. Just as with your vital statistics, if the pulse is dropping and breathing slows, it's time to take action. Understanding what these actions are when developing your KPIs is important in creating standard operating procedures that will empower decision makers within your organization. Although every scenario cannot be anticipated, developing action plans will demonstrate that you've created a valuable KPI.

▶ Keep in mind, however, expectations will change over time and realistic expectations are set based on performance trends. So don't be afraid to adjust expectations midstream if the KPIs are not trending the way you anticipated.

It is important for you to keep in mind that KPIs like those described in this chapter are a beginning, not an ending. Put another way, each of the metrics and measures used to understand behavior across social channels is designed to call attention to emerging opportunities and challenges, not to answer specific questions. Answering questions is the domain of analysts and resources within your organization who dedicate at least part of their time to analyzing data.

SUMMARY

After reading this chapter, you should have a solid understanding of Social Analytics and how to begin thinking about using this discipline in the context of your business. A starting point for wrapping your mind around the vast array of measures and metrics that will unfold during your social measurement planning is to adopt a Triple-A Mindset. This mindset enables you to quantify your Audience, their Activity, and your responsive Actions in the context of your social media goals and objectives. If you simply walk away with this mindset as your launching pad, you'll be well on your way to keeping pace with consumers in ways that resonate with your business.

From there you should ensure the alignment of your corporate goals with business objectives using a Waterfall Strategy. Remember that these corporate goals are probably already set within your organization. Social media doesn't need to radically change your business process, in fact it shouldn't. It's merely the newest, hottest, sexiest channel that customers are using to connect with your brand. By setting a strategy to engage with these customers in a way that will ultimately benefit your business, you will not only satisfy your customers, but your senior brass will be smiling, too.

CHAPTER 5

Using the Social Analytics Framework

Social media has introduced an abundance of new opportunities for businesses to develop closer ties to customers, enlist everyday consumers as brand advocates, crowd source support to the farthest reaches of the globe, and rely on consumers for innovation. Yet, these new methods of operation have the potential to create a paradigm of chaos if businesses attempt to chase down every social media opportunity that arises. Thus, organizations need a framework to assess ideas, create measurement game plans, and execute upon social media strategies that align with business goals and objectives. Although some skeptics may dismiss a Social Analytics Framework as unnecessary, I argue that any business that embarks on a social media initiative without quantifying the costs, risks, and rewards in quantifiable terms is destined for disappointment. This chapter details the process for using a Social Analytics Framework for planning, execution, and improvement of social media activities.

> **NOTE** Concepts for this chapter and for the Social Analytics Framework
> were originally published in a white paper that I co-authored with Jeremiah
> Owyang of the Altimeter Group. Our work titled *Social Marketing Analytics: A New
> Framework for Measuring Results in Social Media* (`www.slideshare.net/jlovett/`
> `social-marketing-analytics`) offered a seminal view of social strategy aligned
> with measures of success.

MOVING FROM STRATEGY TO EXECUTION

> ▶ *Incorporating measures of success is even more important when working with external third parties to ensure tracking for social media campaigns or applications created on your behalf.*

Accountability is imperative to any business, but often in the frenzy surrounding the launch of social media initiatives, projects and programs leave the drawing board with shortsighted measures of success—and sometimes no measures at all. One of the key lessons that I've learned from witnessing countless digital initiatives debut on the Web is that stuffing measurement capabilities into a page, an application, or a video player after the fact is about as challenging as getting toothpaste back into the tube. For this reason, it is imperative that businesses plan ahead to incorporate measures of success within their initiatives prior to launch.

However, organizations that hastily develop lists of counting metrics and spreadsheets full of data to include in their social media efforts often focus on capturing the digital trivia of social media activity. Measures like fans, followers, likes, dislikes, clicks, views, visits, view-throughs, bookmarks, comments, trackbacks, uploads, downloads, time spent, friends, friend volume, and more are for the most part the minutia of measurement. These measures, by themselves and without proper context, typically represent meaningless customer interactions that have no basis for making logical business decisions. Yet, when applied in context of larger business goals—or goals that exist within a Social Analytics Framework—these measures can build upon your awareness of user behavior.

The secret to creating measures of success is to develop multiple levels of metrics that resonate with different audiences. Each of these success metrics must align with the Waterfall Strategy described in Chapter 4, to provide strategic, managerial, and operational details. In this way, your executives should receive only between two and five critical success metrics that reveal the health of your social programs in relation to big corporate goals such as revenue or satisfaction. VPs and directors should receive slightly more metrics that reveal information about comparative performance or performance by channel. Managers should gain details on day-to-day operations, including all the metrics that are reported upstream to senior managers. This will deliver visibility into metrics necessary to accelerate or decelerate specific programs. At the most tactical levels, analysts should have access to all the data from the nitty-gritty minutia to the overarching strategic measures of success. This provides them with the data necessary to perform detailed analysis and find insights within the data.

Companies that do this well, such as you can see in the example provided in the sidebar about Piper Aircraft, demonstrate that social media efforts can provide details about the success of individual social efforts and their contributions to overarching corporate goals.

PIPERSPORT AIRCRAFT SOARS WITH SOCIAL MEDIA

Early in 2010, Piper Aircraft was preparing to launch its newest and most affordable airplane, called the PiperSport, to the general public. The product was set to retail for $140,000 USD and with just a week to go before the launch, the company hired social media consultants to produce a $40,000 USD social media campaign that would span YouTube, Facebook, and Twitter.

As a commercial entity, the primary goal of Piper Aircraft is to generate revenue, yet the objectives for the PiperSport social media launch was to build awareness of the new product using an authentic tone, engaging multimedia content, and emphasis on conversation versus traditional marketing. They took a unique approach to marketing a product with a hopeful side-benefit of enticing potential buyers to purchase the PiperSport online.

The metrics the organization used to measure the success of this social media campaign included video views, Facebook views, Twitter mentions, mainstream media coverage, and ultimately sales. Within a week of launch, the video depicted in Figure 5-1 generated over 7,000 views (today it has over 130,000 hits on YouTube), the story broke across multiple news organizations, and Piper Aircraft achieved mainstream media coverage and actually booked the first sale online. All this within one week!

(continues)

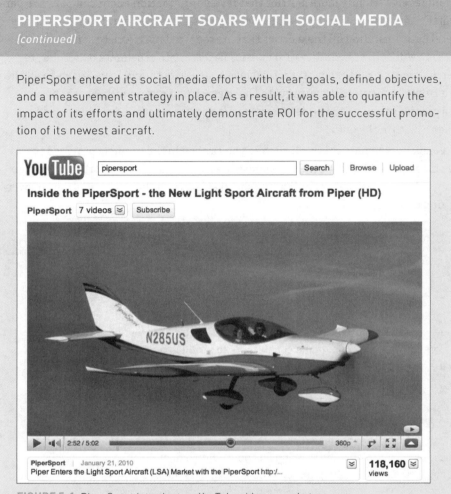

PIPERSPORT AIRCRAFT SOARS WITH SOCIAL MEDIA
(continued)

PiperSport entered its social media efforts with clear goals, defined objectives, and a measurement strategy in place. As a result, it was able to quantify the impact of its efforts and ultimately demonstrate ROI for the successful promotion of its newest aircraft.

FIGURE 5-1: PiperSport introductory YouTube video snapshot.

Making Goals and Objectives Tangible

▶ Jim Sterne has authored seven books on a broad range of marketing topics and is widely recognized as the Godfather of Web Analytics.

Jim Sterne, who is both my dear friend and wise mentor, is the author of the original *Social Media Metrics* book (John Wiley & Sons, 2010). (Jim stated in his most excellent read that there are only three true business goals: raising revenue, lowering costs, and increasing customer satisfaction. While I don't disagree with Jim, I believe it's worth mentioning that not all social media activities have an immediate impact on the bottom line, nor does every effort produce happy smiles on every face. In many cases, social media is the distant precursor to sales, savings, and satisfaction—it just takes a while to get there. For me, the shades of gray leading up to Jim's Big Three Goals contain the mystique of social media. And setting your sights on getting there is oftentimes what makes the trip worthwhile.

FOCUSING ON SPECIFIC OUTCOMES

Operating without corporate goals in mind definitely won't pay the bills, but it will very likely make for a short career. Avoid cutting your career short by focusing on the fundamental measurement concept of setting clear and quantifiable targets. It may be easier to think about these targets as outcomes.

You saw in Chapter 4 that you can learn a lot about an organization by evaluating its mission statement. Yet, the platitudes offered in mission statements often contain little substance worth measuring. Aspirations like inspiring and nurturing the human spirit are entirely nebulous. In a similar way, raising revenue is nebulous too. Is your goal to make $1 more than yesterday? Or is the goal to earn $100,000 more, perhaps? "Oh, I see . . . you meant increasing revenues by 62 percent year-over-year. Now I get it! Let's get to work figuring out how to make that happen." These are the conversations you should be having with individuals in your organization who offer nebulous goals.

Table 5-1 offers a way to think about transforming those nebulous goals into outcome-based goals. Notice that none of these outcomes mentions tactics at all—we're still working at a high level here, and the tactics will come later. But just imagine the impact you'll make when you move from saying that your plan is to build buzz around the new product launch (Zzzzz . . .) to announcing that you met your goal of increasing Share of Voice by 50 percent before the product even launched. (Now that's quantifiable!)

Businesses that succeed with social media are ones that clearly identify what success looks like. Each of these outcome-based goals listed in Table 5-1 specifies desired result and the timeframe for measuring success. Avoid the trap of reporting metrics to your boss or senior managers and being asked the question, "Is that good?" Instead, go into each situation knowing what good looks like and report whether your social media initiative exceeded or fell short of your specific outcome-based goals. So when the boss asks you—"How did we do?"—you can respond by saying, "We crushed our target goal by 35 percent and contributed to our corporate goal of increasing revenues by generating $X to the bottom line." Clearly, not every

▶ Don't tolerate sandbagging! Keep yourself and your peers honest by socializing goals and outcomes so that stakeholders agree. This ensures realistic outcomes and not just easy targets.

initiative will contribute to the financial success of your organization. But by identifying targets and aligning desired outcomes with overarching corporate goals, you will be on your way to quantifying the impact of specific social initiatives in the context of your corporate goals.

TABLE 5-1: Creating Outcome-Based Goals

▶ Outcome-based goals like the examples in Table 5-1 include specific targets and definitive timeframes. These two ingredients make for a measurable goal.

NEBULOUS GOAL	OUTCOME GOAL(S)
Build buzz around new product	• Increase share of voice to 50+ percent during 30 days preceding new product launch
	• Extend conversation reach to exceed internal benchmarks by 20 percent within 60 days of product launch
	• Achieve product placement in three mainstream media outlets within 90 days of product launch
Grow emerging markets	• Gain 20 percent market share for new products in target markets in 2011
	• Increase traffic to new product pages from BRIC countries by 35 percent in 2011
	• Build audience engagement within target markets to 40 percent "engaged visitors" in 2011
Increase revenue	• Generate 100 qualified leads per social media campaign within 90 days of new product launch
	• Convert 5 percent of qualified leads to actual sales of new product within 120 days
	• Achieve sales of $1 million USD within 24 months of new product launch

TAKING A STAND

Many managers working through measurement strategies get stumped before they even begin. The reason for this is because setting measures of success can seem entirely arbitrary given the absence of preexisting data or benchmarks to work from. My advice to social media measurers is to simply pick a target and begin measuring progress against it. While you may not know if it's exactly the right target, it will serve as a milepost to assess progress. Plan to watch your targets closely and refine them as necessary when data accumulates.

This approach requires that the measurement targets you choose are flexible and have latitude for change. In fact, when you're starting out, they must be flexible. As you're creating internal targets for measuring social media initiatives, it's okay to experiment to see what works and what doesn't. Here are three methods that I've used to establish a baseline for measurement and to identify a target goal.

▶ **Use Internal Comps:** Comparable examples from other internal social media efforts can help to set expectations and identify target goals. Of course, this works only if you have something to compare against, but it's a great way to gauge progress. Even if you don't have social media examples to use, explore other past marketing activities to use as a baseline. For example, if your e-mail marketing efforts result in 30 percent click-throughs on average, you might place a click-through rate for a call to action within a social media campaign at 30 percent as well. If this turns out to be extremely high, you can evaluate the cost per click to gauge success in a comparative way.

▶ **Use Competitive Intel:** One of the beautiful things about social media is that many efforts and initiatives launched by your competition are transparent. When your competitor launches a YouTube campaign for example, as an out-sider you can see how many visitors it attracts and how much buzz it creates just by listening. While you may not know how much money they spent to create the campaign, you can determine the traffic it generated and the viral distribution it received by conducting some simple analysis of public You-Tube metrics. Do your competitive diligence to measure yourself against the competition.

▶ **Take an Educated Stand:** If all else fails, establish a target, discuss it with your peers to attain consensus, and watch it closely. When you launch your projects and the metrics begin to stabilize, you can revisit goals and adjust accordingly. For example, if your social media campaign is being tested to gauge interest in an emerging market, perform some analysis to anticipate what level of response you expect to receive. Collaborate with peers to validate a working hypothesis and launch the campaign with expectations. The trick is to adjust expectations and goals with clear communication, but to do so in a proactive manner.

Identifying target goals and specific outcomes is achievable with some work and diligence. While I don't suggest pulling metrics out of thin air, you can use the previous methods to establish a reasonable starting point for defining goals. The best method is to examine your data and get a precise reading on where your metrics are, but this isn't always an option. However, don't let this stop you from getting started. The inability to take action because of instable metrics is no excuse. The age-old wisdom "don't sweat the small stuff" applies here.

▶ Don't get stumped by "analysis paralysis." Pick a target, start measuring, and adjust if necessary.

AIMING FOR PRECISION, NOT ACCURACY

The lies we tell in analytics are white ones. Our numbers, metrics, and Key Performance Indicators (KPIs) are communicated with the best intentions, yet our data oscillates within a range of deviation. This is because the method of counting unique visitors is flawed by the limitations of existing tracking capabilities. An individual who visits a site from work, then from home, and yet again from a mobile device is oftentimes counted as three unique visitors. Although this is somewhat mitigated by using identities and profiles within social medium, inaccuracies in measures of sentiment and other social metrics will continue to exist. As a result, most practitioners have forsaken precision for accuracy and resigned to the fact that the measures provide directional guidance—not empirical facts.

In a perfect world, you would have both accuracy and precision, yet this is rarely the case. *Accuracy* describes how close your expected measures are to the actual number, and *precision* describes how close your measurements are to one another. These terms are closely related but the distinction is huge because to be precise is to have reproducibility. This means that upon multiple tests, you end up with results that are very similar. You can adjust expectations to zero in on the consistent results. As illustrated in Figure 5-2, accuracy is unpredictable because you don't necessarily know by which direction you're off. However, when your measurements are precise, you can refocus your targets to hone in on measures of success that are reproducible. Thus, when you are taking a stand and estimating measures of success, it's more important to be precise than to be accurate.

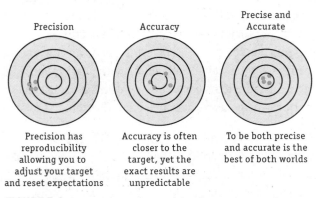

Precision	Accuracy	Precise and Accurate
Precision has reproducibility allowing you to adjust your target and reset expectations	Accuracy is often closer to the target, yet the exact results are unpredictable	To be both precise and accurate is the best of both worlds

FIGURE 5-2: Accuracy versus precision in measurement.

The current measurement practices dance around the issues of accuracy by offering insights at a generalized level, offering shards of intelligence, which undoubtedly are better than none. However, communication tactics require silver-tongued practitioners to educate with accuracy while avoiding the details of precision. Educated marketing guesswork has devolved from the visions of an infinitely measureable web. Still, we persevere because our noble quest for the truth nags our collective conscience in knowing that we can deliver more.

WEB ANALYTICS INDUSTRY VETERAN JIM NOVO SAYS . . .

"I'd argue that given a choice, it's more important to be precise than accurate—reproducibility is more important (especially to management) than getting the exact number right. Reproducibility is, after all, at the core of the scientific testing method, isn't it? If you can't repeat the test and get the same results, you don't have a valid hypothesis. (`http://blog.jimnovo.com/2007/08/28/marketing-attribution-models/`)

Activating Operational Tactics

One of the biggest mistakes you can make with social media measurement is charging headlong into a measurement investment for a single channel. I believe that social media channels will fall in and out of favor and chasing them down in lieu of developing a strategic approach is foolhardy. Building a strategy for Twitter or Facebook is incredibly shortsighted and typically results in a massive effort with few tangible results. Managers that set out to build a Facebook presence or communicate with customers via Twitter should stop and ask themselves how those efforts will support the overarching goals of their organizations. Simply having a Facebook page won't yield positive results unless you know why you're there in the first place. The goals can be as simple as starting a dialogue with your customers, but these goals must be considered before launching.

Operational tactics like the channels you pursue and the specific measures you use should ultimately be the last piece of your Social Analytics Framework.

It's possible that for your specific audience, Facebook is not the best channel to reach customers. Despite that at the time of this writing Facebook has nearly 600 million users, your audience may be more attentive to a forum focused on your specific products or specialized industry. You may find that the interactions you have in these channels are profoundly more impactful than those on Facebook. This is just one example that illustrates why you need to develop a strategy first and then choose tactics that make the most sense.

▶ Putting these components last ensures that you develop a strategy that supports your organization and don't fall prey to the hype of social media.

If it's too late for you already, and you've already invested in specific channels without a social strategy, ask yourself how people currently interact with your social properties. If you don't know or cannot determine what it's doing for your organization, then consider regrouping to focus on efforts that support your company's goals. This may be a hard pill to swallow for social media managers, but blindly proceeding into the social media abyss is no way to get ahead. Consumers will quickly tire of your antics if you cannot offer them compelling reasons to visit, interact, and share with their networks.

Visualizing the Social Analytics Framework

The Social Analytics Framework possibly carries more mystique than what's merited. In fact, frameworks in general are often disappointing to people who look to them for quick wins and overnight success stories. The reality is that the Social Analytics Framework, and most frameworks in general, are merely visual concepts to help you put things in their proper places. In no way do the frameworks assume the responsibility of work required to truly execute on a solid strategy for measurement. That's up to you.

If you're still with me and haven't thrown this book against the wall yet, then I'll take you through the logic behind the Social Analytics Framework, illustrated in Figure 5-3. Essentially, this depicts an inside-out construct where everything originates at the corporate goals of the organization at the center of the Framework. Remember the Waterfall Strategy I discussed in Chapter 4? This Framework includes the same concept; it simply originates in the center and moves outward as tasks shift from strategy to execution. At the center of the framework are your overarching corporate goals that nearly everyone within your organization should be familiar with. All objectives, measures, and tactics that flow from the framework should have a clear link back to those clear and specific corporate goals.

The next layer in the Social Analytics Framework is where the strategy is aligned. Here you'll find the business objectives: Gaining Exposure, Fostering Dialogue, Generating Interactions, Facilitating Support, Promoting Advocacy, Spurring Innovation, and potentially others that are important to your business.

Moving outward from the strategy layer is the management functions. Here is where the specific KPIs manifest and enable social media measurers to watch, benchmark, and report on the health of their social initiatives. I've identified just a few KPIs for each business objective and recommend that three is a good number to

▶ It's important to note that corporate goals may not have each of these six objectives aligned. Some may have more and others fewer, but this is a general starting point for organizations that are seeking a holistic vantage point.

start with. Too many KPIs can easily be ignored and having just a few–the right few–typically leads to more actions when the numbers fluctuate. There will be plenty more measures and counting metrics at the operational level to keep you busy, so don't worry that you won't have enough.

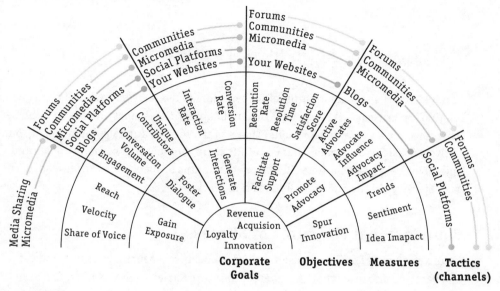

Owned Media ──────●
Earned Media ──────●

Note: Goals, Objectives, Measures, and Tactics presented in this framework are examples. Customize these for your organization.

FIGURE 5-3: The Social Analytics Framework.

Finally, the tactics layer of the Social Analytics Framework is where you decide which channels to use, what measures will fuel your insights, and how you'll assess the most granular details of your social media campaigns. For the most part, this layer of the framework contains the counting metrics that will detail the intricate moves and progressions of your social media operations. And, if measured correctly, the tactics level allows you to immediately identify wins and emergencies as they happen. Managing Social Analytics at the operational level is equivalent to sitting in the virtual Network Operations Center. Few outsiders really know what you do, but your day spent delegating assignments, averting disasters, and satisfying customers is perhaps the most significant with regards to keeping your social media strategy afloat.

CALCULATING FORMULAS FOR KPIS

Formulating the actual measures of success, commonly referred to as KPIs, is a challenging but critical task. As you learned in Chapter 4, KPIs must provide context, set expectations, and mandate actions. That's a tall order for any calculated metric, but entirely possible to accomplish if your KPIs carry the weight of corporate goals and objectives behind them. Here I'll explore the details of specific KPIs that align with the objectives in the Social Analytics Framework.

Foundational Measures of Success

Before you can build KPIs or assign values to specific measures, you must first establish baseline measures that are inherent to future Social Analytics KPIs. The basic math of Social Analytics requires these foundational measures. Each of the five foundational measures defined here can serve as integers within specific success measures, as well as offer high-level insights on their own (see Table 5-2).

My business partner, Eric T. Peterson (who wrote *The Big Book of KPIs*), and I developed these foundational measures to establish a basis for a common vernacular. We did this because in Web Analytics, there are a handful of measures of success that form a common denominator from which all other measures of success are derived. Visitors, visits, page views, and increasingly events are so widely used in online marketing and digital business functions that they have become a common currency against which nearly all efforts are judged. Unfortunately, these foundational measures fail near completely in social media.

▶ Foundational measures can be used across any social media channel and the individual inputs should be modified to fit each distinct channel. By calculating the measures in the same way, you can create consistency across different platforms and channels.

Entire conversations about your brand occur without anyone visiting your site; complete experiences can be built on social platforms like Facebook, Flickr, and YouTube, and your social audience is undoubtedly far greater than the sum of visitors coming to your site. Thus, the new foundational measures for social marketing analytics can act as a performance benchmark to evaluate success across channels and competitors. The foundational measures for Social Analytics include interaction, engagement, influence, advocates, and impact.

TABLE 5-2: Social Analytics Foundational Measures

FOUNDATIONAL MEASURE	CALCULATION
Interaction	Conversions / Activity = Interaction
Engagement	Visits × Time × Comments × Shares = Engagement
Influence	Volume of Relevant Content × Comments × Shares × Reach = Influence
Advocates	Influence × Positive Sentiment = Advocacy
Impact	Outcomes / (Interactions + Engagement) = Impact

FOUNDATIONAL MEASURE: INTERACTION

Social media interaction is the number of people who respond to your calls to action within a specific marketing initiative. It is a measure of the volume of people who are attracted to specific marketing initiative and the rate at which they complete your desired action. It also demonstrates a collective interest in any given effort. Interaction is active rather than passive because it requires sharing, submitting, or transacting. With this definition, consumers can "interact" with a web site or social network by participating in direct conversations, sharing links via Twitter or social bookmarking tools, or by completing transactions using your digital channels. Interaction is a ratio of visitors to converters.

Interaction must be measured against a specific marketing initiative such as a blog post, a campaign, or a program to measure the interaction of each marketing endeavor's call to action. Interaction can be evaluated within specific channels or across multiple channels for comparison. By tracking a composite measure that includes the number of views, unique visitors, shares, and conversions surrounding an initiative, organizations can evaluate the percentage of interactions against a benchmark of all visitors.

FOUNDATIONAL MEASURE: ENGAGEMENT

Social media engagement is an estimate of the degree and depth of participation an individual person displays around a specific topic or marketing initiative. Despite the fact that engagement is widely used, few businesses quantify engagement in the same way. Unlike interaction, which quantifies the ratio of people who complete actions with a marketing initiative, engagement indicates the degree to which a person is invested in a given event. Engagement can be associated with specific

▶ Numerous engagement calculations exist, some of which are as simple as (time + pageviews); others are extremely complex. Find a measure of engagement that works for your business that you can easily explain to senior executives.

marketing initiatives such as a blog post, campaign, or program where people can read, converse, comment, or generally participate. Engagement is a measure of individual attention.

Similar to interaction, engagement should be measured against specific marketing initiatives. This method allows companies to measure engagement within a specific web property or across multiple social channels. Engagement can be calculated as a relative score from 1 to 100, whereby numbers below 50 indicate less engaging topics and numbers greater than 50 indicate highly engaging topics. Specific inputs for engagement can also be weighted (for example, comments and shares are more valuable than time). And depending on your specific channel of measurement, "comments" can act as a proxy for any type of active participation (for example, form completion).

FOUNDATIONAL MEASURE: INFLUENCE

Social media influence is the relative power of a person to affect other people regarding a specific brand, topic, or field of expertise. Influence may be the most popular measure for social media, yet many existing definitions are inherently flawed. Social media influence must not be measured in terms of the sheer volume of fans or followers a person has, but rather the person's ability to demonstrate expertise in a topic and sway others into action. Influence will vary across social media channels since each individual influencer will have his or her platform of choice. Influence is a measure of authority.

▶ The Twitter analysis tool Peer Index does a good job at showing influence within a range of categories like media and entertainment, technology, science, health, sports and so on.

Simply because a person is influential in technology recommendations doesn't mean that you should take fashion advice from them. If this were the case, we might all be wearing pocket protectors. Influence should be calculated according to your brand goals and objectives. Some vendors provide the ability to configure weighted influence calculations with specific inputs for different social channels. These calculations are necessary to surface individuals who meet your criteria for influencers and offer baseline comparatives for identifying influencers across the Web.

FOUNDATIONAL MEASURE: ADVOCATES

A social media advocate is a person who acts as a proponent for a brand or cause. Advocacy is a concept as old as the first marketplaces, but one that is amplified with the rise of social media. A person who advocates for a specific product or service can act independently from the organization, yet more and more businesses are developing advocacy programs to nurture advocates and provide them with perks for spreading goodwill on behalf of their benefactors. The best advocates possess an inherent enthusiasm for your products or services and have influence over their respective social circles. Thus, advocacy is measured using a combination of sentiment analysis, influence, and commitment to the brand. Advocacy is a measure of positive influence.

Advocates should be measured by their ability to create a genuine dialogue about your products and services that fosters interaction, engagement, and impact. This requires that advocates be informed about your business and have a platform to share their opinions within their social networks. There are both significant opportunities and risks associated with advocacy, yet consumers are talking about your company anyway, so an advocacy program is a means to entrust a controlled group to evangelize on your behalf. Develop a successful advocacy by building them on credibility and transparency.

FOUNDATIONAL MEASURE: IMPACT

Social media impact is the ability of a person to guide the outcome of desired events as measured against specific goals, also known as campaign ROI. Impact is the measure that answers the return on investment questions within social media. This measure will reveal the results of an individual person or group of people in translating social media activity into tangible value whether financial or otherwise. Impact measures must be aligned with specific goals and objectives within the organization such that impact can be measured as a percentage of activity. While impact may not always align with an individual person, organizations can measure impact of specific social media campaigns or channels. Impact is a measure of success towards desired outcomes.

Impact must be measured in terms of tangible results against expectations set forth when determining business objectives. For example, if the goal of a specific marketing campaign is to acquire a thousand new customers, impact should be measured as total exposure divided by total new customer acquisitions. Alternatively, if the goal of a project is to supply third-world countries with clean drinking water, then impact can be measured in terms of lives affected. These measures will vary by campaign and specific marketing initiative, yet characteristics that determine impact include conversion events such as sales, leads, downloads, donations, completed projects, and so on. Companies can measure impact using purely digital metrics and attribution tactics or with a mix of qualitative metrics and anecdotal evidence. In either case, measuring impact is a critical component of gauging the overall success of your social media activity (see more on impact in Chapter 9).

Measuring Success by Business Objectives

So by now, you can probably appreciate that calculating metrics is no simple task. This is largely one of the reasons why few before me have attempted to document specific calculations for Social Analytics. Yet, while I have tested and put these measures into practice, they are by no means universal. These calculations are examples that must be tweaked and tuned to fit your specific business and the channels you operate in. While they may work beautifully in certain situations, there is a chance that they may break down entirely in others. The ability to apply foundational measures and business objective measures is dependent on your organization. It will vary by initiative, by the tools you use, and by the analysts you can dedicate to the task of making them work.

However, based on my experience and client interactions, the six objectives identified in Chapter 4 and the foundational measures cited here serve as a starting point for effectively measuring social marketing using an objective-based methodology. The success of these objectives is measurable using KPIs that demonstrate progress toward the goal. Companies are encouraged to adopt these objectives and performance indicators and customize them to adhere to the specific goals of individual organizations.

Exposure Key Performance Indicators

Generating exposure requires brands to leverage the viral nature of social media by seeding topics and ideas to the marketplace. Exposure is the twenty-first century equivalent of brand marketing because it is a measure of how far and wide your message travels via social media channels. In most cases, exposure is about awareness and is considered a precursor to starting a dialogue, engaging consumers, or encouraging interactions. A few success metrics that can be used to gauge exposure include reach, velocity, and share of voice, which are defined in Table 5-3.

TABLE 5-3: Exposure KPI Calculations

BUSINESS OBJECTIVE KPI	CALCULATION
Reach	Seed Audience × Shared Network Audience = Reach
Velocity	Reach × Time = Velocity
Share of Voice	Brand Mentions / Total Mentions (Brand + Competitor A, B, C...n) = Share of Voice

REACH

Reach is the first KPI within the set of exposure metrics because it can tell you the size of the audience that you're marketing to. This metric can be highly effective for planning marketing activities to determine which networks or social media channels have the greatest opportunity for getting your message out there. There are numerous commercial calculations for reach available, and I encourage you to adopt your vendor's methodology if it makes sense for your business. The key is to measure reach consistently to establish benchmarks and effectively set expectations.

While I dive deeper into the details of the reach calculation in Chapter 6, keep in mind that reach represents potential. This is akin to the impressions metric in advertising, because measuring reach is not an exact science. Rather it's an estimation of the total potential audience that may or may not see you message. Reach is about how far your message can travel and therefore is an effective planning metric. You should work to validate your reach assumptions using other metrics like velocity and impact to determine effectiveness.

VELOCITY

Velocity is the speed at which an idea, a campaign, a video or any other concept travels across social media. It's effectively the distance that something travels over time. Recall that I mentioned earlier in this book that social media doesn't always have to re-create the wheel? Well, velocity is a physics term that works just perfectly when measuring social media. By tracking velocity and the relative increase or decrease in velocity over time, you can assess the relevance of your social marketing activities.

In many cases, social media velocity occurs weeks or even months after a campaign leaves your organization. While viral videos like Volkswagen's Super Bowl commercial buck this trend, far more social initiatives gradually gain momentum before hitting the ten-million-viewer threshold. Watch velocity over time and work to throttle up the velocity of your critical messages by accelerating with repetition or by enlisting your advocates to help get the word out on your behalf.

SHARE OF VOICE

Share of voice is the relative percentage of brand mentions in social channels (such as articles, blogs, comments, Tweets, videos, and the like) among a competitive set. Share of voice is a competitive intelligence metric, so expectations can be established from a baseline of market share as determined by revenue or alternative fiscal sources. Share of Voice should be presented as a percentage over a given time period and accompanied by historical comparisons. This metric can also offer competitive

insight when represented as a pie chart showing percentages for the entire competitive set. Additionally, share of voice can be segmented by channel to identify which
social channels have the greatest impact.

When share of voice deviates beyond a reasonable threshold, the first place to
evaluate is the content produced by your marketing organization. If your content
freshness is waning, it shouldn't be a surprise that share of voice is in decline as
well. Alternatively, if your competition is clobbering your share of voice, it's time to
understand what they're up to. A strong marketing campaign or hilarious YouTube
video that's gone viral can send your share of voice plummeting. Knowing why your
indicator is moving offers competitive intelligence that's sure to interest your senior
executives.

Dialogue Key Performance Indicators

Creating dialogue requires that businesses produce relevant and meaningful content
to engage an audience and attract contributors. Organizations must embrace this
element and accept that while dialogue can be initiated by an organization, it often
takes on a life of its own that spirals beyond the control of your blog, site, or forum.
A handful of success metrics for the business objective of dialogue include share of
voice, audience engagement, and conversation reach. Table 5-4 describes these in
more detail.

TABLE 5-4: Dialogue KPI Calculations

BUSINESS OBJECTIVE KPI	CALCULATION
Audience Engagement	(Comments + Shares + Trackbacks) / Total Views = Audience Engagement
Conversation Volume	Reach x Engagement = Conversation Volume
Unique Contributors	Total Individuals Participating per Campaign

AUDIENCE ENGAGEMENT

Audience engagement is the proportion of visitors who participate in a specific marketing initiative by contributing comments, sharing, or linking back. Expectations
for engagement will vary based on traffic and readership, yet you can establish baseline metrics. Organizations with a strong following can expect a consistent volume
of audience engagement and can modify expectations based on advertising, search

efforts, and promotional activity accordingly. Audience engagement is a leading indicator for creating a dialogue about a specific topic or product.

Variations in the audience engagement should serve to identify hot issues and topics of lesser interest. Thus, rather than looking at the absolute metrics for audience engagement, it's important to understand the variations of engagement across unique marketing initiatives. An isolated number alone won't necessarily offer actionable information, yet when viewed in the context of alternative initiatives, it will serve to quantify the impact of a specific initiative and determine if more publicity or promotion is required. Audience engagement should be tracked over time to understand the normal volume of dialogue within a specific channel.

▶ Notice how audience engagement uses the foundational measure engagement, but applies it to specific social initiatives within a channel.

CONVERSATION VOLUME

Conversation volume is the number of unique visitors exposed to a specific brand/issue/topic conversation across one or more social media channels and the level at which they engage. When calculating conversation volume, the first challenge is identifying the scope of the conversation by associating it with a specific marketing initiative, a topic, and/or keywords. Once this breadth of the conversation is clear, companies can forecast the exposure within different social media channels and quantify the expected number of unique voices contributing to the dialogue. Volume metrics and the amplification of volume will be highly variable depending on the topic and should be trended over time. Organizations should formulate a volume benchmark of past initiatives to identify when the volume of participants in a conversation is expanding and traveling beyond your normal ripple of dialogue venues.

Conversation volume can be evaluated in terms of both topic and location across social media channels. When volume metrics exceed expectations, companies should explore the most active channels and influencers, while keeping an eye on sentiment to ensure that the reach is going in a positive direction. Low volume metrics can signify ineffective channels or marketing messages that are murky or poorly received. Conversation volume can also indicate when it's time to spur on your advocate community to add to the conversation.

UNIQUE CONTRIBUTORS

It should be obvious that creating a dialogue requires at least two individual people to get things started. However, you can tell when you have a popular topic or a subject that resonates with the masses when thousands or millions of people want to join the conversation. This is why it's important to understand how many people are contributing to your social media activities. While one or two individuals are capable of initiating a dialogue and creating some noise, the value of these conversations increase as more and more individuals get involved.

You track unique contributors over time to discern how many individuals have come into contact with your given social media activities. While the number of unique contributors doesn't always need to number in the millions, you can use the metric to gauge how many unique contributors are necessary to achieve your desired outcomes. Low quantities of unique contributors could mean that you're seeding your social ideas in ineffective channels or that you need to enlist more advocates to amplify the conversation. In any case, measuring the number of people that you draw into any given social activity will tell a great deal about the long-term success of your idea.

Interaction Key Performance Indicators

Interaction metrics offer a unique perspective on your ability to persuade consumers into action using social media. Once you seed your message in all the right places and then foster a dialogue about your social media escapades, getting consumers to take action is the next critical step. Keep in mind that interaction can be a conversion event like getting someone to register for a webcast or it can also involve a transaction where a consumer turns over money across a social media channel, yet the sheer act of doing something constitutes interaction. Some key metrics to measure interaction include interaction rate and conversion rate. Table 5-5 describes these in more detail.

TABLE 5-5: Interaction KPI Calculations

BUSINESS OBJECTIVE KPI	CALCULATION
Interaction Rate	Total Conversions / Activity = Interaction Rate
Conversion Rate	Total # Completed Actions / Total Engaged Audience = Conversion Rate

INTERACTION RATE

Social media interaction rates indicate the percentage of unique users that start down the path that you've laid out for them. While engagement is a measure of attention and quantifies the depth of interactions, this metric will identify how many people are initiating the process. As one of the foundational measures identified earlier, interaction should be a key metric in your social media measurement bag of tricks.

Keep in mind that interaction rate should identify people that have not only expressed interest in your social media calls to action, but also started down the path of completing them. This is a leading indicator of how effective you are at getting your message across using social channels and how compelling it is to your audience. Further, interaction reveals a great deal about the efficiency of your processes as it requires people to start and complete the task at hand. By watching these indicators, you will learn a great deal about your social programs and what it takes to actually spur people into action.

CONVERSION RATE

Conversion rates should be one of your Holy Grail metrics. This key measure of success indicates whether or not you're actually getting individuals to follow through on the designs you've set out for them. Conversion has been a critical measure for assessing the effectiveness of digital channels since the inception of the Internet. Yet, in many ways conversion rates are flawed because they include far too many variables that are not working toward the desired outcome. Focus the denominator on your targeted audience and then use a numerator of the number of individuals within that audience that completed your desired action. It's important to ensure consistency between these categories to calculate usable conversion rates.

Conversion rates provide immediate recognition of the success of your social marketing activities. Think of this performance indicator as the equivalent of having someone show all signs of buying from you and then asking if they actually made the purchase. By evaluating your conversion rates and performing analysis on individuals who did not convert, you can learn a great deal about your online processes and the ways in which consumers are comfortable transacting with you across digital channels.

Support Key Performance Indicators

Support success metrics are largely focused on your organization's ability to listen and respond to the ongoing conversation about your brand, products, services, and entire company. As mentioned previously, social media creates multiple opportunities for delivering customer support in rapid fashion. Although social support won't eliminate the need for traditional support channels, it can alleviate pressure from existing solutions and empower your staff to respond quickly and efficiently. Performance indicators for customer support can be compared to traditional channels and include issue resolution rate, resolution time, and satisfaction score. See Table 5-6 for more information.

TABLE 5-6: Support KPI Calculations

BUSINESS OBJECTIVE KPI	CALCULATION
Issue Resolution Rate	Total # Issues Resolved Satisfactorily / Total # Service Issues = Issue Resolution Rate
Resolution Time	Total Inquiry Response Time / Total # Service Inquiries = Resolution Time
Satisfaction Score	Customer Feedback (Input A, B, C...n) / All Customer Feedback = Satisfaction Score

> ▶ Whenever possible, set expectations by comparing social media issue resolution with traditional call center metrics. This will provide a baseline of performance and offer strong indicators of channel quality.

ISSUE RESOLUTION RATE

Social media issue resolution rate is the percentage of customer service inquiries resolved satisfactorily using social media channels. The implicit factor within the issue resolution rate is actively determining whether the issue was satisfactorily resolved. To accomplish this, you need to ask your customers or interpret satisfaction using some other means. You can do this with a simple online survey question or other automated method, although results will not be all inclusive.

The issue resolution rate should provide immediate recognition of the quality of your social media support efforts. Low issue resolution rates signify that additional training is required for staff or that the issues in question may require more documentation. Use this metric to take cues on which channels or service agents are most effective and leverage their success throughout the organization.

RESOLUTION TIME

> ▶ Again, expectations can be set based on traditional call center or e-mail response times if available, keeping in mind that social interactions are much closer to real time than other channels.

Resolution time is the amount of minutes/hours/days required to produce a human-generated response to customer service issues posed in social media channels. Customers expect near-instantaneous response to their service inquiries, and while organizations may not have sub-60-second response times, they should strive to respond in a timely manner.

Responses should most likely be measured in hours and benchmarked against baseline comparatives. Also recognize that automated responses are unlikely to satisfy your customers; thus, genuine, quality answers from actual humans are the expected norm.

When resolution time performance declines, the first place to investigate is your front-line social media service representatives. Was there a widespread issue that caused a delay in resolution time or was it an isolated event? In either case, understanding the response times and their contextual circumstances should illuminate potential issues. Although calculating response time for service inquiries may require some simple tabulation of issue start and resolution times, many social media measurement solutions offer basic workflow tools to direct issues to appropriate staff. If service is a primary component of your online social media strategy, a workflow tool baked into your monitoring solution is a must-have.

SATISFACTION SCORE

The customer satisfaction score is an indexed score indicating the relative satisfaction of customers. There are numerous calculations and established methods for determining customer satisfaction; they include inputs such as quality, delivery, perceived value, and overall performance. Any combination of these or other important metrics on a weighted scale should comprise a numeric satisfaction score. It's important to note that social channels should not act as proxies for other proven methods of determining satisfaction, such as surveys. The expectations for a customer satisfaction score should be established on benchmark figures derived from historical performance. If no historical track record exists, a consistent set of scores can serve as the norm.

When customer satisfaction scores plummet, companies should investigate the source of the decline and the channels involved. Satisfaction scores are likely to change less quickly than other social media KPIs and will trend upward or downward over time.

It's important to catch downward movement in trends early to prevent customer attrition and remedy service or site issues before they become pervasive.

Advocacy Key Performance Indicators

The advocacy success metrics are largely focused on the dedicated audience in social media that you can trust to support your brand, products, or services. Not all companies will need to manage advocacy programs, yet the majority of organizations out there will have both advocates and detractors at some time. By developing an advocacy program, organizations can build a stable of genuine enthusiast to support the brand and combat detractors on your behalf. KPIs that indicate the health of an advocacy program include active advocates, advocate influence, and advocacy impact. See Table 5-7 for more information.

TABLE 5-7: Advocacy KPI Calculations

BUSINESS OBJECTIVE KPI	CALCULATION
Active Advocates	# Active Advocates / Total Advocates = Active Advocates
Advocate Influence	Unique Advocate's Influence / Total Advocate Influence = Advocate Influence
Advocacy Impact	# Advocacy-Driven Conversations / Total Volume of Advocacy Traffic = Advocacy Impact

ACTIVE ADVOCATES

▶ # of Active Advocates (w/in past 30 days) / Total Advocates = Active Advocates

Active advocates include the number of individuals generating positive sentiment over a given time frame (for example, the past 30 days). Expectations for the active advocate metric should be established when setting up your organization's advocacy program. This metric will echo the corporate goals you've established for enlisting consumer support by leveraging social media channels. It will provide immediate context on the health of your advocacy program and determine if it's working as designed. Active advocates should be benchmarked over time with annotations and reminders identifying when programs initiate or specific advocacy awards/incentives are offered.

After establishing the appropriate number of active advocates required to keep your advocacy program healthy, taking action on this number becomes routine. Above average numbers require minimal feeding, whereas negative active advocate scores indicate that it's time to reach out to your fans and create some buzz. This metric can be adjusted based on specific programs or campaigns, but should be compared against a benchmark of overall corporate advocacy.

ADVOCATE INFLUENCE

▶ Unique Advocate's Influence / Total Advocate Influence = Advocate Influence

Advocate influence is the relative percentage of influence for an individual advocate across one or more social media channels. Building an advocacy program involves enlisting people who are going to reverberate goodwill about your products on a consistent basis. Yet setting expectations for how far and wide each advocate's message will travel requires an advocate influence calculation. Influence can be measured using the volume of relevant content, comments, shares, and reach. This measure can be used as an input to calculate advocate influence by quantifying the relative influence of any given individual against the standard within your advocacy program.

The advocate influence KPI is most valuable when evaluated in the context of your business objective. While this may sound redundant, it's critical that all success metrics tie back to business objectives. In this way, advocate influence can be used to identify new individuals for your advocacy program, incentivize participants, and penalize/motivate others. This metric will also enable you to identify existing channels and social circles that influencers reach and allow you to identify new territory for soliciting advocates. To do this, establish a threshold for influence and evaluate individuals as compared to the threshold. This will also allow you to segment advocates by varying degrees of influence and associate individuals with specific topics.

ADVOCACY IMPACT

Advocacy impact is the direct or indirect contributions of advocacy on conversions. Calculating advocacy impact is tricky because it quickly becomes complicated as multi-touch conversion events create attribution challenges. So don't expect advocacy impact to be a definitive metric for all conversions resulting from advocacy activity. However, it is still possible to quantify direct conversion events resulting from advocacy programs or even individual advocates. The first step is identifying conversions. Whether they are online sales, document downloads, or requests for information, the calculation will be the same. Track referral information to determine the source of conversion traffic and monitor all traffic generated from advocacy initiatives. Since you'll know where advocates commonly discuss your products and services, this is one method for tracking online activity back to individual advocate sources.

Understanding the impact of your advocacy program, and to a lesser extent the impact of individual advocates, is imperative in determining overall effectiveness of the business objective. Each advocacy program or individual can be armed with specific identifiers that will point back to the influence they have on your online conversions. As stated previously, this won't be empirical due to multi-exposure events, but it can identify last-touch conversion events and can be used to recognize traffic generated by individual advocates and programs. Once this information is apparent, the actions are clear: feed your most impactful programs and fuel your active advocates. Although too much of a good thing can produce diminishing returns, the ability to recognize who is producing will lead to decisive actions.

Innovation Key Performance Indicators

The innovation success metrics are largely focused on your company's ability to recognize and take action on ideas generated by consumers. Organizations that develop methods for harnessing feedback and indirect cues will develop a competitive advantage. Further, organizations that do this in a transparent manner will develop loyal and dedicated customers. Performance indicators for innovation include topic trends, sentiment ratio, and idea impact, as described in Table 5-8.

TABLE 5-8: Innovation KPI Calculations

BUSINESS OBJECTIVE KPI	CALCULATION
Topic Trends	# Specific Topic Mentions / All Topic Mentions = Topic Trends
Sentiment Ratio	Positive : Neutral : Negative Brand Mentions / All Brand Mentions = Sentiment Ratio
Idea Impact	# Positive Idea Conversations, Comments / Total Idea Conversations, Comments = Idea Impact

TOPIC TRENDS

Topic trends include key brand/product/service topics identified by monitoring social media conversations. Topic trends should be evaluated much like keywords because there will typically be a number of popular topics followed by a long tail of less common ones. The ability to pick up on topic threads that fall below the block-buster categories can yield productive ideas for innovation. Organizations will require the help of commercial social media monitoring tools to effectively listen to the vast array of conversations happening across the Web. Yet, the ability to under-stand the context of product and service conversations as well as where these con-versations are taking place is critical for tapping into consumer knowledge. Expect topic trends to have some consistency in terms of leading topics, yet new topics can surface quickly.

Organizations that are fast to react to both positive and negative topic trends will showcase their social media savvy. While popular topics should incite organiza-tions to consider a new lexicon for your product and service offerings, hidden gems can deliver the greatest value. Companies should dedicate time to mining topic trend data on a regular basis to ensure that they are in touch with consumers and to seek out new ideas for innovation.

SENTIMENT RATIO

Sentiment ratio is the ratio of positive, neutral, and negative brand mentions about specific products or services over a given time period. Sentiment ratios should be trended over time and represented as in the context of positive, neutral, and negative. Sentiment is possible to attain using automated analysis available from commercial social media monitoring technologies. However, sentiment is one of the most criticized measures in social media because of its inaccuracy. Yet, all brands hope for positive sentiment. Still, marketers and PR professionals should be able to harness and learn from any type of sentiment, especially when it comes to seeking feedback for new product or service ideas. Expectations should be adjusted according to a baseline of consistent results. However, sentiment can change quickly.

> **NOTE** One salesperson representing a major social media monitoring vendor actually told me that their sentiment analysis was only 60 percent accurate at best. The ability to identify sarcasm, intonation, and intent is extremely challenging for any technology.

Each type of sentiment (positive/neutral/negative) can be analyzed to determine the source and origin of the response:

- **Positive sentiment** can be used to identify advocates and communities where your brand is welcomed.

- **Neutral sentiment** can help to interpret where conversations about your brand can be swayed through reinforcement, dialogue, and advocacy.

- **Negative sentiment** should be addressed directly and countered with support, advocacy, dialogue, or some combination therein.

The ability to recognize these areas and take action on them will elevate your company's ability to innovate.

IDEA IMPACT

Idea impact is the rate of interaction, engagement, and positive sentiment generated from a new product or service idea. It may be helpful to think about the idea impact metrics as the next-generation focus group. Rather than going through the exercise of running ideas through a finite number of target individuals, idea impact enables organizations to leverage the power of the Internet and social media to test the waters. Although the challenge is to do this without revealing your entire secret sauce, organizations can test concepts, prototypes, and other innovation ideas through a wide net of consumers or controlled group of advocates. In any case, the ability to measure the impact of new ideas is paramount for innovation.

Idea impact can be used as an indicator for success in numerous ways. For example, movie trailers released through controlled social media outlets can be measured according to the buzz generated through conversations, shares, and social mentions to accurately predict the box office success. Similarly, consumer product promotions can be measured according to the dialogue generated among target audiences. By using idea impact, organizations can gain insight into how consumers will receive a given product or service. This in turn is a metric for forecasting the success of your innovation efforts.

COMMUNICATING RESULTS

▶ Some will encourage you to think of KPIs as your check engine lights—when they go on, you should probably take a look. Instead, work to create imperative KPIs that are more like a low fuel light, whereby you must do something or you won't be running much longer.

One key advantage to using a framework for Social Analytics is that it offers a method for reporting results in a consistent manner. By knowing that your tactics align with corporate goals and developing your reporting to reflect this, you will inherently be reporting on things that matter to your organization. Further, by collaborating with stakeholders while establishing your objectives and KPIs, you will create a level of awareness of the social media initiatives that you're working on. This awareness will lead to a greater stakeholder understanding of the way in which data supports your quest towards desired outcomes.

Reporting Tips and Tricks To Maintain Interest

When reporting data and results to your organization, it's quite easy to fall into a mundane rut of always reporting the same thing. This happens most often when social media measurers generate automated reports that show counting metrics like fans and followers. Although these measures may draw interest from some as you're getting programs off the ground, the real questions lie deeper within the data. You should be asking what the numbers mean to the company, why they move or remain consistent, and whether the numbers are contributing to your overall goals.

A good way to keep this in perspective is to remember that the social media data you collect is about people. Although the interactions you have with them are digital, effectively your social media efforts are generating conversations and building relationships with your following. Though this may be somewhat superficial, getting to know your customers one by one and collectively is hard work, but also extremely rewarding. The beauty comes when you start to reveal patterns within the data that uncover ways in which consumers, think, act, or use your services that you weren't previously aware of.

BECOME A STORYTELLER

One of the best ways to transform your data from numbers on a page to impression-able information is to shape stories around the data. You can do this by delivering context around your data, thus humanizing the information for your audience. Doing this requires skill, art, and a bit of creative license, but it will be well worth it for you and for recipients of your data.

HOW TO TELL A STORY WITH DATA

This was extracted from a blog post that I wrote in December 2009:

A few weeks ago, my business partner Eric and I attended a basketball game in Minnesota. Eric purchased the tickets a few days ahead of time, and I really didn't have any expectations going into the game except to have a great time. Much to my surprise, our seats were incredible! We were sitting immediately behind the announcer's table in the first row. Now, keep in mind, I'm a Boston sports guy and even when the Celtics were struggling through the 90s and the early part of this decade, you still couldn't get a seat behind the announcer's table or anywhere near the first row without taking out a second mortgage on your house. But, this was Minnesota, and the Timberwolves are not necessarily a big market team.

Anyway, as we enjoyed the game, we struck up a conversation with the woman sitting immediately in front of us who was a coordinator for the announcers. Sitting on either side of her were two official NBA scorers recording all the ac-tion into their computers and generating reports at nearly 10-minute intervals. These reports were printed and handed to the announcers, which ended up in a big pile on their desks in front of them. After a while, our friendly coordinator began handing Eric and I her extra copy of these Official Scorer's Reports. So, like any good Web Analysts would do, we took a look and gave the report a criti-cal review (see Figure 5-4).

We were astounded by how poorly constructed the reports were. Sure, they contained all the critical information on each player, such as minutes played, field goals, field goal attempts, and total points. But there were no indicators of which metrics were moving, who was playing exceptionally well, or even shooting percentages for individual players. The announcers were undoubtedly skilled at their jobs, because these reports did nothing (or at least very little) to inform them of what to say to their television audiences. Clearly, the NBA could benefit from some help from @pimpmyreports.

(continues)

HOW TO TELL A STORY WITH DATA *(continued)*

NATIONAL BASKETBALL ASSOCIATION															OFFICIAL SCORER'S REPORT
															4TH QUARTER AT 8:39

12/09/2009 Target Center, Minneapolis, MN
Officials: #41 Ken Mauer, #40 Leon Wood, #65 Sean Wright

Time of Game: 1:44
Attendance: Not Counted Yet

VISITOR: New Orleans Hornets

NO PLAYER		MIN	FG	FGA	3P	3PA	FT	FTA	OR	DR	TOT	A	PF	ST	TO	BS	PTS
16 Peja Stojakovic	F	30:09	8	12	5	6	0	1	0	3	3	1	0	2	0	0	21
30 David West	F	24:55	6	14	1	1	0	0	1	5	6	2	1	0	1	0	13
50 Emeka Okafor	C	30:56	2	6	0	0	3	4	2	4	6	1	4	2	1	2	7
23 Devin Brown	G	18:49	3	6	2	3	0	0	0	0	0	0	0	1	0	0	8
3 Chris Paul	G	30:09	5	12	1	4	2	2	0	3	3	12	3	0	5	0	13
5 Marcus Thornton		20:32	7	12	2	4	1	2	0	1	1	2	0	2	1	0	17
2 Darren Collison		9:12	0	2	0	1	0	0	0	0	0	3	0	1	2	0	0
9 Darius Songaila		14:26	2	5	0	0	0	0	1	2	3	0	2	2	0	0	4
12 Hilton Armstrong		5:04	0	0	0	0	0	0	0	2	2	1	3	0	1	1	0
41 James Posey		12:33	0	2	0	1	0	1	0	3	3	0	2	0	0	0	0
24 Morris Peterson	DNP - Coach's Decision																
32 Julian Wright	DNP - Coach's Decision																
TOTALS:			33	71	11	20	6	10	4	23	27	22	15	10	11	3	83
PERCENTAGES:			46.5%		55.0%		60.0%		TM REB: 4					TOT TO: 11 (12 PTS)			

HOME: MINNESOTA TIMBERWOLVES

NO PLAYER		MIN	FG	FGA	3P	3PA	FT	FTA	OR	DR	TOT	A	PF	ST	TO	BS	PTS
3 Damien Wilkins	F	18:07	1	4	0	0	0	0	1	2	3	3	0	0	1	0	2
8 Ryan Gomes	F	27:27	9	13	1	1	0	0	0	4	4	1	0	2	3	0	19
25 Al Jefferson	C	28:27	8	12	0	0	0	0	4	10	14	1	0	2	0	1	16
22 Corey Brewer	G	28:18	5	12	0	0	0	4	0	1	1	2	2	2	1	0	10
10 Jonny Flynn	G	24:48	4	7	1	3	2	3	0	2	2	9	2	0	2	0	11
1 Ryan Hollins		10:54	4	5	0	0	3	3	0	1	1	1	1	0	2	0	11
12 Kevin Love		23:56	4	6	1	1	1	2	1	7	8	1	3	1	2	1	10
19 Wayne Ellington		14:30	3	6	0	2	0	0	1	3	4	1	2	0	0	0	6
11 Sasha Pavlovic		5:45	0	0	0	0	0	0	0	1	1	0	0	1	0	0	0
7 Ramon Sessions		14:33	1	3	0	0	0	0	0	1	1	6	3	0	2	0	2
14 Brian Cardinal	DNP - Coach's Decision																
4 Oleksiy Pecherov	DNP - Coach's Decision																
TOTALS:			39	68	3	7	6	12	7	32	39	25	13	7	16	2	87
PERCENTAGES:			57.4%		42.9%		50.0%		TM REB: 7					TOT TO: 16 (21 PTS)			

SCORE BY PERIODS	1	2	3	4	TOTAL
Hornets	29	24	25	5	83
TIMBERWOLVES	29	35	19	4	87

Inactive: Hornets - Diogu, Marks, B. Brown Timberwolves - Hart, Jawai

Technical Fouls - Defensive Three Second
   Hornets: NONE
   TIMBERWOLVES (1): 2:53 3rd

Pts. in the Pt. Hornets 22 (11/25), TIMBERWOLVES 48 (24/36)   Biggest Lead Hornets 6, TIMBERWOLVES 16
2nd Chance Pts. Hornets 7 (3/6), TIMBERWOLVES 8 (4/6)   Lead Changes 6
FB Pts. Hornets 8 (4/5), TIMBERWOLVES 22 (10/11)   Times Tied 4

FIGURE 5-4: Official scorer's report.

So, here is where I get to the point about telling a story with your data. Sometime during the middle of the fourth quarter, a young aspiring sportscaster came running down to the announcer's row and handed off a stack of paper that offered some new information. Finally! His 4th-Quarternotes recap was the first written analysis we'd seen that actually placed the statistics and metrics recorded during the game into meaningful context. The 4th-Quarternotes (in Figure 5-5) showed that:

▶ A win could bring the T'wolves to 3-3 in their last six games.

▶ Al Jefferson was having a good night—approaching a career milestone for rebounds—and posting his 9th double-double of the season.

▶ Rookie Jonny Flynn was about to post his first double-double (which only five rookie players have accomplished), needing only one more assist.

▶ Ryan Gomes was once again nearing a 20-point game with a 58.6 percent field goal percentage in the past five games.

 4TH-QUARTERNOTES

Dec. 9, 2009 vs. New Orleans

Wolves Notes

- With a win, the Wolves would improve to 3-3 in their last six games.
- With 12 rebounds already tonight, Al Jefferson is now just three boards shy of 3,000 for his career. Jefferson grabbed a season-high 14 rebounds the last time these teams met on Dec. 4.
- Jefferson has already posted his ninth double-double of the season.
- Jonny Flynn needs just one more assist to post his first career double-double. Flynn could become just the sixth Timberwolves rookie to accomplish the feat, joining Pooh Richardson, Darrick Martin, Stephon Marbury, Wally Szczerbiak and Randy Foye.
- Ryan Gomes is just one point shy of tallying 20+ points in four of the last six games. He entered tonight's contest averaging 20.2 ppg on 58.6% shooting over the previous five.
- The Wolves already have 22 fast break points tonight. Minnesota's season high is 26 (Nov. 14 at Memphis).

FIGURE 5-5: T'Wolves 4th-Quarternotes.

This method of reporting used all of the same data that was contained within the Official Scorer's Report, but added historical context, which really brought the data to life. This was interesting stuff! Now, T'wolves fans and casual observers alike could understand the significance of Jefferson's 16 points and 28:27 minutes on the floor—or that Jonny Flynn needed just one more assist to achieve a significant feat. After reading this (even as a Boston sports fan), I was invested in the game and had something to root for—go Flynn!

(continues)

HOW TO TELL A STORY WITH DATA *(continued)*

So here's the moral of the story:

► If you're going to produce generic reports with no visual cues, do not show them to anyone because they won't use them. Make sure you hire some good analysts who can interpret these reports and give a play-by-play.

► If you do want to distribute your reports widely, take the time to format them in a way that highlights important metrics and calls attention to what's meaningful so that recipients can interpret them on their own.

► And most importantly—place your data and metrics in context given historical knowledge; significant accomplishments; or some other method to bring the data to life. Give your executives and business stakeholders something to cheer about!

Finally, if you ever have an opportunity to sit behind the announcer's table, make sure you befriend the coordinator so you can get a copy of the reports for yourself.

DELIVER ANALYSIS

I make a clear distinction between reporting and analysis. You should too. And here's why. Reporting is simply providing the numbers to your intended audience and allowing them to interpret, use, utilize (or brutalize) them as they see fit. All too often analytics is an exercise in reporting. And, no offense to monkeys, but any monkey can do it. Don't be a reporting monkey. Instead, offer the recipients of your reports something more. You're in this job because you know something about the data you collect and the meaning that it has to your business. You must make this shine through in your reporting by adding analysis. Analysis, however, requires that you turn on your brain and think about what the numbers mean. It also affords you the opportunity to shape the way that others interpret your data and can illuminate nuggets of insight or monumental revelations about your customers.

For every Social Analytics report that you send via e-mail, deliver in PowerPoint, slam down on your boss's desk, or narrate to your significant other over dinner, ensure that you include analysis. Take the opportunity to explain what the data means, and you will succeed in translating that data into information. This is your one shot at including your brilliance into every report and what makes reporting on data actually fun. You must take the time to include the thinking behind the numbers by placing them into context and revealing how they impact your larger goals.

Don't read this to mean that you can do away with reporting entirely and get away with simply providing your analysis. That's not the case. You need reporting to get the information out to your peers and colleagues. The act of reporting is your responsibility as a social media measurer because it informs your audience as to what's going on. The analysis delivers a greater understanding of that data. It's okay that recipients may interpret your data differently. Be prepared with rationale behind your thinking and be open to other interpretations of your data. You may just learn something in the process.

CUSTOMIZE YOUR REPORTING

Another way to think about presenting data is giving the people what they want. I mentioned earlier that the data you reveal should be more and more detailed as you get closer to the operational level of the project. This is because senior managers typically have less time or interest in the details. They just want to know how your project is impacting the big picture. Also, recognize that different people absorb information in different ways. Whereas some may love spreadsheets of data, others may need a written synopsis and others still a visual representation like the infographics presented in Chapter 2. When creating your reports, consider that you may need more than one way to represent the data.

One nifty little feature for translating data into common English is offered by Webtrends in their Analytics 9 interface. They created "Story View," which automatically transforms data from spreadsheet to narrative. The prose illustrated in Figure 5-6 shows the typical output of Webtrends' Story View, which also calls out specific metrics from exceptional days. This information can be accessed from within the user interface or exported into an e-mail, Word, or PowerPoint document. You too can do this with your social media data by taking the time to think through what the data means and putting it into context. Unless you're using Webtrends, you may not have an automated way to achieve this, but all the same, a minimal amount of effort can go a long way towards getting your message across.

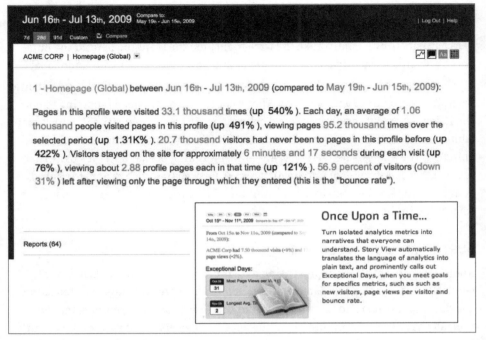

FIGURE 5-6: Webtrends' "Story View."

Using KPIs To Affect Change

Your primary motivation for using the Social Analytics Framework should be to approach social media pragmatically and to use the data output as a means to affect change. If the measures you employ force you to look at your customers in a new light, think about your products differently, or modify the status quo, you've succeeded. The KPIs should not only offer vital statistics on the health of your social initiatives, but they should also tell you when to forge ahead and when to venture into new territory.

Further, you will also need to become a KPI enforcer. This requires taking action from variances in your KPIs so that they don't become worthless metrics. Any KPI that changes dramatically should cause you to either celebrate or go running for help. Understanding what these actions are when developing your KPIs is important in creating standard operating procedures that will empower decision makers within your organization. While you cannot anticipate every scenario, developing action plans will demonstrate that you've created a valuable KPI.

Mitigating Chaos with Consistency

The tendency to chase down every new social media opportunity and launch into quick measurement tactics may be too much for some to resist. However, companies that take a long-term thoughtful approach to measuring against goals and objectives will realize the potential and value of their social efforts with much greater clarity than those that rush to measure. Additionally, I wager that this approach will lead to more productive efforts and money better spent than chasing the next new shiny object.

Brands such as Gatorade, Intel, Starbucks, Discover Financial, MTV, and Dell, which have taken this type of strategic approach, are paving the way to highly effective social media marketing. They're winning by executing on ideas and initiatives with pragmatic measures of success that are reproducible processes. The ability to plan, execute, and deliver in this way makes for a system that can be effectively measured and managed with a high degree of confidence. Additionally, when foundational measures and KPIs are applied in a systematic way, they can be used to benchmark social media initiatives across channels and help plan for investments in the future marketing mix.

SUMMARY

Social media participants are still awkwardly finding their way amid new surroundings. These consumers explore social media with voracious appetites, thus creating measurement challenges for organizations. Yet, every measurable business objective provides an opportunity to learn about consumers and the ways in which they interact with you, your brand, and each other. The Social Analytics Framework provides a scalable vantage point to understand these behaviors, test new initiatives, and improve the overall effectiveness of your social marketing activity. By making learning and continuous improvement your primary goals, your social marketing activity will develop in a positive direction.

I encourage readers to adopt sections of this Social Analytics Framework and modify it to fit your specific business needs. Not all measures and metrics will resonate with each audience nor will this foundational framework give you all the elements necessary for success. Still, the act of pragmatic measurement will offer competitive advantage and differentiate you from the majority of your peers. Companies must develop specific aspects of the framework that align with business objectives. In turn, the framework will offer you the ability to measure, assess, and explain the performance of your social media initiatives.

CHAPTER 6

Deploying a Process of Continuous Optimization

IN THIS CHAPTER

▶ Optimizing your social measurement strategy

▶ Measuring sharable content, engagement, and virality

▶ Shifting channels to meet your audience where they are

▶ Addressing longevity, idea generation, and budgeting

In a socially driven environment, businesses are constantly in flux, so change becomes the constant. For many, this is a difficult reality to accept because constant change requires continuous adaptation. Yet, mere adaptation is not enough to keep socially connected customers satisfied. Organizations must not only improve upon, but also exceed customers' expectations on a recurring basis. And those expectations are set not by your organization alone; they are shaped by external experiences from other brands, by contributions from other consumers, and by macroeconomic factors beyond your control. Thus, the process of continuous optimization is a challenging one.

However, organizations today are succeeding with optimization by using social media metrics to understand behaviors and results. These metrics enable businesses to recognize wildly successful programs and to key in on influencing factors that lead to social resonance and virality. Additionally, businesses that incorporate consumers into their process of optimization can capitalize on the powerful sway of social influence and enlist loyal advocates in the process. These businesses recognize that social media programs and properties must be nurtured with continuous optimization.

OPTIMIZING YOUR SOCIAL MEASUREMENT STRATEGY

Social media is—and will always be—a work in process. Don't fool yourself into thinking that a successful social media initiative is necessarily a long-term asset. It can be, but most efforts have a definitive life span. And a short life span at that. According to a study conducted by Sysmos in September 2010, the average life span of a Tweet is about an hour. They found that 92.4 percent of Retweets happen within one hour after publication, and 96.9 percent of @replies occur within the first hour.[1] This means if your Tweet isn't circulated after 60 minutes, it's likely a goner. Of course you can broadcast with repetition, and there are numerous tools that allow you to automate this process, such as Crowdbooster, or even Hootsuite. Schedule your automated Tweets sparingly so that you don't alienate your audience by spamming them with too many messages. Also know that Twitter is only one channel and life span is something to consider across all channels when planning for social media and for social media measurement. Granted, your 140 character missives may be perishable, but what about the social media page you developed for Facebook, the video you produced for YouTube, or the mobile app that you spent thousands to develop? Will they perish as well? This short answer is yes, most likely. However, you can extend the life of social media initiatives by nurturing them through optimization. The ability to optimize social media using metrics is paramount to pursuing continuous improvement. But before diving into the process of optimizing your social media, let's first explore the ambiguity of marketing optimization.

> **TIP** Start tracking the life span of your social marketing initiatives and optimization efforts to determine whether and when a campaign is worth resuscitating. There's very little research available to inform you of the longevity you'll get out of any given social campaign. And of course your mileage will vary depending on the resources, moderation, and curation you put into each effort. I recommend tracking social campaign life span by channel with some definitive measures such as elapsed time, financial commitment, resource commitment, optimization efforts, and impact. By doing this in a consistent manner and benchmarking campaign success across channels, you'll be well on your way to identifying successful efforts and learning how to focus on your most profitable social media channels.

[1] Source: Sysmos Replies and Retweets on Twitter http://sysomos.com/insidetwitter/engagement.

Deciphering the Art of Optimization

Optimization by itself is an immensely ambiguous term, yet it has reached a buzz-worthy crescendo among marketers and IT professionals alike. By the simplest defini-tion, optimization is the process of making something better. To optimize a process is to improve upon it. Thus, if something is optimized, then presumably it's as good as it gets. However, as the term optimization flutters around business applications, the meaning becomes diluted and often times abstract—so much so that someone recently described a conversation to me regarding optimizing where both parties were in vehement agreement with dramatic headshaking and belabored guffaws. But, the dialogue abruptly ceased when they discovered that they were each concep-tualizing an entirely different manifestation of the term optimization. So how could this happen?

Consider that optimization has been around for quite some time, and despite the common misconception of late that optimization is a technology, it is rather a pro-cess that is aided by technology. Further, the process of optimization can be applied in myriad forms. Take for example, revenue optimization, fulfillment optimization, call center optimization, pricing optimization, search engine optimization, channel optimization, marketing mix optimization; the list goes on. Pretty much any noun (or combination thereof) imaginable can precede the term optimization, and presto, you've got something new to optimize.

The circles I run in, and most likely yours, too, are often referring to marketing optimization. Some may call it online optimization—or perhaps, business optimiza-tion—but these descriptors really don't help to narrow the field of optimization pos-sibilities. So I advise using descriptive language to identify the optimization process you are attempting to improve. Table 6-1 breaks down the category of marketing optimization into components that are easily understood and clearly defined, so that individuals can take responsibility for each piece.

TABLE 6-1: Marketing Optimization Processes

OPTIMIZATION CATEGORY	DESCRIPTION
Interaction Optimization	The real-time dialogue between a visitor and an online channel (web, e-mail, chat)
Search Engine Optimization	The process of associating keywords to content
Web Site Optimization	Improving the navigation, flow, or design of a web site
Ad Optimization	Targeting or tailoring advertising (placement and mes-sage) to attract a specific audience

(continues)

TABLE 6-1: Marketing Optimization Processes *(continued)*

OPTIMIZATION CATEGORY	DESCRIPTION
Contact Optimization	Identifying the appropriate frequency and timing of a customer contact strategy
Channel Optimization	Determining the most appropriate channel to deliver a message, product, or service
Marketing Mix Optimization	Which combination of marketing programs leads to the most profitable outcomes
Social Media Optimization	The process of improving social media initiatives in pursuit of business objectives

Although these distinctions still don't define the entire gamut of marketing optimization possibilities, the next time someone throws out the term "optimization" looking to cash in on the buzz, ask them to describe precisely what they intend to optimize.

MATHEMATICAL MARKETING OPTIMIZATION

▶ SAS Institute also offers a social media analytics tool. Check out http://bit.ly/SAS_SocialAnalytics.

The experts as the SAS Institute describe true optimization as *". . . looking at every single possible combination of factors and determining the absolute best of all possible solutions."* And they should know. SAS is world-renowned for its analytical software and modeling capabilities. When users of SAS products talk about optimization, it's usually something different than most social media marketers have in mind. For SAS users, optimization tools help organizations like the NHL Carolina Hurricanes to determine the optimal ticket price for the 18,680 seats in the RBC Center in Raleigh, North Carolina. Another example is Canada's Scotiabank, which uses SAS marketing optimization to determine the most impactful customer communications. They mine millions of customer records and match offers to customers while maintaining a minimally invasive contact strategy. They've been able to realize growth using this targeted approach of 80,000 to 100,000 incremental accounts above what they would have achieved by waiting for customers to take actions on their own accord.

ONLINE MARKETING OPTIMIZATION

Online marketing optimization is a genre of marketing that dawned circa 2007. The concept was introduced by my former colleague, Suresh Vittal, who popularized his vision of an online marketing optimization suite of tools with several thought-provoking research papers on the topic. His work was readily adopted by vendors such as Omniture, Coremetrics, and Unica, who embraced the notion of using data to fuel marketing operations within a connected suite of interlocking products. With the help of a few strong vendors who put their shoulders behind the online marketing optimization concept, the idea began to flourish. Businesses also gravitated to the notion of marketing optimization suites in part because marketers had no single tool to assist in their increasingly complex task of reaching customers across emerging digital channels. Expect this trend to continue and for social media tools to become indoctrinated into the online marketing optimization suite. This is likely to happen by acquisitions in the marketplace. Yet, as more businesses recognize the value of data in driving business decisions, the tools available to social marketers will be offered and supported by major enterprise software vendors.

In addition to the technologies available in online optimization today, there is also a popular conference series called the eMetrics Optimization Summit that is offered in numerous cities around the globe, including San Francisco, Washington D.C., Toronto, London, Munich, Stockholm, Paris, and Sydney. The conference offers a bevy of marketing optimization topics, from web site optimization to campaign optimization to social media optimization (SMO). If you haven't heard of the eMetrics conference series, it's definitely worth a trip to a city near you. I've had the good fortune to attend and present at many eMetrics conferences (eight and counting!), and they are always great experiences. At the last three I've attended I've spoken on social media, which is always a hot topic and sure to draw a crowd. eMetrics succeeds at capturing social media and being captured by social media in Tweets, blog posts, and videos of on-site events.

▶ To keep this all in perspective, eMetrics and other worthy conferences out there are about real-life social networking. Don't miss the opportunity to get out and talk to like-minded people about your social initiatives and ideas.

> **NOTE** This is an excerpt from a blog post that I wrote summarizing my experience at eMetrics D.C. way back in 2009:
>
> ...the details of the presentations and buzz at the event were all captured tremendously through the help of social media. Yet, the one thing that couldn't be bottled up or summarized in 140 characters was the hallway conversations, post-session chats, and late-night debauchery. These off-the-record activities deliver the real value of eMetrics and similar conferences. So, while you may be able to get the play-by-play sitting by your laptop and chasing hashtags, the real deal is live and in person.

SOCIAL MARKETING OPTIMIZATION

So this brings you back to social marketing optimization. My definition of social marketing optimization is this: *The process of improving social media initiatives in pursuit of specific business objectives.* I readily accept that this definition differs from what others have written, but I stand by my version as the best and most flexible out there today. Alternative definitions state that social marketing optimization is designed with the intent of attracting visitors to a web site, much like the way search engine optimization (SEO) was designed. However, this shortsighted definition doesn't consider that marketers might not always have the goal of driving visitors back to a web site. Social marketing activities that strive to foster dialogue don't necessarily care where that dialogue takes place. Whether it happens on a web site, a social network, an app, or a TV console is irrelevant. Similarly, facilitating support doesn't require that consumers visit a web site for satisfactory completion of the task. Thus, I believe that social marketing optimization is about improving upon the activities, campaigns, and programs that your company produces to attain desired results. Driving web site visitors might or might not be part of that goal.

Savvy readers will also note that I refer back to the social business objectives described in Chapter 4 when I describe the process for optimizing social media because I strongly believe that using objectives as the basis for measures of success is critically important.

> **CROSSREF** See Chapter 4 for details on tying business objectives to corporate goals.

Thus, when you're contemplating what to optimize, or how to best accomplish that task, take the time to revisit your objectives and goals to ensure that there is still alignment and that you haven't lost sight of the original intent. Do this because if you are successful with your SMO efforts, you'll want to point back to the impact that these efforts had on your corporate goals. If you achieve this, you'll be a hero not just in SMO circles, but also in the eyes of your senior leadership.

MEASURING THE UNOFFICIAL RULES OF SOCIAL MEDIA OPTIMIZATION

Dating back to 2006, marketers have been working through definitions for SMO. At that time, Rohit Bhargava, a VP with Ogilvy and founding member of the 360 Digital Influence Group, blogged about the "5 Rules of Social Media Optimization."

His original blog entry was posted on August 10, 2010, on the Influential Marketing Blog and was an instant success, spurring conversation among social media mavens across the globe. Within weeks, multiple tags on del.ic.ious, Diggs, blog post links, and PR mentions occurred. The big idea spawned a Wikipedia page and has since taken on a life of its own.

Four years after his original post, Rohit revisited his "5 Rules of Social Media Optimization" and published his thoughts in another blog post, reprinted with permission here, which remained largely unchanged. His revised post is printed in the sidebar titled "The 5 New Rules of Social Media Optimization."

THE 5 NEW RULES OF SOCIAL MEDIA OPTIMIZATION (SMO)

About a week ago I started seeing a curious number of tweets, links, and Google Alerts to a popular blog post I wrote 4 years ago. The reason was that today happens to be the four-year anniversary of that post, which first introduced the idea of Social Media Optimization or SMO, as it is now popularly known in the world of digital marketing and on Wikipedia. For many of the readers who consistently read my posts today, this SMO post may have been the reason they first stumbled onto my blog. It became an unintentionally big idea that captured the attention of a growing niche of digital marketers who saw themselves at the intersection of working in search engine optimization (SEO) and wanting to branch out into the new world of social media.

In the four years since that post, I have tried to focus this blog on my real passion of sharing insights that could inspire people to create better marketing to sell their ideas to the world. SMO was a point on that journey, and given the interest that this one idea has sparked among digital marketers around the world, it is one that is worth revisiting today. As I thought about this post today, I realized that the ideal way to revisit SMO would be to try and answer the one question I have been asked most frequently by marketers around the world about SMO: **Would you change these "5 rules" today given that the original post was written before Twitter or Foursquare or many other big trends or sites that are now becoming a big part of the social web?**

The short answer is yes. The core change I would make is to add and focus on a word that I think truly describes the social web today in a way that few people

(continues)

THE 5 NEW RULES OF SOCIAL MEDIA OPTIMIZATION (SMO)
(continued)

grasped 4 years ago: **sharing**. So, based on this, here are my thoughts on **the 5 NEW Rules Of Social Media Optimization:**

1. ~~Increase your linkability~~ **Create shareable content:** Four years ago I focused on linkability because the main currency that could drive up your traffic was how many people were linking to your content. Today, content can be liked or tweeted and it is about more than links—it is about creating content that is shareable. The better your content is, the more people will want to share it with their entire social networks whether they link it, like it, dig it, or share it.

2. ~~Make tagging and bookmarking easy~~ **Make sharing easy:** Following from the previous point, tagging and bookmarking only scratch the surface of the many ways that people can share content with others. They can post a short link to their profile, embed a video, send out a tweet, or create a hashtag for a conversation. Limiting the ways of sharing to just tagging or bookmarking doesn't make sense anymore. The core of this rule, however, was the point about making it easy, and that is still at the heart of this new rule. Once you have shareable content, it has to be one-button-easy so people will do it with minimal effort or thinking.

3. ~~Reward inbound links~~ **Reward engagement:** In 2006, the main thing most marketers were concerned about were inbound links. It was a time when Technorati was the standard by which we all measured the performance of our content and many bloggers focused more on their number of inbound links than their readership or traffic numbers. Today the real currency is around conversation or engagement. While there are a million definitions for "engagement" ranging from comments and discussion to posting or sharing content, this is the behaviour that matters most in the social web and the one that we should all focus on rewarding when it happens.

4. ~~Help your content travel~~ **Proactively share content:** This was the weakest of the original 5 rules, as the original rule simply talked about publishing your content in other formats such as PDFs or videos and submitting them to other sites. Instead, the essence of the new version of this rule is all about proactively sharing content in a different way. This encompasses

everything from creating slides to post on Slideshare or documents to share on Scribd—as well as tweeting about your content or offering embeddable versions of it, or using RSS feeds to syndicate it. Proactively sharing even includes posting your content to social networking profiles or creating profiles on video-sharing sites.

5. ~~Encourage the mashup~~ **Encourage the mashup:** The last original rule of SMO is the one that I would leave intact. The concept of the "mashup" where people take and remix your content by adding their own input and voice has only grown over the past four years. The mashup will be around to stay, whether the term continues to be used or not. Allowing people to take an ownership over the social content you publish will continue to be a key way that you can optimize your content for the social web.

On the original 5 rules, several other smart folks jumped in to add 12 more rules to the list... it only makes sense for me to try and invite the same input this time around. What do you think of these updated rules? Are there others you would add to the list?

This blog entry was posted by Rohit Bhargava on August 10, 2010, on the Influential Marketing Blog.

Rohit was certainly onto something with his rules for social media optimization (coined SMO), but these rules were different from other forms of optimization that preceded SMO. Rohit's SMO was about sharing and finding ways to truly optimize the life span of an idea. Thus, rather than thinking of optimization as a process that leveraged historic schools of thought, his "rules" for SMO were not about the math of traditional optimization, nor the continuous improvement of online optimization. Rather, Rohit's concept explored the ability to spread an idea across social medium and for others to take that idea and improve upon it. In response to Rohit's call for new ideas in SMO, four influential social media mavens stepped up to add additional rules, as noted above to take the original 5 to a whopping 17 rules. These rules are as follows:

1. Create sharable content
2. Make sharing easy
3. Reward engagement
4. Proactively share content

5. Encourage the mashup

6. Be a user resource, even if it doesn't help you

7. Reward helpful and valuable users

8. Participate

9. Know how to target your audience

10. Create content

11. Be real

12. Don't forget your roots; be humble

13. Don't be afraid to try new things; stay fresh

14. Develop an SMO strategy

15. Choose your SMO tactics wisely

16. Make SMO part of your process and best practices

17. Don't be afraid to let go of a message or idea and let others own it

(Rules 1–5, 17 contributed by Rohit Bhargava)

(Rules 6–7 contributed by Jeremiah Owyang)

(Rules 8–11 contributed by Cameron Olthuis)

(Rules 12–13 contributed by Loren Baker)

(Rules 14–16 contributed by Lee Odden)

> *Releasing ideas into the "wilds" of the Internet and allowing them to flourish (and hopefully come back) is really what social media optimization is all about.*

These unofficial rules of SMO are still entirely relevant today. And perhaps the one I like best is the final rule, #17 added by Rohit, which enabled me to include his thoughts and the conception of his vision for social marketing optimization in this book. *Don't be afraid to let go of a message or idea and let others own it.* For most marketers, this is an excruciating task and one that is seldom performed. But letting go of messages and ideas will ultimately pay dividends for organizations that heed this advice. Yet, I'll bring this back around to the context of this book and the reason why you're invested in social marketing. The measurability of it all and the ability to quantify your efforts against these SMO rules is essential for determining which tactics worked and which ideas were cast off into the ether without providing benefit for your organization. You can assess the performance of your social-rule-abiding tactics by applying metrics for sharable content, engagement, and virality.

Measuring Sharable Content

There are a number of ways to measure sharable content, but perhaps the best metric is *reach*.

> **CROSSREF** See Chapter 5 for details on calculating reach.

For me, reach extends beyond the number of fans you have or the followers of a given account or RSS feed. Reach is specific to the number of individuals exposed to your idea and the journey your idea takes, from conception to its final resting place. This is relevant to optimization in that your social media activities will have a definitive starting point (hopefully with specific goals, objectives, and measures of success in place) and optimization should occur as these ideas spread, flourish, and take new shape.

REACHING YOUR POTENTIAL

When measuring reach, you must be cognizant of the fact that reach calculations that take into consideration the number of followers in Twitter, fans on Facebook, subscribers to blogs, or even recipients of e-mails represent potential reach; they don't really tell you how many people were actually exposed to your idea or content. Reach, in many cases, is the "promise" of an audience versus the "truth" of how many people actually show up for the gig. It's difficult to discern true value from reach because of this potential audience. It's not the actual number of people you impress, nor the number of people that you call to action; rather it's an estimate. Of course, potential reach can be used for planning purposes to determine where you might have an impact, but for assessing the real effect of your social initiatives on actual humans, you'll have to use interaction and impact metrics.

▶ Key point here: Most measures of reach are about "potential reach" and should be used for planning purposes.

Luckily, metrics do exist that can offer a more realistic view of the impact of reach. For example, social media mentions—which can be tracked using monitoring tools or by simply establishing Google Alerts for your ideas' keywords—can track mentions across the vast expanse of the Internet. Additionally, content distribution can be tracked revealing when external sites pick up your content or repost your ideas using similar tools. Further, if you're working to drive visitors back to your owned web properties, you can identify referral links generated from your socially seeded ideas using Web Analytics tools to track the frequency and source of referrals over time. Each of these metrics enables social media managers to quantify the actuality of reach versus the potential of reach.

CAPITALIZING ON THE SHARE

One tool that I particularly like for both enabling and quantifying reach is Share-This. You've likely seen the ShareThis button on plenty of web sites from the *Financial Times* to *The Onion*, but for those unaware, it's a simple tool for consumers to distribute content with just the click of a mouse across more than 40 social destinations, including Facebook, YouTube, and Digg, to name a few. On the back end, publishers gain the ability to track the distribution of their content after consumers share it via social media channels. ShareThis exposes its data to publishers using the analytics metrics dashboard, which is pictured in Figure 6-1. Yet, ShareThis offers a Social Reach calculation that reveals the number of people who are actually clicking through on content versus just watching it pass by. As I mentioned previously, this is the real power of sharing and one that ShareThis is bringing to the surface through its analytical dashboard.

FIGURE 6-1: ShareThis' social analytics metrics dashboard.

ADVANCING THE REACH METRIC

Measuring reach is one way to understand how many people were exposed to your social media video, but as I mentioned, it tells only a fraction of the story. The smart folks over at Visible Measures, a Boston-based company specializing in online video measurement, came up with a metric that they call True Reach (`http://corp.visible measures.com//true-reach`). This calculated metric includes data from seeded video as well as the viral spread of video across all Internet locations. Thus, it tracks the original video you plant as well as any copies or derivatives that circulate around the Internet. Further, they include the number of views across all these locations to reveal where consumers are engaging with your video content. This information is augmented with sentiment analysis, which tells you how people are reacting to your video message and content.

Lots of firms use this metric to track the effectiveness of online videos and compare results against the competition. But the True Reach methodology is also popularized in rankings published by *Advertising Age*, *Variety,* and Mashable. These sites report on videos that top the charts across categories such as online ad campaigns, film trailers, and webisodes. Thus, the True Reach metric offers an intelligent way to track ideas (conception) and their spread over time (contagiousness), while also offering a competitive view.

Using this methodology allows Visible Measures to track another interesting online video phenomenon, which is the number of videos that attain the prestigious honor of 100 million views. Most sites will allow you to track video views within a single media source such as YouTube or Hulu, but the Visible Measures approach quantifies all views across the Internet. At the time of this writing, there are still fewer than 100 videos in the 100 Million Views Club. The prestige of making this list ranks high among agencies and video producers globally, but as more and more consumers rack up time watching videos online and as the Internet permeates across TV screens and mobile devices, this benchmark will surely rise. Nonetheless, it's worth watching to see if your big hit is good enough to make this exclusive club. Music videos and movie trailers dominate the list, but there are a few instances of consumer-generated videos, video games, and TV spots that make the grade.

Measuring Engagement

Engagement is the lifeblood of social media participation. It determines whether you have the attention of your audience and whether the information you produce is worthy of reply or riposte. I look at engagement as a measure of consumer behavior. As an organization or a brand, you must engage with social media. You have no choice. The alternative is obsolescence and that certainly won't contribute to your corporate goals and objectives. With this perspective, measuring engagement becomes all about the ways in which your audience interacts with your people, your digital properties, your distributed applications, and each other.

Yet, engagement is a slippery metric that ventures into the gray corners of measurement because it seeks to quantify the intangible. It presupposes that social media isn't always about definitively identifying a return on investment (ROI).

Because in reality, many of the activities you launch with social media won't have a direct correlation to ROI. Instead, these are often brand-building exercises, frivolous entertainment offerings, or relationship marketing tactics that will simply provide a good experience for participants. It's important to recognize that not every social media endeavor ends with a pot of gold somewhere over the rainbow. Lots of activity, interaction, and engagement will tangentially support your financial goals. Don't kid yourself into believing that everything ties back to ROI.

ENGAGING YOUR INNER MATHEMATICIAN

Web analytics efforts have been working to quantify engagement for several years. Many large organizations rely on engagement calculations to understand key aspects of their online business. Although one might argue that engagement is best suited for publisher sites or informational sites that don't end with a conversion event, I've witnessed engagement work across a broad spectrum of industries and digital properties. Engagement calculations can run from extremely complex, such as the one offered in Figure 6-2, to simple metrics for understanding activity and time spent. There is some opposition to using engagement as a measure of success, but I contend that engagement, in whatever manifestation you choose, is an essential metric for understanding user behavior. This is especially true in web site analytics as it is in the context of SMO where the perpetuation of ideas depends on engagement for users to converse with, shape, and extend those ideas to new ground.

MEASURING THE IMMEASURABLE

My business partner, Eric T. Peterson, set out to "measure the immeasurable" by creating a formula for quantifying engagement. In 2008, he, along with co-author Joseph Carrabis of Nextstage Group, published a white paper that produced a scientific and highly contested engagement calculation.

The published work included the following calculation:

$$\Sigma(C_i + D_i + R_i + L_i + B_i + F_i + I_i)$$

Figure 6-2 shows the entire calculation for the more mathematically inclined.

$$E = \left| \left(\sum_{t}^{v} \sum_{j=1}^{} \frac{m_j\left(1 + \frac{1}{3}\Delta T_j\right) + \left(\sum_{f} L_f\right) + \left(\sum_{f} F_f\right) + \left(\sum_{i} I_i\right) + \left(\sum_{b} B_b\right)}{m_v} + \sum_{k=1}^{z} \frac{dk}{dz} \right) \right|$$

FIGURE 6-2: Eric T. Peterson and Joseph Carrabis's engagement calculation.

In human terms, this calculation states the following:

"Visitor Engagement is a function of the number of clicks (Ci), the visit duration (Di), the rate at which the visitor returns to the site over time (Ri), their overall loyalty to the site (Li), their measured awareness of the brand (Bi), their willingness to directly contribute feedback (Fi), and the likelihood that they will engage in specific activities on the site designed to increase awareness and create a lasting impression (Ii)."

The components of the Visitor Engagement calculation are as follows:

▶ **Click Depth Index:** Captures the contribution of page and event views

▶ **Duration Index:** Captures the contribution of time spent on site

▶ **Recency Index:** Captures the visitor's "visit velocity"—the rate at which visitors return to the web site over time

▶ **Brand Index:** Captures the apparent awareness of the visitor of the brand, site, or product(s)

▶ **Feedback Index:** Captures qualitative information, including propensity to solicit additional information or supply direct feedback

▶ **Interaction Index:** Captures visitor interaction with content or functionality designed to increase level of attention the visitor is paying to the brand, site, or product(s)

▶ **Loyalty Index:** Captures the level of long-term interaction the visitor has with the brand, site, or product(s)

Source: "Measuring the Immeasurable: Visitor Engagement," September 7, 2008, Eric T. Peterson, Joseph Carrabis. `http://bit.ly/DEMYSTIFIED_engagement_whitepaper`

While the Peterson/Carrabis engagement calculation may not work for everyone, it's a proven method for quantifying behavior and optimizing digital properties to match the characteristics of your visitors. Many companies that I work with will modify the engagement calculation to leverage more simplistic metrics for understanding behavior. I encourage this effort because it is perfectly acceptable to use proxy metrics for engagement that include click depth and duration, which will inform your business about ways that visitors interact with your digital properties. More importantly, if you do adopt an engagement calculation, you will need to explain it to your peers and your executives, so it's imperative that you understand it. And this may require simplification. In whatever form you choose, the ability to recognize engagement on your social media initiatives is a critical first step in optimizing for specific social business objectives.

CATEGORIZING ENGAGEMENT MEASURES

When it comes to measuring engagement from the perspective of consumer behavior, it may be helpful to categorize engagement into passive engagement and active engagement. You should expect that different people will interact with your social media activities at different rates. By categorizing engagement, you can begin to differentiate the wallflowers from the social media chatterboxes. Consider the following categories and corresponding metrics for engagement:

- ▶ **Passive Engagement:** Passive Engagement metrics include the first three components of the engagement calculation and offer a perspective on who is involved with your social media activities. I recommend using a combination of metrics to understand Passive Engagement, including:
  - ▷ Visitors
  - ▷ Views
  - ▷ Repeat visits
  - ▷ Time spent
- ▶ **Active Engagement:** Active Engagement metrics include components of customer feedback, interaction, and loyalty. For each of these measures, consumers must proactively demonstrate attention by participating in your social media initiatives. I recommend using a combination of metrics to understand Active Engagement, including:
  - ▷ Comments
  - ▷ Unique contributors
  - ▷ Downloads
  - ▷ Shares

Measuring Virality

By understanding sharing and engagement, you can track the source of information, how it traverses the Internet, and how people interact with that content. Still, the real magic of social media is measured in the virality, or the spread of content, ideas, and information, from one socially connected individual to another. Virality is the gasoline that ignites a social topic from local knowledge to widespread awareness. Virality can be quantified using a series of metrics so you can link the source, spread, and impact of any given social media initiative.

One U.K. company called UnrulyMedia publishes an online video ranking called the Viral Video Chart. Instead of reporting on total video views, UnrulyMedia tracks the number of video shares across Facebook, Twitter, and blog posts. The breakout by channel allows you to see how well videos are spreading across social medium, offering glimpses of what works and where. Unruly also offers a branded ad chart in partnership with *Contagious* magazine called Most Contagious, which is certainly the clout you want to hold if you're producing ads for branding purposes. This is but one measure for virality, and others exist as well.

FROM VIRAL COEFFICIENT TO K-FACTOR

As with most social media metrics, there are several ways to measure virality, and there are some adamant proponents for the cause. If you're at all squeamish, the thought of virality is enough to make you uncomfortable, yet the parallels between the spread of social media and infectious diseases are just too close to ignore. As such, some measurers of social media have adopted scientific metrics to explain virality within social media.

One measure is the Viral Coefficient, which is explained in simple social media terminology by Robert Zubek as, "a measure of how many new users are brought in by each existing user."[2] Zubek is a game developer and software engineer who has produced a formula for calculating the viral growth of games in social media; he wrote on his blog, "It's a quick and easy way to measure growth: if the coefficient is 1.0, the site grows linearly, and if it's less than that, it will slow down. And if the coefficient is higher than 1.0, you have superlinear growth of a runaway hit." And who doesn't love a superlinear runaway hit?

Detractors of the Viral Coefficient measure take issue with the fact that the calculation does not consider time and that a viral rate calculation similar to velocity is a necessary addition for quantifying virality. There's a litany of additional objections, but the lack of time is one that makes most sense to me. And in fact, velocity is one metric that also resonates with me because it delivers value in a comparative way. Velocity, as described by Jeremiah Owyang of the Altimeter Group, "is the measurement of how fast an idea, embed, widget, or other like unit spreads over web properties. Benchmarked over time, acceleration and deceleration indicate

[2]Abstracted from the Robert Zubek/Blog, Viral Coefficient Calculation, 1/30/2008. http://robert.zubek.net/blog/2008/01/30/viral-coefficient-calculation/

relevancy." Now we're getting somewhere! The analogy he explains compares social media velocity to an ocean wave. As conversations increase and social media activity crests, it acts much like a wave. When more activity is generated, the wave accelerates and when energy is diminishing from the social media initiative, it starts to decelerate. Ultimately, ocean waves lose energy and peter out, or they crash upon the shores with dramatic effect. So, too, do insights within Big Data waves and social media ideas. Ride 'em when the surf's up.

Another measure for virality is the K-Factor, which is similar to the Viral Coefficient. It allows you to understand how far a social campaign spreads and who the key contributors are to this reach. K-Factor is the rate of growth for a social initiative as determined by the average number of people who will share with others in their network. A K-Factor of 1 is considered to be a steady state where the percentage of active users (that is, hosts) remains equivalent to adoption by new users. To explain this, I'll use the example of a social media application, such as one that you'd download from iTunes. As hosts abandon the app through lack of use or deletion, new adopters pick up the app at an equal rate. This keeps the K-Factor in equilibrium. If the K-Factor is greater than 1, then more new users are adopting the app than existing users are retreating, and this is good. If, however, the K-Factor is less than 1, then the app is losing hosts faster than it's gaining new users and thus is in decline.

Figure 6-3 created by Dion Hinchcliffe illustrates a strong K-Factor attained by seeding apps (or ideas) with a critical mass of well-connected influencers. The more

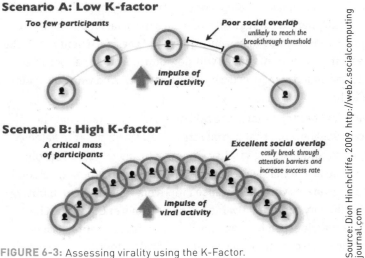

Scenario A: Low K-factor

Too few participants

Poor social overlap
unlikely to reach the breakthrough threshold

impulse of viral activity

Scenario B: High K-factor

A critical mass of participants

Excellent social overlap
easily break through attention barriers and increase success rate

impulse of viral activity

FIGURE 6-3: Assessing virality using the K-Factor.

Source: Dion Hinchcliffe, 2009. http://web2.socialcomputingjournal.com

influential the host of an application, the more likely it is that the host will bring on multiple new adopters. If you have enough of these influencers with substantial reach, then your app or idea is likely to spread in a viral way. Yet, as illustrated in Figure 6-3, having too few participants will fail to generate substantial momentum for your application to go viral. And this points back to Rule #9 in the unofficial rules of SMO, which is know how to target your audience. If you can seed ideas with the right influencers, then you have a much better chance of meeting the definition I've laid out here for SMO.

CATEGORIZING VIRAL MEASURES

Although there are many ways to quantify the viral nature of social media, I recommend bucketing viral measures into four main categories that align with source, spread, impact, and competition. You can combine these to create calculated metrics or simply use them as measures that inform your insights about viral marketing. Either way, these metrics will help to understand what happens to your content once you let go and if you hit the right audience necessary to attract hoards of visitors and prospects. Remember to choose your metrics carefully. Although, it's worthwhile to track all of these metrics at the tactical level, reporting them is another story. Find ways to communicate consistently to your business peers and use language and metrics that they can understand. Also, just because you can measure many aspects of viral campaigns doesn't mean that you should capture everything. The metrics I present here are outcome metrics, so don't feel the need to chase them all down unless you determine that they will be valuable to your business and that you can align them with your goals and exposure, interaction or advocacy objectives.

The viral metric categories I recommend include Conception, Contagiousness, Consumption, and Competition:

- **Conception:** This category of Conception denotes the origin of your social media initiative and the seeds (as well as the seeding strategy) you set forth to allow it to grow. Conception metrics to consider include:

  ▷ Original seed location(s)

  ▷ PR/promotion of original idea

  ▷ Target audience

  ▷ Number of invitations/messages sent

▶ Conception is the planning category. It's important to track metrics at this stage to document your strategy and then be able to replicate activities that work. This type of tracking is largely manual and can be maintained using Excel.

▶ Contagiousness equates to the essence of your viral campaigns. Tracking here requires both manual processes for recording seed data and analytics tools to help quantify visitors and content distribution.

▶ **Contagiousness:** This category reflects how well your idea spreads from conception to other individuals and social networks across the Internet. Contagiousness metrics to consider include:

  ▷ Invitation/message open rate

  ▷ Percent of new visitors/prospects per seed

  ▷ Number of sites propagating your original seed

  ▷ Viral coefficient

  ▷ K-Factor

  ▷ Velocity

▶ Consumption should include your engagement metrics as well as conversion metrics. It's the category that tells you if your ideas circle back around and pay dividends to your company.

▶ **Consumption:** This category indicates how well your idea impacts your business objectives by drawing consumers to take action on your original idea. Consumption metrics to consider include:

  ▷ Opt-ins for future contact

  ▷ Conversion rate

  ▷ Buzz or Share of Voice

  ▷ Financial impact

  ▷ Satisfaction impact

▶ Competition is every executive's favorite. Even if your efforts aren't the best, if they are one step ahead of the competition, that's oftentimes enough. Measure the competition using analytics and social monitoring technologies.

▶ **Competition:** Of course, it's important to keep an eye on your competitors and to see how your viral media efforts fare when pitted against the competition. Competition metrics to consider include:

  ▷ Share of Voice

  ▷ Comparative views

  ▷ Comparative share

  ▷ Category growth

  ▷ Market share

VIRAL APPLICATION OBJECTIVES

It's worth repeating that all of your social media efforts must align with your business objectives. This mantra holds true for viral initiatives as well. Using objectives helps to set expectations for what you want from your viral marketing ambitions and provides a means to determine if you reached your expectations. Yen Lee (@yeeguy) wrote a terrific blog post summarizing work that he contributed to at Stanford University on objectives for increasing the virality of social media applications (http://bit.ly/Viral_App_Objectives_yeeguy). He offers four objectives for why you'd want to encourage virality of social applications and the methods for doing so, which include:

- ▶ Increase active hosts (percentage of people who share apps)
- ▶ Increase contact rate (average number of contacts in a given time period)
- ▶ Increase duration (length of time a host is active)
- ▶ Increase infections (the success rate of hosts spreading the app)

In his analysis, Lee advises

- ▶ Promoting active hosts by offering premium content to users who share your app
- ▶ Increasing your contact rate by creating specific incentives (for example, invite 10 friends)
- ▶ Enabling user-to-user contact to shift the burden of content creation to your audience and to increase the duration of time spent with your app
- ▶ Remaining attentive to the fact that sharing is fundamentally an exercise between two people and the "infection," or virality of an app, is most likely to spread if the contact reinforces the social relationship between two friends

Each of these objectives and recommendations offers solid advice for increasing the virality of your social media applications.

> **NOTE** In addition to explaining his four objectives for viral apps, Yen Lee also offers common ranges for Host Activity, Contact Rate, Activity Duration, and Infection Conversions based on his study of Facebook apps. Visit **http://bit.ly/Viral_App_Objectives_yeeguy**.

SHIFTING CHANNELS FOR SOCIAL OPTIMIZATION

Consumers are spending more and more time online. They're trading use of traditional channels such as television, radio, and print media for their younger and more exciting digital siblings. And you can't blame them. Online media provides an interactive element that fosters a multidirectional experience capable of being shared with friends and family. Thus, it's no surprise that the online population spends the majority of its time using social networks. This is followed by online gaming and e-mail and then shortly down the list comes online video. As marketers and measurers of social media, it's up to you to understand the changing habits of online consumers and to ensure that your optimization efforts meet your new digital audience in their channels and social networks of choice. For many, this begins with video.

> NOTE   Mobile devices such as iPads and smartphones are accelerating this trend as consumers can now take their digital experiences anywhere.

Americans watch a lot of video online. According to 2010 data from comScore Video Metrix, approximately 177 million U.S. Internet users watch online video on average every month. That's about 84 percent of the total U.S. Internet population.[3] And their consumption is astounding, with an average viewing time of nearly 15 hours of online video watching time per month. Given these consumption rates, it won't be too long before the video landmark of 100 million views is surpassed with regularity. Yet creating a video that skyrockets to social media stardom is a challenging feat.

You can throw money at the problem to promote videos across multiple locations, including mass-market media like television. You can invest $3 million dollars in a NFL Super Bowl commercial or perhaps hundreds of millions on a FIFA World Cup sponsorship, but most operators don't have the deep pockets for that. Instead, conceiving plain old good ideas can produce higher engagement and a less sales-y approach. Brands can do this and offer value to video viewers in a genuine way.

[3] Data derived from comScore's Video Metrix service as publicly reported in 2010 U.S. Online Video Rankings press releases issued by comScore. http://bit.ly/comScore_videometrics

PROMOTING REAL PEOPLE, NOT THREAD COUNTS

For example, for one of their online video campaigns, InterContinental Hotels redirected funds from traditional advertising to create videos showcasing the extensive local knowledge of their concierges. The content contained clips of these concierges talking about restaurants, attractions, and hotspots within their geographic regions. The videos were tagged with metadata and made searchable via SEO tactics that led viewers to professionally developed videos that showcased locations and exceptional travel-related content rather than the thread count of InterContinental's sheets. The result was a compelling video campaign that produced more than 700 videos subtly featuring InterContinental and increasing awareness and engagement of the brand across the Internet.

Taking the Social Media Marketing Challenge

Pepsi did something revolutionary in early 2010 when they announced plans to abstain from Super Bowl advertising and instead dedicate the funds towards a social media marketing campaign. The plan was to launch the Pepsi Refresh online program, as shown in Figure 6-4, which would earmark $20 million towards funding "ideas that will have a positive impact." The overall investment was larger than even three one-minute Super Bowl ads, which Pepsi's prime competitor Coca-Cola purchased for nearly $10 million. The investment would serve to jumpstart Pepsi's social media marketing and provide a platform for sustained optimization. Part of PepsiCo's corporate goal of creating sustainable digital efforts within their core business includes delivering "performance with purpose." The timing for this gutsy move was ideal since anything having to do with social media was buzzing loudly in early 2010, and PepsiCo could potentially benefit its shareholders with a strategic investment in a civic-minded social media effort.

From my outsider's point of view (and this is purely speculation), there were a number of social media objectives that Pepsi, who runs second to Coke in market-share, could work towards to deliver on "performance with purpose." Specifically, the company needed a reason (or "purpose") to get people talking about the Pepsi brand in social media circles. This equates to the business objective of fostering dialogue. Undoubtedly, one corporate goal for PepsiCo is to grow market share whenever and wherever possible (read as performance). Thus, a secondary objective would be build-ing loyalty with its social media activity sufficient to tempt soda drinkers enough to choose Pepsi. Of course, philanthropy always tugs at the heartstrings of many. So perhaps the true motivating factor was to demonstrate good corporate citizenship as a method to do the right thing and win favor from people around the globe. Giving back is a noble cause, so even if absolutely no new Pepsi converts come from the effort, PepsiCo made a purposeful contribution and had an impact on many people. If I were running the social media campaign at Pepsi, I would measure the objectives discussed in the following sections.

FIGURE 6-4: Pepsi's social media Refresh campaign site.

FOSTERING DIALOGUE FOR PEPSI

Recall from Chapter 4 that fostering dialogue means creating a dialogue between an organization and its customers and facilitating a conversation between people—in other words, giving them something to talk about. Well, for a company that's been running Super Bowl ads for nearly 25 years featuring A-list stars such as Brittany Spears, will.i.am, P. Diddy, Shaq, and Cindy Crawford (just to drop a few names), it worked. Metrics tracked by SM2, shown in Figure 6-5, reveal that Pepsi definitely popped up in social media conversations following their announcement of pulling their Super Bowl ads in December 2009. Yet, the dialogue continued through January and into February, with a crescendo on the day of the final NFL matchup. Not too shabby for a brand that pulled its Super Bowl ads. They still got the dialogue started and maintained momentum through to the event.

Metrics to watch for Pepsi's ability to foster dialogue include social media mentions (volume), share of voice (competition), audience engagement (shares, trackbacks, referral visits to refresheverything.com), and conversation reach.

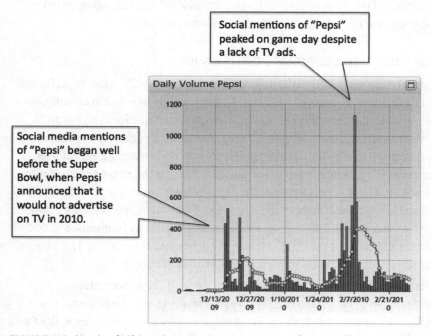

FIGURE 6-5: Alterian SM2 interface showing the number of "Pepsi" + "Super Bowl" mentions.

BUILDING LOYALTY TOWARD PEPSI

In addition to merely getting people to talk about Pepsi and its bold move to pull Super Bowl advertising, the brand is also motivated to gain more devout customers. Loyalty in the purest sense for a brand like Pepsi means forsaking any products other than ones produced by Pepsi at the risk of possible dehydration. It means asking for the product by name and definitely refusing cola beverages that come packaged in any shade of red.

However, social media loyalty is a different beast. To be loyal across social media means participating in social network activities like joining the Pepsi fan page on Facebook, participating in the Refresh Everything campaign, or tweeting your dissatisfaction about a particular venue because they fail to serve your Pepsi beverage of choice. Thus, loyalty across social media is about gaining the positive support of individuals and counting on their patronage.

Metrics to watch for Pepsi's ability to build loyalty include number of returning visitors, number of positive media mentions by individual, participation by individual, engagement by individual, and influence of loyal customers.

EXEMPLIFYING GOOD CORPORATE CITIZENSHIP

So, rather than throwing millions of dollars toward minutes of TV time, Pepsi looked to building a sustainable program that could offer tangible benefits to an audience potentially even larger than the 106 million viewers who tuned into the 2010 NFL Super Bowl. This effort, albeit subtly, declared that Pepsi is committed to becoming a good corporate citizen by engaging in philanthropic endeavors. I'll set aside any ulterior motives for generating profit and just give PepsiCo the benefit of the doubt on this one. At the time of this writing, the Pepsi Refresh online program has funded over 250 ideas to the tune of more than $10 million. Funds have been allocated towards many worthy causes, including raising awareness for autism by funding a $10,000 investment in a film called the United States of Autism and committing $1.2 million toward projects dedicated to cleaning up the Gulf oil spill of 2010.

Metrics to watch for Pepsi's ability to exemplify good corporate citizenship include the number of visitors to the Pepsi refresheverything.com web site, the number of new ideas submitted, the amount of funds allocated, the reach of the Pepsi Refresh products, and the long-term impact on overall sales.

So, the question becomes, did Pepsi succeed with its decision to shift marketing dollars to social media in 2010?

What we do know, according to metrics illustrated in Figure 6-6, is that the buzz created by pulling advertising from the Super Bowl generated more dialogue for Pepsi than Coke received leading up to game day. During the Super Bowl itself, Coke garnered more social media mentions, yet positive opinion (as measured in sentiment) for Coke was stronger during the time period surrounding the Super Bowl. Thus, by analyzing the numbers one might surmise that this was a stunt that gained Pepsi a few more media mentions than it would have otherwise received.

▶ Remember that without knowing the true motivating factors and business objectives behind its social marketing strategy, it's tough to say. The goals of the social media strategy would have been tied to those motivating factors and business objectives.

However, it's my opinion that the real analysis must happen within the Pepsi Refresh campaign. Take a look at the numbers as reported by PepsiCo 9 months after the program launch:

- ▶ 7,500 submitted ideas
- ▶ More than 46 million people have voted for a project
- ▶ 256 projects received Pepsi Refresh project grants
- ▶ Projects are estimated to have reached over 200,000 people nationwide

According to Bonin Bough, who is the global director of digital and social media at PepsiCo, the project was a huge success. He even commented that the project has garnered more votes than the U.S. presidency. Most importantly, months after the Super Bowl, when the commercials have been long forgotten, the Pepsi Refresh project continues to give back to social good.

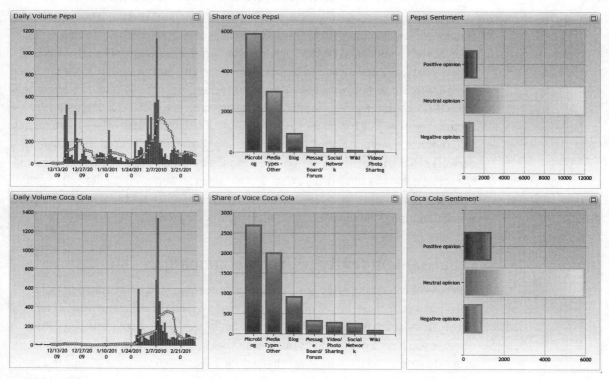

FIGURE 6-6: Alterian SM2 interface showing a competitive view of Coke vs. Pepsi.

IMPROVING BY OPTIMAL DESIGN

As you start to think about your social media marketing efforts and the ways in which you will improve upon projects and campaigns, and their overall effectiveness, consider what role optimization will play. As you've probably discerned by now, I'm pretty liberal in my use of the term optimization and of optimal design. So much so, I'm sure that purebred statisticians will cringe at the thought of applying optimal design without defining statistical criterion. Yet, it's my strong belief that social media is malleable and that it must adapt and change with human behavior. Although you can certainly trend this with statistics and by modeling campaigns using predictive analysis to intercept consumers at precisely the moment of decision, there is nuance involved. This nuance is dependent upon the nature of consumers, who are capricious at best. There's an art to social media that cannot be modeled or predicted within a standard deviation of one or two percentage points.

You can understand the performance of social media marketing if you apply a framework for measurement to identify business objectives and align measures of success with operational tactics. Optimization offers the potential to deliver continually better experiences and to propagate ideas and encourage the spread of those ideas across social networks spanning the Internet. Organizations must plan for this, too. Optimization requires mapping out the life span of a social campaign and determining how it will be fueled for sustained growth or if it will fade off with the sunset. SMO requires generating good ideas and having the foresight to seed those ideas in networks that will facilitate growth. This requires understanding your audience and the social networks where they exist. Optimization for social media depends upon three key ingredients: planning, ideas, and resources. Without these key elements, it's challenging to build sustainable social media initiatives.

Creating Longevity for Social Campaigns

For those of you racing off to launch your optimized social media campaigns and running to your social media monitoring tools to watch the media mentions start rolling in, be prepared for disappointment. Social media requires nurturing. Just because you have a great idea doesn't mean that everyone will think so. And more often than not, social media ideas that extend beyond 140 characters require a spectrum of tools, including a platform for engagement to measure success. All of these things need to be in place before you can really start to build momentum and draw an audience to your idea. In most cases, your idea will need refinement, curation, and some sharp spurs to get it going. Of course, there are notable exceptions if you're willing to throw some serious cash at the problem; if a famous blogger like Robert Scoble happens to owe you a favor; or if you hit the viral video jackpot, you can jump-start your campaign. But in most cases, momentum takes time.

Building momentum also enables measurers of social media to plan for the long-term success of their initiatives. And no, this doesn't mean that you need 60 months' worth of ideas on a whiteboard before getting started, but you do need a means to manage and optimize your efforts. Some social media efforts, like creating a Facebook page or developing a user community, will build momentum and carry much of the momentum on their own, or I should say, through the power of the user community. But they still need guidance and new idea seeds to keep them going. Consider that social media activity is by and large an "upstream" activity. By upstream, I'm referring to whatever it is that you work to guide your web site customers toward, whether that's an online conversion, a download, or a lead. Social media activity is typically the precursor to visitors entering interactions, dialogues or engagement with your company. As such, you need to keep visitors' attention by creating the content or facilitating conversations that gives them a reason to keep coming back.

Succeeding Through Ideation

Social media champions must be willing to relinquish the power of an idea to the collective masses. This means providing your audience opportunities to share ideas and to allow them to determine which ideas are good ones and which are destined to remain unfulfilled. You can see this concept exemplified in Starbucks' My Idea site, Dell's Idea Storm, and the Pepsi Refresh everything campaign. In fact, leaning on consumers to generate ideas is becoming commonplace. Marketers looking to stay one step ahead of the competition will need to create savvy new methods for soliciting ideas and allowing consumers to collaborate on social endeavors of their own. More often than not, this occurs when brands create a platform to facilitate online interaction.

> ▶ No matter how good you are, or how good you think you are, your audience is better.

While building social media platforms is not typically a low-cost endeavor, it does provide a place for visitors to engage with your content and the means to measure their behavior over time. Further, owning the platform also allows you to optimize your efforts over time and to seed new ideas according to what's working and what needs revision. Granted, there are many other ways to do this as well, by leveraging existing platforms and facilitating the conversation there. Sites that are dabbling with social media will likely work toward using existing media before diving into platform-building exercises of their own. Still, it's extremely important to dedicate metrics to your cause so that you can evaluate performance over time and benchmark success.

Budgeting for Optimization

A study called "The CMO Survey" was commissioned by the American Marketing Association and conducted in February 2010 by Duke University's Fuqua School of Business. In this annual study, marketers were asked what percentage of their budget was earmarked for social media. Figure 6-7 shows that in 2010, 5.6 percent represented the mean budget allocated for current spending on social media. This is up 60 percent from the previous year, indicating that spending on social media, albeit still a fraction of overall marketing spending, is on the rapid ascent. These numbers only get better as marketers were asked to look out 12 and 60 months to project social media spending.

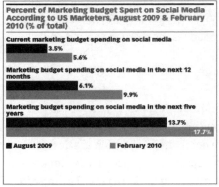

Source: Duke University's Fuqua School of Business, "The CMO Survey" commissioned by the American Marketing Association (AMA), February 11, 2010

FIGURE 6-7: Marketing spent on social media.

▶ Whether you allocate 6 percent, 10 percent, or more of your budget for social media, plan to reserve some of those funds for measurement and optimization.

The challenge I see with this and so many other social marketing campaigns is that budgets are typically defined for specific initiatives, and dollars are spent to develop the idea, produce the delivery vehicle, and launch the campaign. All too often, measurement is an afterthought and optimization isn't even considered.

Companies that want to succeed with their social media objectives must be thinking of ways to measure their success and to reserve funds for making course corrections, adding resources, or promoting social marketing activities along the way. These fundamental steps to developing sustainable social media activities are often abandoned because the money was spent on creative. This must change.

Other research shows that 86 percent of marketers plan to increase their budgets for social media this year. However, the common complaint from the majority of marketers surveyed is that they have nothing concrete to show for their social media efforts to date. I blame this on a lack of proper planning, failure to set proper expectations, and a blatant incompetency in social media metrics. Avoid having to explain to your boss or your organization that you cannot quantify the impact of your hours of hard work spent developing and optimizing social media by using some of the basic tenets of good strategy described in this book.

SUMMARY

Deploying a process of continuous optimization requires that marketers understand what they're trying to achieve and how they will identify success. When working on optimization tactics, keep in mind that this term and many of the concepts of optimization are ambiguous and even foreign to your colleagues who are unfamiliar with marketing terminology. Make it easier for them by clearly defining what you're talking about with regards to optimization. You can accomplish this using general terms like planning, evaluating, and refining your efforts. But when applying measures of success, get specific by using categorization techniques such as bucketing metrics into groups of conception, contagiousness, consumption, and competition. Also remember the key aspects of social media optimization, which include sharing, virality, and impact. Work to ensure that everyone involved in your social media programs understands the metrics you use to quantify success and leverages the same definitions and formulas.

But perhaps most of all, consider that optimization can also be a change in your way of thinking. You optimize your social media efforts to attain continuous improvement. Sometimes improvement occurs by changing your way of thinking. This may require being real, being humble, staying fresh, and letting go of your ideas. In many cases, letting go of social media ideas provides you with important feedback and critical insights that allow you to optimize for improvement.

PART III

FINDING THE BIG SOCIAL MEDIA PAYOFF

Tracking the Elusive ROI in Social Media

If you flipped straight to this chapter in hopes of finding the magic solution for calculating the return on investment (ROI) in social media, let me put a pin in that thought balloon straight away. There is no quick fix here and there certainly isn't a one-size-fits-all approach to quantifying the returns of your social media programs. Although many marketers are getting close to assembling the pieces necessary to honestly evaluate returns on their investments, the nuances and shades of gray clouding this valuation are numerous. However, it is possible to break through the clouds to find your way toward quantifiable returns.

▶ Don't buy the social media ROI snake oil. You can calculate ROI, but not with an elixir, a calculator, or a magic pill.

Organizations that are most successful in summing up the value of their social media efforts establish baselines for determining where they are today and where they end up as a result of social initiatives. Although this harkens back to aligning your measures of success with corporate goals, as explained in Chapter 5, it also requires thinking about your social media activities in non-traditional ways. This chapter explores spending trends in social media; explains how to think differently about the value of your customers; covers success stories from the field; and discusses how to bring it all together so you can understand the impact of social media across your entire business.

DEMONSTRATING RESULTS IN DOLLARS AND SENSE

You can start with a relatively basic and generally agreed-upon formula for calculating ROI.

```
ROI = Gain from Investment - Cost of Investment / Cost of Investment
```

At face value this formula appears pretty straightforward, but once you begin peeling back the layers of this formula, you'll see that each term is loaded with variables. This is especially true with the first one, *Gain from Investment*. Gain implies that you know what your current gains are and that you can directly attribute additional gains from a social media activity. This is incredibly difficult to do. How do you quantify gains on a Tweet? How can a YouTube video with 1 million views and excellent viral distribution be translated into incremental revenue gains? The vast majority of social activities are difficult to quantify because there is often no financial transaction resulting in fiscal gains.

▶ The ROI on social media is rarely straight math. You need to factor in intangibles like exposure, interaction, and advocacy.

Furthermore, costs are relative in that they usually include bought media, but also require consideration for earned media, employee time, overhead, technology, and other elements of process. Thus, even with a simple formula for calculating ROI, you see that it can unravel pretty quickly when applied to social media. For this reason, it's important to apply some common business sense here and recognize that social activities won't always translate directly to dollars, euros, or yen. Instead, you need to determine the value of activities on a more granular level and then associate their contributions to the top or bottom line.

To put all this into context, the next section discusses spending trends in order to allow you to benchmark your social media spending against industry norms.

Budgeting for Social Media

Investment in social tools, tactics, and technology is exploding. As an identifiable segment of media, social media funding had been constrained, that is until now. In early 2010, social media projects began getting funding—if only for experiential projects—as businesses endeavored to make sense of what these tools and technology could do for them. Results came pouring in—brand awareness improved, HR found it much easier to source and qualify candidates, and development listened and found new and exciting ways to improve the product so even more people would be interested in making frequent and expensive purchases. Forward-thinking organizations put metrics in place to begin adding up social media contributions and uncovered even further justifications to deploy social media tools and technology.

eMarketer reports that 88 percent of corporations will be deploying social media for marketing in 2012, up from 73 percent in 2010 (www.emarketer.com/docs/eMarketer_11_Trends_for_2011.pdf). However, with the technology still so new zero-sum budgeting is rampant. Thus, funds need to be begged, borrowed, or stolen from other areas. Although many businesses are now expanding their investments in social media, the reallocation of budgets is often centered in the marketing department. And because they're often stealing funds from one area of marketing to fund social media, many organizations question why social media deserves the hard-fought dollars. The result is that budgets for social media activity are paltry compared to other aspects of corporate spending.

THROWING MONEY AT THE PROBLEM

Fortunately, there's a whole lot of research available on social media spending. Perhaps the most viable source is my former employer, Forrester Research. (See their "U.S. Interactive Marketing Forecast, 2009 to 2014," available at www.forrester.com/rb/Research/us_interactive_marketing_forecast,_2009_to_2014/q/id/47730/t/2). Forrester pegs social media spending (excluding social ads and staffing) at $1.2 billion U.S. in 2011. Even during recessionary times, spending on social media is skyrocketing compared to other interactive marketing categories such as mobile marketing, e-mail marketing, display advertising, and search marketing. Although the forecast included only dollars spent for creating owned social media assets and social campaigns, these activities are poised for the most aggressive growth. The forecast anticipates a 34 percent compound annual growth rate (CAGR) that will launch spending on social media past the $3 billion mark in the next 3 years.

Yet, for many organizations, social media spending still represents only a fraction of their entire marketing budgets. In the previous chapter, I mentioned a study conducted by Duke University's Fuqua School of Business and the American Marketing Association called "The CMO Survey." It found that in 2010 businesses allocated 6 percent of their marketing budgets to social media. Yet, in the next 5 years, this number is expected to grow to 18 percent. Figure 7-1 indicates that marketers, while potentially still experimenting with social media today, are planning to up the ante in years to come. This bodes well for measurers of social media because as budgets increase and dollars flow toward social efforts, quantifying their contributions becomes increasingly critical.

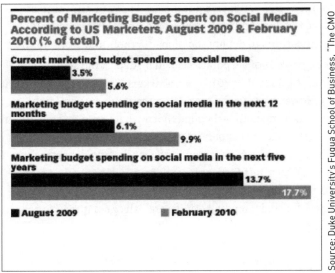

Percent of Marketing Budget Spent on Social Media According to US Marketers, August 2009 & February 2010 (% of total)

Current marketing budget spending on social media
3.5%
5.6%

Marketing budget spending on social media in the next 12 months
6.1%
9.9%

Marketing budget spending on social media in the next five years
13.7%
17.7%

■ August 2009   ■ February 2010

Source: Duke University's Fuqua School of Business, "The CMO Survey," commissioned by the American Marketing Association (AMA), February 11, 2010

FIGURE 7-1: Findings from "The CMO Survey."

> **NOTE** On average, companies are allocating 6 percent of marketing budgets to social media. This skews down for business-to-business organizations, but small businesses are likely to spend much more on social media.

In reviewing the findings from the studies referenced here as well as several other reports, I discovered the following commonalities regarding social media spending:

▶ **Companies of all sizes are betting on social media.** eMarketer reported that 88 percent of corporations will be spending on social media this year, and Forrester reported that 86 percent of marketers expected social media to increase in effectiveness over the next 3 years. So not only is money going to social media creation, but it's also expected to start paying dividends.

▶ **Budgets for social media are steadily increasing.** If this isn't a telltale sign that social media is here to stay, I'm not sure what is. Forrester's projected 34 percent CAGR is astounding. Few technologies are building momentum at such a fast clip. And all signs point to continued growth, as social media is proving its value across departments in numerous organizations.

▶ **Experimentation is giving way to programmatic planning.** I've commented on this already, but experimentation with social media was yesterday's project. Gone are the days of toe-dipping to see if the water is warm. This pool party is jumping, and organizations at every stage of the social media game should be planning for sustainability.

▶ **Resources are a nagging problem.** The most common challenge for organizations embarking on dedicated social media programs is finding and securing staff. Many begin with finite resources and hire external agencies or consultants for both strategic and tactical guidance.

▶ **Measurement is mandatory.** Each of the previous observations points to the fact that companies are building toward greater investments in social media. These increased levels of financial dedication elevate the need for quantifiable measurement tactics. Not surprisingly, ROI appeared as a top trend to watch for organizations investing in social media. With each dollar spent, quantifying returns becomes absolutely critical for protecting and growing social media budgets.

▶ *Done right, social media requires 'round the clock attention and a dedicated internal staff.*

WATCHING YOUR INVESTMENTS AT WORK

So, now that you are convinced that dollars are flowing to social media programs, campaigns, and professionals, the burning question becomes whether or not these activities are paying off. The dilemma here is that to recognize whether or not your social initiatives are working, you need a system for measurement. This is why having solid tracking mechanisms in place, with unique campaign ID codes and specific channel identification methods, prior to launching any initiative is so extremely important. The key metrics you will use to assess the impact of social media should be readily available within your organization. Examples include total number of customers, total number of transactions, average transaction value, and average number of transactions per customer. The list goes on, but you can see that these aren't social media metrics per se. They're business metrics that will enable you to correlate social activity to determine which campaigns had an impact on moving your financial numbers. Now, there are many social media metrics that are "softer" than any of the financial metrics that can illuminate the shades of gray I mentioned earlier. Yet, the key to proving the ROI on social media often boils down to the ability to illustrate precisely which activity contributed to top-line sales.

> **NOTE** Never release a social media campaign into the wild without considering how to measure its impact. Measure social media using tracking methods (such as campaign codes, personalized URLs, unique 800 numbers, and more) to identify the activity and referrals it generates.

▶ Google Analytics, Omniture SiteCatalyst, or other Web Analytics tools are necessary to understand referral traffic that your social initiatives drive back to your owned media properties.

The unfortunate reality is that many organizations forget about all these tracking requirements in their rush to jump into the social media menagerie. According to the "Social Media and Online PR Report 2010" produced by Econsultancy (available at http://econsultancy.com/us/reports/social-media-and-online-pr-report), 72 percent of companies surveyed identified direct traffic as *the* most important metric for assessing social media activity. This implies that these companies are using social media to drive consumers back to their owned web properties, which is a good thing because this traffic is entirely measurable. Yet, to correlate the impact of social activities with increased online traffic, social media measurers need to venture into the world of Web Analytics. This can be easily accomplished with free tools like Google Analytics.

By adding simple tracking codes to your primary web pages, reports like the one shown in Figure 7-2 reveal the volume and origin of traffic. This becomes valuable in determining the effectiveness of social media channels as compared to other traffic acquisition efforts. Google Analytics also allows you to track incoming visitors using unique campaign identifiers so you can get even more specific about the initiatives that are driving people to your web pages. Other services, like URL shorteners offered by Bit.ly, Goo.gl, and others, can be used to track and manage metrics around the origin of visitors. In fact, Bit.ly allows brands to customize short URLs for use across myriad social media platforms. Tracking these short links requires logging into the interface shown in Figure 7-3 to obtain details on referral sources, along with a plethora of other tracking information.

When you start to dig into social media metrics utilization by companies that reveal more than mere visitors and page views, things begin to break down. Although the "Social Media and Online PR Report 2010" offered by Econsultancy does portray some promising nuggets of optimism, there are also areas of grave concern.

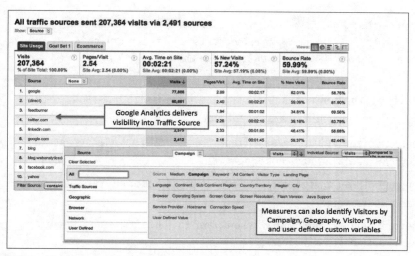

FIGURE 7-2: Google Analytics identifies visitors by source, campaign, and visitor type.

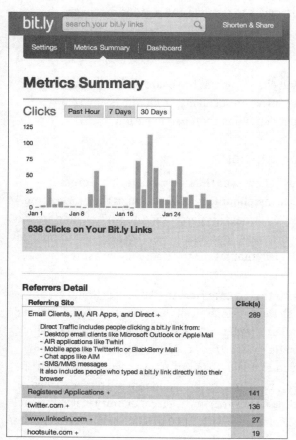

► Add a "+" to the end of any free Bit .ly link (http://bit .ly/my_book+) to see a slew of traffic metrics. Not only is this a shortcut to your own metrics, but it can also offer visibility into how well others are doing.

FIGURE 7-3: Bit.ly interface showing short link referrals by origin.

NOTE You can find a good synopsis/discussion of the "Social Media and Online PR Report 2010" at www.marketingcharts.com/interactive/86-of-companies-plan-social-media-budget-bumps-11248/.

Here are a few of the findings that indicate how far organizations really are from adopting rigorous social media measurement practices:

- ▶ 40 percent of individuals surveyed reported that they have "experimented with social media but have not done much."
- ▶ 19 percent offered that their most senior managers showed "very little interest" in social media.
- ▶ 66 percent replied "don't know" when asked to identify the most important measure of social media success.
- ▶ 20 percent of individuals responding who did know their most important metric said it was engaging customers to respond and provide feedback.
- ▶ 65 percent of respondents reported that they're not using any listening tools to monitor customer conversations about their brand.

I expect that these numbers will change across the board for organizations that recognize that their customers are active on social media channels and that their ability to react and respond is dependent upon their participation.

SPENDING ACROSS YOUR ORGANIZATION

▶ Check out Jeremiah Owyang's presentation on spending and organization of social media at LeWeb 2010:

bit.ly/SocialBusiness_Forma

The research from "The CMO Survey" showed us that, on average, large organizations are spending somewhere in the neighborhood of 6 percent of their marketing budgets on social media activities. Yet, what this percentage doesn't include are the investments in staffing and other organizational expenses, like setting up a virtual Network Operations Center (vNOC) or similar means to effectively measure your social media effectiveness.

Some of the best research on this topic comes from the Altimeter Group, where Jeremiah Owyang continues to push the envelope on all things social. Jeremiah found that among the 140 enterprises he surveyed, most have formulated their social programs only within the last 2 years. He categorized companies by their social media tenure, ranging from beginner, to formalized, to mature/advanced. Across each of these categories, staffing is, in fact, the most costly component of any social media program. This is followed by spending on advertising, then community platforms, and traditional and boutique agencies. Companies with 1,000 to 5,000 employees dedicate, on average, three full-time employees to social media. This is in contrast to the largest organizations with upwards of 100,000 employees, which tend to have teams of 20 or more individuals dedicated to social media. Depending on your corporate pay scale and geographic location, funding these teams can easily reach into the millions of dollars. Figure 7-4 shows the Altimeter Group's findings, which were included in their study titled "Career Path of the Corporate Social Strategist" (available at www.altimetergroup .com/report-career-path-of-the-corporate-social-strategist).

How many *full-time equivalent* staff do you have dedicated to the social media program?:

By # of Employees in Company	Average # of Staff		By Length of Program	Average # of Staff		By Program Maturity	Average # of Staff
1,000 to < 5,000	3.1		Under 1 year	3.9		Beginner	1.0
5,000 to < 10,000	5.2		1 year to < 2 years	7.0		Experimental	3.6
10,000 to < 50,000	5.4		2 years to < 3 years	12.1		Formalized	8.2
50,000 to < 100,000	23.8		3 years to < 4 years	10.0		Mature	20
More than 100,000	20.4		4 years to < 5 years	34.3		Advanced	24.3
			More than 5 years	31.1			

FIGURE 7-4: Altimeter Group data on staffing for social media.

When considering just how much to budget for social media, take the time to understand where your competitors are putting their money to work. Clearly, obtaining the staff necessary to manage and measure your digital initiatives is important, but you must also consider investments in strategy and infrastructure. Although these numbers reported by the Altimeter Group are a reflection of large enterprises, you can see from Figure 7-5 that, after staffing, advertising, community, and external help from agencies are top spending categories for 2011 (www.web-strategist.com/blog/ 2010/12/09/slides-social-business-forecast-2011-the-year-of-integration-leweb-keynote/). Other experts, like Valerie Maltoni, who blogs on the Conversation Agent, agree. Valerie believes that social media is the new agency-client relationship builder (www .conversationagent.com/2010/02/why-social-media-is-the-new-agencyclient-relationship-builder.html). Valerie goes on to say that "Marketing in 2010 is very much about knowing your numbers and having the ability to deliver on the numbers." Hooray! A rally call for social media measurers everywhere.

Research shows that employees are the most expensive item on your budgets, so: What does

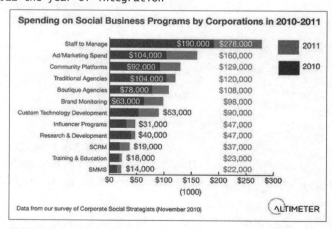

FIGURE 7-5: Altimeter group data on corporate spending on social business programs.

it cost to find that social media team member? Salaries for social media employees can range widely depending on experience, geography, and other factors. A report produced by Social Media Influence called "The State of Social Media Jobs 2010" (http://socialmediainfluence.com/2011/01/03/2011-and-the-rise-of-social-media-jobs/) looked at over 21,000 job postings for social media employees. The study is chock full of interesting findings, and their breakdown of salary ranges in 2010 is as follows:

- ▶ **Community Manager:** $60 to $90K
- ▶ **Analyst/Strategist:** $40 to $60K
- ▶ **Product Developer:** $75 to $100K
- ▶ **Editor/Publisher:** $30 to $45K

Although these are base salary ranges for employees, when calculating labor costs for your social media activities, it's prudent to consider fully loaded costs. For example, the typical organization that offers healthcare, a 401(k), and other employee benefits should plan on adding about 50 percent to each employee's base salary. Additionally, you have overhead expenses, such as setting up a workspace, laptop, and support, that are usually an additional 20 percent on top of base salaries (factor in more for phone, Internet, and home office expenses if the employee works remotely). When you add all this up, the total cost of hiring one Senior Community Manager at the top of the pay scale looks something like Table 7-1.

TABLE 7-1: Cost of a Community Manager (Fully Loaded Costs)

COMMUNITY MANAGER COSTS	AVERAGES (USE YOUR OWN REAL NUMBERS)
Base salary	$90,000 USD
Benefits (additional 50%)	$45,000 USD
Overhead (additional 20%)	$18,000 USD
Total Costs	**$153,000 USD**

▶ Anyone who attempts to tell you that social media is free doesn't practice social media. Some channels may be free to communicate on, but time, ideas, and execution all cost money.

So, the next time you hear someone say that social media is free, ask them who they have working on it. Although some aspects of using the medium don't have direct financial costs, participating in social media isn't free.

Recognizing that Not All Returns Are Legal Tender

I'll just put it right out there and say that not everything you do in social media will have a direct causal relationship to revenue. In a perfect world you could tie everything you do in social media directly to revenue. But sadly, the real world does not work quite that way, and all businesses would do well to remember this fact. Much of what you do in social media is measured in soft metrics that help you understand opinions and attitudes of customers as they communicate about your brand in their social circles. Though I'm the first to point out that opinions and attitudes don't pay the bills, getting straight down to cold hard cash often requires building relationships with consumers to understand their diverse needs and wants. Thus, you arrive at multiple sets of measures that ultimately contribute to a return on investment—sometimes directly, sometimes indirectly. You must clarify these metrics because driving toward some set of arbitrary numbers would deliver only frustration in the workplace.

> ▶ Getting to ROI in social media often requires analyzing the correlation between your metrics and financials. Although the metrics cannot always show causation, they can indicate social media efforts that had an impact.

ACCEPTING TANGIBLES AND INTANGIBLES

The ongoing debate about using "hard" versus "soft" metrics in social media is a feisty one. On the one side, you have stalwart business people who insist upon relating everything back to sales numbers. These traditionalists communicate in the language of cold hard cash, and anything less is a paltry substitute. On the other side, you have more liberal individuals who believe in nurturing a relationship and really understanding what that means before taking their target customers' hard-earned cash. In either case, both of these groups are often left wondering which half of their marketing dollars were wasted.

In my role as a consultant and measurement strategist, I often find myself mediating between these two groups by insisting that both are correct in their thinking. For matters of accounting and fiscal responsibility, there is a real need for tying social media activity to financial returns. The ability to produce accurate data on revenue earned, dollars saved, and overhead costs is a basic tenet of any responsible business. These are the metrics that belong in your executive reports, and you should be able to extrapolate from these metrics to formulate other financial social media metrics like the cost per satisfied customer, cost per qualified lead, and direct revenue per specific social media campaign.

So, although it is entirely possible to quantify such measures in dollars, there are indirect contributions that lead up to these metrics that must be considered. This is especially true for high consideration purchases or buying cycles that extend over weeks, months, or even years. Soft metrics offer visibility into your brand equity,

I highly recommend reporting financial metrics to your senior executives, but no single metric can tell the whole story. Be armed with engagement metrics that illustrate activity and participation as well.

consumer trust, and overall confidence in your ability to service clients. Each of these assets contributes to the financial success of your organization, albeit indirectly. That's why I strongly believe that quantifying ROI for social media requires a mix of hard and soft metrics to fully understand the impact of your activity.

In many business processes there are returns not related to hard dollar sales that cannot be ignored. R&D is one aspect of business that may not show a return with each investment made, but trying to remain relevant to consumers means continuously evolving to meet their changing needs. Peter Drucker pointed out that the two essential elements of a business are innovation and marketing, and for many organizations, innovation requires investment in R&D. Not every idea coming out of the R&D will show results or become a viable revenue-generating product or service. Social media is similar in this way. One of the secrets I've learned from optimizing web sites and social media programs is that it takes a lot of failed ideas to arrive at a single great one. For this reason alone, innovation is an essential element that needs regular funding to achieve even a small percentage of success.

Several critics have attempted to paint social media as immeasurable or as a media form that should not be measured in the first place. This mode of thinking is blasphemy, and luckily most measurers of social media are tossing this idea to the curb. These silly notions are being replaced with strategies, tactics, and tools that help quantify engagement in social media that can show returns on specific business objectives.

CALCULATING RETURN ON EVERYTHING

Despite the fact that not every social media initiative will produce a direct line to the top or bottom of your balance sheet, you need to measure every one. You need to do this because understanding the ways that customers interact with your brands across social and traditional channels is critical to understanding why they eventually buy from you. If your products and services are so good that you're able to sit back and simply wait for customers to buy again and again, perhaps you don't need to understand why. But the rest of us have to work to entice consumers into buying. More important to continuously deliver top-notch products and services, you need to constantly innovate to stay a step ahead of your consumers. This requires understanding the nuances of digital behavior that act as prerequisites to revenue. It also requires listening to customers and considering their feedback as you work to improve. But ultimately, it all comes back to understanding what you want to gain from your social media activities in the first place.

Measuring the returns on social media requires that you know what you're working toward and how much you're spending to get there. When the ultimate goal is a dollar, it becomes obvious because we all appreciate the value of a dollar. However, when the goal is increasing dialogue, engaging with customers, promoting advocacy, or elevating customer satisfaction, identifying the returns on these intangibles is much more difficult because we don't have a common definition for how these intangibles should look. So that's where you begin: by defining the social media objectives you're working toward and the outcome values these objectives deliver to your organization. For example, if creating a dialogue with your customers is important to your company, you need to identify the costs associated with that activity.

▶ **Return on Interaction:** Interactions can be defined in many ways, but you should take the time to decide what an interaction means to you. If you engage in Twitter conversations with your customers, an interaction can simply be an @reply exchange between your team and an individual. Alternatively, if you manage a community site, an interaction might be someone visiting the site and posting comments or creating new threads containing original content. Interactions are activities that your team, your customers, and your prospects perform across any given social media platform. As I described in Chapter 5, interactions are the gateway to conversions in whatever form your conversions may be. Whether it's a download, a phone call, or an online transaction, interactions are the digital tasks performed leading up to these events. Thus, it's important to understand these activities and catalog them to refer back to at a later time. Interactions are the activities that precede a conversion event, and only when an individual accomplishes one of your stated objectives is the sum of their interactions meaningful in the context of ROI. By looking backward from a conversion event, you will be able to see interactions that led up to the event and then evaluate the cost per interaction against the sum of your financial gains.

▶ **Return on Engagement:** Thinking about your return on engagement can get incredibly complex in a hurry, as you read back in Chapter 6, yet it doesn't need to be. Engagement can simply be a method to understand how actively customers or prospects are interacting with your social offerings. Building off the previous definition for interactions, engagement is simply the sum of several interactions. For example:

▷ On a social network, users could be considered engaged if they spend over 10 minutes on the site and click though a minimum of five links.

Remember that calculating return on objectives is an introspective exercise. Don't take my definitions here, but instead adapt this methodology to fit your business.

> ▷ For a community platform, engagement could be defined as multiple visits in any given time period, or the number of threads someone reads and the number of responses posted.

> ▷ Or if you are using micromedia channels for delivering customer service, engagement could be defined as the number of @replies or mentions of the brand in social channels.

In each of these instances, you should have specific goals in mind for visitor and user interactions, and those goals can be quantified using a measure of engagement.

▶ **Return on Satisfaction:** The ability to quantify a return on satisfaction is dependent on your ability to survey your customers in a systematic and repeatable way. Lots of digital survey tools exist out there, and understanding the satisfaction of your customer base is critically important to providing good products and services. When working to assess the satisfaction of customers across social media channels, it's a good idea to ask them if they accomplished what they set out to do. If the answer is yes, dig deeper to determine if they were satisfied. Although I'm oversimplifying here, the ability to assess whether you met a customer's expectation is a valuable piece of data. From this, you can begin to understand your percentage of satisfied customers and even extrapolate the value of a satisfied customer in financial terms when correlated to sales data.

▶ **Return on Advocacy:** When thinking about a return on advocacy, the place to start, as with all calculations of return, is to know your baseline costs and then measure the impact of your advocates. Impact can be determined by referrals, positive sentiment, or goodwill that a brand ambassador shows toward your organization. Although advocacy may not appear on the bottom line of your P&L, you can assess the effectiveness of your advocacy programs by making correlations to advocacy and subsequent sales. For example, analyze data from your social advocates to determine whether members of their social graph are indeed becoming your new customers.

▶ Though this may require a social media monitoring tool and some skilled analysis, it's not too much of a stretch to make inferences about how new customers were exposed or influenced by your stable of loyal advocates.

CAUTIONING AGAINST ROI CALCULATORS

A query on your favorite search engine for a social media ROI will produce tens, if not hundreds of thousands, of results in just fractions of a second. There are numerous books on the topic that go into far greater detail than I do here. Many of those authors are vehement about the fact that there are precise formulas for defining ROI.

Some even develop social ROI calculators as well. But what the multitude of search results won't tell you is that calculators are only as good as their assumptions and the data that you enter into them. Be wary. Although some will tell you that $99.99 will buy the best ROI calculator money can buy, you must recognize that success usually can't be measured adequately with an off-the-shelf product until you customize it to fit your business. Success, or in this case ROI, needs to be quantified according to your goals and calibrated to your efforts.

One individual's effort to produce a social media ROI calculator was deftly shredded by Olivier Blanchard on his BrandBuilder Blog. Blanchard is overtly skeptical of calculators in general and perhaps overly harsh toward the one referenced in his blog post, "How NOT to Calculate Social Media ROI." (You can see the full critique at http://thebrandbuilder.wordpress.com/2009/05/29/how-to-not-calculate-social-media-r-o-i/.) Although the calculator in question is flawed in several ways, Blanchard points out that the major flaw is absolutely no inclusion of revenue metrics.

Olivier's blog post helped me to think through some important concepts about quantifying social media ROI that I feel are worth reiterating:

▶ **Don't fall victim to inside-the-box thinking.** Attempting to measure social media in the context of impressions and page views is the wrong way to go here. Using antiquated measures of success just because your executive team—or technophobe colleagues—understand them is just plain lazy. Take the time to explain that social media is about the interaction between your brand and your customers, and then develop measures that establish the strength of these interactions and how they correlate to revenue over time.

▶ **Don't assign arbitrary value to activity; valuate your calls to action!** Don't kid yourself into thinking that your social conversations are contributing directly to your top-line revenue. For most businesses, conversation is the allure, but only *some* conversations will have a definitive call to action that results in a conversion. I say *some* here because you shouldn't be selling at every social media street corner, unless you aspire to be a snake oil salesman. Conversations can be effective for answering questions, attracting eyeballs, and drawing attention, but remember that these are not the metrics you report to your executives until you convert the conversations into dollar signs.

▶ **Social media is about engaging and communicating with people and this is a cost of doing business.** If you're good at engaging and communicating across social media channels, you may benefit from cost savings or even incremental revenue. But more often than not, the returns that you gain from social media activity are precursors to cash. You participate because it's where your customers are, and you can build relationships with them by offering genuine interaction and vehicles for feedback, entertainment, or commerce. However, you must evaluate the value of these relationships and your social media output. Once you can attribute the value of your activities as they relate to your objectives, you can plot their impact on financial sales numbers over time.

Making a Business Case for Social Media

▶ Offer a financial focal point for each social media initiative. It should include costs, a timeline, and expected returns. Additionally, the focal point must include a plan for how you will measure results.

We are advocates of social media applied to business; making a case for social media is what we do. Experience shows that the foundational component of building a case for social media at the C-suite must include timelines and financial terms, despite what I just wrote about calculating a return on everything. Those metrics are for you. Business stakeholders and executives need a financial focal point to make decisions regarding social media. When you cannot quantify the exact return that you anticipate from any social media activity, the next best thing is to offer precise costs, a precise plan for measurement, and an impact projection. This impact projection should be a well-formed hypothesis founded in data that shows what you expect to achieve and how long a timeline you need to get there.

Increasing revenue is an outcome near and dear to the heart for executives. Lowering cost is another, and establishing compliance with a government regulation is yet another. Each of these has an impact on the net income and the ability to conduct business; so when discussing a business application for social media with a business person, be sure to start and finish with one of these key drivers.

KNOWING YOUR COSTS

▶ Start quantifying social media costs on a napkin if you must, but quickly arrive at a legitimate spreadsheet. Use this as a tool to identify fixed social media costs, as well as labor and campaign level variables, and be sure to track them over time.

Okay, these are the basics, folks. Take the time to know your costs. Don't guess, don't estimate, don't ballpark—nail them down. If you haven't figured this out already, take the time to perform some cocktail napkin calculations to determine how much your social campaigns cost. Then ditch the cocktail napkin and start working on a spreadsheet. You should know every fixed cost (such as business overhead and labor) as well as every campaign cost (such as cost per campaign and promotional/advertising costs) and be able to track them over time. Without a solid understanding of these expenses—or at minimum, realistic quotes for services that you are considering—you will never get to ROI. You must know your costs.

Consider the following social media cost categories when working toward calculating ROI:

- **Labor:** Yes, social media requires actual people who will perform the actual work. Social interaction is a cost of doing business today. It's certainly not a pet project that you assign to an intern. Social media programs require people, and the bigger the rock star, the more they cost.

- **Training:** In addition to hiring the right people to work on your social media programs, you also need to offer them adequate training to perform their jobs. Although this does apply to your front line social media employees, it should extend to your entire organization as well so that they are familiar with social media policy and know what's permissible and what's taboo regarding social exploits.

- **Development:** At some point, your company will develop methods to leverage social media. These efforts may include community sites, blogs, YouTube channels, Facebook fan pages, and many, many other types of properties that haven't even emerged yet. Each of these will cost something, and it's your job to calculate what those costs will be.

- **Campaigns:** Once you've got the platform for deploying social media and getting the word out, you need to start executing. Each initiative you deliver will have costs associated with it, from strategy, to creative, to measurement, to deployment, to ongoing management. Do your homework to find out how much time and creative horsepower is required for each initiative so that you can accurately calculate costs.

- **Social Technologies:** I've offered examples of numerous tools that you can use to measure and monitor social media throughout this book, and more will be detailed in Chapter 8. Although some are free, others can be quite expensive. Understand the base costs associated with any investment in technology (such as data fees and implementation expenses), and also consider the ongoing costs (such as data storage and professional services). Few technologies have a single payment and most will require implementation fees, ongoing maintenance, and other services. Don't underestimate.

- **Agencies and Consultants:** For most organizations social media is a team effort that utilizes both internal and external resources. Understand that any time you bring in external resources, there will be costs. Ensure that you establish the entire scope of work that your external partners will deliver, including training and ongoing support, so that you don't have any surprises.

▶ **Business Overhead:** All businesses cost money to operate and yours does too. How much of the business overhead you include in your ROI calculations will vary based on the accounting practices at your company. Take the time to sit down with your financial officers to understand what elements of overhead should be included in your ROI calculations and work with consistent methods for inclusion on an ongoing basis.

Table 7-2 offers a simple worksheet for calculating costs. Use this worksheet as a starting point or get more elaborate, but ensure that you're tracking both projections and actual costs.

TABLE 7-2: Social Media Cost Category Worksheet

CATEGORY	PROJECTED COST	ACTUAL COST
Labor		
Training		
Development		
Campaigns		
Social Technologies		
Agencies and Consultants		
Business Overhead		
Other Expenses		

Blogger Mack Collier assembled a pretty good list of costs associated with launching social media programs. He also does a great job in his blog post "How much does Social Media cost companies in 2011?" to help organizations think about the desired outcomes for their social media activities. Whether you create a program to increase awareness or develop a campaign to generate leads, be sure to understand what you're getting into with regard to the time and effort it will take to manage these social activities and then think about the actual costs of getting in the game. Here are a few of the pricing guidelines that Mack offers:

▶ **Blog:** Design and develop, outsource some content (average $3,000/month)

▶ **Twitter:** Establish and build following, training included (average $2,000/month)

▶ **Facebook:** Create a fan page, with initial training (average $3,000/month)

Mack goes on to deliver much more detail and guidance than I've shared here, so check out his blog at http://mackcollier.com/how-much-does-social-media-cost-in-2011/ to learn more about his experience with costs associated with social media setups.

MEASURING YOUR ACTIVITY

You must quantify all your social media efforts to have any semblance of tracking progress toward your goals. And, if you want to calculate how much this actually costs and the returns on your investments (which you should), measuring your activity is paramount. I'll argue till I'm blue in the face that this applies to tangible measures that offer visibility into the direct impact of social efforts on sales as well as the intangibles, like engagement and satisfaction, that contribute to your overall social media program success.

That said, I want to offer the following three ROI metrics you can't live without:

▶ **Quantity:** This is a measure of volume and treads dangerously close to counting metrics that I derided previously because of their inability to provide clear and comprehensible value to your most senior executives. Yet those who were paying attention will recall that such metrics are the granular building blocks of other calculations that do add up to business value metrics. You need metrics like quantity of visitors, quantity of new visitors, and quantity of engaged visitors to help you measure the effectiveness of your actions. You also need quantity metrics to calculate the impact of each individual's cost and potential value.

▶ **Cost:** Once you know the quantity of visitors/leads/re-Tweets/what-have-you, you can calculate the costs associated with these actions. Keep in mind the caveats I mentioned earlier about fully loaded costs, but use these cost calculations to determine how much you're spending on each effort. In some cases, these will be the metrics you build from that allow you to reach quantifiable ROI calculations. Examples include cost per interaction, cost per engaged visitor, and cost per satisfied visitor. Understanding the costs you incur to achieve your desired actions will enable you to clarify what is required to derive revenue.

▶ **Conversion:** Conversion is the gold we all so desperately seek. Whether your conversion events are financial or figurative, they should represent quantifiable value to your organization. Make these the metrics that you follow closely and that everyone in your organization understands. In some instances, a conversion event can be downloading a form or answering a call to action, but like financial conversion events, these too should have a monetary value. Don't guess at it, but actually do the work to quantify what it means in dollar values. For example, if 20 percent of the individuals who download your whitepapers end up as truly qualified leads in your sales cycle, you can determine their value based on this data.

CONVINCING YOUR BOSS

Katie Paine likes to say that if you really have to justify social media, you're doing something wrong. I agree with this statement for getting started with social media, but the reality is that to secure more dollars for your efforts and to grow beyond startup social media programs, you have to demonstrate returns. This is the only way that a fiscally responsible organization will appreciate the value of your social media efforts. Thus, you do need to prove it to your boss and your boss's boss on a recurring basis. As with any digital initiative, you will have successes and failures, but if you do things right, the former will outweigh the latter.

This is why it's critical to develop your social tactics in the context of business objectives and corporate goals. When proving the value to your senior leaders, use examples and metrics of social activities that contribute to company goals. Consider HR, for example. Recent stats show that 95 percent of companies use LinkedIn to find and attract employees. A personal account on LinkedIn is free and a business account starts at $25. If using this channel, quantify cost savings of using social media versus employing a contract recruiter. For product development, a great example is Dell and its IdeaStorm.com community. As of January 2011, over 15,000 ideas have been submitted by members, and other members have given those ideas a thumbs up/thumbs down over 700,000 times and made comments on them 90,000 times, resulting in 430 ideas implemented to date. These are ideas that engineers may well have come up with on their own, but by harnessing the power of the community on IdeaStorm they let their community vote on what was important to them, and this was a product of social media. These contributions have value.

Gary Vaynerchuk of WineLibrary.com and the author of *Crush It* one time decided to establish the power of various media to generate new orders for his wine distribution business. He made legitimate investments in direct mail, display advertising, and Twitter. The results (Table 7-3) put in sharp contrast the ability of the various media to create revenue.

TABLE 7-3: WineLibrary.com's Channel Comparison

MEDIA	LABOR COST	CAMPAIGN COST	NEW CUSTOMERS
Direct mail	$2,500 (est)	$15,000	200
Display advertising	$2,500 (est)	$7,500	300
Twitter	$2,500 (est)	$0	1,800

The cost for fulfillment from any of these channels is the same, so the equation can be directed more at the pre-production and development cost. For direct mail and billboard, pre-production and creative costs would be comparable, but is the cost for Gary's Twitter presence really $0? Not by a long stretch. If you consider that the cost of Gary's time is in the hundreds of dollars an hour, and that the time spent developing his 800,000+ followers has taken many, many hours, you then can approach what the actual costs are.

Gary didn't make these investments based on an ROI equation. He's an entrepreneur and justifies investments of time, effort, and dollars into social media tactics to promote his business. I applaud this level of executive decision-making. But recognize that it's possible because Gary sits atop the food chain at WineLibrary.com. The rest of us can encourage entrepreneurial business decision making, but at some point the ability to make a more quantifiable decision is needed. Here is where you can begin to look at specific aspects of the customer life cycle and evaluate the benefits.

SMASHING YOUR MARKETING FUNNEL

It's my opinion that marketers have been kidding themselves for quite some time now by entertaining the notion that consumers adhere to linear buying patterns. The delusion is commonly visualized using a funnel that welcomes customers in with enticing acquisition whispers and ushers them through the narrows of the funnel, with conversion tactics leading to the ultimate green pasture that is revenue. This funnel sounds appealing, and marketers, Web Analytics professionals, and myriad sales personnel have used it in attempts to understand customer behaviors. Yet, the reality is that consumers don't follow anything close to a funnel when considering or purchasing products and services.

This funnel metaphor is defunct because consumers today have an abundance of choice. Previously, when there were fewer brands to choose from or fewer services to deliberate over, the funnel may have worked for understanding the buying stages of

▶ There is no marketing funnel. Consumers engage with their social networks first. Then, if you're lucky, they consider your brand along with a multitude of others when making buying decisions.

a typical customer. But these conventional modes of thinking no longer hold true. Yet all of them are predicated on the funnel as a visual tool that helps show where your ROI comes from. This couldn't be more misleading. That's why I advise you to smash your conversion funnels and your outdated methods of marketing and accept a new paradigm for understanding outcomes by interacting with customers wherever they are in their purchasing life cycles.

Funneling Doesn't Work

Traditional customer life cycle proponents will have you believe that individuals progress through several definitive stages on their way to delivering your ROI. Most often the path they paint begins with acquisition efforts that work to build awareness, attract attention, and serve as methods to get potential customers through your virtual front doors. These efforts are the basis of myriad marketing efforts, and entire teams of people are dedicated to customer acquisition efforts. In fact, the entire $20 billion search marketing industry has evolved on the notion that you can pay for traffic to your web site and use this as a means of adding new prospects to your pipeline. I'm not condemning search marketers or the way they do business, because in fact search is one of the most calculable media. You can quantify your return on search marketing investments because you know your costs and you know your returns. Further, you dictate the price at which you are willing to pay for traffic based on keywords and either toggle up or down depending on your budgets. Using a relatively simple conversion analysis process, you can determine the value of each of your newly acquired customers and compare referral channels against each other.

These acquisition efforts aren't the problem, but rather the problem is people who think they can simply pour individuals into the top of the funnel and watch as they fall out the profitable side. It doesn't work this way.

FUNNELING INTO A FALLACY

Consider that the average online conversion rate of a retailer is 3 percent. Although organizations that practice testing and conversion optimization will routinely outperform this number, it's ridiculous to think that an effort with only 3 percent effectiveness is a viable means of conducting business. That's dysfunctional to me. The next part of the funnel fallacy exists in the "so-called" consideration stage. Carefully constructed images like the one in Figure 7-6 would have you believe that during the consideration phase, prospects are nicely contained within the walls of your funnel and are progressing their way through to conversions. The obstacles typically presented in this phase are poor online processes, lack of intuitive web sites, and malfunctioning online order forms. Although these are real concerns for individuals who are researching your products and working their way through your corporate information, this happens only after a decision to purchase has been made! Unless something is really broken, such obstacles are rarely impediments to conversion.

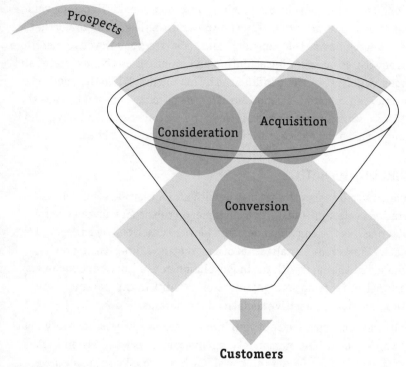

Customers

FIGURE 7-6: The marketing funnel concept is flawed.

The reality is that 90 percent of customers research online prior to making purchases. They use social media and digital channels as a means to gather information about your company, your products, and your customer service track record. Yet, as you saw in Chapter 3, research shows that consumers trust each other more than they trust you. And they'll reach out to their social networks for guidance and advice during the course of their research. This means that these customers aren't contained within the walls of your funnel at all. They're out on social networks talking to peers, reading reviews from strangers, and keeping their options open during their process of deliberation. Another stark data point that becomes important here is that 40 percent of individuals will research products on one site and then go elsewhere to buy.

► Even the best Web Analytics tools are challenged to create accurate funnels because visits occur over multiple sessions and customers rarely follow the exact sequence of steps you anticipate.

Seasoned marketers will know that these concepts aren't really all that new. This has been an issue for some time, and I'm not the only one calling it out. David Edelman wrote a similarly themed article for the *Harvard Business Review* called "Branding in the Digital Age: You're Spending Your Money in All the Wrong Places" (http://hbr.org/2010/12/branding-in-the-digital-age/ar/1). In his piece, David illuminates the consumer decision journey by showing consumers considering and evaluating across multiple brands prior to making any purchases. He goes on to say that marketers often overemphasize the "consider" and "buy" stages of the customer life cycle. Edelman advocates for spending attention and resources on the "evaluate" and "advocate" stages, which are entirely influenced by new media. When this method is effective, consumer relationships strengthen after the purchase in what he calls the "loyalty loop." This loop creates the bond between the customer and the brand, and if it is strong enough, this bond entices the customer to become a loyal fan.

CHASING A CIRCUITOUS PATH

Rather than following a linear path that begins with an acquisition effort, flows into a consideration cycle, and ends with a customer on the other end, or even following a circular one like the consumer decision journey described by Edelman, I offer an alternative. Take your visualization of a marketing funnel, turn it on its side, and commence smashing it with the biggest hammer you can find. Consumers don't follow a funnel and forcing your organization to think in this paradigm will limit your ability to deliver innovative social media programs.

► To become engaged with your brand, consumers must first have exposure to it. Consider generating exposure one of the precursors to accruing revenue.

Instead, consumers become aware of your brand through advertising, everyday exposure, and word-of-mouth recommendations from members within their social graph. Rather than setting their sights on one single brand and learning all they can about it, a more realistic scenario shows that consumers first become aware of products and services by observing them in the world around them. These casual encounters may include things like noticing a sleek new model sedan while sitting in highway traffic, or talking with a neighbor about their satisfaction with a particular brand of barbeque grill, or spotting the new packaging of a familiar product on a supermarket aisle end-cap. All of these touch points serve to build a consumer's exposure to a brand and its products and offerings. These exposures happen in both the real world and social media channels.

The consumer mentality begins to change when individuals are actually in-market for making a purchase. This is the point when individuals actually decide that they are going to buy and begin their process of winnowing down the choices. Brands with high exposure may enter into dialogues with these prospects, but diligent consumers will likely expand their knowledge to consider other available alternatives as well. The influences at this dialogue stage of the customer journey are plentiful, and brands that make the first cut are accelerated into the interaction stage, where research becomes more diligent. I should mention here that the scenario I present won't hold true in all circumstances, and depending on your products or services, some stages of the customer buying cycle may be more important than others. For example, if a consumer is purchasing a pack of gum, the timeline for consideration, research, and purchase is compressed into several seconds. The bulk of work occurs during the branding and advocacy stages, where you really have to win over customers. Alternatively, when consumers are purchasing new televisions, they may deliberate for weeks or months before making their final purchase decisions. This holds true for business-to-business organizations as well. Knowing your audience and the lead time to purchase is important to understanding where to focus efforts.

The overall point here is that consumers don't follow a straight path to conversion and ROI. Thus, it's extremely challenging to calculate ROI for all of your efforts with simplistic methods. Most individuals interact with your brand across multiple touch points, both online and off, and even after purchases are made the relationship they have with your brand is still tenuous. If that piece of gum was the most terrible thing they ever tasted, you may just hear about it. Social media plays a critical role in shaping the impressions that consumers have of your brand.

▶ When consumers are "in-market" for a product or service, your social exposure and dialogue campaigns lead them to you so they can interact.

ANSWERING THE SOCIAL PHONE

Marcel LeBrun of Radian6 likens the social media listening process to a phone call; he calls it the "social phone." Imagine for a moment that you're a business of just a few years ago and the phone rings. The usual protocol is to pick up the phone, signify you are present for the call ("Hello, how may I direct your call?"), and then listen to find out who is calling and why. If the call is concerning an opportunity to sell a product, you forward the call to sales, if the call is about a return, you forward the call to customer service, and so on.

In social media, the very same processes are at work, but most businesses are still figuring out that the social phone is ringing and ringing—all the time. Consumers, employees, prospective customers, and stakeholders of every ilk are talking about your company, your brand, and your products. Every post, message, and update is a call on the social phone. Regardless of whether your customers are talking to you, they are talking about you. Imagine where business would be if that shopkeeper picked up the phone and simply laid it quietly on the counter. The caller would talk, request service, want product information, or want to place an order, to no avail.

▶ Your social media phone is—or will be—ringing off the hook. Even if consumers aren't dialing you directly, they are most definitely talking about you.

They would want to talk to a manager or customer service representative and never get through. Not because they were not asking for service, but because the business was not listening to those calls. The social media phone is ringing, but at many businesses, the phone is not being answered. It takes only a few customers realizing that the phone is not being answered to establish a reputation of poor service—and guess where they're going to talk about it?

Yes, you may stumble into some discussions about your brand and your company, but if you are not listening for them, you will most certainly miss many opportunities. Make sure that you listen for the phone and by all means, answer it, engage with the callers, and make smart business decisions based on what the customers want.

Measuring Outcomes, Not Funnels

▶ Adopt a new customer life cycle paradigm focused on outcomes that includes five critical customer attributes: Exposure, Dialogue, Interaction, Support, and Advocacy.

So, if the marketing funnel is broken, how should you look at customers to understand the ways in which they interact with your brand? What I encourage you to do is to look at your marketing programs (especially your social media programs) with specific outcomes in mind. *Outcomes* are the actions that you desire and they are why you develop strategic objectives. As you saw in Chapter 4, numerous objectives can exist, but in the context of quantifying ROI, you can think about your objectives in terms of their resulting outcomes. Potential outcomes that you may look toward when engaging with customers across social media include exposure, dialogue, interaction, support, and advocacy. Although there are certainly other factors that come into play, these five categories can help you to put your social media activities into a measurable perspective.

The new consumer marketing outcome paradigm isn't linear, and it tends to amplify or diminish over time as consumers go in or out of market for new products and services or as the seasons change. For example, someone might ask me in the middle of the summer what brand of snow skis I prefer. Although I'm sure to have an opinion about this and offer my guidance to anyone inside or out of my social circle, I'm not likely to be proactive about touting my favorite brand of skis, boots, or bindings in the heat of summer unless prompted to do so. Conversely, if I've just walked off the slopes from a fresh powder day, I'm more likely to talk about my experiences with my equipment unprovoked.

Figure 7-7 illustrates the five categories of social marketing outcomes and shows that consumers do indeed follow a circuitous path to purchase. In almost all cases, true ROI doesn't kick in until the initial purchase is made, and thus the work you do as marketers and measurers of social media must be quantified as contributions that indirectly lead up to that sale. The next sections consider possible outcomes and how you might evaluate them.

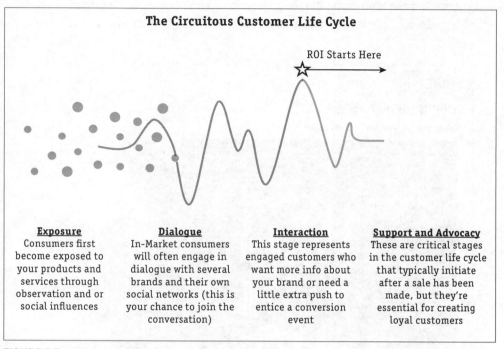

The Circuitous Customer Life Cycle

ROI Starts Here

Exposure	**Dialogue**	**Interaction**	**Support and Advocacy**
Consumers first become exposed to your products and services through observation and or social influences	In-Market consumers will often engage in dialogue with several brands and their own social networks (this is your chance to join the conversation)	This stage represents engaged customers who want more info about your brand or need a little extra push to entice a conversion event	These are critical stages in the customer life cycle that typically initiate after a sale has been made, but they're essential for creating loyal customers

FIGURE 7-7: Evaluating desired outcomes along the customer purchase path.

AMASSING EXPOSURE

Exposure is gained by putting campaigns out into the field, empowering your advocates to speak on your behalf, and ensuring that you engage in activities in which your brand will be visible. Exposure opportunities vary wildly across industries and channels. If you work for a major consumer packaged goods brand, your opportunity for exposure will be much greater than if you work for a small business. Yet, amassing exposure is dependent upon your ability to find your audience and determine which social media channels they utilize—and to focus your programs accordingly.

Example: Blendtec is a pioneer in the category of growing awareness. Their relatively obscure blender company is a social media darling that has attracted millions of YouTube viewers by destroying coveted items such as the iPad, shown in Figure 7-8, to showcase the power of the Blendtec.

Calculating returns for Blendtec: For this exposure campaign, my calculations for ROI would weigh the production costs associated with generating the videos and purchasing the soon-to-be-blended products against the visitors exposed to the videos. I would track video views and their correlation to sales over defined time periods.

FIGURE 7-8: Blendtec's highly effective YouTube video.

CREATING DIALOGUE

Dialogue is different from exposure because it's your opportunity to ignite conversations about your brand, products, and services in the marketplace. Although you may not always initiate the dialogue, nor can you control the conversation entirely, you can deliver accurate and consistent information. Many brands are sparking dialogues with their customers on Facebook, and Webtrends recently conducted a study that showed that Facebook fans are more likely to purchase.

Example: Coca-Cola is one of the top brands on Facebook, according to FanPage-List.com, and with over 23 million fans, I should hope so. But what Coke is doing with their social marketing initiatives on Facebook is offering a way for their fans to communicate with the brand and with each other. The dialogue may go in many directions, yet the benefit to the brand is that it is all centered on Coke.

Calculating returns for Coca-Cola: Finding the ROI for large brands that sell in multiple locations, such as Coca-Cola, is challenging indeed. The exposure they gain from Facebook can be weighed against the costs of generating dialogue with similar customers using traditional marketing channels. Those costs will typically amount to far less than the costs of traditional outlets, especially when you factor in the cost of having customers speak on your behalf.

FACILITATING INTERACTION

Facilitating interaction is perhaps the most active component of the new social engagement paradigm because this is the stage at which you need to listen and respond to your customers across social channels. Remember that you're exploring these stages in the context of consumer buying cycles, and when customers interact with you, it's your chance to create a resounding impression and help them through their decision process with direct human interactions and authentic guidance. Interaction with consumers across social media can happen at any stage of the customer life cycle, from new prospect to longstanding customer, so this is the one category that never sleeps.

Example: The Home Depot interacts with customers regularly across social media channels. Figure 7-9 shows a disgruntled customer's Tweet that received a response within 20 minutes. You don't have to look far these days to witness social interactions in real time.

Calculating returns for Home Depot: In this example, Home Depot should be comparing costs of traditional call center operations against what it costs to maintain and interact using social media.

FIGURE 7-9: The Home Depot reacts to customer Tweets in near real time.

It's important to acknowledge that true financial returns on investments in these stages of the customer journey won't typically manifest until the actual sale is made, or the service is delivered. Yet, each stage in the process is essential in building the confidence and credibility that's required for initial customers to enter the cycle and for existing customers to remain loyal.

Channeling Your Social Outcome Measurement

I strongly advise against developing strategies for specific channels, but it can be beneficial to evaluate progress toward your desired social outcomes across channels. So it's not smart to develop a Facebook strategy or a Twitter strategy, but it is wise to understand how these channels and others can help to contribute either directly or indirectly to your customer life-cycle objectives.

Although it's likely that you will participate in numerous social channels, attempting to force ROI metrics from all of these channels may prove futile. Instead, evaluate each channel from the perspective of a key initiative. It is critically important that the perspective early on within the organization be one of discovery, trial, and education rather than trying to drive to some artificial outcome (such as number of followers, posts, Tweets, and the like). As the information comes to light from the effort, only then can proper metrics, performance against those metrics, and revenue-related outcomes be established.

As the connections to revenue are established and the most profitable tactics for you and your audience are uncovered, you can manage, tweak, push, and pull the levers within the outcome-based model to affect results. Using the Key Performance Indicators (KPIs), you will be able to quickly see what affects revenue and drive investment into those aspects of the program that provide an optimum result.

BUILDING OUTCOME-BASED RETURN METRICS

The metrics used to help manage the customer life-cycle process need to be crafted so that people can understand them and so that the data can be applied in a meaningful way. The information derived from the data needs to helps businesses identify changes in key performance areas such as acquisition, retention, and loyalty. The information needs to give managers insight to make informed decisions about the business and their capital investments; this includes human capital, monetary capital, and, increasingly, reputation capital.

What represents a measurable metric? At the basic level, simple data such as visits, time on site, pages viewed, members in a community, followers, and so on. At a higher level the computed metrics of conversation, engagement, and satisfaction from Chapter 5 provide a more relevant set of metrics that can be communicated more quickly to management and coworkers. The need to build a metric that is communicable and meaningful is essential to the monitoring effort regardless of the focus social media is being applied to—marketing, customer service, or HR—they all have relevant metrics that can be developed and traced. Table 7-4 identifies a series of outcomes and the metrics that you can use to track both progress toward these outcomes and the ROI associated with each.

▶ Calculating ROI requires knowing what you're working toward and how much you spent to get there. Many outcomes won't have direct ROI, but you must track costs to understand their ultimate contribution to the bottom line.

TABLE 7-4: Social Media Outcomes and Associated Metrics

OUTCOME	PROGRESS METRICS	ROI METRICS
Exposure	Reach, Media Mentions, Virality, and Publication Activity	Cost per Exposure Campaign
Dialogue	New Visitors, Referral Sources, Relevant Links, Active Users, User Growth Rate, Trending Brand Topics, and Trending Brand Keywords	Cost per New Visitor Cost per Qualified Lead
Interaction	Time Spent, Pages Viewed, Games Played, Contests Entered, Apps Downloaded, Messages Sent, and Comments Submitted	Cost per Interaction Cost per Engaged Visitor
Support	Return Visitors, Visit Recency, Visit Frequency, Satisfaction Score, and Ratio Positive Reviews	Cost per Satisfied Customer
Advocacy	Content Syndication, Likes, Shares, Bookmarks, Community Status, Influence, Clout, and Top Commenters	Cost per Advocacy Campaign
Revenue	Total Customers, Average Order Value, Average Orders per Customer, and Customer Lifetime Value	Cost per Campaigns Revenue per Customer Total Revenue

RECOGNIZING RETURNS WHEN YOU SEE THEM

Clearly, there are many shades of engagement and not all of them lead to financial returns. I've already offered ways to quantify some of the non-financial measures of success by looking at critical stages of the customer buying cycle. But, you should be asking yourself how to recognize—without a shred of doubt—when a social media initiative is bringing back a return for your dollar. Let's look at a few examples of real-world companies that are reaping the benefits of social media (from http:// www.briansolis.com/2010/08/roi-doesnt-mean-return-on-ignorance/).

▶   Domino's Pizza UK credits social media and its Foursquare initiative with roughly $26 million in pre-tax sales (http://mashable.com/2010/07/12/ dominos-uk-social-media/).

- Dell Outlet Twitter sales continue to grow, and the company last reported $6.5 million in direct microformat-driven sales (http://mashable.com/2009/12/08/dell-twitter-sales/).

- Houston's own The Coffee Groundz doubled its client base and increased sales by 20 to 30 percent with aggressive marketing activity on Twitter.

- Blendtec sales have increased by 700 percent since the company posted its now-famous videos on YouTube (http://www.socialens.com/wp-content/uploads/2009/04/20090127_case_blendtec11.pdf).

- IKEA credits tagging Facebook photos from salespeople and consumers with driving a 15 percent lift in sales.

- Pizza Hut's iPhone app is expected to drive 50 percent of all online sales, and the app already delivered $1 million in revenue in its first three months (http://christianlouca.com/2010/08/18/pizza-hut-exec-claims-mobile-accounts-for-50-percent-of-orders-mobile-commerce-daily/).

- Intuit's TurboTax launched a Twitter campaign to answer consumer questions and found that customers were 71 percent more likely to recommend the product because of these interactions on Twitter (http://econsultancy.com/us/blog/6091-cast-study-turbotax).

Read Brian Solis' blog post, "ROI Doesn't Mean Return on Ignorance".

bit.ly/Solis_ROI.qrcode

Although this section focuses on quantifiable financial returns, the returns you get may start elsewhere before they show up in either the top or bottom line. Imagine that the social media implementation is designed to improve sales, which it does, but only by a small percentage. In the same time period, however, the costs of handling customer service in the call center drop by double digits because customers discover the online community and post questions there instead of calling in to a customer service representative. Likewise, customer satisfaction scores improve because people feel like they are being listened to and their questions are being answered in a way they want them to be.

Revenue goes up slightly and costs fall, resulting in a better bottom line. If stakeholders were unprepared for the impact in improved revenue and were only looking for top-line revenue growth, they might consider the implementation less than successful. Closer evaluation gives a clear picture of the impact of the initiative, which is why the program needs to monitor both "above the line" and "below the line."

"Above the line" infers returns that will come prior to actual revenue; examples include blog posts as well as comments and posts about the company, products, and personnel. All these posts contribute to an online presence that enhances other online efforts such as search engine ads. "Below the line" issues are the returns that come from purchases and other income opportunities. Keeping an eye on both will help establish the breadth and depth of engagement with your customers.

Exposure Case Study: BMC Software

BMC Software was a $2 billion business with a major identity problem. According to Mark Strouse, Global Communications Leader, "If a sales guy runs into a customer and the customer says, 'I don't know who BMC is,' that's a problem that stalls the sales process. If, by our work, we ensure that never happens, then we have made a powerful contribution to sales productivity." And that's what Mark set out to do. Prior to his arrival at BMC Software, the company had very little visibility in the marketplace. His goal was to increase exposure and awareness of the brand to a national scale.

One of the first things that Mark did was to shift the mentality of the PR staff to think and operate more like salespeople. He did this by assigning quotas to each staffer based on a point system he developed. Points were awarded when stories about BMC Software were published in media outlets, with scales that varied based on length of the article, positive sentiment, and overall exposure. One example explained that "a feature story in the *Wall Street Journal* might be worth 5,000 points—double that amount if the story is positive—while a normal IT trade story might get 500 points." Strouse worked closely with his team to align its PR efforts with upcoming product development and marketing activities, thereby collaborating across the organization to improve exposure and effectiveness.

All the while, Strouse was motivating his staff with traditional sales productivity tactics like managing a pipeline and calculating the potential for accruing points. The result was remarkable. The communications team exceeded point quotas and generated 375 placements of the company in media outlets around the globe. Efforts continued to elevate the exposure and awareness for BMC as evidenced by coverage in both mainstream and tech industry publications. And the organization recognized the increased visibility by expanding budgets and continuing to support the communications program.

For more information on this case see www.lucidagency.com/docs/Social_Media_Success_Stories.pdf.

ROI across the Organization Case Study: Dell

When Michael Buck looks at social media he sees that "marketing has become the new finance" for Dell. He has a determined focus on developing and managing a social presence that has real ROI associated with it. As the Director and General Manager for the Global Online SMB (Small to Medium Business), Michael can muster support for most any of its initiatives because they have a model that helps them demonstrate on a consistent basis what the return on the marketing investment is. As long as they can continue to show those returns, the executive suite will continue to make investments in his efforts to connect Dell to the small to medium business community.

Michael believes they achieved such an enviable position by paying attention to the four pillars of Dell's online presence:

▶ **Pillar 1 — eCommerce platforms:** This is the place where the consumer can make an investment and purchase Dell products and services, engage with Dell for customer service and support, and more.

▶ **Pillar 2 — Branded communities:** IdeaStorm.com is a Dell-sponsored community that helps Dell connect to and have a dialogue with its customers around the products themselves. To date the interactions there have generated over 15,000 ideas, which have generated 736,000 user thumbs-up or thumbs-down and 90,000 comments. From those 15,000 ideas, Dell has adopted 430. A scoreboard that sits on the front page of the community lets visitors know that their input is valuable.

▶ **Pillar 3 — External conversations:** Some of the most valuable conversations about Dell do not happen on the Dell web site, nor will they happen on the primary web site for most businesses—they occur in places like Facebook, Twitter, and others. The sites where its customers usually hang out—Dell goes there and engages.

▶ **Pillar 4 — 10,000+ internal advocates:** The staff of Dell—this includes Michael Dell at the top all the way down to line employees who interact with customers on a daily or hourly basis. It is the involvement of these staff people that helps Dell present a human face to its customers.

Through the use of social media, which is pervasive in Dell's website, as seen in Figure 7-10, Michael and his team have effectively shown that they can impact the organization's top line (revenue) and bottom line (expenses). With a business model that impacts both, you can see why Dell management is willing to invest as much as they can in their social and online marketing efforts.

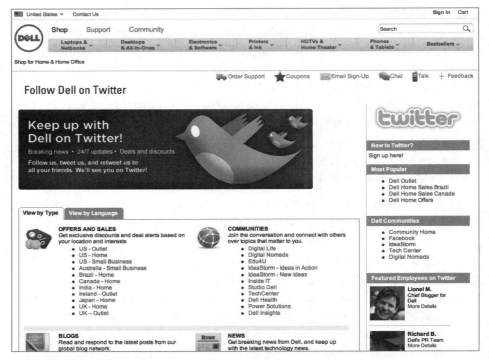

FIGURE 7-10: Dell offers consumers myriad ways to follow and contact the company across social media.

SUMMARY

In researching this chapter, I scoured nearly everything that's ever been written about finding ROI in social media. I can save you time and considerable effort by telling you that there is no magic formula tucked away on some corner of the Internet that has the precious answer.

The problem for social media marketers is that much of what we do does not result in direct revenues. We are building relationships between people, and it's hard to place a valuation on that. You can work toward that end by quantifying the value of a customer and predicting the likelihood of generating new customers from any given activity. Yet, these are still projections and estimations of attributable value.

Thus, what you do is define what you're working toward with social media to establish desired outcomes. You track progress toward these outcomes with metrics that reveal ongoing progress toward the outcome goal, as well as contributions such as adding new customers and growing existing customers. Then you make correlations to determine how these activities impacted overall sales and savings. The most successful efforts plan for this correlation by tracking all efforts and identifying when they pay dividends. Yet, because so much of what we do in social media is about building relationships between people, the ROI can remain elusive. Take the time to establish outcomes and measures of success so that you can understand the results produced by your investment in social media.

Taking the Corporate Plunge

Whether you work for a large enterprise business, a small mom-and-pop shop, or anything in between, social media will change how you operate. I write this chapter for those of you engaged in social media at any stage because the topics herein are essential for getting started, but they're also worth revisiting if you're underway.

In Chapter 3 I mentioned that you can get away with listening to your customers across social media with free tools, ingenuity, and hard work as you're getting started, but to maintain a world class social presence you will need tools that span the gambit of social interactions. That's why I set out to paint a picture of the spectrum of social technologies and define what each technology category can offer to your business. Understanding the differentiating capabilities for the multitude of social media technologies out there will save you time and energy when it comes to selecting vendor partners. This chapter will help you do just that—it also offers an insider's view into seven leading Social Analytics tools in the marketplace. I assessed these technologies by developing a 75-criterion evaluation matrix that you can carry with you to any vendor demo to determine if they have what I deem to be the critical elements of a robust Social Analytics solution.

As you roll all this up to determine your social readiness, you're advised to have a pre-flight checklist at the ready. But before taking off, I also strongly encourage you to address consumer privacy, because the metrics you collect in social media are inherently about people, and keeping the details and personally identifiable information out of the wrong hands is your responsibility. Regardless of the dubious acts of exposure consumers inflict on themselves, inevitably you're accountable for the data you keep, and you need to know what that means and how to secure it. If this sounds like something that might help you get off the ground, or perhaps help you gain assurance that you've done things correctly, then it's time to dive into this chapter.

SEEING THE SOCIAL TECHNOLOGY SPECTRUM

▶ As your social marketing programs mature, you absolutely will need multiple tools to manage your offerings and analyze your data.

Some might tell you that measuring social media requires only a keen sense of knowing what you're after and applying some good old-fashioned hard work to go out and get it. They'll tell you that fancy tools only make things more complicated and that they can be a waste of time. They're partially right. Sometimes keeping an ear to the ground is better than using a fancy tool, but not always. I'm all for a simple method of setting your sights and going after your social media targets, but you absolutely need technology to help you get there quickly and efficiently. More important, if you're working on social media for a large enterprise, the tools will allow you to scale your social media programs in ways that you just can't do without a technology assist. Thus, while you can start out by simply paying attention to the world around you using basic tools, participation can become an integrated part of the business process if you have the right technology partners in place.

The way I see the social media measurement market shaping up is that its tools allow you to listen to the conversation and engage with participants, but also facilitate workflow processes to delegate actions to different departments across your organization. Further, the tools you use for listening to social media should also provide you the ability to understand segments. By this I mean that simply hearing the chatter is a good start, but you must also be able to perform analysis to determine which channels are most active, determine which influencers are shaping the conversations, and decide which ideas can be seeded for future products or campaigns. Although many firms today offer slices of these capabilities, there's still no single vendor that's delivering a unified end-to-end solution.

That said, there currently isn't, nor will there probably ever be, a single, ultimate social media tool. The best vendors in the marketplace are delivering tools that do several tasks very well, but there will almost always be a need to use a combination of tools. Think back to the previous chapter on finding the elusive ROI in social media. That chapter offers a glimpse into why multiple tools are necessary. You can obtain Social Analytics data that point directly at outcomes that you're tracking by campaign on a very detailed level. Yet to understand how well these metrics succeeded at increasing traffic to your web pages, you need a Web Analytics tool. And further, to see the impact of visitors who were guided to the site from a social media campaign and determine when your social initiatives actually pay off, you will likely need to tie these tools to a transactional system of record. And then, when you want to do some fundamental analysis or merge some data, you may find that Excel is the best tool for the job. Although vendors like Radian6 are doing well at enabling integrations with Web Analytics tools, they are further ahead than most. The fully integrated one-stop-shop has yet to manifest, nor do you necessarily want it to. The fact is that you really want your best analysts taking data from social technologies and performing analysis in tools like SAS, SPSS, or R that can help to segment, slice, dice, and visualize data further than what's available from today's bevy of Social Analytics vendors.

If one tool is sufficient for collecting *all* your social media metrics and performing *all* your analysis, you're not asking enough hard questions. Creativity will require that you use a plethora of tools to find insights, tease out findings across social media channels, and make correlations that offer value to your business.

> ▶ Conducting predictive analysis on social user behavior is a task performed with a combination of data collection, analysis, and modeling tools. The right set of tools and skillsets changes the game from listen and react to learn and anticipate.

> ▶ The best social media insights will come from metrics and analysis that mix, mash, and mingle disparate data sets.

Learning from Social Media Requires a Spectrum of Tools

There are literally hundreds, if not thousands, of social media tools in the marketplace, and new ones are springing up every day. This fertile technology playground is rife with big ideas on how businesses can interact with consumers on established social networks or build their own custom social media sandboxes. Each one is spewing out data faster than most organizations can keep up with. Unfortunately for the modern marketer, the abundance of choice among vendors and the propagation of unlimited data do not help in the decision making process. Marketers, managers, and social media measurers need tools that will allow them to perform their jobs to the best of their abilities and enable their businesses to participate and profit from social media. Yet, therein lies the challenge because tools have become specialized to the point where tending to your growing social media presence requires a shed full of tools, not just one.

The approach I take to helping businesses understand the social media technology landscape is different than most. Today, you can find big lists of tools and technologies on the Internet, but most don't help you to understand which tool is right for any given situation. My perspective starts from inside the business, where the core goal of social media is to learn. Learning requires knowing where you are today and where you want to go. Knowing this is fundamental to your measurement. Thus, the tools I'll talk about are primarily designed for business use. Although this chapter will delve deeply into the Social Analytics category, all of the tools within the social media technology spectrum offer some degree of data capture, metrics, and measurement.

For a business to immerse itself fully into the social media arena, five core technology categories are required. These five technology categories reflect stages of social media participation and internal business process, and are as follows:

Discover > Analyze > Engage > Facilitate > Manage

Figure 8-1 shows the social media technology spectrum, which includes the five core social technology categories and vendors associated with each one. The first thing that you should notice is the big LEARN in the center of the spectrum. Each of these technologies helps organizations to learn. Whether during the discovery phase or during execution, learning should be a constant part of the social media process. That's the metrics perspective on this social technology spectrum, because learning comes from evaluating your results, which should happen at every stage of your social interactions, management, and optimization. And as you already know, you cannot do this without first incorporating measures of success. The vendors that populate the outer ring of the social media technology spectrum are a starting point that includes only a fraction of all the vendors vying for position in this space. Keep in mind that there are many, many more that I didn't include here, but that also have a place in the social technology spectrum.

Given the wide range of technologies displayed, it's probably worthwhile to elaborate briefly on each category represented on the social media technology spectrum.

> ▶ The social technology spectrum includes tools ranging from social search to social CRM and everything in between. Large organizations that are weaving social media into the fabric of their cultures use many tools across this spectrum.

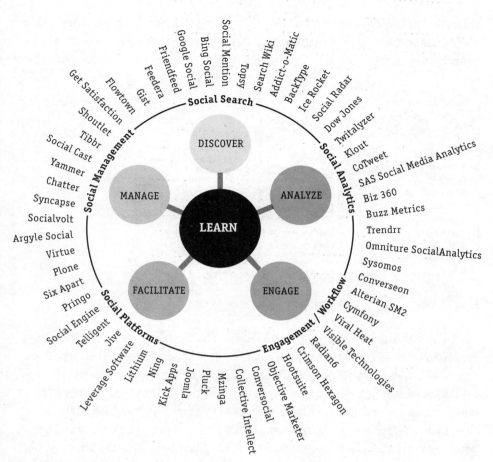

FIGURE 8-1: The social media technology spectrum.

THE DISCOVERY TOOLS (SOCIAL SEARCH)

You already know that social media pervades every corner of the web and searching the Internet using common search engines like Google, Yahoo, or Bing will turn up results from social media destinations across the globe. Even before you can listen to social media, you need to know where to focus. Discovery technologies allow you to find conversations and get a glimpse of social activity as it's happening—or as it happened in the past. Google facilitates this process by allowing users to filter search results using many presets including images, videos, places, blogs, and discussions, among other things. Google's search algorithm is tuned to pick up original content but also now picks up Tweets. In fact, as shown in Figure 8-2, typing **Twitter** into the search field will produce actual Tweets in the results. At the time of writing this chapter, Bing is already out with its Social Search beta release, which allows users to access a summary of search results across shared links, public updates, and other services.

FIGURE 8-2: Google is getting into the social search arena.

Numerous firms are emerging that specialize in helping businesses and consumers discover social content. Many are channel-specific social search tools like Tweet-Scan, BackTweets, TweetSpectrum, Topsy, and hundreds more. Yet, others still are taking social search and social discovery technologies further by scouring not just one channel, but multiple channels. Vendors in this category include Social Mention, IceRocket, and SocialSearch.com. Again, this category is exploding and the good news is that many of these services are free. The downside is that free typically means no saving queries, no downloading, and no exporting results. Yet, these tools can be effective at getting quick hits and discovering the information you're looking for in a hurry. Although they definitely don't carry the depth or functionality of social analysis tools, they can serve a purpose for exploring social mentions. And if you're really bootstrapping it or just gathering data to prove a point, these tools can provide immense value. Expect to see a lot happening in this space, with new contenders popping into the mix and established search behemoths guarding their turf.

> **NOTE** Social discovery tools can be extremely valuable for researching or getting quick results. But this category of tool is a gateway to social media monitoring that includes programmatic methods for tracking multiple queries, analyzing results, and measuring progress.

THE ANALYSIS TECHNOLOGIES (SOCIAL ANALYTICS)

When the tools make the substantial jump from single search terms to multiple branded terms and keywords that can be filtered and segmented in myriad ways, you enter the Analyze category. These tools are most commonly associated with listening platforms, and the range of capabilities is about as large as the 200 or so vendors that are competing for market share in this category. In many ways, listening tools are social search engines on steroids. They almost all start with a query-based approach to listening and will point their hearing aids at any number of media types. Some tools, like Lithium's Scout Labs, perform queries on the fly and actually search the web in real time to produce a lot of information, whereas others routinely gather pre-defined query data from the web and store it for local access and local analysis within their own proprietary databases.

Although almost all of these tools possess social search engine functions, they typically extend much further to not only scrape and present data in its raw form but also to offer counts and calculated metrics like reach, volume, sentiment, and influence. These capabilities represent the heart of Social Analytics and enable measurers of social media to assess, explain, and make recommendations for action. Although most offer a predefined set of standard metrics and calculated KPIs, they tend to fall short in the area of customization. This requires analysts to leverage additional tools for creating business value metrics. Still, vendors like Adobe's Omniture Business Unit with their new SocialAnalytics offering, SAS with their Social Media Analysis, and Sysomos MAP are taking analysis further with deep-dive access to underlying metrics and individual contributors. And some, like SAS, are beginning to deliver on predictive elements of social media like the Social Forecast capability shown in Figure 8-3.

As you work your way around the social technology spectrum, tool capabilities become more geared toward interacting with consumers. Technologies within the Analyze category that enable workflow processes that allow users to assign social inquiries to specific individuals are tunneling straight through from analysis to engagement. Workflow within social media technologies usually consists of the ability to assign tasks to members of your organization, such as follow up, investigate, or be aware. Many sites use the workflow capabilities within their social monitoring tools to delegate activities.

> ▶ Remember that Social Analytics is the discipline that helps companies measure, assess, and explain the performance of social initiatives in the context of specific business objectives.

> **NOTE** Innovative vendors effectively build tunnels from the Analyze stage to the Engage stage by offering direct interaction to all the social channels with imperceptible fluidity. Doing this enables direct consumer response without leaving the primary business user interface.

► Omniture's
SocialAnalytics
product layers
powerful analysis
capabilities
atop social, web,
and marketing
optimization
intelligence.

FIGURE 8-3: SAS's social media analysis tool offers forecasting.

Although not all vendors are taking this approach, ones that do will succeed in this marketplace. The ability to triage incoming social media data and assign responsibility and action to business users is where the analyze tools get really exciting. This workflow functionality not only offers the ability to provide recommendations for action, but also enables users from any department within the company to see the incoming data (or Tweets, blog posts, comments, or social policy infractions) and make informed decisions about what actions to take. This functionality alone propels Social Analytics tools well beyond what many other technologies have been able to accomplish because it includes an alert, a call to action, and the critical information necessary to make a decision. This triumvirate (alert, call to action, decision) of social business knowledge is powerful.

THE ENGAGEMENT PLATFORMS (ENGAGEMENT/WORKFLOW)

Admittedly, the line between the Analyze and Engage stages is blurred, as many vendors in this space are delivering functions that include both capabilities. This is actually a really good thing for businesses as you learned way back in Chapter 3, because analysis should always result in a recommendation or in calls to action. Thus, as more vendors extend their Social Analytics capabilities to include workflow delegation and engagement capabilities from directly within the interface, it places more controls at the fingertips of your internal business users. As you already know, you're here to communicate with consumers and to help them communicate with each other. Including methods to accomplish this from within the primary data collection and analysis tools is a fantastic way to achieve this goal. Tools that offer only listening and no outbound engagement are essentially like phones on mute. Currently, the range of capabilities in this area spans from no outbound engagement, to spawning windows outside the interface to interact, to fully integrated engagement from within the social media technology user interface.

Needless to say, I am a fan of vendors that deliver interaction capabilities from within their interfaces because this is the function that ties data to action. Radian6 is currently the best in the business at engagement. They've developed a console, shown in Figure 8-4, that enables users to interact directly with consumers; users can also assign tasks and categorize issues within their engagement console. Yet, competitors like Sysomos and even HootSuite (specializing in Twitter) are hot on the heels of Radian6's direct engagement capabilities from within their interfaces. All vendors that offer engagement functionality founded on analytics will enable businesses to make smarter decisions. Ultimately, these functions will be the catalyst that elevates social interactions to become a business function as familiar and as critical as the telephone.

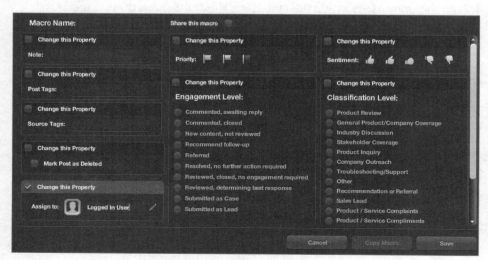

FIGURE 8-4: Radian6's engagement console.

▶ Social technologies that enable fluid communication between consumers and organizations with interface access to any social channel will become an indispensible business mandate.

Engagement technologies that really shine will be those that capture inbound messages in whatever format they're delivered and offer the business a mechanism to formulate the best response, assign responsibility for follow-up, and respond to the message in a timely manner. These tools will also track ongoing status and evaluate results all the way through to ROI using a single technology. This is the workflow and analysis process that you should be working toward.

THE HOSTING AND FACILITATION TOOLS (SOCIAL PLATFORMS)

As I've described the social technology spectrum thus far, I've been focused on finding, analyzing, and engaging in social conversations that exist on non-owned properties and channels across the Internet. But as organizations progress toward actually offering a social media destination that is owned (or at least controlled) by the business, social media platforms are required. I call these hosting and facilitation tools because examples include everything from hosting a blog on Wordpress and facilitating comments, to developing a Facebook fan page with interactive functions, to constructing a full-blown social community like P&G's BeingGirl.com.

In order to construct these social media properties and facilitate a conversation, technology is required. I won't spend much time diving into the details because they are plentiful, but it's worth mentioning that many social media facilitation platforms will offer baked-in analytics and analysis tools. Although most of them offer thin metrics when compared to the Social Analytics tools on the marketplace, you can get by using data provided by these vendors. Software vendor Jive does a good job of providing analytics and platform metrics within their interface. Figure 8-5 shows the management

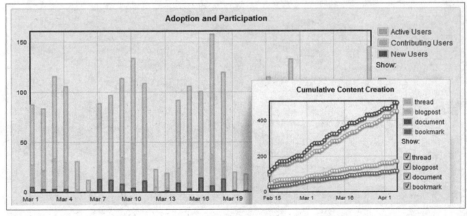

FIGURE 8-5: Jive Software's analytics offers multiple views into data, including metrics on your community.

interface within the Jive platform that offers users a view of how many people are active within the community and the type of content they're producing. Just keep in mind that performing analysis within the walls of these tools will be an isolated exercise unless you find a way to integrate your data and findings with your primary Analyze technology.

THE MANAGEMENT SOLUTIONS (SOCIAL MANAGEMENT)

I include the Manage function within the social technology spectrum because any business participating in social media that is looking to gain a competitive advantage will have established processes for managing its efforts. And you absolutely need technology to do this. This group of technology offerings includes social customer relationship management tools, internal collaboration solutions, and social media aggregation services that enable businesses to manage their social media efforts in an orchestrated way.

This is a big bucket of technologies and is likely to overflow as more and more businesses find the need to manage their social efforts. Yet, forward-thinking vendors like BatchBook are enabling small businesses to integrate social media into the business process, whereas companies like Yammer or Salesforce Chatter offer internal business solutions for allowing colleagues to be social with one another. Others still, like Flowtown, shown in Figure 8-6, enable businesses to integrate their customers' social profiles into a larger data set of information that includes holistic contact data from traditional, web, e-mail, social, and other channels about a customer. Evolutionary development of these types of technologies and services will manifest in what I've described as "true profiles," which contain not only contact information, but behavioral data as well.

As I described in several of these categories, the seams where one category stops and another begins are very much blurred. Vendors will continue to offer capabilities from multiple categories, much in the way that Jive, Lithium, and others already do today. It's also important to recognize that the social technology spectrum is much deeper than what I've initially described here. There are many vendors and technologies that I didn't mention, including vendors that specialize in individual social media channels who build extremely valuable tools for niche applications. For example, there are a slew of Discover technologies such as Topsy, IceRocket, Social-Mention, and Blecko that are laser focused on scouring the web for social banter. Similarly, for technology vendors within the Analyze category, many firms such as Twitalyzer, Klout, BackTweets, and Peerindex are exclusively focused on Twitter.

> A critical component of successful corporate adoption with social media is personal experience using social platforms. Technologies like Salesforce Chatter and Yammer familiarize internal employees with social interactions.

FIGURE 8-6: Emerging vendors like Flowtown offer creative social media solutions.

I expect that as demand for social tools and technologies increases and dollars begin to flow toward measuring social media, we will see extensive merger and acquisition activity. Acquisitions have already begun with Lithium buying Scout Labs, Jive purchasing Filtrbox, and Attensity snatching up Biz360, and undoubtedly more have happened since writing the pages of this book (see the "Stop the Presses! Acquisition Alert!!" sidebar). Within the next 5 years, there will be hundreds of new entrants into this fertile marketplace and consolidation will be profuse. Leading vendors will consume niche players with specialty capabilities that they don't deliver themselves. And enterprise software vendors will develop proprietary solutions or cherry-pick the best of the best to add to their arsenals. Today, software vendors far and wide are getting into the social media game, as demonstrated by offerings from SAS, comScore, Webtrends, Adobe, and ForeSee Results; the list goes on. One ambitious marketer named Ken Burbary created a wiki to track all firms involved with social media monitoring solutions. The list has nearly 150 firms on it to date, and it's sure to advance and recede many times over.

▶ Check out Ken Burbary's wiki of Social Media Monitoring Solutions: http://wiki .kenburbary.com/.

STOP THE PRESSES! ACQUISITION ALERT!!

In between the time that I initially wrote this section and my editorial review of it, Radian6 was acquired by Salesforce.com for $326 million U.S. That's by far the largest social media measurement technology acquisition to date. On an investor call following news of the acquisition, Mark Benioff, Salesforce .com's CEO, stated that Radian6's revenue was $35 million at the time of the acquisition. This means that Salesforce.com paid a nearly 10x premium for the Canadian software maker. As a leader in the market, Radian6 claimed half of the Fortune 100 as customers. Yet, this valuation sets the bar extremely high for other mergers and buy-outs in this space. It also underscores the importance of social media and the promise of big business benefits for companies that employ social measurement technologies. More details on the acquisition are available from TechCrunch (`http://techcrunch.com/2011/03/31/why-salesforce-overpaid-for-radian6/`).

Deciding Which Technology to Use When

Hopefully, you can see pretty clearly that the technologies within the social spectrum are vast and deep. There's a lot to sort through and understand as you journey to build out a social media program. Each vendor category across the social technology spectrum will offer metrics to provide visibility into performance. Much in the same way that these tools will be deployed and used by different functional areas across your organization, the metrics, too, will serve various needs.

There is certainly some overlap across technology categories, and vendors are likely to broaden their capabilities through development or acquisition. Yet, each category in the social technology spectrum serves a very real business need. The trick is determining when you need to go out and source each one. Further, understanding which technology category can help with your social business escapades and what you can expect in return is key to making important technology decisions. Table 8-1 is a simple table I created to help you better understand which technology fits where.

TABLE 8-1: Social Technology Category Overview

	GENERAL CAPABILITIES	VENDORS TO WATCH	METRICS TO EXPECT
DISCOVER	Social search functionality delivers quick results on brand or topic queries	Google, Bing, Social Mention, SearchWiki	Trending Topics, Keyword/Brand Occurrences, Number of Unique Sources
ANALYZE	Social Analytics functionality captures data and enables exploration of social channels, topics, influencers, and competitors	Crimson Hexagon, SAS Social Media Analytics, Omniture, Sysomos	Social Mentions, Share of Voice, Sentiment, Influence, Authority, Loyalty, Impact
ENGAGE	Social interaction functionality allows businesses to monitor, assign, and respond to social media inquiries	Radian6, Lithium/ Scout Labs	Comments, Likes, Shares, Interaction Rate, Virality
FACILITATE	Social platform development tools enable businesses to create online destinations for consumers to interact and engage	Telligent, Jive	Registered Users, New Users, Community Growth
MANAGE	Social aggregation, internal collaboration, and governance tools provide unified management solutions	Yammer, Saleforce Chatter	Social Media Effectiveness, Customer Lifetime Value

CHOOSING YOUR SOCIAL ANALYTICS VENDOR

Recognize that there are five core vendor categories within the technology spectrum that I defined, but also realize that each category offers metrics of one kind or another. The Analyze category will deliver the richest Social Analytics information that enables you to dig into consumer behaviors, understand the effectiveness of your social media marketing, and quantify the impact of your efforts. This is where the business value and outcome-based metrics reside. Opportunities for measuring exposure, dialogue, interaction, support, advocacy, and innovation are most readily available from these Social Analytics tools. For this reason, I've chosen to focus on this area of the technology spectrum. In this section, I'll elaborate on specific vendor offerings and describe what's available on the market today. I evaluate only a short list of seven vendors in this section, including Alterian SM2, Converseon, Cymfony, Lithium, Radian6, Sysomos, and Trendrr. There are many others out there and new ones are emerging at an astounding rate. The information regarding vendor capabilities in this chapter should be viewed as a snapshot in time. This snapshot includes only features available at the time of my review in January 2011. Each vendor that I spoke with had extensive product development roadmaps and big plans for where they are taking their products and services in the future.

That said, I chose to evaluate a short list of leading vendors in the Analyze category based on three selection criteria: 1) their visibility in the market, 2) sustained presence, and 3) viability as a solution that I'd recommend. Although there are numerous others that I would definitely recommend to smaller or mid-sized organizations, or even large enterprises with specific business requirements, these firms represent the most firmly established vendors in the space and, as a result, cater to large enterprises and the Fortune 1000. Several of these vendors also offer capabilities within the Engage category because they have components of direct interaction that enable users to reach out to consumers through their primary user interfaces.

Throughout my analysis I looked for several features, including setup options, standard metrics, analysis filters, key functions, data sharing options, and integrations. The following section details my findings in each category.

▶ Follow the #SocialAnalytics hashtag on Twitter to read the latest buzz about vendors and happenings in this market.

Setting Up Your Social Analytics Tool

Vendors of Social Analytics tools have segregated into three distinct modes of operation: managed service, self-service, and hybrids. The first is the managed offering, where the vendor aids its clients through the entire setup and tool-configuration process. For many, this makes the difference between a tool that spews noisy data without value and one that captures relevant and useful information straight out of the gate. Remember that social monitoring tools need to be fine-tuned to pick up on topics, issues, and social destinations that are meaningful to your company—and this requires skill. Managed solutions deliver this skill to your organization throughout their professional services teams. However, managed setups can also be the most expensive route. All but one of the vendors I evaluated have managed service offerings.

▶ Before you invest in a social monitoring tool, make sure that you know the level of support you will receive—initially and ongoing—as well as how much you can modify the setup on your own once it's complete.

The alternative is allowing clients to set up their own social monitoring projects in a self-service fashion, entering keywords and listening parameters on their own. This method offers the greatest flexibility for seasoned veterans who know what they're looking for in the social atmosphere and know how to hone the tools to find what they want. For less skilled measurers of social media, this process may end up taking more time, but can result in a strong familiarity with the technology interface and the nuances of setup and maintenance. Although some vendors don't let their clients manage the setup and data collection components of their own tools, each of the seven vendors I evaluated offers self-service capabilities, which I deem to be important.

The third option is a hybrid approach, where vendors deliver a predefined amount of support during setup and clients have the option to pay for more. This is potentially the best of both worlds in that you have the ability to tweak the tool to your own desires, yet have the experts share best practices from their extensive experience.

Other key considerations when evaluating the setup components of any Social Analytics offering is how far back each tool will go for data collection. As you're setting up these tools, you are defining the parameters for searching the extensive corners of the Internet for mentions of your brand and other valuable issues and topics, yet just how far back in history that search extends varies among vendors. Vendors range in this capacity from a 30-day default to 180 days, but many will go 365 days or even multiple years upon request and for a fee. Almost all of the vendors we spoke with maintain data for the life of the client engagement. This is a key differentiator between companies that deliver Discovery and those that deliver Analyze tools.

Another important consideration regarding Social Analytics tool setup is the speed of data processing. This feature will define the amount of time it takes to see data such as Tweets, blog comments, or any social mentions within the interface. Seventy-one percent of vendors I evaluated (five out of seven) do this in real time, whereas a few still maintain a lag in delivery. Consider the importance of this function if you plan to deliver customer service across social media, because real-time access to data will be a prerequisite for maintaining Service Level Agreements.

> **TIP** Unfortunately, you often need to start using tools in order to recognize lag time. For example, when monitoring Twitter, I use both HootSuite and TweetDeck, yet messages will show up more quickly in TweetDeck. Although both are technically real-time, when every second counts some tools are simply faster than others. If this is something that's important to you, ensure that you put this on your list of questions to ask vendor reference clients.

Other criteria I looked for included keyword limitations, access control privileges, number of languages, and media types monitored. Each of these factors will have different priority levels for organizations depending on how many employees you have, whether you operate globally, and how many brands you're tracking.

Figure 8-7 shows the vendors evaluated and their specific capabilities in the area of setup as of January 2011.

	Alterian SM2	Converseon	Cymfony	Lithium	Radian6	Sysomos	Trendrr
Managed Offering	Yes	Yes	Yes	No	Yes	Yes	Yes
Self-Service Offering	Yes	Yes	Yes	Yes	Yes	Yes	Yes
Historical Data Default	365+	180 days	365+	180 days	30 days	30 days	other
Data Expiration/Roll-off	Never	Never	other	180 days	Never	Never	Never
On Premise or SaaS Delivery	SaaS	SaaS	SaaS	SaaS	SaaS	SaaS	SaaS
Data Processing Frequency	<24 hrs	Real-Time	Real-Time	Real-Time	Real-Time	<24 hrs	Real-Time
Keyword Limitations	Unlimited	Unlimited	Unlimited	Unlimited	1000	Unlimited	other
Languages	20+	20+	14	English Only	15	20+	English Only
Access Rights Controls	Yes	Yes	Yes	Yes	Yes	Yes	No

FIGURE 8-7: Social Analytics vendor setup criteria.

Working with Metrics

The common denominator measurement among all social media monitoring and analysis tools is volume. Volume is the base measure upon which many others are founded and it applies to many metrics. Volume reveals the frequency of mentions, the buzz surrounding your brand, and the overall social worthiness of any given topic. Volume can also illuminate much about your brand and the exposure and awareness that your organization enjoys. Almost all of the filters discussed in the next section apply to volume, since they are methods used to zero in on your audience and understand the nuances of your social media programs and interactions.

Chapter 5 covered the foundational measures for Social Analytics, which includes interaction, engagement, influence, advocates, and impact. These metrics offer a common vernacular for social media measurers around the world to evaluate and benchmark their efforts. Unfortunately, social media vendors have been slow to adopt all of these foundational measures, leaving practitioners to their own devices for implementing them as measures of success within their respective social measurement programs. A handful of the vendors evaluated do offer an engagement score, and several more are deriving their own influence metrics or borrowing from external sources like Klout. A scant few are delivering loyalty metrics that begin to approach the advocacy metrics that I typically customize for my own analysis. Granted, delivering on calculated metrics with accuracy is no easy task, but the more cunning vendors are beginning to pick up on the need for advanced Social Analytics metrics.

The majority of vendors in this small sample set are offering out of the box many important components of a solid social measurement program. As detailed in Figure 8-8, the specific metrics include influence (86 percent), authority (57 percent), share of voice (86 percent), sentiment (100 percent), loyalty (29 percent), and impact (43 percent).

	Alterian SM2	Converseon	Cymfony	Lithium	Radian6	Sysomos	Trendrr
Standard and Calculated Metrics							
Social Mentions (Volume)	Yes	Yes	Yes	Yes	Yes	Yes	Yes
Engagement Score			Yes		Yes		Yes
Influence	Yes	Yes	Yes		Yes	Yes	Yes
Authority		Yes	Yes		Yes	Yes	
Share of Voice	Yes	Yes	Yes	Yes	Yes	Yes	
Sentiment	Yes	Yes	Yes	Yes	Yes	Yes	Yes
Sentiment Override	Yes	Yes	Yes	Yes	Yes	Yes	
Loyalty		Yes	Yes				
Reach	Yes	Yes	Yes		Yes	Yes	Yes
Impact		Yes	Yes		Yes		
Custom Metrics		Yes	Yes		Yes		

FIGURE 8-8: Standard and calculated metrics.

Utilizing Analysis Filters

Analysis filters comprise a core function that almost all vendors within the Social Analytics category are delivering. These filters enable you to slice and dice social metrics so that you can explore the details behind their conversations, interactions, and social media campaigns. The ability to perform meaningful analysis is contingent upon the ability to filter data to get to the most meaningful information and, subsequently, insights which can be delivered to managers and executives as recommendations.

Across the vendors that I reviewed, filtering capabilities varied in their ease of use, but 100 percent did offer this function to their clients. Filters that I look for are detailed in Figure 8-9 and include language, media type, geography, tags, demographics, keywords, and contributors.

Analysis Filters	Alterian SM2	Converseon	Cymfony	Lithium	Radian6	Sysomos	Trendrr
Date / Time	Yes	Yes	Yes	Yes	Yes	Yes	Yes
Keywords	Yes	Yes	Yes	Yes	Yes	Yes	Yes
Language	Yes	Yes	Yes		Yes	Yes	Yes
Media Type	Yes	Yes	Yes	Yes	Yes	Yes	
Geography	Yes	Yes	Yes		Yes	Yes	Yes
Demographics	Yes	Yes	Yes		Yes	Yes	Yes
Domain / URL	Yes	Yes	Yes	Yes		Yes	
Tags	Yes		Yes	Yes	Yes	Yes	Yes
Sentiment	Yes	Yes	Yes	Yes	Yes	Yes	Yes
Top Contributors / Influencers	Yes	Yes	Yes		Yes	Yes	Yes
Workflow Stage	Yes	Yes	Yes		Yes	Yes	
User Defined / Custom	Yes	Yes	Yes		Yes	Yes	Yes
Business Function	Yes	Yes	Yes		Yes		

FIGURE 8-9: Social Analytics analysis filters.

Leveraging Key Functions

The key functions offered by many of the vendors considered in this analysis are what separate the Analyze vendors from the Engage vendors. These criteria include both interactive analysis capabilities like alerting functions and the ability to annotate charts for adding additional key information, but also the ability to perform workflow tasks.

▶ Both alerts and annotations are, in my opinion, absolutely critical capabilities.

Unless you're scouring your Social Analytics metrics multiple times throughout the day, things will slip past. I guarantee it. Thus, alerts can assist you in calling out key occurrences within your social and brand monitoring activities. For example, an alert can notify you when negative sentiment spikes, allowing you to quickly pick up on and respond to crises as they are happening. Additionally, alerting functions can be used to inform others within your organization who don't necessarily want to log into the social media technology interface. Providing alerts can serve as a means to educate and inform individuals across departments within your organization.

In addition to alerts, I strongly believe that annotations are critical for any data analysis tool. The ability to annotate a report within your social media tool affords you the opportunity to explain gaps in data or spikes resulting from a video that went viral or from that time when your servers crashed and all those nasty complaints rolled in via Twitter. These handy notes, when delivered correctly, will persist across data views so that you are reminded during your analysis of what happened and, perhaps more importantly, so that others who aren't as familiar with the data as you are can be informed about why something appears the way it does.

Other key functions offered by leading vendors include engagement with consumers directly through the technology interface. You can not only see a full stream of social mentions about your brands and keywords, but also respond with Tweets, blog comments, or even Facebook wall posts. This is the future of Social Analytics tools because regardless of the medium, consumers want to have a conversation with brands, and the corporate response to this should be channel agnostic. Although doing this requires a high degree of sophistication in the vendor delivering the service, it streamlines the communication, management, and efficiency of working across many social channels.

As you explore the realm of Social Analytics, one function that you will definitely stumble upon is text analytics. Keep in mind that much of the basis for Social Analytics is founded upon the ability to discern meaning from the written word. One glance at sentiment accuracy will tell you that this is no easy task for machines to conquer. Thus, many social analysis companies emerged with core functionality in natural language processing (NLP). Although some vendors, like Cymfony, incorporate this within the root processing systems of their tools, others, like Sysomos, expose their text analytics functions to their users. Both tactics ultimately benefit their clients by delivering greater accuracy in results and deeper insights into the things that consumers say and mean about brands in the marketplace. Figure 8-10 shows the key functions of vendors evaluated.

Key Functions	Alterian SM2	Converseon	Cymfony	Lithium	Radian6	Sysomos	Trendrr
Alerts		Yes	Yes	Yes	Yes	Yes	
Workflow Assignment	Yes	Yes	Yes	Yes	Yes	Yes	
Workflow Comments	Yes	Yes	Yes	Yes	Yes	Yes	
SLA Tracking			Yes			Yes	
Direct Engagement (from interface)	Yes				Yes	Yes	Yes
Annotations	Yes	Yes	Yes		Yes		
Text Analytics	Yes	Yes	Yes	Yes	Yes	Yes	Yes
Word Clouds	Yes	Yes	Yes	Yes	Yes	Yes	Yes
Keyword Comparison	Yes	Yes	Yes	Yes	Yes	Yes	Yes

FIGURE 8-10: Social Analytics key functions.

Getting Data In and Out of Tools

The ability to import and export data is an extremely important function for any data analysis tool. In many cases, you will want to take data from the Social Analytics tool and perform additional analysis on it using tools like Excel, or incorporate it into a database for modeling or predictive analysis. This requires the ability to export data via HTML, XML, XLS, or CSV formats. Similarly, the ability to evaluate external data sources, like Web Analytics clickstream data or traffic metrics, from within your Social Analytics interface will enable you to make correlations and comparisons of effectiveness over time. Currently, four out of seven vendors reviewed offer APIs to get data out of their systems, and the ability to import data from external sources is present in several, but limited overall.

▶ At the time of this writing, Radian6 offers the best data integration from Web Analytics tools, yet still allows import of only five metrics.

For early stage social media measurers, the ability to integrate data either within or outside of the primary Social Analytics user interface will become a competitive differentiator. Integrations are the key to unlocking cross-functional insights, thus allowing social media activity to pervade all areas of an organization. Additionally, integrations will lead to the ability to trigger automated actions or feed customer life-cycle cues to marketing automation solutions so that the technologies can harmonize and deliver superior digital experiences for customers in real time. These sophisticated acts of automation are possible only with data integrations. We're still in early days for these capabilities, but expect to see significant advances in the next few years where data intake from social interactions is translated into automated responses using highly relevant messages, dynamic content, or even connections to live service agents. Figure 8-11 shows the current state of data sharing and integration capabilities among vendors I reviewed. Although these numbers may not be impressive today, this will undoubtedly be an area of growth and development in the near future.

	Alterian SM2	Converseon	Cymfony	Lithium	Radian6	Sysomos	Trendrr
Data Sharing Options							
HTML	Yes	Yes		Yes	Yes		Yes
XML	Yes		Yes		Yes		Yes
XLS	Yes	Yes	Yes				Yes
PDF	Yes	Yes		Yes	Yes	Yes	Yes
TXT	Yes		Yes			Yes	Yes
CSV	Yes	Yes	Yes	Yes	Yes	Yes	Yes
Email	Yes	Yes	Yes	Yes	Yes	Yes	Yes
Dashboard Sharing	Yes		Yes	Yes	Yes		Yes
Integrations							
Data API	Yes		Yes		Yes		Yes
Compete.com	Yes		Yes		Yes		
Google Analytics					Yes		
Alexa	Yes		Yes			Yes	
Other (please describe)		Custom			Webtrends, Omniture, Salesforce		

FIGURE 8-11: Social Analytics data sharing and integration options.

Assessing Your Needs

When you are thinking about vendor partners to work with, my best advice is to define your business requirements and reporting needs prior to engaging in conversations with vendor salespeople. If you are able to prioritize a list of requirements and capabilities, deciding which you can and cannot live without makes winnowing down the list of vendors slightly easier. Vendor solutions should align with your requirements through appropriate offerings or customization—not by shoehorning you into their standard capabilities. Luckily, most are willing to work closely with clients to make this happen.

▶ Don't fall victim to vendors that require you to conform to their capabilities, but rather, work with those that offer flexibility and customization opportunities.

One of the analogies that I like to use when helping clients assess technologies is as follows. You're headed out to the corner store to pick up a few things. Do you choose to take a bike, a car, or a jet airplane? Each will probably get you there, but certainly the jet is overkill and choosing between the bike and the car probably depends on factors like the weather, time of day, number of items you're picking up at the store, and so on. Choosing a social media vendor is somewhat similar in that you probably don't want to buy the jet airplane because it would be too much for your organization to take full advantage of. You also want to be wary of the bike because it may service your needs today (assuming the sun is shining and you only need a gallon of milk), but it may not suffice in the long term.

Thus, when you're deciding which social media technology solution to go with, take the time to define your requirements list, map out a rough measurement plan, and ask yourself a series of questions that will help you to make the right choice.

Selecting a Social Analytics Vendor—Tips and Tricks

When you're ready to begin sorting through the multiple vendors on the market that offer Social Analytics tools, start by assessing your technology needs. In my consulting practice, I frequently perform vendor selection engagements because the landscape is incredibly confusing. With hundreds of vendors vying for your precious dollars, and more popping up all the time, selecting the perfect match can be a daunting task. By the time you determine exactly what any given Social Analytics technology can do, there's something new to look at and consider in your evaluation.

Additionally, the process of assessing multiple vendors requires diligent note taking, screenshots, and copious questions to get to a real understanding of market differentiators. The next sections list a few tips and tricks I picked up along the way that will help you make the right decision.

NOTE The dirty little secret of vendor capabilities is that in mature (or maturing) markets, the vast majority of critical functionality is commoditized. Despite vehement objections by vendors worldwide, it's true. Going down a checklist of features and functions will often result in frustration because when you take into consideration all the nuances, variances, and caveats that ride along with each tool, most perform in similar ways—or at least they can be customized to do so. This is no accident either. Competition in the measurement marketplace is extremely high, and I can guarantee that each vendor delivering a product is keeping a close eye on the competition.

In many cases, selecting a vendor comes down to preference and usability, and these are things that are best discovered during an extended test drive. Put your vendors to the test with head-to-head challenges to see which one performs best. Selecting a measurement vendor is a task that you should not take lightly. On average, Web Analytics solutions are utilized for 2 1/2 years before being replaced by a new solution. It's likely that social monitoring tools will follow a similar trend. Additionally, the fact that implementation will require some work to get the tool up and running in the first place is reason enough to take the decision seriously. But also consider that the data you collect and the metrics you generate with your social media measurement tool will become the basis for comparison over time. Benchmarks are typically specific to the tool from which they are produced. Although this is not always the case, calculated metrics will very likely change from one solution to another, and you should know that switching vendors may mean losing historical data.

IDENTIFYING "NICE-TO-HAVES" AND "MUST-HAVES"

The best way to identify what you want and what you really need is to make a list that defines your "Nice-to-Haves" and "Must-Haves" for social media measurement. Set aside the fact that vendors might not be able to fulfill either list; this is a blue-sky exercise to explore the boundaries of what's possible. Anyone who has shopped for a house has gone through this process: for example, you'd be willing to do without the garage in favor of the deluxe kitchen or forego the expansive back yard in trade for a friendly neighborhood and curb appeal. Shopping for vendors is similar in that you should make a list of ideal features and functions and then make your compromises to fit the situation.

Social media platforms that add value will be ones that enable companies to customize the data collection methods to meet their unique business requirements. Additionally, the ability to perform true ad hoc analysis against a flexible database is paramount to attaining insights from Social Analytics. A valuable tool would also include data collection from owned and non-owned media properties. This data could be written to a database and enabled with calculated metrics, such as the KPIs mentioned previously, that demonstrate progress toward desired outcomes. The system would also contain workflow processes and alerting functionality to delegate tasks to specific individuals and create imperative calls to action for specific triggered events.

REQUESTING A DEMO

Whenever you're trying on a new tool for size, insist that the vendor provide you a live demo of the technology and allow you access to the tool so that you can actually play with it and take it for an extended test drive. Most vendors will allow you to access a demo account when considering a potential purchase.

Be wary of vendors who don't offer trial access to tools.

However, it's best not just to dive right in; rather, get the instructions from a pro on how to use the technology in its intended way. Demos are awesome and I definitely recommend them, but remember that watching a skilled salesperson navigate a cached graphical interface via WebEx is different from bumbling around on your own. Although you too can likely become proficient at navigating the interface with skill and grace, this tends not to happen out of the box. Even so, there's no substitute for digging in and using the tool on your own. I guarantee that you'll need to spend some time exploring tabs, drop-downs, and filters to get the tool singing on key. For most, this will take some practice and some time. I'm constantly tweaking the tools I use and learning new things about features and functions all the time.

Yet, it's important that you demand that the tool is configured to track keywords, metrics, and influencers that matter to your business. Any social tool will look great if you use a household brand as an example search parameter. There will be lots of mentions about the product, and there's probably a broad smattering of examples that extend across a multitude of digital channels, making for lots to look at. But if your brand is a small B2B business, or you operate a regional retail store, or even if you're a large mid-sized company without tremendous notoriety, then looking at a household brand isn't going to illustrate how the tool will perform for you. This is why you must demand during your analysis phase that the tools be configured to your branded terms and keywords that matter. Doing this will not only give you insights into the volume of data you'll be working with, but also will reveal the noise that each tool picks up relative to your searches. Of course, you can fine-tune tools to get mostly signal in your listening technologies, but you'll need to look at the tools through the lens you'll actually be using them with. Try out these products with a sense of how you plan to manage your social media programs in order to get a full sense of how they will deliver.

When demoing vendors, be sure to track the same keywords across all tools so that you get an apples-to-apples comparison. Results will vary.

CONSIDERING SETUP, TRAINING, AND SUPPORT

Many of the social media monitoring and Social Analytics tools out there won't let you go it alone when it comes to setting up and managing your technologies. Perhaps they learned some lessons from failed Web Analytics implementations, or possibly they're just tuned in to the complexity of Social Analytics technologies. Either way, unless you're a seasoned Social Analytics veteran, this can be a good thing. Getting your listening technology tuned to the right frequency takes some time, and there's nothing better than having a pro help you through this process.

One of the first things that you need to consider is who's primarily going to be using the tool and who the secondary users are going to be. The primary users should be the ones getting the demo and must have a firm grasp on what they want to measure and how they'd like to get there. Although you don't need to have everything figured out at your first demo, make sure that you get the most out of the process by knowing what you need and where the fluff is. Also keep in mind that the primary user will likely have to pull data, deliver reports, and teach others within the organization how to use the tool and how to understand the data. The ease with which you'll be able to accomplish this is somewhat dependent on the vendor you choose.

Another point to consider is the extent of training that is offered by the vendors you're evaluating and how much that training will cost. It's great to get a deep-dive training session upon first signing on with a tool, yet knowing that you've got additional modules available to learn specific tricks or to take a closer look at some advanced capabilities is good too. Although this is also part of knowing your total cost of ownership, be sure to understand how many support hours you will receive from your vendor and what's included in these sessions. The last thing you want after purchasing a tool is to find out that the training session you were counting on to educate your business peers about using the tool is going to cost you $1,999 per person.

Any good social media program is going to grow, evolve, and change over time. Thus it's important to know how you can make changes to your monitoring and analytics technology as modifications become necessary. Some vendors will enable self-service access to create "projects" or campaigns as needed, whereas others will require you to call your account manager to make a change. You'll need to know what your vendor allows in this case and if they're going to charge you for the change.

► Don't be surprised by hidden costs; make sure you understand the total cost of ownership for vendor services.

ASKING ALL THE RIGHT QUESTIONS

Make sure that you go into each evaluation with a predetermined set of questions that you want to get answered. This list will inevitably grow as you look at the first set of tools, but having something to look at to ensure that you're getting all the things that you need is critical. Here's a short list of questions to keep in your back pocket as you go through the process of evaluating vendors:

- ► How much is the total cost of ownership?
- ► Does the company offer managed services, self-service, or a hybrid approach?
- ► How far back does the tool track historical data?
- ► Can the company offer reference clients for you to speak with?
- ► What new features or functions are on the product development roadmap?

THINKING LONG-TERM

When you are interviewing vendors to determine what will fit the bill as your social media monitoring solution, it's important to ask about their long-term roadmap and vision for the company. This line of questioning should reveal how the vendor is thinking about their products and where they see the next big thing in social media measurement. For vendors that are on their A-game, it will reveal what they see as possibilities in the market and potentially open your mind to things you might not see coming. On the other hand, if their responses are lackluster or nonexistent, you should question their dedication to supporting your measurement efforts over the long term.

Many people ask me to speculate on the longevity and staying power of vendors in the digital measurement marketplace. Short of peering into my crystal ball and rattling off Nostradamus-like predictions, it just plain tough to predict how these things will go down. What you can expect is that the vast majority of vendors developing social media monitoring solutions are looking to get paid someday. This typically means that they're working to build a viable solution that fulfills a need within the marketplace today. Whether they deliver this as a bootstrapped startup, venture-funded innovator, profitable independent, or publicly traded company, the goal is to make something you can use and benefit from with bottom-line results.

> ▶ This places the onus on you to help your vendors be the best that they can be by delivering feedback and insisting on requirements and features that you deem important.

However, before the final bell sounds, anticipate that an acquisition of your measurement vendor is a highly likely scenario. Acquisitions validate the hard work and years of effort that software developers pour into their ideas and hopefully make all the effort seem worthwhile. You simply do not have any control over whether the vendor you select today is snatched up by a rival or larger enterprise software company tomorrow. So my advice is to not worry about it.

EVALUATING YOUR SOCIAL MEDIA MEASUREMENT READINESS

Despite the variation and confusion among vendors, there are certainly areas of strength among the competitive offerings. Currently, the strongest area for the leading social media listening vendors is their ability to capture conversations and brand mentions across a broad scope of Internet activity. These capabilities help organizations "learn" and serve a very necessary component of social media measurement. Some solutions require users to point the tools at a finite set of keywords and essentially know what they're looking for. Others capture a much wider range of social interactions and aid in the discovery process as well. Many commercial tools available today also offer the ability to track trends within conversations and reveal many interesting facts about social media activity across a broad spectrum of the web. Yet, in all cases, you need to be equipped with the knowledge of what you want to measure and how you plan to enlist the help of vendors to accomplish your measurement goals.

It's worth repeating that there is currently no single vendor that can effectively measure all aspects of social media. Although many vendors in this space offer capable tools with usable interfaces, the reality is that businesses turn to multiple solutions for capturing, analyzing, and interpreting their social media activities. Most use an amalgamation of commercial solutions geared for capturing social buzz, free tools offering limited information, and a whole lot of manual intervention for aggregating and analyzing social media data. Don't expect this to change in the near future.

Defining Your Requirements

As I mentioned earlier, social media tools can perform many different actions and deliver functionality in myriad ways. The vendor landscape can be overwhelming unless you know what you're looking for in a lasting relationship. I recommend developing a list of questions to ask before entering into any vendor demos or negotiations. Creating this will help you to think through the things that are important to your social media measurement challenges and to potentially begin the collaboration process across your organization. Although this may not sound relevant to social media metrics, it is in fact critical to collecting the right data and answering questions that are pertinent to social media measurement.

Here's a list of questions to get you thinking in the right frame of mind:

- ▶ Who is your target audience?
- ▶ Which social channels do you *think* are important?
- ▶ Which social channels are mission critical?
- ▶ How many brands/campaigns/projects will you be watching?
- ▶ What keywords are relevant to your brand?
- ▶ How much volume will your keywords generate?
- ▶ How frequently will you conduct analysis?
- ▶ How will you share data across your organization?
- ▶ Which companies are included within your competitive set?
- ▶ Who are the internal stakeholders you'll be serving?
- ▶ What are your stakeholders' specific goals and data needs?
- ▶ Will stakeholders access data themselves or receive it via reports?
- ▶ How much support will you require from IT or other resources?

You can see by this list that there's a lot to think about. But keeping it simple can also help you make your decisions. Selecting the right vendor is never an easy task.

ALWAYS SELECT VENDORS TO MEET YOUR BUSINESS NEEDS

For one client, I faced an interesting challenge of selecting a Social Analytics vendor that I would use to provide social media oversight, comparative benchmarks, and strategic guidance. My client (a nonprofit foundation) operates an annual challenge where they offer millions in grant money to fund projects that deliver innovative ideas that benefit their cause. In all cases, the ideas must leverage social media and look toward developing new and innovative ways for connecting people to one another. My task was to set up individual measures of success for the 12 distinct projects that received grant money and formulate comparative benchmarks to evaluate the entire cohort of grantees. The Social Analytics data would be used to assess progress toward their desired outcomes and to make tactical decisions on a daily or weekly basis.

So, like any diligent measurer of social media embarking on a new journey, I set out to find the perfect vendor. I purposefully sidelined my preconceived notions of each vendor's capabilities and looked at the field with a fresh perspective that focused on my specific needs for this engagement. I knew what I wanted and how I wanted to get there, so I formulated a requirements list that would help me decide which vendor best suited my needs and where I might have to make compromises. My list consisted of the following:

There are 12 specific projects/brands in my assessment

Each project will have between 5 and 25 keywords

I want to correlate Google Analytics data with social mentions

Visits to web properties were estimated at <10k uniques per month

Social mentions were estimated at <1k mentions per month

Key business objectives for each project included:

- ► Gain Exposure

- ► Foster Dialogue

- ► Engage Community

- ► Promote Advocacy

- ► Spur Innovation

(continues)

ALWAYS SELECT VENDORS TO MEET YOUR BUSINESS NEEDS
(continued)

Specific metrics that I wanted to report on included:

- Reach
- Engagement Score
- Influencers
- Authority of Influencers
- Share of Voice (among projects)
- Sentiment
- Impact

Projects will include web and social media and offline channels.

Social media channels to monitor include:

- Twitter
- Facebook
- Mainstream News
- YouTube
- Others

Solution must have ability to send to PDF reports and e-mail to recipients.

Budget is less than $2,000 annually.

This was my requirements list—or simpleton RFP (if you will)—for selecting a Social Analytics vendor. Going into it I knew that I probably wouldn't get everything I was hoping for given my limited budget, but that's the harshness of the real world. Right off the bat, many of the vendors I reviewed in the Social Analytics Capability Matrix were ruled out because they were focused on enterprise businesses, and my 12 mini-projects didn't add up to size large, no matter how hard I squinted. So, I dug into the vendors on the matrix that would toggle down to support a consultant's project view and opened the evaluation list to include additional vendors such as Filtrbox, PostRank, Social Radar, Sprout Social, uberVu, and Viralheat.

I gave each of them an honest go, and as you might expect, I found plusses and minuses for each. Without going into the gory details, I can tell you that I ended up going with uberVu (see Figure 8-12) because it consistently picked up news sources that I wasn't seeing elsewhere; it did not bring back much noise; I was able to measure many of the specific metrics I wanted; and on a subjective note, I liked the user interface. Things I left on the table during my bargain Social Analytics shopping adventure included no integration with Google Analytics, no calculated engagement score, and no measure of impact. I intended to work around these limitations using other tools in conjunction with uberVU. But what I did get for the low price of $1,979.98 for the year was the right tool for this specific project and for my client. It just goes to show that sometimes the best tools are not the ones that cost the most money, but the ones that fit the job.

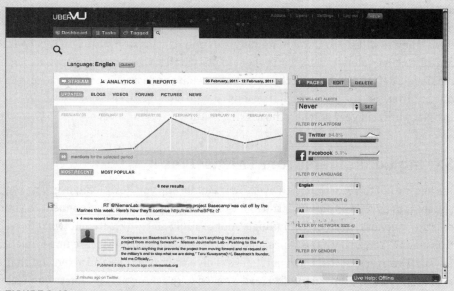

FIGURE 8-12: uberVu's social media monitoring dashboard.

PROTECTING PRIVACY AT ALL COSTS

One of the issues that must not be overlooked by any business venturing into social media is privacy. It's my belief that Internet privacy concerns will crescendo in the next 12 to 24 months, and businesses will face consequential decisions about how they manage the consumer data they collect from web sites, advertisements, and social media activities. Like it or not, if you collect data or compile metrics from social media activities, this affects you and your business. In most cases, the data you harness about social media activity will be entirely benign, yet consumers will make the ethical responsibility (and perhaps legal obligation sometime in the near future) of stewarding customer data an increasingly difficult task.

Consumers readily participate in social media antics with little regard for personal privacy. They post pictures on photo sharing web sites like Flickr and Blipfoto .com for all to see, they Tweet about everything from personal details to the mundane, they're willing to share religious views and relationship status on Facebook, and oftentimes allow others to tag them in photos that they post for all to see. Social media has definitely changed the way that we share and consume information about one another, yet the privacy implications that go along with this newfound level of intimacy are still very much in the making.

Saving Consumers from Themselves

It's beginning to seem that with every new mobile app you download, every network you join, or every web site registration, the site asks if you'd like to connect to your existing network. Prudent individuals should stop and think, "Hmm… what does this mean?" Yet, in my experience, most of these connect requests are impediments to what I started out to do, so I don't always give them the time and attention that I should. However, I force myself to read what they're asking permission to connect to and what personal information I might be exposing—and if I'm really feeling skeptical, I'll explore through to read the privacy policy if they offer one. However, the last time I did this, I ended up looking at a 36-page legal document with a comprehension level equivalent to something published in Wingdings font. I didn't spend much time reading through the policy, but I did accept it because I wanted to use the new service on the other side of this online permission gate. I personally haven't conducted research to determine if I'm an outlier in my ways of operation regarding accepting connect requests, but my anecdotal evidence tells me that I'm certainly not alone. That said, I'm also probably more cognizant than most.

I believe that consumers today are reckless about exposing details, images, and locations of their private lives. Although some are making conscious decisions when they commit these acts of unregulated immodesty, others do so unwittingly. And even those who are careful about information that they expose across social and digital channels may not always be informed about the depth of information that really is out there.

OVERCOMING DUBIOUS ACTS OF IGNORANCE

Stories of infamy are widely available about individuals who commit unparalleled acts of ignorance using social channels. In Chapter 2 I mentioned ways that businesses can commit colossal acts of stupidity online, so here are a few tidbits about individuals that were snatched from the headlines of real-world occurrences.

First is a Tweet that tanked the job opportunity before it started. See http://www.msnbc.msn.com/id/29901380.

Then there was the Facebook post that lost the job while underway. See http://www.telegraph.co.uk/technology/facebook/6027302/Woman-sacked-after-abusing-boss-on-Facebook.html.

And most recently, a French court upheld the dismissal of two employees for participating in the *"club des néfastes"* (club of the "evildoers" or "ill-fated" employees). In this instance, employees were granted access to the *club des néfastes* for making it exceedingly difficult on HR managers within their organization. Three employees engaged in a Facebook discussion on the matter, one of whom allowed "Friends of Friends" to see wall postings. As a result, a company representative saw the online discourse and the employees were terminated. The case was brought before a French Conseil that ruled in favor of the employer because the comments were publicly accessible and defamatory to the organization that the individuals worked for. See http://www.crossborderemployer.com/post/2010/12/08/Discharge-for-Facebook-Postings-by-Employees-in-France-Upheld-by-Labor-Tribunal-Barbera-v-Societe-Alten-SIR3b-Southiphong-v-Societe-Alten-SIR-.aspx.

Perhaps in response to the dubious (or ignorant) acts of consumers using social media, there are web sites out there working to help consumers recognize the shady acts of privacy they unknowingly commit. One such site is PleaseRobMe.com (Figure 8-13), which was deployed as a method to educate consumers about over-sharing on location-based services like Foursquare and Gowalla.

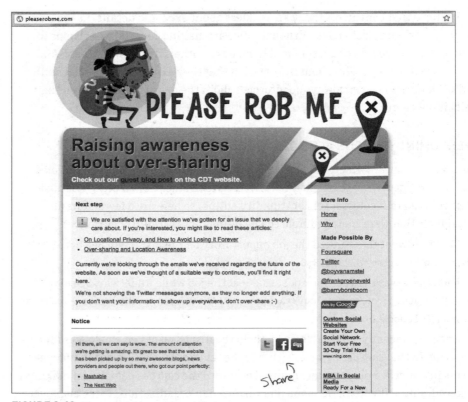

FIGURE 8-13: PleaseRobMe.com's public homepage.

The founders of PleaseRobMe.com are Frank Groeneveld, Barry Borsboom, and Boy van Amstel, and they penned the blog post "Over-sharing and Location Awareness," which was published on the Center for Democracy & Technology web site and which I've included in the accompanying sidebar.

OVER-SHARING AND LOCATION AWARENESS

Over the last few years the consensus about privacy on the Internet seems to have changed a lot. A few years ago, people were still hesitant about using their real names online, but nowadays people are comfortable sharing their exact location with the whole world.

Over the last few years the consensus about privacy on the Internet seems to have changed a lot. A few years ago, people were still hesitant about using their real names online, but nowadays people are comfortable sharing their exact location with the whole world.

Where does this change in consensus come from? Are people starting to feel too comfortable? We're not sure, but over-sharing might result in more risk and unintended consequence than one might think, especially in the long run.

The issue with location-based information is that it exposes another layer of personal information that, frankly, we haven't had to think much about: our exact physical location at anytime, anywhere. If you're comfortable being a human homing beacon, that's fine, we just want you to be fully aware of what that means and the potential risks it might involve.

Social networks have increased enormously in size and number. Most of them allow you to relay messages between different sites and it's easy to lose track of just how much information you might be giving away and how many people have free access to it. These new technologies make it increasingly easy to share potentially sensitive personal information, like your exact location. People might be over-sharing without knowing about it. For example, you might relay your Foursquare location to your public Twitter account and by doing this expose the message to the whole world (Twitter: "Our default is almost always to make the information you provide public").

Most social networks have good search functionalities. People use such search features to find their friends or things they might be interested in. However, this means others can find them and their information as well. It's important to be aware of privacy settings, to control the reach your messages have. If you allow your messages to travel between different social networks, this becomes more complicated. Information you trust to your friends might end up somewhere else.

The rate at which new technology develops allows us to do more amazing stuff every day. It's important to reconsider basic things like privacy at the same pace.

www.cdt.org/blogs/cdt/over-sharing-and-location-awareness

I applaud these guys for their successful effort in building awareness of our increasing public profile exposure through new social technologies. Education is one of the foundational elements of protecting privacy, and most consumers are too impetuous in their online actions.

The Electronic Frontier Foundation published a whitepaper entitled "On Locational Privacy, and How to Avoid Losing It Forever" (available at https://www.eff.org/wp/locational-privacy). This paper describes ways in which everyday electronic conveniences like electronic toll payment devices, cell phones, smart parking meters, public Wi-Fi services, and social media check-in platforms can pose potential threats to personal privacy. Before you dismiss these researchers as tinfoil hat–wearing loonies, consider for a minute the implications of these "convenient" services. The study points out that any social deviant, ex-boyfriend, debt collector, or radical activist could use data from these services to answer the following questions:

- Did you go to an anti-war rally on Tuesday?
- Did you walk into an abortion clinic?
- Did you see an AIDS counselor?
- Have you been checking into a motel at lunchtime?
- Did you skip lunch to pitch a venture capitalist?

Social media is offering visibility into these activities and in some cases trivializing the severity of consumers' actions by making games and awarding badges for checking into locations. Although consumers are certainly doing this of their own volition, this affords a high degree of exposure with potentially damning consequences. The paper goes on to describe methods by which technology providers can obfuscate personally identifiable data to show information only in aggregate. While I am a fan of this practice (which is common in Web Analytics solutions), I don't agree with the authors' conclusions.

They surmise that "democratic action and lawmaking" should be the deciding factor in when we retain our location privacy. Although this may be an inevitable consequence, I advocate that self-regulation is an immediate imperative for all companies that are collecting data and facilitating location-based services. If we can collectively exemplify that the technologies available and our collection, storage, and public reporting of consumer data is conducted in a way that is predominantly managed by the individual consumer, then we're offering a choice. Either participate or don't, but recognize that your participation will result in information being publicly available about you and your whereabouts.

WHEN TRANSPARENCY BITES

Sound bites from a survey conducted by Vovci on American's attitudes toward using social media data for market research revealed some harsh criticism (see `http://blog.vovici.com/blog/bid/28663/Consumer-Attitudes-towards-Social-Media-Market-Research-casrotech`). Although 95 percent of this sample of adults from the western United States were concerned about their privacy, 40 percent were very or extremely concerned. Comments from the most incredulous included:

▶ "I don't like the idea that companies can follow me around on the Internet and identify me personally. I don't mind being part of a generic demographic, but when they can identify me, follow my activities about everything I do on the Internet, and target me specifically, then it's gets a little scary and I worry about my privacy."

▶ "Spying, lying, snooping, and watching for no good reason."

▶ "A little too close to 'Big Brother is watching.' But you should know enough to never post if you don't want others to read it."

▶ "I don't like that they invade our privacy in the first place. If we wanted them to know, we would contact them."

▶ "I like nothing about this. If it is social media, it should be social media and not for research."

▶ "It is skeezy and lecherous stealing data that they would otherwise have to pay for."

▶ *These perceptions can be mitigated with education and transparency.*

RISING ABOVE THE FEAR, UNCERTAINTY, AND DOUBT

When it comes to matters of online privacy, it's unfortunate that many mainstream media outlets like the *Wall Street Journal* fan the flames of consumer Fear, Uncertainty, and Doubt (FUD). The *Wall Street Journal* has been publishing a series of articles under their "What They Know" series that I feel paint a negative picture of the tracking methods of businesses today. Of course I'm coming at this from the perspective of someone who is helping organizations to understand online consumer behavior and how to use that knowledge to deliver more effective web sites and social media offerings. I also preach for ethical practices in data collection and utilization (see the next section entitled "Advocating for Ethics"). Yet, some businesses do have questionable practices, so it is certainly worth investigating. By no means do I condemn the series, yet I do look for them to offer an unbiased account.

For example, in their "What They Know – Mobile" story, the *Wall Street Journal* calls out one application that I use frequently, which is Pandora music (http:// online.wsj.com/article/SB10001424052748704694004576020083703574602.html? mod=what_they_know). This company has been largely successful and even announced an initial public offering in February 2011. Yet, the *Wall Street Journal* highlights the fact that they routinely sell customer information to third parties. The user data passed off by Pandora includes age, gender, location, and phone identifier number. Information is not linked to the individual name, but rather is used in aggregate primarily for ad targeting purposes. To complicate matters, application distributors like Apple, with their App Store also have a vested interest in the distribution and data collection from the apps they deliver. The article reads:

> Apple targets ads to phone users based largely on what it knows about them through its App Store and iTunes music service. The targeting criteria can include the types of songs, videos, and apps a person downloads, according to an Apple ad presentation reviewed by the *Journal*. The presentation named 103 targeting categories, including: karaoke, Christian/ gospel music, anime, business news, health apps, games, and horror movies.

This was also written before Apple was exposed for retaining location-based data on consumers iPhones, iPads, and other devices. So what can you do about all this? Well, if you're working for any type of organization that collects data about customers who use your online products, services, applications, and web sites, you should reveal how you intend to use that data. If you don't know, drop this book now and go find out!

Some may fear that full disclosure in this way might lead to fewer sales, fewer downloads, or fewer customers. However, I can tell you with absolute certainty that betraying the trust of your customers by not telling them will cost you much more in the long run.

▶ That's the first requirement to gaining consumer trust—telling them what data you're collecting and how you plan to use that data.

Demonstrating Corporate Responsibility

As a measurer of social media, to a certain extent, you're stuck between what your organization decides to do and what regulatory factions decide is best for all of us. Yet, don't take this predicament as something that renders you helpless. In fact, I believe it's quite the opposite. You, as a measurer of social media, have the power of knowledge. You know what's being collected about the consumers you interact with on a daily basis; you know how that information is stored (or not) within your organization; and you know the extent to which consumer data is used to deliver customer service, product innovation, or better social media experiences. You are not helpless at all; you are powerful! Yet, the extent to which you control your own destiny is determined by how well you communicate to your organization. If you work for yourself or a small organization, getting everyone on board might be as simple as holding a meeting and explaining how you're planning to govern consumer privacy. Yet, if you work for a large corporate entity, you'll likely face bigger challenges. The next sections explain a few ways that you can take the privacy reins and steer your tactics in the right direction.

SAFEGUARDING CONSUMER DATA

First off, accept the responsibility that if you're collecting, storing, or analyzing social media data about consumers that can be deemed personally identifiable, you must take precautions to safeguard that information. Safeguards come in many forms, which can range from fully obfuscating personally identifiable information to provisioning access only to authorized individuals within your organization. The degree to which you safeguard data is dependent upon what you collect and how you make it available for use. When we look specifically at social media data, most instances will reveal only what consumers themselves offer through the social channels that they participate in. Yet, how you choose to use that data is where you need to be careful.

> NOTE Personally identifiable information (aka PII) refers to information that can be used to uniquely identify, contact, or locate a single person or can be used with other sources to uniquely identify a single individual.

For example, if you manage a Facebook fan page, you will likely have access to a wealth of information about every individual who chooses to become a fan of your permission-based page. When an individual accepts the relatively discrete permission for Facebook, the organization that owns the page gains access to profile information, friend information, and a bevy of other personal details that could be used for diverse marketing purposes. Most commonly, this type of information is used for behavioral targeting purposes and to make digital experiences better and more relevant for individual consumers. Yet, selling this type of data to third parties so that they can use it to serve up ads on the network of advertisers is where most people object. Although Facebook will do this within their own ecosystem, there are many, many behavioral ad networks that routinely purchase consumer data for targeting purposes.

PREEMPTING PRIVACY REGULATION

As someone who measures social media—hopefully with virtuous intentions—you have the means to act responsibly on behalf of your organization. Although your individual actions may not avert regulation in the long term, if enough of us take matters into our own hands and practice ethical data collection, establish best practices, and educate consumers, government agencies, and our employers, we do have a fighting chance.

My former JupiterResearch colleague, David Card, wrote about the need for self-regulation in a GigaOM report. The following sidebar includes a blog post that accompanied his research.

SOCIAL MEDIA AND PRIVACY: GET SERIOUS OR GET REGULATED

Privacy isn't just Facebook's problem. As I write over at GigaOM Pro, the entire consumer Internet and media industry had better get its collective act together on the privacy front or get ready to face serious consumer backlash and, perhaps worse, government regulation.

For the second time this year, Facebook is at the center of a privacy controversy. Many popular apps on Facebook, including social games from Zynga, have been transmitting Facebook user IDs to third parties. Some of those companies are data aggregators or data miners that create profiles of users or groups and sell them to marketers.

A Zogby poll showed that 87 percent of those surveyed were concerned with the security of their personal information online, and 80 percent were bothered by advertisers tracking them. In another survey, 96 percent of respondents said online companies shouldn't be allowed to share or sell that info to third parties without permission, even though nearly half admitted they don't read privacy policies.

Members of Congress are questioning Facebook on its current snafu. These are the same people who went after the "zombie cookies" highlighted in yet another *Wall Street Journal* story. Even before that, online privacy bills had been proposed in the House, and European regulators are passing fresh proposals around the EC. I doubt the online media industry wants to rely on congressmen understanding the nuances between zombies and other cookies; a ban on cookies would completely destroy ad targeting and optimization.

In short, the online media industry needs to rev up its lobbyists (Google spent $1.2 million on lobbying this quarter; Facebook, $120,000), explain what's going on to legislators and to the public, and seriously consider self-regulation. Additionally, the industry should:

▶ Explain what they're already doing about consumer information, and not on developer blogs. These stories need to be on home pages and in ad campaigns.

▶ Go after real bad guys publicly. Facebook, for instance, is suing spammers.

▶ Use the publicized information outlined in the first two points to create a set of best practices and an audited seal of approval.

▶ Use an organization like the Online Publisher's Association—rather than the Internet Advertising Bureau or the Direct Marketing Association—as a hub for public campaigns. It would be better PR coming from the publishers, who shouldn't be afraid to play the "democracy needs a viable press, and the press needs viable advertising" card.

http://gigaom.com/2010/10/28/social-media-and-privacy-get-serious-or-get-regulated/

RELINQUISHING COMPLETE CONTROL

Undoubtedly, there will always be individuals who choose not to use your products or services or even visit your digital destinations if they're ultra-wary about privacy. In most cases, they can configure their browser settings to refuse cookies or other tracking devices, walk around with limited-functionality mobile devices, and generally relegate themselves to suboptimal online experiences. Trying to stop these individuals isn't worth your time. Rather, offering some methods of privacy control and data collection knowledge to your customers, visitors, and potential prospects is a much better way to go. By making your data-collection practices accessible in non-legalese language, offering methods to opt out of behavioral targeting, or tracking and demonstrating that your organization is committed to upholding the privacy of each and every individual that you come into contact with, you will, by and large, accommodate all of the objections that could be lodged against you.

Advocating for Ethics

One initiative that I've personally crusaded for is the Web Analyst's Code of Ethics. As a long-time industry analyst and consultant in digital measurement technologies, I perennially advise my clients, colleagues, and professional acquaintances to practice ethical data collection and utilization methods. Not only do I feel that it's the right thing to do, but my job depends upon it.

▶ The simple act of creating metrics and evaluating behavior across any digital medium—including social media—places a burden of responsibility on the keepers of those data.

Any individual or organization that partakes in digital data collection that includes any personally identifiable information treads a dangerous line of trust with end users. We as measurers of digital medium have the potential to know a great deal about individuals, which means that cautionary measures and diligent governance must be put in place. For these reasons, I decided to do something about it and collaborated with my business partner at Web Analytics Demystified and with the Web Analytics Association (WAA), where I am a board member, to establish a set of self-regulation principles.

LAST CHANCE TO SHAPE THE WEB ANALYST'S CODE OF ETHICS

Posted by John Lovett, WAA Director and Senior Partner, Web Analytics Demystified

I'm pleased to report that we've made incredible progress on the Web Analyst's Code of Ethics. Thus far, nearly 50 individuals contributed comments and suggestions for improvement to the first draft of the Code of Ethics originally posted on September 12, 2010. We formed a sub-committee within the WAA Standards group to discuss the specific changes required to make the Code of Ethics more understandable and something that we can collectively stand behind as web analysts dedicated to protecting consumer privacy. We were interviewed by the *Wall Street Journal*, who posted our point of view in their Digits blog post called Web Analysts Push for Privacy Standards. And finally, I've been on a personal quest over the past six weeks to evangelize the Code of Ethics in Europe and across the US by seeking feedback from numerous practitioners, vendors, consultants, and end users about our ability to change the perception about the ways in which we collect and use data about consumers.

The following document [Web Analyst's Code of Ethics (`http://bit.ly/ Code_of_Ethics`)] represents the culmination of these efforts in a document that captures the spirit and commitment we hold true with regard to upholding consumer privacy. Special thanks go out to all the contributors to this body of work, including Eric Peterson, Christopher Berry, Hemash Bhatti, Anna Long, Jodi McDermott, Judah Philips, and the many, many others that contributed to this work.

Version 2 of the Web Analyst's Code of Ethics will be open for public comment and review until November 18th, 2010, when we will finalize it for publication and distribution to web analysts far and wide. Please take the time to read, comprehend, and comment on this very important industry document.

PRACTICING ETHICAL DATA COLLECTION

In my opinion, practicing ethical data collection is simple. Follow these guidelines every time:

1. Tell consumers *what* you're going to do in clear, concise language regarding data collection and utilization practices.

2. Inform them *why* you are doing these things and what benefits they will receive as a result.

3. Empower them to *opt out* of these practices if they so choose.

4. *Do what you say* you are going to do regarding data collection and utilization practices.

5. If customers ask, *tell them what you did* with the data you collected about them.

It's not rocket science here; it's called accountability!

By simply making your intentions clear and allowing individuals to decide whether or not they will allow you to act in this way, you are acting responsibly. Any attempts to veil your efforts or dupe consumers into offering up more information than they are comfortable with will ultimately come back to haunt you. Most consumers won't notice or take the time to read your policies, so you have the responsibility of doing right and offering information to this end.

ADHERING TO FIVE CORE TENETS OF DATA PRIVACY

Basically, when collecting and using information through social media you should pledge to adhere to the following core tenets:

▶ **Privacy:** I agree to hold consumer data in the highest regard and will do everything in my power to keep personally identifiable consumer data safe, secure, and private. To this end I will never knowingly transfer, release, or otherwise distribute personally identifiable information (PII) gathered through digital channels to any third party without express permission from the consumer(s) who generated the data. I will also work with my clients/employer where applicable to enforce a cookie and user identification policy that is appropriate and respectful of the consumer experience.

▶ **Transparency:** I agree to encourage full disclosure of my client/employer consumer data collection practices and to encourage communication of how that data will be used in clear and understandable language. To this end I will work with my clients/employer to ensure that the privacy policy is up to date and provides a clear and truthful reflection of our collection, use, and storage policies about digitally collected data. Without divulging proprietary or competitive information, I will be transparent, honest, and forthright regarding the data collected and how it is used to improve the overall consumer and customer experience online.

▶ **Consumer Control:** I agree to inform and empower consumers to opt out of my client/employer data collection practices and to document ways to do this. To this end I will work to ensure that consumers have a means to opt out and to ensure that they are removed from tracking when they request it. Further, I will do my best to use tracking and browser-based technologies in the way they were designed and not otherwise circumvent consumer control over their browsing experience.

▶ **Education:** I agree to educate my clients/employer about the types of data collected, and the potential risks to consumers associated with those data. To this end I will make every effort to inform my peers of the commitment to data privacy and to educate staff, especially senior management, of current data collection capabilities, data definitions, and potential data risks. Further, I will educate my clients/employer about how these technologies could be perceived as invasive.

▶ **Accountability:** I agree to act as a steward of customer data and to uphold the consumers' right to privacy as governed by my clients/employer and applicable laws and regulations. To this end, I will work with appropriate teams as necessary to ensure that data access lists are up to date and that anyone with access to these systems understands how that data can and cannot be used. I will do my best to comply with all practices governing ethical use of consumer data.

COMMITTING TO EDUCATION

Perhaps the single most important thing that you can do, next to committing to hold consumer privacy in the highest regard, is to also commit to educating those around you. For consumers, the message is crystal clear—don't blog, Tweet, post, reply to, comment on, like, or do anything on social media that you wouldn't feel comfortable having as a part of your permanent record. Social media has created a new and indelible record of all your escapades. Society as a whole may be lenient toward online acts of dubious behavior, but these acts will linger for anyone who is curious or determined enough to look for them. On the flip side, as a business that's collecting data about consumers, you have a responsibility to hold data security, consumer personal privacy, and governance over data in the highest regard. Failure to do this will have repercussions, and those are the conversations you don't want to have.

SUMMARY

Still ready to take the corporate plunge? I hope so. Even though there's a lot to consider in this chapter, all of it is extremely worthwhile. The metrics and measures of success that will ultimately help you identify successful social media initiatives are founded upon making good corporate decisions and doing so with diligence and consideration.

Recognize that you will likely need tools from multiple categories of the social media technology spectrum to effectively manage all aspects of your social operations. There really isn't a silver bullet for social measurement and management. Take this into consideration as you evaluate vendors for the job and weigh the must-haves against your wish list items. I also strongly encourage you to consider the privacy implications of collecting and storing data about your customers. As privacy regulations heat up in the months and years to come, the best thing you can do about it as a business is to ensure that your practices are ethical and above board. Getting ahead of this now will likely save you headaches in the future.

CHAPTER 9

Planning for a Socially Networked Future

IN THIS CHAPTER

▶ Building a culture of measurement
▶ Refining your social media measurement strategy
▶ Gaining advantage by anticipating social trends
▶ Measuring what really matters: impact

Throughout this book, I've shared numerous secrets about measuring social media and the metrics that are required to accomplish this substantive task. Yet, as you plan forward and think about your socially networked future, there are several key ingredients to developing effective social media metrics. The first is a level of preparedness that comes with knowing what you're getting into when engaging with customers across social media channels and educating your organizations about what to expect. There's also the ideology that change is the constant within social media and any program, initiative, or measure of success that works today might not work tomorrow. Thus, measurers of social media and those executing tirelessly on campaigns and programs may feel as if they are chasing an impalpable ghost. However, with diligence, pragmatism, and some sound measurement strategy, you can get there.

This final chapter explores how to create a measurement mentality within your organization. You'll take a peek into the future as I reveal what I believe are the trends to come in the not-too-distant future. Finally, I'll leave you with some critical questions to ponder as you shape the metrics that will ultimately define your social media measurement strategy.

CREATING A MEASUREMENT MENTALITY

During my day job and through my consulting practice, I routinely advise companies on building cultures of measurement. In most cases, I start off in the exact same way, by emphasizing that building culture takes time. This is particularly true when it comes to digital measurement and social media, which interjects juxtaposition from the outset. How do you maintain the lightning speed of social media interaction, while moving at the glacial pace of corporate change? The answer is immersion. Immerse yourself and those around you into the social media mentality by getting involved at the corporate as well as the personal level.

Insisting upon Participation

Fortunately for measurers of social media, the medium should be familiar to many individuals within your organization, including rank and file employees as well as everyone up to the executive suite of your company. Your first task as an evangelist for social media is ensuring that everyone has a firm grasp of the medium and that they're familiar, or better yet, comfortable using it. This may mean helping to establish Twitter profiles for senior management to listen to the chatter about your brand; or demonstrating the types of conversations that occur on your corporate Facebook pages; or even coaching key team members on the subtleties of corporate blogging. Yet, participation is the fastest route to understanding. By encouraging individuals within your organization to personally use social apps, social networks, and mobile devices, you can instill a deep sense of understanding.

▶ If your organization is new to social media, or executives are generally averse to new digital media, you can assume the role of internal evangelist to help establish personal accounts and get individuals started using social media.

The good news is that in many cases this immersion is fun. Although it's often a learning experience for individuals, it can be a corporate method for building camaraderie among peers. Some organizations take this to heart and enable immersion by not only providing the social applications to use, but also issuing devices for access, such as iPads and/or smartphones, to employees across their organizations. According to Apple, the iPad has been tested or deployed at 80 percent of Fortune 100 companies, which demonstrates that mobility is looming as an enterprise mandate.

If you look at this trend in the most liberal sense, you can infer that large enterprises and household brands are leveraging iPads and other mobile devices to improve experiences for their customers. One example is Mercedes Benz, who is stepping into the digital dimension by empowering its sales teams with mobile devices and social applications that bring contemporary technologies to their customers. They use iPads loaded with their proprietary financial software to perform credit checks and search for promotions directly from the salesroom floor (www.macstories.net/ipad/ mercedes-benz-dealers-will-use-the-ipad-as-a-sales-tool/). Although these applications are not social apps per se, they enable a brand to interact with its customers in real time with a technology assist. This is a huge convenience for customers as well as a useful tool for employees because it allows them to interact and engage with customers in a genuine and meaningful way.

Other businesses and institutions are using mobile devices such as iPads in creative ways as well. Business schools and universities now issue iPads fully loaded with digital textbooks for the semester, cutting down costs and the weight of backpacks substantially. SAP is reportedly issuing 17,000 iPads to employees worldwide. And JPMorgan now issues iPads to associates within their global investment banking division. These businesses and others like them are on the cusp of a digital transformation. While in these cases the device is the first step, how soon before each organization empowers its employees with social applications that will become a critical part of their everyday jobs? According to an e-mail obtained by Bloomberg News, it's purported that JPMorgan executives offered the following statement as the rationale behind issuing iPads to their associates: "We believe there are real benefits in our working environment that can be realized using this device—as well as the personal productivity and enjoyment that come as part of the package" (www.bloomberg.com/ news/2010-11-30/jpmorgan-gives-its-investment-bankers-ipads-in-challenge-to- rim-blackberry.html). I think it's safe to assume that social technologies will be part of that productivity as well.

GETTING YOUR BUSINESS SOCIALLY FUNCTIONAL

At Best Buy, two executives, Barry Judge (CMO) and Brian Dunn (CEO), are rumored to have a friendly competition to see who can amass the largest Twitter following. Currently, Dunn (@BBYCEO) has a long way to go with 8,565 followers, and Judge (@BestBuyCMO) is well ahead with his 17,049-person following. However, as shown in Figure 9-1, both executives have a Klout Score of 52, so depending on how you're counting, Dunn's influence hasn't gone unnoticed. I use this example not because I think that the number of followers they have is important (really it isn't in the grand scheme of making Best Buy money), nor because I think that Klout is a bellwether for influence, but I mention it because each of these senior leaders is practicing social media. They aren't just passive listeners, either. They're engaged with their audiences and immersing themselves into the digital world. Best Buy has recognized that social media is how many of their customers choose to interact with the Best Buy brand, and they've stepped up their response by personally engaging. Although not every C-level staffer will choose to maintain a personal identity across social channels, those who do will inevitably have a much firmer grasp of the medium and its power.

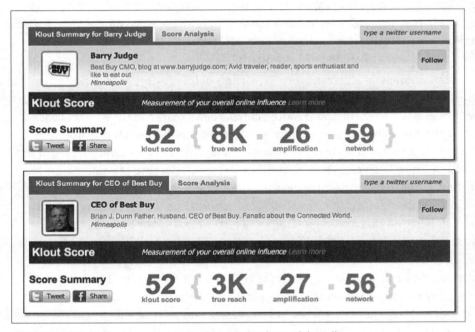

FIGURE 9-1: Best Buy executives embrace and practice social media.

But it's not just the executives at the top of your company who need to be socially active; it's all employees. It won't be long before organizations issue standardized employee Twitter accounts that conform to corporate standards along with their company-issued laptops and mobile devices. I can envision a not-too-distant future when social media access and compliance with protocol are mandatory tools for new hires at companies across the globe. Clearly today, we see that human resource managers are checking employee Facebook accounts and Twitter streams prior to extending job offers, but soon these social platforms will become part of the job. Yet, with all these individuals now representing an organization across a medium that largely emerged as a means for interacting personally with friends and colleagues, there had better be some governance. This is why I encourage all organizations to develop and implement social media policy.

ESTABLISHING A CORPORATE SOCIAL MEDIA POLICY

All organizations, whether large or small, should invest the time to create a social media policy. It's a best practice for large companies to protect themselves from liability. For small companies, it instills some common sense into employees and serves to remind them of their responsibilities. Ford Motor Company offers sound guidance for its employees regarding their use of social media (www.scribd.com/doc/36127480/Ford-Social-Media-Guidelines). Ford's social policy consists of the following guidance:

1. Honesty about who you are

2. Clarity that your opinions are your own

3. Respect and humility in all communication

4. Good judgment in sharing only public information

5. Awareness that what you say is permanent

These core points should be a lesson to us all about how to conduct ourselves when using social media.

Chris Boudreaux is an executive at Converseon who created a web site called socialmediagovernance.com that includes, among many other valuable resources, a list of 164 social media policies. The list includes links to social media usage policies from organizations such as the American Red Cross, Best Buy, Coca-Cola, and U.S. military forces like the Navy and Coast Guard. These policies are as different as the organizations that created them, but they tend to share some common principles—most of which are common sense, with a bit of motherhood and apple pie thrown in to boot. I spent some time parsing the social media policies on the list and weaved a conglomerate of snippets shown in Table 9-1 that reflects my beliefs about what a social media policy should include. If you're looking for insights or guidance on how to build out yours, I suggest that you consult Chris's list to see what your peers and competitors are up to. The full list can be found at http://socialmedia-governance.com/policies.php.

▶ If you want employees to read and adhere to your social media policies, ensure that they're written in plain English and not legalese. Ford's Social Media Guidelines are a great example of how to do it well.

TABLE 9-1: Social Media Corporate Policy Snippets

ORGANIZATION	EXCERPT FROM POSTED POLICY
Best Buy	"Guidelines for functioning in an electronic world are the same as the values, ethics and confidentiality policies employees are expected to live everyday, whether you're Twittering, talking with customers or chatting over the neighbor's fence."
Capgemini	"What you post will reflect on you, so be consistent with the way you would wish to portray yourself to friends, family, colleagues and clients."
IBM	"Be mindful that what you publish will be public for a long time— protect your privacy and take care to understand a site's terms of service."
Thompson Reuters	"The distinction between the private and the professional has largely broken down online and you should assume that your professional and personal social media activity will be treated as one no matter how hard you try to keep them separate."
U.S. Air Force	"Replace error with fact, not argument. When you see misrepresentations made about the Air Force in social media, you may certainly use your blog, theirs, or someone else's to point out the error. Always do so with respect and with the facts."
University of Michigan	"If you join a social network, make sure you are contributing valuable insights. Don't hijack the discussion and redirect by posting self/organizational promoting information."
Cisco	"Because you are legally responsible for your postings, you may be subject to liability if your posts are found defamatory, harassing, or in violation of any other applicable law."
National Public Radio	"Realize that social media communities have their own culture, etiquette, and norms, and be respectful of them."
Intel	"If you're about to publish something that makes you even the slightest bit uncomfortable, don't shrug it off and hit 'send.' Take a minute to review these guidelines and try to figure out what's bothering you, then fix it."
State of North Carolina	"Employees should be mindful that inappropriate usage of social media can be grounds for disciplinary action."

```
http://www.bby.com/2010/01/20/best-buy-social-media-guidelines/
http://www.capgemini.com/terms/socialmedia/
http://www.ibm.com/blogs/zz/en/guidelines.html
http://handbook.reuters.com/index.php/Reporting_from_the_internet#Social_media_guidelines
http://www.af.mil/shared/media/document/AFD-090406-036.pdf
http://voices.umich.edu/docs/Social-Media-Guidelines.pdf
http://blogs.cisco.com/news/ciscos_internet_postings_policy/
http://www.npr.org/about/aboutnpr/ethics/social_media_guidelines.html
http://www.intel.com/sites/sitewide/en_US/social-media.htm
http://www.records.ncdcr.gov/guides/best_practices_socialmedia_usage_20091217.pdf
```

Each of the examples cited in Table 9-1 is merely a snippet of larger social policies of these organizations. Each goes to great lengths to explain that we're living in a changing world, and in both their personal or professional lives, employees at these organizations are part of that new world. The codes of conduct, social policies, and new media guidance serve to inform, educate, and protect organizations and their employees about the benefits and pitfalls of social media engagement.

DEMONSTRATING THE IMPORTANCE OF CONNECTEDNESS

One sure-fire way to immerse your organization in social media adoption is to embrace corporate productivity tools that function much like social media applications. I'm thinking here of technologies such as Yammer, Salesforce Chatter, or many of the other tools in the Manage category of the social technology spectrum. These technologies typically allow corporate users to create profiles, access information, communicate with each other, and generally incorporate work tasks into a closed and secure corporate social media platform.

According to a study conducted by Yammer, which included 10,000 of their users, the results of using these enterprise social networking technologies revealed many benefits. Keeping in mind that this study was conducted by Yammer itself as a marketing device, Figure 9-2 illustrates their findings, and I'll share with you a few of the key nuggets that internal social platforms offer:

▶ More open communication

▶ Better new employee onboarding

▶ Increased connectedness between employees

▶ Higher productivity and lower attrition

Certainly, there are other ways of attaining similar accomplishments within an organization, yet using a tool like Yammer or Chatter can accelerate these internal corporate benefits. More importantly, users of Yammer and other solutions like it are participating in social networking. By following colleagues, joining and creating groups, and sharing information within the corporate social platform, they're acclimating themselves to social media. Although this may sound mundane to the social savvy reader, just think of the computer illiterate in your organizations, those who barely know how to send an e-mail without pressing "reply all." These folks are getting an education every time they log in to your internal social platforms.

▶ Internal social media platforms like Yammer or Salesforce Chatter can serve as training wheels for the socially inept.

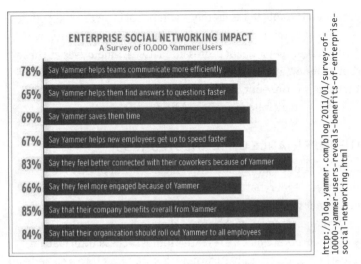

FIGURE 9-2: Benefits of enterprise social networking using Yammer.

Delivering a Scalable Measurement Strategy

"However beautiful the strategy, you should occasionally look at the results."
—Winston Churchill

This bit of wisdom from Winston Churchill was prescient in many ways. Developing a strategy that you can be proud of and use to rally your comrades is possible only if you achieve positive results. And in almost all cases, success or failure cannot be identified until your programs have left the building. Thus, it's critically important to develop a social media measurement strategy that captures metrics that allow you to assess your progress against big, audacious corporate goals as well as the nitty-gritty details that will help you to fine-tune your effectiveness. Although I've repeatedly recommended using only a few metrics to communicate your progress to the executive suite within your organization, it's a good idea to build up a bevy of metrics to fall back on if you're just starting out.

CREATING A STRATEGIC MEASUREMENT TO-DO LIST

So, if you're starting a program from scratch or even breathing new life into an existing program, I recommend the following measurement secrets to get you headed in the right direction and to get your social media measurement program off to a good start.

► **Make your programs impossible to refuse.** Take the time to do your homework and ensure that the digital measurement strategies that you suggest are not only feasible and in line with corporate objectives, but also low-risk for your organization. Here is where alignment against corporate goals is critically important because it's your chance to illustrate to your superiors that you'll be demonstrating how these new-fangled social media activities contribute to meaningful goals like revenue, satisfaction, and support. By planning precisely how your measures will map to big picture goals you will minimize objections. Additionally, know what you're up against and plan a response to any potential objections. For example, if you know that there's no budget for a social monitoring tool, suggest free solutions that will allow you to initiate a measurement program with an agreement that if it works, you will petition for funding for future projects.

▶ When launching a new or untested social media initiative, start with a small-scale pilot to demonstrate proof of concept. This minimizes risk and allows you to establish a track record.

▶ **Gain the support of at least one senior champion.** Championing an initiative like social media measurement can be challenging if no one understands what you're up to and no one is in your corner offering support. For this reason, it's critical to identify a senior level individual in your organization who will champion your cause. In many cases, this will be your direct manager or boss, but it doesn't always have to be. In fact, I've seen cases where an aspiring digital measurement analyst made a convincing case to an executive outside his team, who was then instrumental in ushering an entirely new measurement program into existence. By finding individuals who will benefit from your measurement programs and enlisting their support by asking for guidance, including them in your planning processes, and oftentimes acting as a protégé, you can accomplish great things.

▶ Identify possible champions for your measurement activities and begin building a relationship by piquing their interests or helping with their projects. Once you gain their confidence you can ask for support on your social media measurement ideas.

▶ **Don't get lost in the shuffle.** Remember that almost everyone in your organization will be busy with their own tasks, projects, and responsibilities, and yours will be just another moving part in the machine. While in many cases there will be a spotlight on the social media programs that you're measuring—especially if they are new and untested—there will be other times that your efforts go unnoticed. Ensure that you don't get lost in the shuffle by keeping every vested party up to date on the progress of your social media measurement activities. That's not to say that you need to pester stakeholders with incessant e-mails, but rather keep them informed by sharing interesting findings or anecdotes from your measurement analysis. It's best if you can establish a regular reporting routine up front so that your colleagues will know that you'll be keeping them informed, but coloring your informational reports with key highlights, interesting findings, and your insights will make a world of difference.

► **Report on your wins and your losses.** Of course reporting on your successes is one of the benefits of your job, but there are times when we have to hang our heads and face the music, too. Although no one likes to be the bearer of bad news, your responsibility as a measurer of social media is to report on the good and the bad. In my experience, I've found that it's often best to break bad news when it happens to mitigate further damage or take immediate actions for course correction. That said, don't wield the bad news without first understanding what happened and devising a plan or a series of options about how you can remedy the situation. Granted, you may not always have a crackerjack solution to every turn of events, but take the time to understand why something went wrong and how not to repeat it in the future. This will demonstrate that you're earning your stripes as a measurer of all things digital.

► **Demonstrate how you're improving over time.** Every good social media program has good and bad days. That goes for campaigns, ideas, and social media programs as well. By maintaining a record of your social actions and the programs you put into the field, you should be able to establish performance benchmarks over time. These benchmarks will enable you to identify when initiatives perform within normal ranges of expectation and when an idea is a viral sensation. Use your historic data to explain what's good and what isn't in a way that enables you to speak from a position of authority. All too often, I see companies making subjective claims about the effectiveness of this campaign or that, when in reality they have no basis for comparison. By establishing a scalable social measurement program, you'll be equipped to report on what works, what doesn't, and how you're improving over time.

Once you're successful at selling your social measurement programs internally, you'll find that stakeholders will rely on you for information about what to measure and how to launch new ideas into the field. Oftentimes, I find that the measurers of digital media are empowered because they hold the insights from past performance and can advise colleagues on what's likely to work and what isn't. These negotiations require tact and grace, but marketers who understand the performance of digital campaigns and why they worked are typically good allies when attempting to replicate success.

BENCHMARKING SUCCESSES AND FAILURES

In social media, benchmarks can be tough to come by. You cannot simply perform a Google search to come up with historic data that enables you to assess your status or

> Sometimes reporting bad news early can make a huge difference in recovery efforts. Don't hide from the inevitable; report both good and bad facts, but include recommendations for improvement.

> For some social media measurers, assuming the role of internal consultant to key stakeholders is a great way to ensure that measurement is included during the planning stages of social campaign development.

measure your progress against a set of comparable peers. In most cases, you have to build measures of success over time because your metrics will inherently be specific to your unique business. When clients press me for strategic benchmarks straight out of the gate, I assure them that I will deliver benchmarks; I just tell them that they'll get their benchmarks exactly when we have some definitive results to compare against. Benchmarks are really just a line in the sand that enables you to compare performance of one activity, or channel, or competitor against another.

Yet benchmarks, like other elements of your social media programs, need to develop over time. While you may be able to make comparisons within a few months of collecting data, I recommend amassing several months' worth of data to allow time for the metrics and the medium to stabilize. This accumulation will allow you to distinguish between the trends and the anomalies. I recommend benchmarking operational processes, key success metrics, and results. In this light, social media measurement does afford some metrics that can be evaluated in the context of competitive performance. Because the medium we operate in is often exposed to the public, there are ways of benchmarking success outside your own organization to map against the competition.

STANDARDIZING ON TERMS AND TACTICS

One key component of any social media measurement strategy is ensuring that all parties within your organization know what you're talking about when you rattle off measures and metrics. This is a classic crime in traditional Web Analytics. I've seen it happen countless times, when a Web Analyst begins spewing terminology like "unique visitors," "bounce rates," and "page depth"—for us measure geeks this is great stuff, but the vast majority of individuals' eyes will glaze over at the first mention of analytics vernacular. Avoid this costly mistake by ensuring that your metrics and the terms you use to describe them are sensible. That's not to say that you cannot have meaningful terms like reach and influence; just be prepared to offer a clear and concise answer when someone asks you what it means. My friend Bob Page likes to say, "If you're explaining, you're losing." Keep it simple whenever you can.

That said, the nature of metrics and digital measurement is such that we sometimes do need complex terms and formulas to explain or calculate what's going on. Yet, most of what we do is founded in the logic of numbers and therefore can be explained and replicated with precision. The best way I've seen to do this is by creating a data dictionary. A *data dictionary* is just what it sounds like: a dictionary that defines terms, formulas, calculations, and any other functions that need to be commonly understood by a group of people. Once you have this handy reference guide, it will become a valuable part of your corporate mentality. Make sure it's accessible through your internal social media platform, and don't be afraid to add to or revise the data dictionary on an ongoing basis. New terms will emerge all the time, and as a measurer of social media, you should work to ensure that everyone within your organization has a shared understanding of what you're measuring and what it means.

Introducing Accountability into the Mix

Any program of digital measurement should have some level of accountability attached. If it doesn't, you're merely collecting data without purpose. Accountability doesn't have to mean winning or losing jobs, but it should mean that data collected from your social media measurement carries enough value to red-light programs that are performing poorly or identify initiatives that should be celebrated for their contributions to the organization. To do this, companies need a high degree of confidence in their data and there must be widespread alignment on what success looks like.

In a lot of ways, this is why social media measurement should be a function within your internal organization and not outsourced to an agency or other outside party that's actually executing on your social programs. It's a bit like asking the fox to watch the henhouse if you turn over measurement to the same individuals who deliver your programs. Instead, make sure that you work closely with them to agree upon measures of success and what social media metrics are important to your organization. They should be willing to help on this account, because the metrics you use to quantify social initiatives will ultimately determine the effectiveness of your partners. Be wary of external parties that are reticent to relinquish control of social media metrics to your internal measurement pros. Before you retreat to your respective safe zones, know that there are ways to remain cooperative and accountable for your social media programs. Let's explore some possibilities.

COLLABORATING FOR BUSINESS SUCCESS

▶ Use internal social media platforms to get the word out about your measurement operating procedures.

Whether your social media activities are cooked up entirely in house or you work with dozens of partners, collaboration is key to success. And by collaboration, I mean talking, meeting, and sometimes sparring with stakeholders until you gain an understanding of the goals of each social initiative, what they consider to be a success, and how you will measure it. While you're working on building up the corporate mentality that places digital measurement at the front of every employee's mind, you will be constantly fighting to implement metrics into social media initiatives. However, as I've witnessed at numerous organizations before, there will be a point where measurement isn't an afterthought and you will be consulted before programs are about to hit the streets. However, this requires a widespread awareness of your measurement program, and your standard operating procedures for implementing metrics and measures.

Recognize that some of your forays into social media will be experimental, but this shouldn't stop you from creating metrics to measure each aspect of them to determine their effectiveness—rather, it's even more reason to do so. This is especially true when working with external agencies and paying for your social activities. By collaborating with marketers, developers, and strategists about what you're working toward, you can establish agreeable metrics that will allow you to recognize when you've hit success. This is impossible to do in a vacuum and, thus, collaboration is a requirement.

HOLDING EVERYONE'S FEET TO THE FIRE

Once you've established your measures of success and defined how you will measure your social marketing activity, make sure that everyone involved is aware of the status on an ongoing basis. By this time, this should be no secret, as much of what I discussed in previous chapters is about setting expectations and communicating your results. By introducing accountability to these concepts you're merely holding everyone to their commitments in social media and their ability to deliver on promises. As you learned earlier, this is no longer a trivial medium and big dollars are at stake. Thus, a robust measurement plan with clearly defined metrics and widely understood measures of success is paramount to any program.

One senior executive that I spoke with informed me that analytics was moved at his Fortune 100 company from marketing to finance because the fundamentals were so similar to other tasks within the finance department. He described the act of collecting data, analyzing results, and using the information to make business decisions and pointed out the parallels between digital data and financial data. For him, the processes were largely the same, and moving the digital analytics team into finance not only made sense, but also elevated the level of corporate accountability. This was especially important because the company encouraged a high level of testing and experimentation. Each new trial initiative was measured using analytics to determine its effectiveness. The results determined whether the idea would be rolled out to production or squashed at the germination stage.

Now, when anyone within the organization reports on information at any level, they are expected to do so with evidence revealed from data. While this was somewhat of a cultural change at the organization, employees are beginning to adopt this as a standard practice. However, according to the executive I spoke with, he had to

▶ Some enterprises are beginning to place analytics within the finance departments of their organizations to leverage similar financial data processes and elevate accountability.

step on a few throats to make examples out of employees who experimented with campaigns and failed to implement measures of success because there was no way to validate the true effectiveness of the idea without data to support the results. After just a few tough-love examples, employees across the organization are now making better use of data and using it to support their ideas and hypotheses. Now that's accountability!

LOOKING AHEAD FOR THE NEXT BIG TREND

To peer into the epicenter of social media opportunity is akin to staring at the molten core of the sun. Its power will fuel growth, innovation, connectedness, and new life for things we can't possibly even imagine to come in the digital era. Like the telephone did for the 19th century, social media will transform our lives in profound ways.

Yet, instead of burning your retinas in search of the answers for what's to come, take a look at the emerging disciplines in the world around you. What I see is data amassing at an astounding rate and organizations drowning in the deluge. Those that do float to the top will identify ways to find meaning within the data and leverage conjoined data and ideas to reveal astounding new discoveries. We'll look to data visualizations like the ones depicted in Chapter 2 to help us rapidly process this wealth of new data and for a new breed of data artists to lead the charge.

Additionally, the proliferation of mobile devices will allow us to untether from the constraints of yesterday's computing relics and enter a new realm of mobility and social connectedness. This will give rise to liberating social location-based services that open conduits for infinite interactions between colleagues, friends, and strangers. These services will emerge alongside of privacy measures that place individuals in control of their own data.

> **NOTE** Although enterprises and organizations will still yearn for and maintain stores of information about their customers, personal data, preferences, attitudes, and experiences will become a new currency that's traded by individuals in a fair value exchange across digital media.

I'd be remiss if I didn't point to one of the most encouraging trends that I see unfolding in the near future. Whereas most companies are actively trying to monetize their social media efforts and ratchet up the levers of customer satisfaction, service, and revenue, others are working (oftentimes simultaneously) toward less self-absorbed goals. Here I'm talking about the emergence of social good. Never before have we had an opportunity to reach, inform, and engage others at the scale that social media offers. Individuals and organizations that are using this medium for philanthropic efforts are forging new ground and creating a genuine impact in areas across the globe. As some companies chase new friends and followers for financial gains, I expect that the socially conscious will offset their capitalist pursuits for humanitarian gains.

In this section I will touch on these burgeoning social media trends: data mashups, location-based social activities, and social good. But before getting started, I thought I'd share a question and answer exchange that I had with an aspiring graduate student looking to cash in on some expert secrets for the venture capital firm where he was interning.

SOCIAL ANALYTICS INTERVIEW QUESTIONS

I'm often asked to peer into my crystal ball and make predictions about what I believe will happen with measurement technologies in the future. Not too long ago, I was approached by a student seeking just this sort of prognostication. His motivation was to impress a VC firm in Montreal where he was interning by tapping into the wisdom of a select few in the digital measurement field. I offered some thoughts on the condition that I could repurpose them in this book.

A Response to Antoine Meunier, Graduate Student at HEC Montreal Business School by John Lovett (JL)

Q: Studies show that CMOs care more and more about social media in their marketing mix. Considering your experience as a consultant, what kind of information interests CMOs (or analysts) the most? What are their expectations?

JL: I agree that CMOs are beginning to place more faith in the value of social media. It's not because internal marketers are convincing their organizations to invest in social media, but because customers are increasingly speaking with words and actions across social channels. The cacophony of social chatter is jarring and brands must take notice. Thus, the information most critical to marketers is understanding customer behavior across both new and existing channels and deciphering customer needs within a multichannel, multinational context.

(continues)

SOCIAL ANALYTICS INTERVIEW QUESTIONS *(continued)*

*According to a 2009 survey conducted by **www.thecmosurvey.com**, 88 percent of CMOs will focus on getting closer to their customers in the next 5 years. Getting closer requires meeting customers in channels where they interact. This is increasingly happening at off-site locations and on social networks. The challenge for the CMO is to understand customer behaviors at an individual customer level across these channels to reach them in the most meaningful way. Thus, the expectation of CMOs is that the technologies they use to collect and analyze data about customers is capable of integrating within individual customer profiles that portray a comprehensive picture of interactions across channels. I call this complete view a "true profile" of an individual customer. Further, it's my belief that CMOs harbor the expectation that marketing automation technologies should be capable of accessing these unique customer true profiles for targeted marketing across numerous customer touch points, including social channels.*

Q: Do you consider CMOs' expectations to be fully satisfied by the products that are available in the market? Is there still something missing?

JL: The expectations of integrated customer data and unified "true profiles" of individual customers are far from satisfied. For most they have not even begun to manifest. To date, no single technology solution is able to fulfill this integration and identification problem seamlessly. Companies that are succeeding in this way are assembling technologies and developing custom solutions to meet their needs.

Q: How would you differentiate an innovative social media analytics platform (potentially interesting for venture capitalists) from one that adds no value?

JL: Social media platforms that add value will be ones that enable companies to customize the data collection methods to meet their unique business requirements. Additionally, the ability to perform true ad hoc analysis against a flexible database is paramount to attaining insights from social analytics. A valuable tool would also include data collection from owned and non-owned media properties. This data could be written to a database and enabled with calculated metrics such as Key Performance Indicators that demonstrate progress toward desired outcomes. The system would also contain workflow processes and alerting functionality to delegate tasks to specific individuals and create imperative calls to action for specific triggered events.

Thus, the system would function as an analysis, reporting, and action tool that could be used by numerous teams across an enterprise. These capabilities could emerge in some form of hybrid social media monitoring/Web Analytics tool. Yet, to my knowledge, none have been developed to date that possess the full extent of capabilities I've described here.

Q: Which technologies do you consider to be relevant and reliable today?

JL: Technologies from companies such as Radian6, Visible Technologies, Twitalyzer, Klout, Kontagent, and others each possess elements of the technology capabilities I've described herein. There are shards of brilliance within each of these, and undoubtedly others that I have yet to see.

Q: In your opinion, what is the next step for social media analytics from a technological standpoint?

JL: In addition to the capabilities I described previously, social media management requires what I've termed a "virtual Network Operations Center" for effective orchestration. This command center would act as a listening post for all brand-related conversations or topics taking place on the Internet; a triage center to delegate tasks; an aggregator of unique customer true profile data; and a campaign management hub for automated activities.

This virtual NOC would enable an enterprise to communicate with customers across both inbound and outbound marketing vehicles in a coordinated, consistent, and highly personalized manner. The data accessible to the virtual NOC would also be available to analysts for propensity modeling, predictive scoring, and hypothesis testing. Governance over this solution would be mandatory, but the output of such a system would enable a highly efficient and highly relevant means of facilitating customer interactions.

Mashing Data Futures

One of the beautiful things about living in a Big Data world that's connected via social networks is that there are many opportunities to mix, mash, and combine data sets in interesting ways. Oftentimes these data mashes can offer glimpses into businesses, consumers, and society as a whole. Although data integration techniques have been around for a very long time, the introduction of social data creates new opportunities for businesses, researchers, and average consumers to learn from and explore the vast expanse of digital data.

INTEGRATING CUSTOMER PROFILE DATA

One challenge that I'm frequently asked about by clients is the ability to socialize customer data across the enterprise. In many cases, organizations have substantial data about their customers from a single channel of record. These businesses may have rich data stores within their customer relationship management (CRM) databases that offer details about customer purchase histories, credit profiles, propensity to purchase, affinity for certain products, and many more details about their interactions with the organization. Yet, in most cases, this data is locked within a specific CRM silo that reveals only one side of customer behavior. Oftentimes, there is no link to web data, which may be the primary method in which customers gain their information, research products, and deliberate about new services. Organizations that bring these two data streams together often learn revealing details about customers' preferences, interests, and intentions, all through their implicit digital actions.

Taking this one step further, organizations that integrate customers' social media profiles into their data sets can open even greater reams of knowledge about customers' likes, dislikes, and inherent preferences based on what they say and the company they keep within their social networks. If this is all starting to sound a little scary to you, don't worry. The integrated customer profile should be governed by strict privacy protocols to ensure that painting this complete picture of the customer across channels is done with the customer's permission and used in a manner that is consistent with how customers want to be contacted. This tenuous statement is the linchpin of this concept that I call the "true profile."

▶ A true profile of a customer gathers together customer data from multiple sources to give an organization a more relevant and useful picture of the total customer.

A true profile is the convergence of customer data from customer relationship management (CRM), web site browsing, social media, and other sources to create a single unified profile of any given customer. I call this the true profile of the user, as shown in Figure 9-3.

The art of profiling customers to drive more relevant communications has been a marketing mainstay for decades. Whether this tactic consists of being sized up by a used car salesperson upon walking onto the lot, or accumulating records of long-term customers across multiple interactions, the premise is the same—understanding customer needs, wants, and desires with the goal of delivering goods and services to meet those needs. Yet, as consumers increasingly turn to the Internet and other digital channels to interact with brands, the art of profiling customers becomes extremely complex. Thus, the true profile is a solution that offers a contemporary understanding of customers by managing data from interactions across multiple channels (that is, physical locations, call centers, web sites, mobile devices, social networks, and so on) within a unified customer profile.

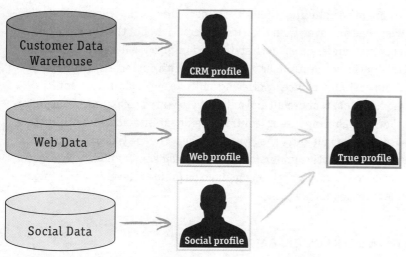

FIGURE 9-3: The true customer profile.

True profiles can be assembled using a variety of techniques, but the underlying method consists of three key components:

▶ **Capturing Customer Data:** The foundation of the true profile begins with customer data, which is something that most companies have in abundance. Customer data sources include traditional CRM databases, sales force automation records, financial transaction information, Web Analytics data, and social media mentions, just to name a few. Yet, the majority of organizations maintain customer interactions occurring across these disparate channels in isolated silos that reveal only a portion of true customer behavior.

▶ **Analyzing Customer Behavior:** Once data is aggregated within a true profile, internal teams of Customer Marketers or Web Analysts can access records to understand how individuals interact with brands across various channels. For example, analysis might reveal that customers with high profitability tend to research products and services online first and then make transactions by phone with call center agents. Or alternatively, customers with products nearing the end of their life cycle are 10 times more likely to respond to an e-mail message by clicking links to newer versions of their products. These insights can be used to generate marketing campaigns and outreach methods that are highly relevant and highly likely to have an impact on your bottom line.

▶ **Deciphering Customer Intent:** The key component within the true profile is the ability to amass knowledge of implicit and explicit customer behavior for

▶ True profiles break the silos of data by integrating pertinent sales, marketing, and behavioral information about individual customers within a centralized record.

the purpose of deciphering intent. Customers' intentions will undoubtedly shift over time and even with each new interaction, but the ability to build upon customer preferences, both stated and inferred, will serve marketers by ultimately building stronger relationships with customers. This includes respecting customer choice by offering multiple methods of communication such as phone, chat, or e-mail and adhering to stated communication preferences. Yet, deciphering intent requires intelligent interactions with customers based on what you know they want and what they're likely to respond to based on your collective understanding of customers. The ability to direct this knowledge toward a customer using true profiles elevates marketing to a higher level of sophistication.

COLLIDING DATA SETS FOR BIG BANG IDEAS

While combining customer data sets across channels is definitely something that I see headed your way in the near future, I also believe that this data can be used in context for customers across social technologies as well.

One company that is revolutionizing consumer access to data mashups is Siri. After incubating in Stamford's Research Institute and consuming $200 million in early-stage research and development, the fledgling company secured two brief rounds of funding that added an additional $24 million to its development coffers. While still gaining inertia in its early days, the technology attracted some major attention from industry insiders like Robert Scoble, who quipped, "This is the future of the Web." After receiving these accolades, the company was quickly snatched off the market by Apple (APPL) in April of 2010 for a rumored acquisition price in the neighborhood of $200M (http://blog.programmableweb.com/2010/04/28/apple-buys-siri-largest-mashup-acquisition-ever/).

The Siri service, as shown in Figure 9-4, is available today as an app that is billed as a personal assistant that interprets voice commands to conduct real-time searches. You can voice a request such as, "Where's the best place to eat around here?" or "Book me a flight to Phoenix," and the application will work to accomplish your request. It works using voice recognition software from Nuance and by querying open APIs from services such as Yelp, OpenTable, MovieTickets.com, and Rotten Tomatoes, to name a few. The service can not only find locations, but can also scan reviews to recommend the best option based on user reviews. When it needs more information, the app will ask questions, and remarkably, it even gets to know you over time. Much like a human assistant would begin to know your preferences over time, Siri does the same. Functionality also enables users to set up alerts and reminders for everyday occurrences.

FIGURE 9-4: The Siri personal assistant mashes data from open APIs.

The nifty little app allows users to enter a whole new world of data mashing and socially accessible possibilities. Theoretically, that is. I've been "teaching" my app, and well, let's just say that it's still an apprentice. It is good at sourcing restaurants and will allow me to book a reservation at a local eatery, all with a few clicks on my iPhone. But complicated queries with multiple facets still trip it up.

According to views expressed during Scoble's interview with the founders, the "tentacles" of the Internet aren't linked at this time. This prevents sharing of information and social context. When these information sources are linked and synthesized in real time, the possibilities include a device capable of understanding commands and orchestrating information and events. This will be one app to watch, and undoubtedly, the underlying technology will manifest in other ways as well. Hopefully we have the slick usability of an Apple product to look forward to once it's perfected.

NOTE If you're interested in data mashups and API access, check out Programmableweb.com.

Mobilizing Your Social Marketing

One area of social media that is poised for explosive social growth is the utilization of location-based services (LBS). These social solutions, offered by companies like Foursquare and Gowalla, allow registered users to "check in" to locations across the globe. Mobile devices capture each user's precise coordinates, and users typically receive recognition for their check-in efforts. Recognition can consist of anything from badges, as offered by Foursquare, to cold cash discounts at local stores and restaurants. Most early iterations of LBS services have shown sprouts of whimsy and gamification, yet they are turning into big business in a hurry.

MAKING SENSE OF LOCATION-BASED SERVICES

If we're in agreement that social media as a whole is still in its early days, social location-based services (LBS) can certainly be considered a newborn that's still wet behind the ears. The most recognized operators in this space, Gowalla and Foursquare, have only been around since 2007 and 2009, respectively. LBS technologies first emerged from Palm in 1999, which delivered early apps from weather.com and Traffic Touch that made use of the ZIP code level positioning information. In the past decade, LBS solutions have become indispensible for personal global positioning devices, and recently, they're finding their way into apps and social services.

The social media incarnation of LBS includes sites that allow users to broadcast their current location to the world at large. Think of users checking in on their mobile devices to say, "Hey, I'm at Starbucks!" or "I'm at Fenway Park." At the time of this writing, the most popular LBS offerings are Foursquare, Gowalla, and Facebook Places. So, you may be asking yourself why in the world anyone would want to participate in LBS and divulge their whereabouts to the masses at any given time? Well, you're not alone. Many question the value of these game-like applications, yet as with many nascent technologies, the inherent potential for permission-based marketing to consumers using the relevance of their location holds enormous opportunity.

Keep in mind that the entire market for social LBS is estimated at $20 billion, despite the fact that adoption of these services is very low. A study conducted by Pew Internet found that in 2010 only 4 percent of American adults participated in location-based services (www.pewinternet.org/Reports/2010/Location-based-services.aspx). Yet, by my estimates, there are approximately 40 million active users of social LBS at this time. However, that number does include Facebook Places, which represents exactly half of all active LBS users. Table 9-2 shows current active users across networks and funding to date for the most popular social LBS solutions.

TABLE 9-2: Social Location-Based Services

	YEAR FOUNDED	REPORTED FUND-ING TO DATE*	ESTIMATED USERS**
Facebook Places	2010	n/a	30 million
Google Latitude	2009	n/a	10 million
Foursquare	2009	$21.4M	7 million
Loopt	2005	$17M	4 million
MyTown	2008	$29.5M	3.1 million
Where.com	2004	$18.5M	3 million
BrightKite	2009	$1.42M	2 million
SCVNGR	2008	$19.8M	1 million
Gowalla	2007	$10.4M	1 million

* As reported by CrunchBase
** Sources:
http://siliconangle.com/blog/2010/09/27/where-com-acquires-localginger-marking-the-shift-to-location-based-flash-sales/
http://techcrunch.com/2010/07/09/loopt-4-million/
http://www.engagedigital.com/2011/02/10/gowalla-nears-1m-users/
http://mashable.com/2011/02/22/scvngr-1-million/
http://techcrunch.com/2011/02/21/foursquare-closing-in-on-7-million-users/
http://www.readwriteweb.com/archives/brightkite_universal_check-in_foursquare_gowalla.php
http://networkeffect.allthingsd.com/20110201/google-latitude-adds-check-ins-how-2009/
http://www.businessinsider.com/facebook-places-may-have-30-million-users-but-none-of-them-use-it-very-much-2010-10

Excluding the 800-pound gorilla that is Facebook, Foursquare is the fastest growing social LBS on the market today. According to a report that the company issued in early 2011, they grew 3,400 percent in 2010. And the burgeoning service is showing no signs of fatigue. As illustrated in Figure 9-5, Foursquare had 381 million check-ins in 2010 from every country on the planet and one reported check-in from outer space. Check-ins by time and category reveal that most users are reporting their whereabouts at eateries, offices, and shopping locations around the world.

If this social LBS craze still has you scratching your head, you're not alone. The fascination of sharing your location and revealing personal information for little benefit except fame and fictitious mayorship is beyond the grasp of most. Yet, companies that do venture into location-based marketing should be measuring their efforts. From venue owners looking to cash in on the LBS bandwagon to brands tracking their users' locations, the ultimate goal should be to quantify the contributions of location-based services to your corporate objectives. Although I've already offered some metrics that you can use to track social LBS in Chapter 1, you should be thinking about how these mobile networks can be measured against your business goals. Most offer APIs that allow users to access historic data about check-ins. Marketers should be working to gain information of this nature in aggregate as well. Here are a few links to developer sites that offer details on how to access LBS APIs.

▶ **Foursquare:** `http://developer.foursquare.com/docs/users/checkins.html`

▶ **Gowalla:** `http://gowalla.com/api/docs`

▶ **Facebook:** `http://developers.facebook.com/docs/reference/api/`

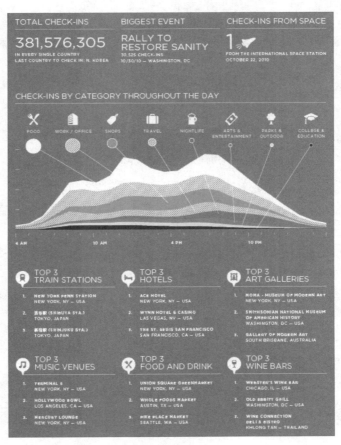

FIGURE 9-5: Foursquare's 2010 statistics.

CREATING A VALUE EXCHANGE IN HYPER-LOCAL MARKETS

Most marketers I know want data. Oftentimes, they want it so badly that they're willing to pay for it to get closer to their customers. Yet data accuracy is often a problem, so there's nothing better than convincing consumers to give up explicit data about their location, preferences, and details of their likes, dislikes, and social spheres of influence. How do you do this? Offer them a deal. We humans are so tempted by the idea of a deal that we're often willing to spend more and purchase more frequently when products, promotions, and services are presented as deals.

We're seeing this in manifestations of Groupon and LivingSocial, both of whom dropped big bucks on marketing and advertising in 2011. Groupon wasn't so successful with their Super Bowl commercial, but regardless, the company has managed to accrue $2 billion in revenues in just two short years. As more and more individuals adopt smartphones and tablets to leverage social media on the go, marketers will find ways of attracting their attention and wallets.

LOOKING AHEAD AT LOCATION-BASED SERVICES

It's my belief that location-based services will become ubiquitous when businesses adopt near-field communication technology that transmits a wireless signal that opens worlds of possibilities. Tasks such as paying a grocery bill with a scan of your phone or checking into a hotel with the click of your mobile device will become commonplace as more businesses adopt these services. Yet, the opportunity for near-field communication services transcends LBS solutions because of the ability to convert customers into loyal users. They benefit from convenience and brands win by gaining more data from their customers.

Some, like the authors of the *Loyalty in 4D* paper (www.a-g.com/4DLoyalty/Loyalty_in_4D_White_Paper.pdf), predict a collision of data streams that include the conversation stream (that is, status updates), the location stream (that is, LBS check-ins), and the purchase stream (made possible by burgeoning solutions like Blippy and Swipely). According to the report, "The conversation stream provides the attitudinal profile for the consumer and more. We not only learn their interests and their profession, but who their friends are, who influences them and what brands they are willing to interact with. The location stream tells us where they actually go. We learn about brand stickiness and place loyalty. The purchase stream tells us what brands they purchase, whether they remain loyal to brands or are offer-sensitive and gives us a coveted look at the size of their wallet and the share by each brand." This convergence of social, mobile, and transactional data could open a treasure trove of insights for marketers.

Doing Social Good

The next big opportunity I see for social marketers is the ability to give back to their communities, to charities, to non-governmental organizations (NGOs), and by extension, to their customers by doing *social good*. The concept of social good leverages social media and the ability to connect users to unite in support of worthy causes. It includes philanthropic efforts that grow through social networks. And, it's becoming a very big deal.

Of course, philanthropy isn't new by any stretch of the imagination, as organizations like the Gates Foundation have been doing this for years. Yet, many companies are accelerating their philanthropic efforts using social media. What's more, brands, media outlets, and everyday consumers are taking notice. Several companies have dedicated web sites or sections of their sites to promoting social good. Examples can be found at Causes.com, Causecast, DoSomething, Epic Change, Global Giving, KULA, socialIMPACT, and Mashable's Social Good, just to name a few. This list doesn't include hundreds of organizations and bloggers who are working to make a difference using social media.

Organizations are stepping up their game when it comes to social good and corporate social responsibility. Seventy percent of executives surveyed by Webber Shandwick reported that they use social media to communicate their corporate social responsibility to their customers and the public at large. Among these executives, 60 percent reported that their efforts in this regard have had a positive impact on the quality of communications and helped to reach a broad and diverse audience (www.slideshare.net/wssocialimpact/crowdsourcing-social-impact-in-csr). Webber Shandwick is the firm behind many social good initiatives, such as the Pepsi Refresh project, the MasterCard Foundation, Best Buy's @15, and Stand Up To Cancer, among many others. This organization and others like it are training businesses and nonprofit organizations to use social media to amplify their messages and activate the masses.

EXTENDING GOODWILL THROUGH SOCIAL MEDIA

Examples of social good are plentiful. I'll relate a few that I find particularly interesting. One example of a social good project is an initiative sponsored by BHH New York, which offered up a mere $1,000 dollars to three interns who developed a project with the goal of "doing something good." They developed Underheard in New York, which is a modest 30-day endeavor to give homeless people in New York City a voice and a platform to be heard. Four individuals living without shelter in New York were given cell phones and Twitter accounts to share glimpses of their lives. Despite the fact that the project was designed as only a short-term initiative, the experience has undoubtedly changed the lives of many individuals involved.

Over the course of 30 days, the four men involved in Underheard in New York shared their stories and reached a community of followers. For the men shown in Figure 9-6, their lives were forever changed by the experience. The project enabled the men to improve aspects of their lives, ranging from the newfound ability to "crack a little smile sometimes," to finding jobs, to being reunited with long-lost family members.

FIGURE 9-6: Underheard in New York offers a voice for the homeless.

Another social good initiative that has had a significant impact on many people is called charity: water. It started with one individual's idea to donate his birthday proceeds, and he asked that his would-be gifters donate $20 to provide drinking water for people around the globe who don't have access to clean water. Seven hundred people showed up and the entire sum of the money was donated to build six wells in

Uganda. This simple gift profoundly affected the lives of hundreds of individuals. But the idea didn't stop there; they kept going and asked that others share in this idea to help those around the world who don't have access to clean water by donating to remedy the situation. The idea spread like wildfire and the initiative has surpassed all expectations.

The beauty of this social good initiative is that communities banded together to contribute to this cause. This was the case for a small community of digital measurement professionals that I'm a part of as well. One advocate from our group, Jason Thompson, decided to donate his birthday proceeds to charity: water and set out with a goal of $500 as his target. According to Jason, word got out entirely through social networking. He described what happened in this way:

> "I Tweeted a couple times about my birthday campaign and things took off from there. I was really focused on marketing to the digital measurement community I work in, we go by #measure in the Twitterverse. There was a small group of five people that really jumped on board and took over all the marketing efforts. Before I knew it, I was seeing links from Facebook, Twitter, LinkedIn, etc., all pointing to my charity: water birthday campaign. It blew me away how involved other people got in the effort."

As more and more people began donating money, it became apparent that Jason would easily surpass his target goal of $500, so he upped it to $1,000. Yet, the social media momentum was on and donations kept pouring in. Dollars from members of the digital measurement community kept pouring in up until the day of Jason's birthday, which signified the end of the giving period. He shattered his $500 goal by 10 times and raised $5,074 for charity: water. Metrics showed that this donation will provide 25 years of clean drinking water for over 250 people, water that is accessible right in their village. Jason was quoted as saying, "This will literally change the way of life for an entire village." But it changed Jason too. When we talked about it, he shared that the experience gave him a new perspective on life by allowing him to put the things that he takes for granted, like clean drinking water, into perspective. Thus, not only did this project, which was made possible by social media, change the lives of the inhabitants of an entire village, it also changed the lives of everyone involved.

Jason's story is just one of the episodes in charity: water's history. To date, they've raised over $7 million and directly affected the lives of over 1.7 million people. The image in Figure 9-7 shows just how far one man's idea has traveled, primarily using social media, and they're tracking it using metrics. Now that's what I call social good.

FIGURE 9-7: charity: water's social good efforts affect hundreds of thousands.

PERSONIFYING GOOD

However, like your commercial efforts, all this social good must be measured to understand the progress and impact that it has on recipients. Organizations like charity: water and others are adept at tracking donors and donations, yet unlike charity:water few have the means to effectively measure their efforts on a detailed level. However, this is changing.

One initiative that I'm particularly proud of is called the Analysis Exchange. I happen to be a co-founder of this organization that helps nonprofits and NGOs by delivering free Web Analytics services. Our idea was to solve a massive pain point for organizations that typically had finite resources but plentiful data. Our idea was to create trios, pairing nonprofits with aspiring Web Analysts who were eager to learn and mentors who had experience in the field of digital measurement. The concept behind the launch of the Analysis Exchange program was to train a new breed of digital measurement professionals using an innovative approach that allowed mentors and students to give back to the nonprofit community and everyone to benefit from a productive learning exercise at the same time. Our efforts have been wildly successful to date. In the first 12 months of the program, Analysis Exchange has helped hundreds of nonprofit organizations (including charity: water) to measure the impact of their digital offerings. Figure 9-8 shows a map of participants in the Analysis Exchange program.

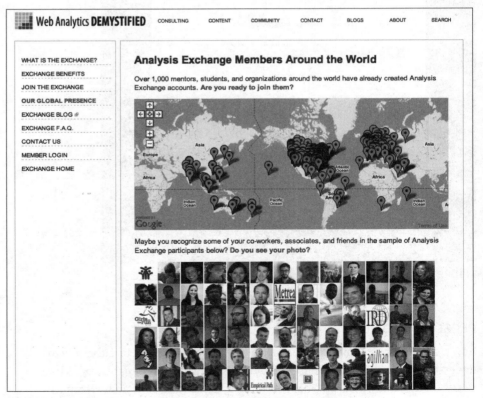

FIGURE 9-8: The Analysis Exchange network of students and mentors.

I summed up my thoughts about how analytics can help nonprofits for our partner organization the NTEN, the nonprofit Technology Network. The accompanying sidebar is what I wrote.

HOW CAN THE COMMUNICATIONS STAFF AT A SMALL TO MEDIUM-SIZED NONPROFIT USE WEB ANALYTICS TO MAKE THEIR JOBS EASIER?

Communicating in today's real-time, socially connected, tech-savvy world is a whole lot more difficult than it used to be. Not only do you have to watch what customers do at your events and in your physical locations, but now you need to be aware of their online behaviors, how they interact with your web sites, and where they spend their time on social networks. The challenges are even more pronounced for small and mid-sized nonprofits, which operate on limited budgets with finite resources. Yet, failure to embrace online channels as a means to reach your audience will result in inferior results.

That's why so many nonprofits are turning to Analytics to help them understand the digital channels that have the potential to impact numerous aspects of their organizations, especially communications. By analyzing visitor traffic to web pages using analytics, small organizations are able to recognize which content captures the attention of their audiences and when it drives visitors to act. With just a limited amount of time, a small communications staff can analyze their inbound traffic to determine which channels (such as e-mail, search, or social media) are delivering visitors who volunteer and contribute to their cause.

Armed with this knowledge, communications teams can craft messages that are tailored for each channel. Using the web pages you already have, these messages can direct visitors to profitable content using direct links within your outbound e-mails, advertisements, or newsletters. In this way, Analytics can take the guesswork out of marketing by helping to identify the best message for the right channel. Many nonprofits and non-governmental organizations are working with the Analysis Exchange program, which is a service that provides absolutely free analytics services to accomplish these tasks. Visit **www.analysis-exchange.com** to learn more about how Web Analytics and the Analysis Exchange can accelerate your online communications.

MEASURING THE MOST IMPORTANT METRIC: IMPACT

Perhaps one of the most important things that you can do when measuring social media is to remain cognizant of the overall impact that your efforts have on your business, your customers, and in some cases, society at large. I saved this little secret for the end of this book because impact is quite frankly the hardest aspect that you will ever work to measure. While impact can sometimes be quantified in terms of financial impact, customer satisfaction impact, and other tangible terms, impact often eludes digital tracking mechanisms and occurs at a much more personal, ana-log level.

Some might try to argue that measuring impact is a fool's mission and cannot be accomplished. I dismiss this notion and contend that measuring impact requires a combination of discipline and determination, as well as many of the measurement tactics that I've outlined throughout this book.

Measuring impact in the simplest terms requires knowing where you begin and where you end for any given initiative. The savvy marketer will document the journey and learn from the process to avoid pitfalls and replicate success.

Knowing Where You Are Today

> My advice is to do this early on to identify your internal strengths and weaknesses.

To effectively measure impact, I recommend that you take stock in where you are today with regard to your social marketing programs and your measurement practices. In my consulting engagements I help clients understand where they are starting from by per-forming an assessment of their current technology, their staffing levels, the business processes in use, and the governance they have over these activities. Although I use a 200-point evaluation matrix to quantify these aspects of social media readiness, you can opt for a simpler method of identifying your resources and knowing your capabili-ties. Most often, social media marketers have this information at their fingertips, yet few take the time to organize their thoughts into a strategic plan.

Ask yourself the following questions to determine your social media readiness and to ensure that you have a shared understanding of where you're starting from with social media measurement:

> - What human resources are available for measuring your social media programs?
> - What is the skill level and experience of your social media measurement staff?
> - What is the budget for social media monitoring and analysis?

- What level of importance does your organization place on social media at this time?

- Is the allocated budget proportional to the importance of social programs?

- What level of awareness does your organization have about social media measurement?

- How much education and training will you need to perform to bring your colleagues up to speed?

- What tools are available for measuring and analyzing social marketing activity?

- Does your executive team support your social media measurement program?

- Which programs, tactics, and channels have succeeded for your organization and which have failed in the past?

If you are satisfied with the majority of your answers to these questions, you're well on your way to kicking off a successful social media measurement program. If, however, your answers are lacking, take the time identify your shortfalls and work with internal managers and peers to remedy the situation. In either case, use this list of questions to set proper expectations.

Agreeing Upon Where You Want to Go

Once you have a firm grasp of your social media resources and capabilities, you can begin to map out where you want to go. This process of mapping your destinations requires knowledge of overarching corporate goals and tight alignment with objectives and desired outcomes. This method of alignment was described as the Waterfall Strategy in Chapter 4, whereby all social media initiatives are aligned with a greater purpose. In doing this, you will ensure that your programs and tactics are working toward something beneficial for your company. Your task is to ensure that the measures and metrics you put in place accurately track progress toward those goals.

- Does your organization have specific and measurable corporate goals?

- Does everyone within your organization know what the corporate goals are?

- Is your social media measurement plan aligned to support corporate goals?

- Have you collaborated with key business stakeholders to capture their social media data needs?

- ▶ Do you work closely with stakeholders to establish measures of success for each social marketing initiative prior to launch?
- ▶ Do your measures of success accurately reflect the progress and impact of social marketing campaigns?
- ▶ Once established, do you use measures of success to set and maintain expectations?
- ▶ Have you established thresholds for acceptable performance on key success metrics?
- ▶ Do you have a process for optimizing social media programs while they are in the field?
- ▶ Are your stakeholders and marketing peers held accountable for the goals they set and the commitments they make?

Recounting the Journey of How You Arrived

As you saw earlier, most social media campaigns have a finite shelf life. This can be bad for social marketers because they continually need to develop the next great idea, yet it's typically good for the social media measurer because it offers an opportunity for reflection and assessment of existing measures of success.

- ▶ Have you developed a process of regular reporting to keep stakeholders informed and minimize surprises?
- ▶ Did you establish milestones that signify key accomplishments during the life of the campaign?
- ▶ Did you reach your stated goals? If not, what prevented you from getting there?
- ▶ Were your metrics meaningful enough to mandate changes during the active program period?
- ▶ Did you learn anything about the measurement and planning process that you can apply to future initiatives?
- ▶ Are you building and maintaining benchmarks to evaluate progress over time?
- ▶ Did you incorporate feedback from colleagues and customers to assess the perceived success of the program?

- ▶ Do you have a competitive perspective that enables you to assess progress against that of the competition?

- ▶ Do you have established methods of sharing stories of success and failure with peers across your organization?

Acknowledging that Social Media Is About People

I want you to think back to Chapter 3 and recall why we started this crazy social media measurement ride in the first place. We did it to understand people and how they behave using new technologies. Their behaviors—while sometimes bizarre and often unpredictable—are made possible by social media and an infinitely connected society. We use the measures and tactics throughout this book in an attempt to make sense of their actions and go to great lengths to catalog behavior in hopes that this will benefit us in future endeavors. Yet, amid all the metrics and measures, it's very easy to lose sight of the fact that we are talking about humans and the ways they leverage modern communication vehicles to share ideas, express emotions, research opportunities, purchase products, and entertain themselves.

Yet, measurement itself is not the goal. It's simply a method of informing you whether or not you reached the end you were angling for in any given social marketing initiative.

It's also important to recognize that amassing a Twitter following or racking up YouTube views isn't the end either. These are activities involving people that can help you to reach your stated goals of more revenue and increased satisfaction, or whatever yours may be.

▶ *Measurement reveals the path toward your desired outcome. It's not the end game.*

- ▶ Social media metrics are a starting point.
- ▶ Metrics allow you to measure progress toward goals.
- ▶ Metrics are passive; you must be active.
- ▶ Measurement frameworks provide consistency.
- ▶ Consistency makes comparison possible.
- ▶ Not everything maps back to ROI.
- ▶ Change is constant and metrics must change.

SUMMARY

Measuring social media is a challenging and rewarding exercise. The challenges are identifying the metrics that matter to your business; collaborating with stakeholders to not only educate them about the potential for social media but also to align on metrics that will truly identify progress toward their business goals; finding the right tools for the job; and ultimately quantifying the impact of your social media efforts. Rewards come in the form of interacting with customers in new and innovative ways; watching an idea sprout from conception to fruition; and allowing your advocates to take your idea and transform it into something bigger and more meaningful than you ever imagined. Social media can do all of these things, and measuring it is key to understanding just how far your ideas can go.

Throughout this book, you've explored ways to ride the wave of Big Social Data that is headed your way; how to make sense of information and translate that information into insights and recommendations; how to activate your business to accept and embrace social media in a genuine, human way. You also read about embracing the concept of Social Analytics and using a framework to measure your success, and then ultimately tracking metrics that matter to your business to determine if your investment in social media reaped the reward that you hoped. All of these tasks are within your grasp. By tackling social media measurement in a pragmatic and thoughtful way, you can find great success in your programs and benefit from the ability to communicate those successes to your organization. Your task is to start measuring, and to take the concepts and secrets that I've laid out in this book and adapt them to your unique business. I wish you luck in your measurement pursuits and many prosperous social media activities.

Index

F

Facebook, 13, 16, 19, 46
  advertising, 12
  audience, 45
  avatars, 91
  brand, 49, 258–259
  businesses, 25
  Coca-Cola, 259
  content, 17, 48
  costs, 248
  data, 30
  Dell, 265
  demographic data, 43
  engagement, 209
  Gnip, 36
  Hadoop, 33
  IKEA, 263
  metrics, 131–132
  Nestle, 79–80
  Piper Aircraft, 163
  privacy, 301
  size, 44
  social graph, 88–89, 91
  translation, 44–45
  video, 9
  virality, 213
  Zuckerberg, Mark, 12-13, 88-89
Facebook Places, 336-338
facilitation, 110, 282
FDA, 114
Fear, Uncertainty, and Doubt (FUD), 305–306
Feedback Index, 211
filters, 286–287
Filtrbox, 280, 298
finances. *See also* budgets; costs; revenue
  impact, 216
  metrics, 241–242
Fitzpatrick, Brad, 89
"The 5 New Rules of Social Media Optimization" (Bhargava), 203–206
"5 Rules of Social Media Optimization (Bhargava)", 202–203
Flickr, 36, 300
Flowtown, 280
fMRI. *See* functional Magnetic Resonance Imaging
Ford Motor Company, 317
Foresee Results, 280
Forrester Research, 15, 233
fortitude, 19
foundational measures, 10
  advocacy, 174–175

channels, 172
  engagement, 173–174
  impact, 175
  influence, 174
  interaction, 173
  Social Analytics Framework, 172–175
Foursquare, 13, 209, 262, 336-338
free channels, 240
Friendster, 47
FUD. *See* Fear, Uncertainty, and Doubt
functional Magnetic Resonance Imaging (fMRI), 22

G

Gain from Investment, 232
Galaxy Zoo, 38, 39
Gates Foundation, 340
GigaOM, 308-309
Global Giving, 340
Gnip, 36
goals. *See also* corporations; objectives
  outcome-based, 165–166
good corporate citizenship, 222–223
Google, 38, 141
  discovery, 273–274, 282
  Gnip, 36
Google Alert, 129, 207
Google Analytics, 236-237
Google Latitude, 337
Gowalla, 336-338
Greenpeace, 79–80
Groeneveld, Frank, 302
Ground Control, 71–72
Groupon, 339
Guardian.co.uk, 33
guerilla monitoring tactics, 134

H

Habbo, 46
Hadoop, 33–34
hard metrics, 241–242
Harrison, Chris, 63–64
Harvard Business Review, 254
hi5, 46-47
Hierarchy of Analytical Needs, 41–43, 128
Hierarchy of Digital Distractions, 61
Higgingbotham, Stacey, 37
Hinchcliffe, Dion, 214–215
Home Depot, 78, 259-260
Hootsuite, 277, 284